The sociology of Karl Mannheim

The sociology of Karl Mannheim:

With a bibliographical guide to the sociology of knowledge, ideological analysis, and social planning

Gunter W. Remmling
Professor of Sociology
Syracuse University

Humanities Press

First published in the United States of America 1975
by Humanities Press Inc.
171 First Avenue
Atlantic Highlands, N.J. 07716

Library of Congress Catalog Card No. 74-31028

Printed in Great Britain

To Elba

Contents

One might still indeed live a self-contained and unblemished life if one were to use as a foundation certain earlier positions whose residues still survive among us. But the pressures which spring from the contemporary situation, once they have penetrated our consciousness, permit now only a going to the limit. In this process, one must demolish all firm foundations under one's feet, and all one can do is to grasp the eternal as a component of the most immediate temporal problems. This means that the prophet and the leader themselves become guilty, but it may be hoped that the radicality of the commitment will compensate for the temporal limitation of the objectives.

Karl Mannheim

We are at a curious juncture in the history of human insanity; in the name of realism, men are quite mad, and precisely what they call utopian is now the condition of human survival.

C. Wright Mills

Preface

Karl Mannheim occupies a prominent position among the founders of the sociology of knowledge – among men who were lone wolves refusing the easy intellectual reassurance and social respectability which are commonly the rewards of the academic specialist who applies a standardized method to a limited, well-circumscribed area of research.

When Max Scheler and Karl Mannheim established the sociology of knowledge during the second decade of the twentieth century they left the safe and tried path leading to quick scholarly success; unafraid of rocking the boat they began asking the gut questions about the modern world – questions that aim at understanding the complex interdependence of cultural elements, at the mapping of human behavior in the intricate landscape of the social situation at large, at the meaning of intellectual production, political power, economic force, and the march of history.

In their self-willed confrontation with the problems generated by the transformation of contemporary culture and society, Scheler and Mannheim were heirs to the most vital ideas in the sociological tradition and ultimately fulfilled the function of the intellectual and writer which Jean-Paul Sartre defined in *Situations II* as an effort to make sure that no individual may remain in ignorance of the world, that no man 'may call himself guiltless of what goes on in it'.

Mannheim eventually arrived on a level of thought where concern for the quality of life emerged as the major motivating force of intellectual work. The quality of life could only be improved after the liberation of people from want and anxiety. For Mannheim freedom was the corollary of human solidarity which alone could bring about worldwide security. The upgrading of the quality of life had to proceed with the help of a technological civilization humanized by the infusion of spiritual-intellectual values.

Marginality and cosmopolitanism combined to leave their imprints on the life of Mannheim which spanned three cultural traditions: Hungarian, German, and British. Károly Mannheim was born in Budapest on March 27, 1893, as the only surviving child of a Jewish middle-class family; his father, Gustav Manheim, was Hungarian, his mother, Rosa Eylenburg, was German.

During his university life in Budapest Mannheim associated with 'leftist' intellectuals who played a leading role in the post-First World War revolution. His scholarly development began under the influence of Hegelian and Marxist thought and in the company of the Hungarian intellectuals Georg Lukács, Béla Zalay, Béla Fogarasi, Béla Balázs, Erwin Szabó, and Sándor Varjas. On November 9, 1918, the University of Budapest awarded Mannheim the degree of Doctor of Philosophy. In March 1920, Admiral Miklós Horthy, leader of the reactionary Hungarian counter-revolution, took over the government and Mannheim migrated to Germany hoping to achieve there the free intellectual growth which the advent of a political tyrant had made impossible in his native country.

As a student Mannheim was profoundly influenced by the German scholars Emil Lask, Heinrich Rickert, and Edmund Husserl; in his research he confronted issues raised by Emil Lederer, Max Weber, Alfred Weber, Ernst Troeltsch, Max Scheler, Wilhelm Dilthey, and Karl Marx.

Again, it was a political tyrant – Adolf Hitler – who terminated Mannheim's academic career in Germany, which had begun in 1926, with an unsalaried lectureship (*Privatdozentur*) at the University of Heidelberg, and ended at the University of Frankfurt am Main, where, in 1930, he had succeeded to the chair of Franz Oppenheimer as Professor of Sociology and Political Economy.

In 1933, having been dismissed from the University of Frankfurt, Mannheim joined the London School of Economics and Political Science as a lecturer in sociology. As late as 1945, he was appointed to the premier chair in education at the University of London and started to teach the sociology and philosophy of education.

Mannheim's migrations left their imprints on his work. The collapse of the Hungarian republic and the steady deterioration of German political life during the years of the Weimar Republic represent elements of an existential insecurity finding reflection in Mannheim's first major theoretical effort which was haunted by the shadow of intellectual dissolution cast by his relativistic sociology of knowledge.

In England the refugee turned to the social and political consequences of the crisis of liberalism, entering a second phase of his intellectual career. Mannheim stared down the specter of social dissolution with a rational theory of societal planning; he thrust a large share of the responsibility for the sane development of social life upon social scientists, whom he visualized as the last cohorts standing between contemporary populations and the irresponsible cunning of power-mad *condottieri*.

During the Second World War, Mannheim began a third phase of intellectual development: the fanaticism of the fighting German masses convinced him that democratic societies also needed a strong measure of ideological unity to survive in the struggle against totalitarian social systems. He, therefore, turned his attention to the ethical and religious values of Western humanism and pondered the role of mass education in the mobilization of the emotional and volitional forces which had to augment – as he now realized – the hitherto overly rational paradigm of social planning.

Mannheim's fourth theoretical phase was inspired by the chilling spectacle of the cold war confrontation of two superpowers dedicated to the paranoid race of nuclear overkill. Toward the end of his brief life Mannheim forged the rudiments of a political sociology which aimed its sights at the arrogant abusers of politico-military power and the resulting danger of the Third World War; at the same time he sounded the trumpet call for the necessary counter-attack under the banner of planning for freedom on behalf of militant and fundamental democracy.

Mannheim died in London on January 9, 1947, at the age of fifty-three; there is a foreboding touch in the description which John Middleton Murry narrates from his personal acquaintance with the emigrant: 'one felt that he was profoundly tired, his heart as it were soaked through with the weariness of bitter disappointment; yet he was indefatigable, determined to spend himself to the uttermost, in his mission of spreading awareness of the human predicament.'

Murry at the same time believed Mannheim to be an heroic figure; customarily the assessment of such personal traits does not fall within the province of the sociologist. What the following analysis of Mannheim's life work is intended to reveal above all is the fact that he was a seriously committed sociologist whose thinking was at all times relevant to the central problems of the twentieth century. His professional stature and the persistence of the problems which enraged and engaged his sociological imagination are accepted by this writer as sufficient reasons for the presentation of Mannheim's changing intellectual development which will hopefully result in a complete intellectual profile of this itinerant scholar.

In concluding I would like to express my gratitude to Professor Max Horkheimer, Professor Ernest Manheim, and Professor W. A. C. Stewart who provided valuable comments from their personal acquaintance with Karl Mannheim. For helpful biographical information I wish to thank Mr J. Alcock, Academic Secretary of

The London School of Economics and Political Science, Mr Krau and the *Kanzler* of the Johann Wolfgang Goethe-Universität at Frankfurt am Main, and Dr Weisert who directs the Universitätsarchiv, Heidelberg. Once again, I am indebted to my wife Elba Valdivia who assisted me in library research and in the preparation of the text.

G.W.R.

Acknowledgments

The author and publishers would like to thank those listed below for their kind permission to reprint material in this volume: from Karl Mannheim, *Essays on the Sociology of Knowledge*, London: Routledge & Kegan Paul, and New York: Oxford University Press, 1952; from C. Wright Mills, *The Causes of World War Three*, New York: Simon & Schuster, 1958; from Gunter W. Remmling, 'Philosophical parameters of Karl Mannheim's sociology of knowledge', *Sociological Quarterly*, vol. 12, no. 4, Autumn, 1971; from Karl Mannheim, *Ideology and Utopia*, London: Routledge & Kegan Paul, and New York: Harcourt Brace Jovanovich, 1936; from Karl Mannheim, *Essays on Sociology and Social Psychology*, London: Routledge & Kegan Paul, and New York: Oxford University Press, 1953; from Karl Mannheim, *Man and Society in an Age of Reconstruction*, London: Routledge & Kegan Paul, and New York: Harcourt Brace Jovanovich, 1940; from Karl Mannheim, *Diagnosis of Our Time*, London: Routledge & Kegan Paul, 1943; from Karl Mannheim, *Freedom, Power and Democratic Planning*, New York: Oxford University Press, 1950, and London: Routledge & Kegan Paul, 1951.

1 The significance and development of Mannheim's sociology

Ancient data such as the Code of Hammurabi, the Old Testament, the Confucian Classics, and Plato's *Republic* document that to a large extent social thought owes its origin and continuation to the dialectical interplay of the human desires for social order and social reconstruction. The relationship between stability and change, between social peace and social justice, was precariously balanced in the ancient and medieval systems of social philosophy, anchored as they were in tradition, values, and religion. Modern social theorists witnessed the revolutionary transformation of political, social, and economic institutions as well as the flight of the gods and the relativization of values. These experiences explain both the Machiavellian flirtation with anarchy and the Hobbesian romance with a totalitarian guarantee of social order.

The further development of social contract theory, especially the transition from John Locke to Jean-Jacques Rousseau, sharpened the confrontation between the guardians of order and the champions of change. By 1789, the scales were rigged heavily in favor of the desire for novelty, and the Jacobinic mentality consummated its victory over the intellectual and social structures of the *ancien régime* in the chaos of revolution and terror.

Sociology arose as an attempt to transcend the alternatives presented to modern men by stability in conservative corruption and instability in radical disruption. Especially Auguste Comte, in naming the new discipline sociology, thought of it as an application of rational-scientific principles to social life; such application, he hoped, would harness the dynamics of change to a vehicle that was not hell-bent for chaos but followed the lodestar of order and stability.

Until the First World War Comte's optimistic equation of scientifically controlled evolution with orderly, unilinear progress retained a persuasive hold on the imagination of most sociologists with the notable exception of social Darwinist or Marxist conflict theorists. The business class and working class ideologists continued the Jacobinic confrontation: they either exploited evolutionism as a rationale for the continuity of existing institutions or rejected evolutionary imagery in favor of revolutionary mystique.

The problems challenging the intellectual community as a result of the great French Revolution were compounded by the devastating experience of the First World War. By 1918, intellectuals were bedeviled not only by the tenuous relation of change and stability; most of them were compelled to admit that the barbarism of total warfare had debunked as illusionary the twin beliefs in evolution and progress.

Sharing the grievous disillusionment of their intellectual fellow workers most sociologists abandoned interest in the discovery of scientific patterning of developmental change. Instead they turned to an empirically delimited investigation of the operation of nonrational forces which were apparently stronger determinants of human behavior than rationality.

The chaos of relativities

The emphasis on the nonrational regions in social action and intellectual activity coalesced with the muscular force of ideological analysis to create a novel climate of opinion which achieved an historical dimension through the admittance of intellectual outsiders to a position of centrality. The fascination of Claude Adrien Helvétius and Paul Henri Holbach with the misuse of authority appeared as contemporary as Friedrich Nietzsche's reduction of psychic and social life to the will-to-power and Karl Marx's economic determinism. The re-examination of traditional interpretations of reality proceeded along different lines. Sigmund Freud's psychoanalytical theory devalued the conscious region of the mind and reduced social and cultural behavior to functions of instinctive mechanisms denuded of historical and spiritual significance. In similar fashion Vilfredo Pareto emphasized the centrality of nonlogical social actions which manifest the biopsychic qualities of residues; such actions are justified by nonlogical theories which have their surface manifestations in derivations, that is, in pseudological explanations of nonlogical conduct.

Despite their substantive dissimilarities and notwithstanding their dependencies on a variety of intellectual antecedents, the Marxian, Nietzschean, Freudian, and Paretian paradigms combine to establish a co-ordinate system for the consciousness of twentieth-century men that achieves the quality of novelty because of the massive factuality of its givenness. In this new co-ordinate system cognitive acts directed towards cultural objectifications are deflected from the interpretation of objective meanings which are rooted in the structural principles of cultural objects themselves; instead cognition is directed to the understanding of what Karl Mannheim calls 'documentary' meaning. Cognitive acts directed to the understanding of documentary meaning have a new intent: they interpret cultural objects as surface manifestations which 'document' the existence of deeper and larger complexes of reality.

Max Weber's interpretative fusion of scattered items of documentary meaning in overarching general concepts such as 'spirit' and even more generally 'rationality' moves brilliantly in the space of the new system of co-ordinates. His analysis points away from and beyond the objective meaning of surface phenomena to underlying socio-cultural forces.

The new attitude to cultural manifestations brings with it a detachment of the cognitive act which forces the interpreter to remain largely 'without' the intended object so that its external connections with other realities will not be obscured by undue fascination for its internal complexities. The new 'extrinsic' interpretation of cultural objectifications is markedly similar to the optic of sociology which remains clear only as long as those who use it cut themselves off in thought – to use Herbert Spencer's formulation – from all their 'relationships of race, and country, and citizenship'.[1] The spread of the novel mode of extrinsic interpretation provoked the growth of ideology-consciousness which stimulated logical positivists and semanticists to develop their peculiar form of language-consciousness while it drove Mannheim to his particular manner of intellectual self-consciousness.

Ever since Napoleon Bonaparte's use of the term ideology for aggressive purposes the realities of political conflict have been associated with the further development of this concept. The deployment of ideology as an intellectual weapon matured to deadly precision in the guerrilla tactics of Marx and the Marxists who discredited the thinking of their adversaries as an anticipation of their unconscious interest, a distorted reflection of their existential situation. In mounting their counter-attack the anti-Marxist forces answered in kind and contributed to the proliferation of ideological weapons and the escalation of political conflict.

Mannheim realized that the reciprocal unmasking of the unconscious roots of intellectual existence contributed to the erosion of man's confidence in thought as such. Surrounded by the political self-consciousness and cultural neuroticism of Weimar Germany Mannheim however permitted the thrust of his intellectual energy to carry him beyond the political confines of the ideological zone. He turned the weapon of ideological analysis against himself in the attempt to lay bare the social roots of all theories including his own.

In this process Mannheim not only developed his sociology of knowledge but also gave methodological precision to the time-honored search for the meaning of history. This search had lured German intellectuals before him into the luminous depths of historicism where all world views reveal themselves, in the words of Wilhelm Dilthey, as 'historically determined, therefore, limited, relative'.[2] From the historicist philosophy of Dilthey also stems the insight that all intellectual workers who define their labors as relative modes of perceiving their objects within an historical horizon must face them as a 'chaos of relativities'.[3]

Mannheim seems to belong to those intellectuals who derive their creative strength from the act of standing close to an abyss. Arthur Schopenhauer dared to think in the awareness that 'before us there is certainly only nothingness'.[4] Nietzsche was haunted by his knowledge of the limitless passion and drunken frenzy of Dionysian forces threatening to destroy all forms and norms in a fiery orgy of primitive life. Chaos is the name of the specter that stalked Mannheim throughout his intellectual career. Continually he pitted the cunning of his reason against the growing shadows of mental and social dissolution.

Mannheim's encounter with the chaotic forces of dissolution and disorder occurred in two major ways. The first engagement was fought on the theoretical plane where chaos manifested itself in the 'gliding of standpoints' brought about by the dragon of relativity. Mannheim battled the intellectual chaos of relativities with a variety of conceptual weapons ranging from the restructuring of epistemology to the construction of a *consensus ex post* made possible by the synthesizing activities of the 'socially unattached intelligentsia'. The second engagement was fought on the empirical plane where chaos appeared in the guise of social disorder fashioned by the ogres of economic exploitation and social injustice. Mannheim opposed the threat to the coherence of modern industrial society with the double-edged sword of social planning.

Order and progress

The question concerning order and progress assumed a central position as soon as realistic analysis had persuaded a majority of people to accept as irreversible the great transition from feudal-theological society to industrial-scientific society. Feudal-theological society had bought order at the price of progress; industrial-scientific society wanted both order and progress. Since God had disappeared along with feudal-theological society philosophers were necessarily transformed from theologians into anthropologists. In a godless universe men were thrown back upon themselves; they were forced to exchange the metaphysics of spiritual transcendence for the rhetoric of the social contract. The first modern philosophers still straddled the old and the new world; among them Thomas Hobbes, convinced of the sinful nature of men, felt compelled to replace the needed but unavailable tyranny of God with the needed and available tyranny of the State. By the time of Rousseau the anthropological rhetoric of the social contract had become part of the revolutionary baggage of the *philosophes* and Jacobinists which disgusted Henri Saint-Simon and his interpreters sufficiently to drag in the grab-bag of 'positive' philosophy as an antidote to the 'negative' philosophy of the pre-revolutionary and revolutionary intelligentsia.

Saint-Simon developed the principles of positivist philosophy to protect progress by restraining the corrupting egoism of the rich; at the same time he intended this philosophical rationale for the rule of a scientific-technological-industrial élite to safeguard order from the disruptive rebelliousness of the poor. There was to be no radical change in the basic structural arrangements of society; the task of equilibration was not to be performed by the hardware of revolution; the equilibrating principle had to be soft and Saint-Simon found it in a secular equivalent of religion, destined to grow into his *Nouveau Christianisme*. In his *Système industriel* there emerges the lofty ideal of brotherly love as the vehicle that would diffuse the agglutinant of moral unity across class lines, throughout society. Comte was even less willing to blame basic economic and political institutions for social evils which he saw originating in corruptive and insurrectionary ideas and manners. He, therefore, steadily moved toward a position from where the thrust of positive science could be directed to the task of establishing a new intellectual order justifying the imposition of the State as supreme moral authority between the leaders of society and the working classes.

Émile Durkheim apparently conceived of his intellectual position as an uneasy balance between the extremes of Comtean and Marxian thought. Comte had been sufficiently close to conservative reactionaries such as Louis de Bonald and Joseph de Maistre to share their fear of the anarchic tendencies in the new division of labor spawned by the godless industrial-scientific order; this fear had persuaded Comte to champion the State as the means of effecting the necessary superimposition of moral unity. Drawing closer to Saint-Simon, Durkheim set out to demonstrate the possibility of an organic, non-authoritarian process for the development of a moral order appropriate both to the principles of stability and progress and the novel socio-technological conditions. This process allegedly resided in the industrial-scientific division of labor itself. Against the Marxian call to class struggle and, as he feared, anarchy, Durkheim raised his own voice on behalf of the higher principle of 'organic' solidarity. In an ironically Marxian-like recourse to historical transcendence he saw the development and survival of his higher principle guaranteed by the movement of socio-technological reality itself. On the plane of implementation he relied heavily on the functional efficacy of allegedly non-authoritarian principles such as moral education and moral discipline. These principles were to facilitate the inevitable adjustment of individuals to industrial-scientific society which represents their unalterable destiny.

The feudal-theological order had died in the ashes of the great French Revolution. After the passage of more than one hundred years the new industrial-scientific order showed no signs that the promises of its theoreticians were about to materialize. The promise of progress was no match for the unbridled insolence of bourgeois profiteering. The message of order was dwarfed by the growing shadow of working-class rebelliousness; it disappeared into the poisonous fogs of the First World War which catapulted Europe's hungry workers into the role change from industrial to military cannon fodder and from there into open revolt.

Saint-Simon and his disciples had promised order and progress; but their indifference to significant corrections of structural inequities explains why they merely provided ideological justification for the replacement of an old order of privilege by a new élitist order. The old order had catered to aristocratic-clerical privileges. The new order served the interests of an industrial-capitalistic élite. Saint-Simon's principle of Christian brotherly love was to begin with an ethereal guarantor of progress inviting the kind of savage ridicule which Marx addressed to the bourgeois ideologists of his native Germany. Marx dismissed their half-hearted suggestions for reform as 'a bleating of sheep' which mirrors nothing but the wretchedness of social reality.[5] Comte, in his plan for social reorganization had made it quite clear that the actual administration of the temporal power should be in the hands of businessmen and bankers. The leaders of business and finance were to maintain social control; they were to assure political, social, and economic justice and to sustain public morality. The sociological priesthood, on the other hand, was to be devoid of any material power to enforce its decisions and recommendations. Durkheim's 'progressive' conception of moral discipline surreptitiously presupposed that poverty recommended itself for its efficacy in the inculcation of moral restraint and the containment of anomie as his statistics on suicide rates seemed to indicate. These statistics after all had 'revealed' that regionally 'the more people there are who have independent means, the more numerous are suicides'.[6]

While the real estate profiteer Saint-Simon was preparing the positivist celebration of the emergent industrial-scientific establishment as the harbinger of a free and rational society, G. W. F. Hegel joined the attack of German idealist philosophers upon the idolatry of factual reality. This attack began with Immanuel Kant's move against the British empiricists; it had the objective of liberating men from their dependence on blind natural and social forces. Men were offered a new role: to be masters of their world and their own development. In a letter to Friedrich Schelling the young Hegel celebrated the disappearance of 'the halo which has surrounded the leading oppressors and gods of the earth'. Hegel's Jacobinic opposition to the given state of affairs and the critical negativity of his dialectics attracted the attention of Marx.

Hegel's career as a radical intellectual was short-lived and ended with his co-optation by the Prussian establishment. It was, therefore, left to Marx to activate the revolutionary potential of Hegel's fact-transcending conception of reason which had described reality as an historical process leading to ever fuller states of correspondence between existence and the potentialities of men. From such premises Marx drew the conclusion that the full development of mankind presupposed the complete, and of necessity revolutionary, transformation of the world. In its given factuality the world permitted only the kind of human impoverishment that Marx had meant to express in the phrase 'the less you *are*, the less you express your life, the more you *have*'.[7]

The drums of revolution

The sociological formula which Comte had suggested with his correlation of order and progress fell apart in the political conflicts of the early twentieth century. The theoretical fascination with the superstructure, with ideas and morality, distinguishing the sociological tradition stemming from Comte and Durkheim found its empirical correlate in the political behavior of the majorities in industrial societies. The common fascination with *order* led to alliances between established upper classes, emerging middle classes, and trade unionists among the working classes. On August 4, 1914, the German Social Democratic party's delegation to the Reichstag voted for the war credits; in France and Great Britain the majorities in the Social Democratic and Labour parties also supported the war efforts of their respective countries. On November 10, 1918, the German Social Democratic leader Friedrich Ebert entered into an alliance with the Supreme Command of the army and promised to support the aristocratic officers' corps so that the country might be saved by the army from Bolshevism, disorder, and civil war.

The mystique of *progress* increasingly attracted the radical minority of Independent Socialists who shared Marx's fascination for the socio-economic substructure, taking his revolutionary call for sweeping structural change seriously. On January 11, 1919, the Spartacists – members of the just founded Communist party of Germany – took to the streets and the rooftops of Berlin tenements to fight a short-lived, bloody battle against *Freikorps* volunteers and regular army men who were directed by the former trade-union leader Gustav Noske.

The anarchy unleashed by the Berlin Spartacus rebellion – neither the first nor the last engagement fought by the champions of progress against the guardians of order – showed the serious dislocations brought about by the collapse of the order-progress formula: order was not progressive enough, progress was not sufficiently orderly. Anarcho-Communist experiments had bloody consequences in Bavaria where Noske's troops from Berlin liquidated the short-lived Republic of Soviets in late April, 1919. In Mannheim's native Hungary a Communist revolt led by Béla Kun brought down the new republic in March 1919. The Hungarian Communist republic in turn was crushed by Rumanian troops in August 1919, and in March 1920, Admiral Miklós Horthy, leader of the reactionary Hungarian counter-revolution, restored the old order. The fugitive Béla Kun finally disappeared in the Russian purges of 1939, which accompanied Stalin's offensive against 'Trotskiism'. In the Soviet Union, too, the mystique of order had come to dominate the historical imagination and the cry for progress had turned into distant murmurs which fluttered forlornly in the cold winds sweeping across Stalinist labor camps.

Karl Mannheim – immersed in an empirical reality where the promise of progress and the assurance of order rode on sequential waves of terror – concluded that all ideas had been scandalized. This assumption informed the intellectual labor invested in his sociology of knowledge which took shape as the theoretical description and reflection of Weimar culture. Many exiles from the ill-fated German republic surrendered their lives to the feelings of futility and doom which overcame them in a Paris tenement, in a Brazilian hovel, or in the grey light of a New York hotel room; unlike them Mannheim found strength in his new English environment. This strength enabled him to gradually develop the outlines of a new synthesis which he believed capable of accommodating the twin desires of people for lasting order and progressive structural change.

The sociology of Karl Mannheim

Mannheim's intellectual development appears as a process involving the transition from relativist socio-cultural theory to instrumental planning theory, the subsequent reinterpretation of the functions of institutions and values, and the final attempt at a redefinition of military-political reality.

Strictly formulated, Mannheim's thinking underwent four changes. These changes will be referred to as phases of his intellectual development: they are schematically approximated and briefly described (see Table 1).[8]

TABLE 1 *The development of Karl Mannheim's sociology*

Stage of development	*Major interest*	*Major work**
First Phase 1918–32	Philosophy Sociology of Knowledge	*Ideology and Utopia*, 1929 (German edition)
Second Phase 1933–8	Sociology of Planning	*Man and Society in an Age of Reconstruction*, 1935 (German edition)
Third Phase 1939–44	Sociology of Religion Sociology of Values Sociology of Education	*Diagnosis of Our Time*, 1943
Fourth Phase 1945–7	Political Sociology Sociology of Power	*Freedom, Power, and Democratic Planning*, 1950 (posthumous)

* English editions: *Ideology and Utopia* (translated by Louis Wirth and Edward Shils; preface by Louis Wirth), 1936.
Man and Society in an Age of Reconstruction (translated by Edward Shils), 1940.
German editions: *Diagnosis of Our Time* (translated by Fritz Blum), 1951.
Freedom, Power, and Democratic Planning (translated by Peter Müller and Anna Müller-Krefting), 1970.

First phase: as a representative of the liberal, avant-garde intelligentsia of post-war Central Europe Mannheim accepts during the 1920s an absolute historism as the basis of his interpretation of sociocultural reality. In the ideational force field generated by intellectuals of the Weimar Republic and eventually in uneasy proximity to the Frankfurt *Institut für Sozialforschung* he develops his radical sociology of knowledge which claims, in contrast to Max Scheler's moderate view, that all thoughts in the humanities and social sciences are determined in form and content by non-theoretical factors. An awareness of general ruthlessness in social-economic-political conflict and the desire of his generation to unmask the hypocrisy of established power positions combine into a personal motivational complex which drives him to expand the suspicion of ideology: he therefore widens Marx's total but special concept of ideology into his own vision of ideology which is not only total but also general. In Mannheim's radical optic the knowledge of all social groups appears as socio-existentially determined. In the brilliant flash of this epistemological explosion we witness the final shift of the intellectual seascape into contemporaneity: there are no longer any privileged social positions with regard to ideational truth or general intellectual reality-adequacy. In answer to the charge of relativism Mannheim develops a series of defensive arguments. These include the reconstitution of traditional, static epistemology on the basis of change-conscious modernistic dynamism, the reconceptualization of relativism as relationism, the accumulative effect of a *consensus ex post* in the non-partisan sifting of reliable knowledge and the related, well-publicized function of the 'socially unattached intelligentsia'. This group, which Alfred Weber singled out for special attention with the controversial concept *sozialfreischwebende Intelligenz*, has supposedly a more comprehensive vision of truth since its members are relatively free from the otherwise general attachment to specific socio-existential positions.

Second phase: in 1933, Mannheim joins the exodus of the German intellectual élite. Soon after his arrival in England his epistemological, ontological, and methodological theorizing that led to the formulation of his radical sociology of knowledge and to the global suspicion of ideology gives way to a novel interest in the crisis phenomena of the twentieth century. While the night of barbarism settles over Germany, Mannheim responds to the pragmatic and experimental openness of his English environment: he develops a theory of democratic social planning as his answer to the problems besetting advanced industrial societies. Significantly he demands that man himself be reconstructed to insure a lasting reconstruction of society. The achievement of these two interrelated goals depends to a large extent on the transformation of 'functional rationality' into 'substantial rationality'. Industrialization gave rise to functional rationality which is an élitist organizing force capable of relating the social actions of associated individuals to objective ends. The instrumental limitation of this form of rationality is to be overcome by substantial rationality which would enable the majority of people to grasp the interrelations of social facts and processes. Democratic social planning is expected to give rise to this substantial rationality which would, on the basis of individual insight into the interrelations of events, elevate interactional behavior to higher levels of autonomy and intelligence.

Third phase: the experience of the Second World War contributes to the lessening of Mannheim's fascination with rationality which has so far dominated his thinking. During the early 1940s Mannheim comes to believe that his earlier emphasis on rationality was one-sided and inadequate to the task of a fuller understanding of human personality. Moving closer to the complexities of psychic phenomena he integrates emotional and volitional variables into his hitherto predominantly rationalistic model of social planning. This change in intention leads to a novel focus of attention upon the social meanings of values and the functional significance of the institutions of education and religion. Values, religious behavior, and meaningful education are seen in close correlation with the human will and human feelings; they are therefore capable of enlisting the active support of men for the planned construction of a fundamentally and militantly democratic society. At this point Mannheim is mainly interested in the creation of a viable value system and the rejuvenation of public education and Christianity in the interest of social reconstruction.

Fourth phase: Mannheim's transition to his last phase coincides significantly with the end of the Second World War. As the chill of the Cold War spreads over and beyond the ruins of Europe, Mannheim redirects his attention to the problems of political and military power. Although he retains his paradigm for social planning as ultimately developed in the third phase, he once more shifts his interest to a new field of inquiry and sets out to formulate his critical sociology of power as a unique presupposition for a realistic political sociology. This stage of intellectual development remained somewhat rudimentary as a consequence of his untimely death in 1947.

2 Philosophical parameters of Mannheim's sociology of knowledge

The road that leads from philosophy to sociology has been well traveled. Comte mapped sociology in the framework of Saint-Simon's positivist philosophy.[1] Spencer's sociological reflections form part of his synthetic philosophy. It was the philosopher Émile Boutroux – teacher of Bergson and Blondel – who stimulated Durkheim to view society as a distinct area of investigation. Durkheim's sociological theory of knowledge is strongly influenced by the phenomenological neo-criticism of Charles Renouvier. Durkheim identified himself as a scientist of moral behavior but the overarching awareness of the moral philosopher never faded from his quantitative universe of social facts. Ferdinand Tönnies's *Gesellschaft* presupposes the rational-contractual conception of society propagated by Thomas Hobbes whose philosophy provided the German sociologist with his point of departure. Tönnies's contrasting societal type of *Gemeinschaft* is anciently rooted in Aristotle's doctrine of social origins and invites comparison with the social philosophy of the romantic conservatives of the nineteenth century; these other philosophical traditions emphasized the naturalness of social development and the spiritual intimacy of kinship and neighborhood which Tönnies attributed to social interaction in the community. Georg Simmel's opening question: 'How is society possible?' is deliberately posed in the manner of Kant's philosophy. Max Scheler has roots in Edmund Husserl's phenomenological philosophy – and so does Karl Mannheim, exponent of a relativistic sociology of knowledge.

Mannheim's preoccupation with philosophy and the sociology of knowledge constitutes the first phase of his intellectual career, spanning the years 1918–32. Specifically his *early* work may be subdivided into a largely philosophical stage, extending from 1918 to 1924, and an essentially sociological stage, delimited by the period 1925–32.

The philosophical stage begins with the lecture, *Lélek és Kultura* (soul and culture), published in 1918 at Budapest; the predominantly philosophical stage ends with the article on 'Historicism', published in 1924 in Germany. Mannheim made the transition from philosophy to sociology in 1925, when he published his article, 'The problem of a sociology of knowledge' in the famed *Archiv für Sozialwissenschaft und Sozialpolitik*. The early sociological stage climaxed in 1929 with the appearance of *Ideologie und Utopie*, drew to a close with the article 'Wissenssoziologie' (1931), and ended in 1932, almost like an afterthought, with the short book, *Die Gegenwartsaufgaben der Soziologie* (Contemporary Tasks of Sociology).

A mapping of the philosophical parameters of Mannheim's sociology of knowledge necessitates the direction of attention to the philosophical stage in his early work: here occurs the shaping of the major philosophical dimensions which give depth not only to his philosophical beginnings, but also to his subsequent sociology of knowledge in the strict sense of the word.[2]

The metaphysical dimension and the shifting of realities

Mannheim began his career as a philosopher in proximity to the Hungarian philosopher and literary critic Georg Lukács who, in 1910, published an essay collection on 'The soul and forms' (*A Lélek és a Formák*). Mannheim's lecture on 'Soul and culture' (*Lélek és Kultura*) was given in the fall of 1917 to introduce a series of lectures combining his own efforts with those of other members of his generation including Frigyes Antal, Béla Bartók, Béla Fogarasi, Arnold Hauser, Zoltán Kodály, and Georg Lukács. A comparison of these publications reveals that Lukács and Mannheim have similar intellectual roots reaching into neo-platonism, *Lebensphilosophie* (Dilthey, Simmel), phenomenology (Husserl), and neo-Kantianism (Rickert, Lask, Max Weber). In 1920, Mannheim reviewed Lukács's *Theory of the Novel* which had made its first appearance in a literary journal in 1916; since Lukács dates his conversion to Marxism-Leninism as a process occurring between 1917 and 1919 his early influence on Mannheim was that of an idealistic, marginally bourgeois metaphysician.[3]

The early Lukács worked toward an idealistic philosophy of history as an embracive explanatory device for the illumination of manifold culture contents and their interconnections – an attempt bordering on the elevation of aesthetics to the rank of an absolute metaphysical principle. Similarly Mannheim identified himself to his Budapest audience as a metaphysical idealist and concluded with expressing the hope that a new, comprehensive system of metaphysics would appear to light up the formative principles governing the emergence of novel cultural manifestations.[4]

Mannheim politely dismissed Marxism as a valuable, but decidedly outmoded frame of reference; he was to remain silent on the issue of Marxism until 1924, the year of his article on 'Historicism'. Here, on the threshold of the sociology of knowledge, he, for the first time, acknowledges the vitality of Marxist analysis and in particular Lukács's role as a Marxist intellectual – Lukács, who so far had only been recognized by Mannheim for his pre-Marxist contributions to aesthetics.[5]

Despite denigrations of Marxism, psychology, and sociology as 'low' sources of insight into the 'heights' of artistic-intellectual creativity, the central theme of 'Soul and culture', which reveals the influence of Simmel's 'Tragedy of culture', shows Mannheim groping for concepts and ideas which are destined to grow in volume and clarity in the subsequent works of his philosophical stage and to reach maturity in his sociology of knowledge. Mannheim diagnoses Western civilization at the dusk of the First World War and sees the central problem in the estrangement of men from their non-material culture – from their 'objective culture' which surrounds them in increasingly formalistic and theoretical fashion as a distant constellation of spiritual artistic-intellectual manifestations. It may not be particularly important that the young philosopher anticipated the advent of a new metaphysics capable of closing the gap between the individual and his culture; significantly, however, he realized that it was the historical situation of his generation which sensitized its thoughtful members to the irrelevance of formalistically estranged culture content. In Mannheim's case this awareness was fated to grow into the embracive principle that all thought products are socio-existentially determined in form and content.

Mannheim's review of *The Theory of the Novel* – which marks the beginning of his scholarly career in Germany – continues the metaphysical dimension; Lukács is praised for his intuitive grasp of the full meaning of the novelistic art form which reveals itself only to an observer who is located at the high mental altitude of metaphysical contexts. But, again, there is a luminous undercurrent of reflections with implications for the future: Mannheim approximates the phenomenological attitude which will lead him into the challenging, positive-negative proximity of Max Scheler; he discovers the heuristic efficacy of an approach to mental products which relates them not to one, but to several structural contexts and prepares the ground for his novel interpretation of epistemology, his situational conceptualization of different types of meaning, and his relativistic principle concerning the 'gliding of standpoints'.[6]

Mannheim's interest in the work of Georg Lukács has personal roots.[7] Upon his return to Budapest in 1915 Lukács formed a circle which met every Sunday in the home of the writer Béla Balázs to discuss the problems of contemporary European culture. For three years Mannheim and other Budapest intellectuals, including the art historian Arnold Hauser, experienced the kind of stimulation and intimacy which Lukács had enjoyed in Max Weber's house in Heidelberg, where similar regular meetings brought together the leading minds of the time. The thirty-one-year-old Lukács enjoyed early fame as a literary critic and author of works in aesthetics when Mannheim joined his circle of admirers.

Mannheim had spent his formative years in Budapest, where he was born on March 27, 1893, the only surviving child of a Hungarian-Jewish father and a German-Jewish mother. He spent his childhood in the country's capital and graduated in Budapest from a humanistic high school. But, when he met Lukács, he was no longer untravelled. In 1912, after a few semesters at the University of Budapest, he had gone to Berlin where he had taken courses with Georg Simmel. Then, he had followed friends to the universities of Freiburg and Heidelberg; he had also spent a shorter period of studies in Paris.

Shortly before the beginning of the First World War, Mannheim returned to his native city; somewhat later, in 1915, he began his fateful association with the Lukács group. In 1917, the men and women of the Lukács group established the Free School for the Humanities and began to offer public lectures and seminars which propagated metaphysical idealism while simultaneously attacking the crass materialism and shallow positivism of modern civilization.

Mannheim's allegiance to the Lukács group did not prevent him from continuing his long-standing participation in the activities of the Society for Social Sciences and those of the Martinovics Lodge of Freemasons which were devoted to the opposing ideals of positivism and rational-scientific progressivism. Meanwhile Mannheim developed his thesis on 'The structural analysis of epistemology' which was to result in the degree of Doctor of Philosophy, awarded by the University of Budapest on November 9, 1918.

Mannheim's involvement with these different groups brought him into contact with nonconformists of diverse backgrounds. Some of the innovating young intellectuals belonged to the reformist 'Social Catholic' movement, others came from the small liberal group of the impoverished gentry, but most of them, including Lukács, stemmed from the Jewish middle class.

The young reformist students and critical intellectuals formed a thin stratum that remained isolated from the bulk of the population; their academic and somewhat élitist orientation permitted only marginal contacts with the nascent working class and the peasantry; their pronounced Hungarian national feelings prevented all connections with the numerous national minorities of the country.

Therefore, the reformers and critics remained in a state of political impotence that lasted until the end of the war.

Until the 1890s Hungarian society resembled a sea of complacency which also engulfed the small intelligentsia of Budapest. At the turn of the century modern, nonconformist ideas began to change the intellectual and artistic climate of the capital, but had no impact on the rest of the country. The widespread complacency was partially due to the political backlash which followed the failure of the revolution of 1848, the defeat of the Hungarian armies in Kossuth's War of Independence, the period of repression and reaction, and the Austro-Hungarian Compromise of 1867. Hungarian complacency was reinforced by thc measure of prosperity that came in the wake of the compromise with Austria. This prosperity was unevenly divided and mainly benefited the ruling class of cosmopolitan aristocrats, whose large estates provided the resources for their courtly life styles, and the tiny commercial middle class of the capital. The small, but growing industrial proletariat lived under miserable conditions. In 1913, three-quarters of Hungary was held in estates belonging to the socially and politically dominant magnates who were the favorites of the court.

Several factors combined to prevent expressions of discontent. Even after the electoral reforms of 1913 franchise was restricted to less than one-third of Hungarian men who had to vote openly and who were, therefore, susceptible to freely applied official pressure. The administration of power was centralized in ministries staffed with narrow-minded members of the impoverished gentry who hated all modern ideas and lorded it over the bulk of the people in alliance with the Church. This oppressed majority consisted of economically exploited, disenfranchised, illiterate, and docile peasants. The media of communication were mainly controlled by the Budapest middle class whose financial and commercial interests prohibited the publication of anything capable of offending the sensibilities of the ruling aristocracy and gentry. It took the privation of the First World War and the stimulus of the Russian Revolution to bring the deep cleavages and bitter discontent in Hungarian society into the open. Toward the end of the war people began to listen to Count Mihály Károlyi, leader of a faction of the Party of Independence, who combined the long-range goals of social and political reforms and concessions to the nationalities with the immediate goals of repudiating the German alliance, making peace with the entente, and becoming independent from Austria.

In October 1918, the people revolted against the war and the monarchy; subsequent events led to the establishment of a republic under Károlyi's presidency. The new Hungarian government was composed of a dubious coalition of Károlyi's bourgeois followers with Radicals and Social Democrats. Caught between Allied intransigence and Communist agitation the new president was incapable of realizing his goals. Faced by the extreme territorial demands of the Allies the government resigned on March 20, 1919, and the Social Democrats fused with the Communists. On the following day the Hungarian people found themselves in a dictatorship of the proletariat, allied with Soviet Russia and led by Béla Kun, a Soviet agent of Hungaro-Jewish origin.

These events significantly changed the activities and fortunes of Mannheim's mild-mannered circle of friends. The reformist intellectuals of the Society for Social Sciences worked for the moderate Károlyi government. The more dramatic development occurred in the hitherto apolitical Lukács group; a number of members joined the newly formed Communist party, following the example which Lukács had set in December, 1918. The activities at the Free School for the Humanities also changed after the proclamation of the Hungarian Soviet Republic which had taken place on March 21, 1919. Idealistic philosophy was replaced by revolutionary agitation and most of the students and lecturers entered the party of the proletariat. Lukács served the new government as Commissar of Education. Mannheim did not follow Lukács and other friends into the Communist party, but, like most lecturers at the Free School, he taught at the University of Budapest after its reorganization by the Communist government in April 1919.

Béla Kun's dictatorial regime alienated the bourgeoisie and failed to attract the peasants; it was violently opposed by the old ruling class and the Allies. Kun's unsuccessful attacks on the Czechs and Rumanians sealed his doom and on August 1, 1919, he and his major supporters fled to Vienna. Two days later, looting Rumanian troops occupied Budapest. On November 16, Admiral Miklós Horthy de Nagybánya entered the capital at the head of a national army; with him came the cadres of a counter-revolutionary government which had been formed by bourgeois émigré committees whose members had escaped the Kun régime to Vienna and French-occupied Szeged. Horthy's arrival unleashed the White Terror: counter-revolutionary detachments engaged in violent acts of revenge which victimized Jews and the leaders of the workers. The wave of terrorism drove many intellectuals from Hungary, sparing only the most docile advocates of reactionary conservatism. Georg Lukács began his many years of exile, first in Austria and Germany, later in Russia. On March 1, 1920, the monarchy was restored in Hungary and, pending the clarification of the position of the throne, Horthy took the office of regent which he never relinquished until his forced abdication on October 16, 1944. Mannheim was among the refugees from the White Terror; he had taught philosophy at the reorganized

University and was, therefore, marked with the sign of complicity in the former Communist government.

When Mannheim arrived in Heidelberg in 1920, German society was still in the throes of revolution and counter-revolution.[8] As in Hungary the German revolution followed in the wake of the military catastrophes triggered by the Allied offensives of July and August, 1918. By October, Emperor William II and the German High Command were sufficiently unnerved to allow the formation of a parliamentary government and to prompt its chancellor, the liberal Prince Max of Baden to request President Wilson to take steps for the restoration of peace. The half-hearted maneuverings of the German leaders and the Allied desire for Germany's total defeat prolonged the privations of the war and in late October and early November sailors of the imperial battle fleet at Kiel mutinied to prevent a suicidal engagement with the English. By November 4, all German battleships flew the red flag and disgorged armed sailors who spread the revolution from the ports to other cities. The soldiers who were sent against the mutineers refused to take action and many of them joined the revolt. On the morning of November 9, Berlin was in revolutionary turmoil: crowds of workers and soldiers had transformed the Reichstag into an armed camp; Karl Liebknecht, the Spartacist leader, prepared to proclaim a soviet republic from the balcony of the imperial castle; Philipp Scheidemann, a leader of the Majority Socialists, countered this move by proclaiming the German Republic from a window of the Reichstag; Prince Max handed over the office of chancellor to the Social Democrat Friedrich Ebert. On the following day William II fled across the German border to Holland and at 5.00 a.m. on the morning of November 11, 1918, four reluctant German delegates signed the armistice.

On the day of the emperor's departure the Berlin convention of the workers' and soldiers' soviets voted to support Ebert's 'social republic'. On November 10, as well, Ebert was informed by General Gröner that he could count on the collaboration of the Supreme Military Command. A disgusted Liebknecht denied his support, but the Independent Socialists joined with the Majority Socialists to create a cabinet. The provisional German government, which commenced its activities as the 'Council of People's Representatives', lost the co-operation of the Independent Socialists after Ebert had ordered troops to Berlin on December 24 for an unsuccessful attempt to clear the palace of revolutionary 'people's sailors'.

Ebert's conservative Majority Socialists began to long for a return to law and order by means of a national assembly, elected not only by Socialists, but by the entire population; elections for a constituent assembly were fixed for January 19, 1919. When Ebert tried to dismiss the president of Berlin's police, the Independent Socialist Emil

Eichhorn, the Communists joined the Independent Socialists in the manifesto of January 5, 1919, calling upon the German proletariat to stage a great mass demonstration against the government of Ebert and Scheidemann. These developments unleashed the Spartacus Rebellion which transformed the German capital and other cities into battle zones, where radical Independent Socialists and Communists fought against the supporters of the Ebert government. Ebert appointed the former basket weaver and trade union leader Gustav Noske as Supreme Commander of a volunteer corps; led by bloodthirsty career officers of the old imperial army Noske's troops entered the center of Berlin on January 11. The Spartacist strongholds succumbed to heavy fire and by January 15, the volunteers of 'blood hound' Noske had cleared the last snipers from Berlin. The same day the Spartacist leaders Karl Liebknecht, Rosa Luxemburg, and Wilhelm Pieck were arrested and beaten by staff members of the *Garde-Kavallerie-Schützendivision.* Liebknecht was murdered by *Kapitänleutnant* von Pflugk-Hartung; Luxemburg was gunned down by *Leutnant* Vogel; Pieck survived to participate in the affairs of the Weimar Republic as a Communist delegate. He returned to Germany from his Moscow exile in 1945 and became president of the German Democratic Republic in 1949.

The elections for a national constituent assembly were held, as scheduled, on January 19 and on February 6 the national assembly met at Weimar, the city of Goethe. On February 11, Ebert was elected president of the *Reich* that was commonly called the Weimar Republic. The next day Scheidemann formed a coalition government made up of Social Democrats, the Catholic Center, and the Democrats. After approving Scheidemann's cabinet, the assembly began drafting a new consitution which was adopted on July 31, and signed on August 11, 1919.

Ebert's alliance with the High Command of the old army had served its purpose of clearing the way for a democratic republic; but in fighting the extreme Left the new government bent so far to the Right that it became an accomplice to the defeat of the social revolution. The Weimar coalition neither achieved public control over Germany's reactionary, monopolistic industrialists, nor did it succeed in breaking up the huge landed estates which were the power bases of feudal-minded agrarian overlords. From the beginning, therefore, the democratic leaders of Weimar Germany had sealed their own doom: their actions preserved the economic arrangements and military values of imperial Germany, leaving excessive power in the hands of cartel bosses and *Junkers*, who hated the Republic and worked for the return of an authoritarian régime. Many workers, disappointed by the failure of social reform, strengthened the Left-wing opposition of Independent Socialists and Communists who attacked the Social Democratic Party and the Republic from the other corner of the ring.

The year of Mannheim's arrival in Germany marks both the beginning of full-scale Rightist counter-revolution and the last successful demonstration of working-class solidarity. In March, 1920, a Rightist conspiracy, headed by the self-proclaimed 'Reich Chancellor' Wolfgang Kapp and supported by the rebellious troops of the Ehrhardt Brigade, a *Freikorps* unit, assumed power in Berlin for a few days. The Kapp putsch was defeated by the refusal of the higher civil servants to collaborate with the rebel 'government' and by the crippling blow of a general strike called by the Social Democratic party and carried out by all labor unions.

German labor failed to reap the benefits of its success in the Kapp putsch; the Socialist parties refused to co-operate with the victorious trade-union leaders who called for the establishment of a labor government as the unified expression of the will of the entire working class. The rebuffed trade unions accepted the return of the ineffectual Weimar coalition, beginning their disastrous policy of compromising with the ruling groups. While the workers' leaders permitted organized labor to skid to a secondary power position the double-dealing General Hans von Seeckt, chief of the army command, used all his cunning to build the army into a state within the state. From then on it was not the life-giving strength of productive labor, but the death-oriented power of the army that was to exercise the decisive force in the Republic.

At the end of June 1920, the Social Democrats lost their dominant position in Germany; the Weimar coalition was replaced by the new combination of the Center, the Democrats, and the German People's Party. The parliamentary delegation of the German People's Party was led by Gustav Stresemann who contributed signally to the further development of Weimar Germany as a bourgeois-capitalist democracy. From August, 1923 to November, 1923, Stresemann held the offices of chancellor and foreign minister; afterwards – until his death in 1929 – he acted as foreign minister.

Stresemann began his political career in the Republic under difficult circumstances. The population was embittered by the severe demands of the Treaty of Versailles which had become effective in January, 1920. Public dissatisfaction was deepened by Allied insistence on reparations payments, more than six billion gold marks annually for forty-two years, and by the French and Belgian occupation of the Ruhr, on January 11, 1923, in retaliation against technical German defaults on reparations obligations in the delivery of timber. People were unnerved by the steady deterioration of the value of German currency and the subsequent inflation which culminated on November 20, 1923, when the mark sank to the value of 4·2 billion to the dollar.

Stresemann's patient negotiations and careful policies of stabilization averted the worst consequences of these developments; he called off the passive resistance against French occupation forces and ordered the resumption of work and reparations payments. On November 20, 1923, a new currency, covered by a mortgage on Germany's entire agricultural and industrial resources, ended the inflation; in 1924, the Dawes Plan reduced annual reparations payments and provided the German government with an international loan of 200 million dollars. Strengthened by the Dawes Plan, the German economy began its remarkable recovery.

During these years of crisis and slow recovery the Rightist opponents of the Republic missed no opportunity to strengthen their position; free from the responsibilities of government they peddled cheap and unrealistic slogans designed to incite chauvinistic emotions among the voters. Undaunted by the miserable Kapp putsch Right-wing conspiracies, such as Organization Consul, elevated murder to an expression of patriotism; many republican leaders fell victim to *Fememord.* On August 26, 1921, Matthias Erzberger, Catholic Center politician and chief signer of the armistice, was gunned down in the Black Forest; on June 24, 1922, Walter Rathenau, Jewish industrialist and foreign minister, was attacked in suburban Berlin-Grunewald with guns and hand grenades. Rathenau's death motivated chancellor Wirth to a Reichstag speech in which he announced that the 'enemy stands on the Right'. Despite mass demonstrations and measures such as the Law for the Protection of the Republic, assassination remained a favored mode of Rightist politics. Ominously, the courts of law developed a tendency to show incredible leniency toward Rightist terrorists, while severely punishing even minor infractions on the part of Leftist individuals. Indicative of this tendency was Hitler's brief and comfortable stay at Landsberg prison – a virtual sabbatical for subversives – which was the only consequence of his Beer-Hall Putsch of 1923.

The professional army of Weimar Germany did not fail to turn republican problems and achievements to the advantage of anti-republican militarists. The economically significant treaty of friendship which was signed between the Soviet Union and Germany on April 16, 1922 at Rapallo provided the chance for military activities in Russia which the Treaty of Versailles withheld from the volunteer army that the Allies had limited to 100,000 officers and men. In 1920, the army delighted in putting down the workers' revolt in the Ruhr; in 1923, the army again made itself 'useful' by suppressing attempted Communist coups in the working-class strongholds of Saxony and Thuringia.

Mannheim spent these turbulent years at Heidelberg where Alfred Weber strongly influenced his thinking; at Freiburg he attended

Heidegger's lectures. His life as a private scholar was made possible by his parents who provided him with an income. Among the Heidelberg faculty he befriended Emil Lederer, the theorist of revolution, but otherwise he stayed clear of political involvements. Mannheim's social 'location' in Germany was detached from fighting interest groups and his early writings displayed a rarified abstractness. As a progressive intellectual, however, he struggled on the theoretical plane for meaningful forms of attachment to the creative social forces of the twentieth century.

The epistemological dimension

It is no coincidence that Mannheim began his scholarly career with a dissertation on *The Structural Analysis of Epistemology*, published in Germany in 1922. His theory in particular and the sociology of knowledge in general presuppose Kant's epistemological innovations.

Kant defined reality as the product of man's own activity. His forerunners in the field of epistemology had centered knowledge in the object of cognition; they expected the mind to reflect the nature of outward, independently existing phenomena. For this process the empiricists relied on sense perceptions, the rationalists relied on the logical powers of reason. Kant, however, expected the objects to conform to the human mind; he demonstrated that human thought *formally* created its cognitive objects. The empirical world around us was *epistemologically* our own product: nature derived its structure, its very distribution in time and space, from the cognitive constitution of the human mind. In this sense the knower inevitably imposed his epistemological conditions on the objects of his cognition.

The sociology of knowledge presupposes Kant's critical elevation of epistemological theory: sociologists of knowledge claim after all that human thinking is connected with social reality. This assumption could not be made if Kant would not have elevated epistemology above the level of crude realism which confronted the knower with autonomous objects to be registered in the manner of photography. Epistemological realism did not permit the knower to influence the objects of his cognition. With the Kantian assumption that the stuff of knowledge is constituted via the creative act of perceiving man such influence is however entirely conceivable.

Mannheim would later claim that there are no objects in themselves: knowing men have different desires, expectations, and interests due to their varying life situations and experiences; therefore the objects in the empirical world appear in many different refractions which correspond to the varying orientations of men.[9] More generally, sociologists of knowledge could not raise their particular questions if Kant would not have affirmed the object-constituting function of cognition. The pre-objective data of the social sciences and humanities become objects of cognition only in the method-conscious processes of perception and conception.

Mannheim's *Structural Analysis of Epistemology* is based on the neo-Kantian interpretation of logic as the science of concepts, judgments, and systems. Equally neo-Kantian is his concern for the logical worth or 'validity' of scientific assertions and conceptual systems; as a young philosopher Mannheim claims a-temporal validity for the theoretical sphere. But his absolutist stance is an uneasy one: he senses the tensions between the intellectual polarities of historical understanding and timeless validity.

Even more significant for Mannheim's future development is his assertion that knowledge may be analyzed in three major ways: as a psychological datum, as a logical entity, or as an ontological (metaphysical) problem. Epistemology, therefore, is not an autonomous science capable of providing its own criterion for the distinction between truth and falsehood. The epistemologist can only analyze knowledge that has (allegedly) been achieved elsewhere and trace this knowledge back to its sources of origin in the fundamental sciences represented by psychology, logic, and ontology. Early in his career Mannheim, then, devalues epistemology as a self-contained critique of knowledge by making it dependent on other sciences; later he will add the decisive thesis that sociology is the fundamental science providing the criteria for the validity of socio-existentially determined knowledge.

The historical dimension

Mannheim's unorthodox view of epistemology, however, did not prevent him from later expressions of his awareness that Kant's philosophy has signal importance for the development of the sociology of knowledge. In his *Ideology and Utopia*, Mannheim credits the philosophy of consciousness, especially Kant's version of it, with the elimination of an outmoded ontological dogmatism. Thanks to Kant the world is no longer seen as an unalterable aggregate of definitive forms existing independently of men; on the contrary the world exists because of its connections with the mind of the knower whose cognitive activity determines the form in which reality appears. Hegel also interpreted the world as a unity which is conceivable only because of its connection with the mental activities of men. Importantly, however, Hegel took the next step in the direction of the sociology of knowledge: he described the world as an ongoing process of historical change in search of equilibrium on increasingly higher levels of development.[10]

For Mannheim thinking is a process which explains the world by placing the world's constituent elements in their developmental levels within a total structure. This Hegelian approach informs Mannheim's doctoral dissertation; in the *Structural Analysis of Epistemology* he attempts to understand socio-cultural phenomena by systematically placing them in their larger logico-meaningful contexts.[11] The name of Wilhelm Dilthey must be added to those of Kant and Hegel; the philosopher of life and systematizer of the cultural and social sciences had a lasting influence on Mannheim's thought.

Dilthey shared Kant's interest in the logical and methodological ordering of scientific activity. Significantly Dilthey also shared Hegel's interest in the logico-meaningful investigation of aspects of reality which Kant had not sufficiently explored because of his fascination with the physical sciences. For Hegel the physical reality of nature formed part of the total structure of the world; but unlike Kant he derived his most important insights from the study and conceptualization of human life, society, culture, and history. Dilthey accepted these Hegelian concerns and proceeded to clarify the methodological prerequisites for the needed establishment of the cultural and social sciences which he identified with the celebrated concept *Geisteswissenschaften*. In these sciences human thought intends *meanings* and intellectual activity therefore depends on the method of *understanding* by means of typological constructs. The physical sciences, on the other hand, intend *facts* which are approached from the outside by means of the method of *explanation* permitting the formulation of causal laws. Whereas the physical scientist relies on the controlled experiment, the researcher in the cultural and social sciences understands his objects in acts of immediate intuition by linking meaning with meaning. The apprehension of meanings is possible since the researcher himself is a denizen of a world of meaningful relations.[12]

The methodological dimension

Dilthey's neo-Idealist approach to scientific methodology was opposed by the neo-Kantians – especially by Wilhelm Windelband and Heinrich Rickert – who accepted causal-law explanations for *all* the sciences and merely admitted that an historical approach called for special attention to unique, nonrecurrent configurations with regard to values. The fusion of neo-Idealism and neo-Kantianism was achieved in Max Weber's methodology which established sociology as the science which links the *interpretative understanding* of social behavior with *causal explanations* of its course and effects. Weber had moved sociology into a position of centrality: this lesson was not lost on Karl Mannheim.

In his essay 'On the interpretation of Weltanschauung', which immediately followed the publication of his doctoral thesis, Mannheim attempted to improve Max Weber's methodological position. He notes that Weber's recognition of causal explanation, expressed in his theoretical works, has not been given sufficient play in Weber's historical writings which are largely based on the method of interpretative understanding.[13]

Mannheim suggests that every social event, every cultural product conveys *three* levels of meaning. Cultural products and social events possess (1) *objective meaning* which the observer can grasp by virtue of his knowledge of the objective social context wherein the data of perception coalesce into a meaningful whole. The understanding of objective meaning can be achieved from the 'outside' and does not presuppose any knowledge of intentions or states of consciousness. The understanding of (2) *expressive meaning*, however, presupposes knowledge of the subjective intentions on the part of the actors in social situations. Social and cultural analysis may move from the interpretation of objective meaning as reflected by the observable social act or cultural product and from the interpretation of the subjectively intended expressive meaning to the level of (3) *documentary meaning*. This type of interpretation is neither concerned with the objective structure of an action nor with the subjective intentions expressed by it; documentary meaning reveals what an action *unintentionally* documents about the actor's total personality.

In this analytical frame the act of charity, for example, may be interpreted as 'social assistance' (objective meaning), as 'sympathetic intention' (expressive meaning), or as 'hypocrisy' (documentary meaning). With regard to cultural products, such as paintings, the analytical progression would move from the interpretation of objective visual content (treatment of space and mode of composition) to the interpretation of the expressive meaning (the subject matter of the painting) and from there finally to the interpretation of the unintentional documentary meaning which may be represented by the particular treatment of the artistic medium and its subject matter. On the level of *documentary* meaning interpretation points *beyond* the immediate behavioral or cultural data to a larger universe of facts which coalesce into a total personality configuration, or total sociocultural context. The interpretation of the act of charity as hypocrisy presupposes knowledge of many other behavioral data which also reflect the hypocritical aspect of the actor's personality. The interpretation of a painting as the reflection of medieval mentality is derived from the observer's larger knowledge of this particular world view in which the artist unconsciously participated.[14]

Documentary interpretation, that is, the attempt to understand the central attitudes, the 'spirit' of an era, represents a method which shows the way leading from philosophy to sociology.[15] All theories derived from the method of documentary interpretation reflect the social structure.

Why?

Because theories of this type are inevitably affected by the interpreter's location in social space and historical time. Whenever we attempt comprehensive reconstructions of meanings we must fall back on the comprehensive socio-cultural structure which gives meaning to our own experiences since substance can only be comprehended by another substance.

The methodological problems surrounding documentary interpretation foreshadow the relativistic implications of the sociology of knowledge: the scope and validity of a documentary interpretation of the French Revolution, for instance, are determined by the social and historical standpoint of the interpreter. The validity of this method is therefore limited to individuals who share the interpreter's location in social space and historical time. Differently worded, each social and generational group must perform new documentary interpretations of the 'same' historical 'reality'.[16]

Further pursuit of this theme will lead Mannheim eventually to a central assumption of his sociology of knowledge: the space- and time-bound perceiving subject is inescapably anchored in the historical-social process of life in a specific way. Consequently, an object of cognition never totally discloses itself to man; rather every perceiving subject sees only a partial aspect of the object and that only from his particular cognitive standpoint. In the social sciences and humanities all objects of cognition rest on meta-empirical world view presuppositions and can only be seen and conceptualized in perspective contexts.

This theme has additional roots in Mannheim's review of Erich Becher's book, *Geisteswissenschaften und Naturwissenschaften* (1921). In opposition to Rickert, Becher utilizes criteria suggested by Alexius Meinong and Husserl to justify the classification of scientific disciplines into *Idealwissenschaften* (mathematics, geometry) and *Realwissenschaften* (natural sciences, human and social sciences, metaphysics). In Mannheim's estimate the central issue is represented by the question concerning the adequacy of classificatory schemes in general. Becher does not evade the issue, but fails to live up to the standards which his reviewer tries to establish. According to Mannheim different sciences, or, for that matter, all objects of classification may be grouped on the basis of numerous points of view. The development of this assumption is crucial, not necessarily for the hoary topic of classificatory logic, but definitely for the genesis of Mannheim's theoretical awareness. Formal logic fails to provide criteria for judging the adequacy of these viewpoints and the systems of classification associated with them; such criteria can only be provided by the inner structure of the objects of classification themselves. Mannheim was quick to suspect the relativistic implications of this position since theorists can only grasp the inner structure of objects, that is, their essence, in different perspective variations or standpoint-determined shadings. Mannheim was unwilling to further pursue the problem of relativism in the context of this review, but the problem was inescapable and would soon return to haunt him throughout his career as a sociologist of knowledge.[17]

Emergence of the social world

Mannheim's relativistic approach to intellectual activity and the products of such activity collides with basic assumptions of Kantian epistemology. In his search for the timeless validity of intellectual activity Kant had found it necessary to anchor the object-constituting principles of general, *a priori* validity (the categories) in a pure, original, and unchangeable consciousness as such (the transcendental apperception). In his *Critique of Pure Reason*, Kant had made it abundantly clear that the existence of a basic speciate universe of discourse was in no way affected by psychological and social influences. Mannheim was fully aware of these Kantian assumptions; at the same time he was equally aware of Dilthey's attempts to relativize the very core of Kantian epistemology. In view of Mannheim's own attempts to accomplish the transition from philosophical thought to social thought it is not surprising that he found Dilthey's particularistic argument more convincing than Kant's universalistic paradigm.

First of all, Dilthey transferred Kant's epistemological paradigm to the human and social sciences which deal with the world of ideas and human life relations. This transferral was legitimate since Kant had limited his epistemological paradigm to the physical and mathematical sciences which deal with the world of inanimate objects and quantitative relations. In transferring Kant's epistemological orientation to new fields of inquiry Dilthey also tried to reveal the basic categories of understanding since he, as well, thought it necessary to identify the transcendental elements which constitute the ordered structure of the mental-human world. Significantly, however, the pure concepts of the understanding which Kant had originally identified did not survive Dilthey's act of transference unchanged. In the new fields of inquiry they re-emerged as 'modes of evaluation' reflecting the particular world views of different thinkers and knowers. These modes of evaluation were no longer universally anchored in a 'consciousness as such'. In Dilthey's novel paradigm the evaluating knower approaches the empirical, pre-objective material of the human and social sciences with the *a priori* of his world view and makes his selections among these mere data in correspondence with *his* particular world view *a priori*. Obviously this world view *a priori* is different from the original, universal, speciate *a priori* of Kant's epistemology. In Dilthey's description the *a priori* is a particular *a priori* which corresponds to the knower's specific position in historical time and social space.

This reformulation of critical epistemology, amounting to a *historicization* of the *a priori*, permitted Dilthey to point out the unity of theory and practice, of science and life. This unity of theory and practice is reflected in the methodology which Dilthey wants to govern the human and social sciences: in these fields each researcher experiences and evaluates his specific historical and social position in the larger frame of reference provided by the totality of life and, consequently, arrives at specific forms of world interpretation and world view. The different world views are the existential bases for varying perspectives which determine the shaping of the ideal world taking place in the cognitive processes of the human and social sciences. The humanist scholar and the social scientist employ a dynamic method which makes the researcher's own social and historical position part of the cognitive goal. This method is brought to bear upon the theories of other scientists as well and, consequently, the objective intention upon the cultural, historical object matter is always accompanied by the subjective intention upon a thinker's specific social and historical position.

These methodological considerations reflect Dilthey's historicism, his sensitivity for the flux and flow of life, his awareness of the relativity and subjectivity of all historical positions. Mannheim drew the full consequences of this kind of historicism in an article first published in 1924.[18]

The development of absolute historicism

In his article on 'Historicism', Mannheim describes this theoretical principle as the only possible modern world view which determines the individual's inner reactions, external responses, his forms of thought, and most of his scientific activities. Historicist theory in Mannheim's description does not merely owe its centrality to the fact that it reflects a world which is historicist in its own mode of development; more importantly he believes that historicist theory will permit modern men to penetrate the 'innermost structure' of the world's historicist reality and help them discover an 'ordering principle' behind the seemingly anarchic manifestations of all-pervading change.

The change in social conditions brought about by the French Revolution and the growing acceptance of the concept of evolution were major factors which combined to create novel modes of historical analysis.[19] More specifically the alterations of social existence and intellectual conceptualization supported the development of two rudimentary types of historicist analysis, permitting the study of historical structure and order from two methodological positions: (1) the evolutionary-vertical method and (2) the organic-horizontal method.

The first method may be applied to any cultural element for the purpose of revealing the 'law of change' which governs the development of all the different elements of culture. A contemporary institution for example may be traced back to historically earlier stages of existence so that the logico-meaningful order of its evolution may be reconstructed. The second method may be used to describe the mutually conditioning, 'organic' interaction of all major cultural elements at a given point in time.

The evolutionary-vertical method has historical depth but produces a mere aggregate of isolated evolutionary lines; the organic-horizontal method reveals the functional interplay between major culture parts, but produces a configuration without evolutionary features.

Fully developed historicism must, therefore, combine both of these methods so that historical analysis will derive from the study of complex socio-cultural reality an understanding of its evolutionary change, as well as of the organic structure of its functional balance.

The major conceptual resources of Mannheim's historicism can be found in Dilthey's historicist philosophy of life, in Hegel's relativistic philosophy of historical meaning, and in the historical sociology of his contemporaries Ernst Troeltsch and Alfred Weber.

In 1904, Troeltsch published an article on 'Modern philosophy of history' which contains the rudiments of his theory of historicism; this theory was later elaborated in his book, *Historicism and Its Problems*.[20] Mannheim showed special interest in two elements of Troeltsch's theory. First, he was attracted by Troeltsch's attempts to submit all data and problems simultaneously to historical and systematic analyses; these attempts represent, indeed, significant approximations of the methodological fusion which Mannheim conceptualized as the confluence of the evolutionary-vertical and the organic-horizontal method. Second, Troeltsch worked toward a 'contemporary cultural synthesis' to provide the disillusioned denizens of the twentieth century with an optic capable of revealing the meaning of history. These intellectual labors suggested to Mannheim that the understanding of historical-cultural meanings can only be achieved within a three-dimensional time perspective which fuses past, present, and future with the agglutinant of modern man's action-oriented pragmatism: 'Only out of the interest which the subject at present acting has in the pattern of the future, does the observation of the past become possible. The trend of historical selection, the form of objectification and representation only becomes understandable in terms of the orientation of present activity.'[21] From Troeltsch's arguments on behalf of a contemporary cultural synthesis Mannheim derives insights which stimulate his own theory of historicism; these insights also foreshadow in limited form a basic assumption of his subsequent sociology of knowledge: 'that historical knowledge is only possible from an ascertainable intellectual location (*Standort*), that it presupposes a subject harboring definite aspirations regarding the future and actively striving to achieve them'.[22]

The specter of relativism

Mannheim's historicism invites comparison with pragmatism; it also affords tenancy to relativism. Mannheim accepted his kinship with the pragmatist philosophers, but under the spell of German Idealist philosophy he made various efforts to convince his audience that historicism actually '*veers away from relativism*'.[23] In the neo-Fichtean tradition of Heinrich Rickert's philosophy this brand of historicism still accepts 'organically' developed standards represented by 'concrete' values. The intuitive *Verstehen* method, developed by Leopold von Ranke, Johann Gustav Droysen, Wilhelm Dilthey, and Max Weber, is credited with the ability of transporting the historical observer into the very core of values and standards which allegedly gave meaning to the existence of bygone societies. In his *Grundriss der Historik* (1867), Droysen characterizes *Verstehen* as the essence of historical method; the possibility of understanding by means of this type of investigation stems from the similarities connecting the historical observer with the recorded material of history. In the process of *Verstehen* outward historical records are projected into the observer's inner experience where they release intellectual and emotional processes similar to those experienced by the historical actors of bygone eras.[24]

On a higher level of conceptual sophistication Mannheim acknowledges his indebtedness to Edmund Husserl's hypothesis that *spatial* objects can only be viewed from definite local positions from where their properties present themselves to the observer only in one-sided 'profiles', in partial perspective variations. By analogy with Husserl's approach to everyday physical nature Mannheim argues that historical, cultural, and psychic objects present partial mental-psychic profiles to the observer who is himself inevitably rooted to a limiting mental-psychic perspectivic standpoint. Again, historicism is steered away from relativism: Mannheim claims that the various historical insights presented by differing mental-psychic profiles are not contradictory or conflicting. On the contrary they represent a progressive series of insights on the road to a 'higher' truth and simply 'encircle the same materially identical given historical content from different standpoints and at different depths of penetration'.[25]

Mannheim's refusal to live with a relativistic historicism put him into the embarrassing position of having to shop around for a meaningful pattern of evolution. The desired evolutionary pattern would have to show that the thoughts and actions of individuals were not only mirror images reflecting their particular social and historical environments, but links in a 'great chain of being', significant elements in an overarching cosmos of historical relevance.

Mannheim's search for a pattern of historical evolution betrays a tendency that will become more pronounced as he moves deeper into the sociology of knowledge: this is his tendency to see man mainly as an agent in connection with abstractly conceived collectivistic processes. This approach leads to Mannheim's neglect of man as an 'inter-personal agent', or his failure to clarify how collectivistic-existential conditions actually infiltrate individualistic-discrete mentalities. Therefore, several sociologists in the United States, including Louis Wirth, Robert K. Merton, John C. McKinney, and Peter Berger have suggested that the (European) sociology of knowledge needs an adequate social psychology, specifically a realistic social theory of mentality capable of fusing psychical and institutional process.[26] Mannheim's American critics seem to imply that the sociology of knowledge would benefit most from symbolic interactionism – especially George Herbert Mead's version of that theory. A fusion of European sociology of knowledge with Mead's social psychology would, however, have to accommodate a number of basic differences between these diverse intellectual attitudes. For example, Scheler, Mannheim, and nearly all other Europeans writing for or against them evidence a great fear of relativism which frequently borders on 'epistemological neuroticism'. By contrast Mead displays a calm bordering on 'sociologistic indifference' to the relativism problem. Furthermore symbolic interactionism – *a theory of intersubjectivity* – seems mainly interested in the social construction of reality to explain the role of *individuals* in a given world; in pursuit of this interest Mead and his followers failed adequately to conceptualize social structure. European sociology of knowledge – *a theory of interobjectivity* – seems largely concerned with the role of *social groups* in the construction of a cosmos of historical significance; Mannheim developed an adequate concept of social structure, but failed to conceptualize personality structure. Ironically, during his English period, Mannheim gained more than sufficient insight into social psychology to entertain questions concerning the internalization of social reality – but, by then, he was no longer sufficiently interested in questions concerning the sociology of knowledge.

In his early search for a pattern of historical evolution Mannheim rejected the Hegelian paradigm as unrealistically logical and the frameworks of life philosophy, irrationalism, and phenomenology as irresponsibly fragmented. The Hegelian paradigm freezes the world in conceptual abstractions, the irrationalist paradigm dissolves the world into a bundle of intuited configurations.

Caught between two unacceptable alternatives, Mannheim fell back upon scientific method in much the same way as Wilhelm Windelband, whose rectorial address of 1894 had served to reject Dilthey's object matter-oriented distinction between the physical and human sciences.[27] To begin with, Mannheim accepted as relevant the distinction between a 'process of civilization' and a 'movement of culture' which Alfred Weber had made in an article published in 1920.[28] Weber's distinction between *Zivilisation* and *Kultur* or, to use the words of Robert K. Merton, between utilitarian and non-utilitarian (expressive) culture alerted Mannheim to the possibility of developing what he considered a realistic typology of socio-cultural life patterns.

Weber's 'culture' refers to psychic-emotional phenomena such as art and religion which are essentially irrational; methodologically these phenomena are best approached through intuition and the holist representation of their organically evolved configurations. As demonstrated by von Ranke and other writers of the historical school psychic-emotional phenomena change their meanings and each intellectual generation must reinterpret them on the basis of the generation's unique psychic-cultural situation. Weber's 'civilization' conceptualizes the cumulative, linear progress through which a given technological and scientific system is gradually being built up. The quantitative methods of the physical sciences are best suited for the explanation of progressively rational intra-system development. As implied in the Enlightenment theory of evolution the progressively rational systems in the civilizational sphere are neither subject to changes in basic meaning nor to historico-temporal and socio-spatial relativity.

At this point Mannheim claims that Alfred Weber's distinction between culture and civilization does not afford tenancy to phenomena in the strictly philosophical and historical sphere. There are, in other words, basic, essential questions in philosophical and historical interpretation which confront one generation of intellectual workers after another. These perennial issues, however, undergo alterations to the extent that their material correlates and their functional meaning change from generation to generation. Essential philosophical and historical problems are, therefore, neither understandable as unique manifestations of 'culture', nor do they fit the linear paradigm of progressive evolution embodied in the concept of 'civilization'. Philosophical and historical analysis has its own evolutionary dynamics which Mannheim characterizes in analogy to Hegel as 'dialectical-rational' development in which problems not merely recur, but in which a succession of new systematizing centers of awareness provides them with novel modes of systematization and organization.

Dialectical-rational development is of special importance for Mannheim since he believes that this concept permits the formulation of a dynamic position without relativistic implications: it is true that the succession of systematizing centers reflects the inevitable shifts of existential positions, but each novel center of intellectual organization 'represents a higher position than the preceding one'.[29] In this manner 'dialectic-systematic' rationality leads to a 'dialectical-dynamic' utopia or the claim 'that the overall philosophical process does possess its truth'.[30]

Mannheim's conclusion stresses the dynamism of his intellectual position: the methods originating in the cultural, philosophical-historical, and civilizational spheres are freely interchangeable since each socio-cultural phenomenon contains a psychic-emotional, dialectically-rational, and progressively-rational stratum. Under the influence of changing existential conditions the socio-cultural phenomena themselves change positions: 'The "state", for example, in certain epochs had a largely "psychic-cultural" character; but this does not mean that, at other times, it cannot pass more and more over into the "civilizational" sphere.'[31]

Mannheim's final remarks on the problems of historicism are significant for two reasons: first, it becomes increasingly clear that his methodological analysis leads to the sociological correlation of socio-cultural phenomena and processes with social classes or their correlates. The sphere of culture with its organic-intuitive method affords tenancy to conservatives; civilization with its progressive, technicist overtones is the product and reflection of liberal, industrial middle classes; the industrial proletariat appears as a product of the philosophical-historical process and its political action is most effectively guided by dialectically-rational methods. Second, Mannheim seems fascinated by the muscular vitality of dialectically-rational conceptualization and applauds both the 'profound' work of the proletarian intellectual Georg Lukács and the possibility 'that at the present time the activistic-progressive tendencies are behind a gradual elaboration of the rational dialectic method'.[32]

As Mannheim moved beyond the frontier of philosophical speculation to seek his fortune among sociologists, he encountered the 'cult of the proletariat' which attracted an influential segment of the artistic-intellectual cadres of Weimar culture; this cult was an important source of strength and vitality for many creative individuals who looked to the proletarian masses for release from a social situation offering them only two choices: to exist as playthings for the rich, or as tools for bourgeois economic interests. For a brief moment of history there was the intellectual 'who came out of the cold'; Weimar culture permitted the artist and intellectual to play a new role, that of the 'outsider as insider'.[33] With the large-scale defection of the masses to various types of overt and covert totalitarianism the chill of alienation returned to haunt artists and intellectuals. In particular the second half of the twentieth century seems marked by an increasing estrangement of the intelligentsia from the proletariat. This process creates novel anxieties and hostilities and motivates some change-conscious intellectuals and their youth-oriented adherents to question the existential relevance of the industrial working classes and their leaders. While the ragged masses of the classical Marxist imagination have 'disappeared' beyond the frontiers of the Third World and the crumbling walls of the Black ghettos, the workers in the remaining societies of the developed world have become suspect of co-optation by locally dominant military-political-industrial establishments. The new intellectuals and youthful activists view these establishments as existentially irrelevant, that is, they see them as anti-life forces which freeze existence into an anticipation of violent death or the practice of patient suffocation behind steel desks. Because of these changes on the frontier of social analysis it may become necessary to attempt a combination of the sociological imagination *à la* Mannheim with the philosophical-psychological imagination of Jean-Paul Sartre's existentialism. Upon immediate reflection the thinking of Mannheim converges with several major interests pursued by Sartre. Both men view intellectual activity as cognitive mapping of the experiential universe, both establish human experience as the source of knowledge, both demand that individuals accept their engagement with the world and other men, and they both discover the final test of meaning in action whereby they transform the history of man into the history of man's *vita activa*. Significantly, however, Sartre brings into this intellectual scenario the mature skepticism of his 'pessimistic humanism' and the psychologist's insight into the depths of human irrationality. Drawing closer to the mood of the waning twentieth century Sartre redefines social action and social reconstruction by casting the existentially committed individual in the role of ethical protester. The modern rebel denudes the flagrant injustices and callous abuses perpetrated by the icy, but brittle holders of power. In contrast to Mannheim the French philosopher does not cast the existentially committed individual in the role of the social engineer directing men into conformity with the rationally designed paradigms of a perfect, utopian social order. Existentialism is a philosophy which condemns the human being to a freedom that is tied to a responsibility for himself and the entire world.[34]

Mannheim began the major reflections of his first intellectual phase with the fateful assumption that the world of modern men can only be grasped historistically. His struggle against the relativistic consequences of this thoroughgoing historicism ends equally fatefully with the admission that there remains nothing in the end but commitment to ethical and political pragmatism: 'only a philosophy which is able to give a concrete answer to the question "what shall we do?" can put forward the claim to have overcome relativism'.[35]

Mannheim attempted to answer this question by investing the intellectual energies of his later years in the development of a comprehensive program of social 'planning for freedom'. Increasingly contemporary sociologists ask similar questions. Since the days of C. Wright Mills some energies have flown into uncovering the intelligentsia's complicity with the military-industrial establishment; at times more subterranean forms of complicity have been suggested in a rather personal manner.[36] There is a growing literature on the sociologist's social and political responsibility and the possibilities of his dual role as observer and change agent; so far nobody has matched the consistency and directive force of Mannheim's answer to the question 'what shall we do?'

3 The development of the conceptual matrix

Mannheim fully developed his paradigm for a sociology of knowledge during the sociological stage of his early work which extends from 1925 to 1932. There was something peculiar about the manner in which Mannheim entered the sociological scenario, for his entry was simultaneously subtle and dramatic.

In his work on 'Historicism', performed during the last, transitional period of his philosophical stage, there occurred the subtle transformation in his thinking which motivated Mannheim to announce his intention of abandoning the philosophy of history for sociology. When Mannheim crossed the bridge leading from philosophy to sociology he was guided by a vision promising the novel correlation of knowledge, culture, and life with empirically identifiable social groups. What he saw emerging, at this point, was a new dimension of historico-philosophical interpretation: 'the social stratification of the cultural process, and the identification of cultural trends with social classes'.[1]

At this point, however, there also occur announcements of dramatic changes in the orientation of sociology, for Mannheim foresees 'the need of replacing its generalizing method, developed in the image of the natural sciences, with a historico-philosophical method'. This new method will take Hegelian dialectics and Marxist sociology for its point of departure and, once further developed, promises the transformation of sociology into a science capable of maintaining its relevance in the storms created by shifts in the intellectual seascape and the 'successive re-patternings of the experiential substratum'.[2]

Mannheim's assumption of the sociological role was documented by his article, 'Das Problem einer Soziologie des Wissens', published in April 1925. On June 12, 1926, he habilitated as a *Privatdozent* in the philosophical faculty of Heidelberg University; at his side was his Hungarian wife whose expertise in psychology and psychoanalysis was to leave significant traces in his later work. Mannheim had married Juliska Láng in 1921 and she remained his lifelong adviser and collaborator; she was to survive him by nine years.

For Mannheim's adopted country the year 1925 brought prosperity and further international reconciliation; on the front of internal politics the year spelled disaster. The Dawes Plan of 1924 had initiated a flow of foreign investments and short-term loans to Germany, which stimulated a wave of modernization affecting large portions of the country's industrial apparatus. Rising production and wages were accompanied by decreasing unemployment and by the end of 1928 Germany had become the leading industrial power in Continental Europe.

The internal political disaster began on February 28, 1925, when Friedrich Ebert, president of the Republic, died at the age of fifty-four. On March 29, 1925, the Germans went to the polls to elect a new president, but, as could be expected, not one of the seven candidates achieved the required majority on the first ballot. For the second round of voting the republican groups supported Wilhelm Marx of the Center Party as the single candidate of the *Volksblock*; the German Nationalists rallied the forces of the Right around the retired Field Marshal Paul von Hindenburg and their major spokesman Admiral von Tirpitz persuaded the seventy-seven-year-old Junker to run; the Communists renominated their own candidate, party chairman Ernst Thälmann. By the slim margin of 904,151 votes, the elections of April 26, 1925, gave Hindenburg the simple plurality which the law required for a second-ballot victory. The self-professed monarchist Hindenburg received 14·6 million votes, while 13·7 million votes went to Marx, supporter of the Republic. Thälmann received the crucial 1·9 million votes which withdrew strength from the republican forces and ironically helped the Rightist cause by making possible the election of a man who personified Prussian militarism, German nationalism, and agrarian Junker conservatism. Kurt Tucholsky, one of the company of Left-wing intellectuals associated with the radical, but independent Berlin journal *Weltbühne*, remarked after the election of Hindenburg that the Germans now had a 'republic until further notice'.

This 'notice' was not given until 1930 and for five years parliamentary principles continued to govern the political life of the German Reich. The period 1925–8 was not only a time of prosperity, it was also the core of the 'Stresemann era', those 'golden twenties', which Mannheim viewed as the reincarnation of the age of Pericles.[3]

While Stresemann acted as foreign minister he signed three major treaties on behalf of Germany, contributing to the development of an era of international good will. The *Locarno Pact*, signed on October 16, 1925, guaranteed the status quo of Germany's western frontiers, re-affirming in particular the German renunciation of Alsace-Lorraine. In response the Allies began to withdraw their military units from the Cologne zone of the occupied Rhineland; on September 8, 1926, Germany was admitted to the League of Nations with a permanent seat on the council. On April 24, 1926, Stresemann signed the *Berlin Pact*, extending the original Rapallo agreement with the Soviet Union; the new Russo-German agreement calmed Soviet fears with regard to German complicity in an anti-Soviet bloc, but renewed suspicion of Germany in most other European nations. On August 27, 1928, Stresemann signed the *Kellogg-Briand Pact* to outlaw war and was warmly received by the Parisians.

The sincerity of Stresemann's intentions has been questioned by historians and the problem of his political morality may never be satisfactorily resolved. His policies of international reconciliation, however, combined with economic prosperity to create a period of relative stabilization. In the 1928 elections to the Reichstag voting practices indicated strong popular support for the original design of the Republic: approximately 65 per cent of the ballot went to political parties that were loyal to the Weimar constitution; the Communists received 11 per cent of the votes and Right-wing parties less than 25 per cent. On the right the Nazi party received no more than 3 per cent of the valid votes.

The Social Democrats, who had received 30 per cent of the ballot, supported Stresemann's foreign policy, but opposed the strong influence which industrialists and businessmen exerted on the government. Especially ominous was the consolidation of monopoly capitalism which gave far-reaching power to such gigantic trusts as *I. G. Farben*, *Siemens*, and *Vereinigte Stahlwerke*. The Right-wing Nationalists, who had received 14 per cent of the vote in 1928, fought violently and vociferously against international reconciliation. The Communists remained suspicious of Stresemann's policies and attacked what they considered his plotting against the Soviet Union; when Germany entered the League of Nations they denounced this move as an anti-Soviet alliance between German capitalists and an international 'consortium of imperialist bandits'. There was, then, sufficient strife and fluctuation during the Stresemann era to inspire such relativistic and power-oriented conceptualizations of reality as Mannheim's sociology of knowledge.

The problem of a sociology of knowledge

When Mannheim published his article, 'The problem of a sociology of knowledge', in 1925, he openly divorced himself from the concerns of his philosophical stage; moreover, he represented his novel alliance with sociology as legitimized by the intellectual and practical life problems of his time which he saw pointing 'toward a temporary fading out of epistemological problems, and toward the emergence of the *sociology of knowledge* as the focal discipline'.[4]

Specifically, Mannheim identifies four basic factors and explains the ascendancy of the sociology of knowledge as a result of their interplay. First, modern men increasingly view knowledge as a partial sphere which is dependent on the more comprehensive sphere of social reality. This temporal and socio-existential conditioning of the development and structure of knowledge is conceptualized as its 'self-relativization'. Second, modern men act in the practical force field of class struggle which renders questions about the immanent truth or falsehood of theoretical propositions irrelevant. In a social reality dominated by the struggle of social classes there emerges the 'unmasking turn of mind'; this additional form of relativization does not aim at the mere theoretical refutation of the ideas of the class enemy, but treats them as components of an ideology. The extra-theoretical function of an opposing ideology, which is an impersonal socio-intellectual force, is 'unmasked' in order existentially to corrode the ideology and destroy its practical effectiveness. Third, in industrial societies the immanence of theoretical meaning is transcended in the direction of an 'ontological terminus' represented by the historico-social sphere centered around the socio-economic process. Fourth, modern men strive toward 'total relativization' which is a process demonstrating the socio-existentially determined character of an *entire* idea system or global world view.[5]

Mannheim realized that work in the sociology of knowledge may originate in various centers of methodological and conceptual systematization. At the close of the first quarter of the twentieth century positivism stood out as a philosophic-scientific system that had been particularly active with regard to research in the sociology of knowledge perspective. The 'vulgar Marxists' represented proletarian positivism; Émile Durkheim, Lucien Lévy-Bruhl, and Wilhelm Jerusalem were notable bourgeois positivists. The two variants of positivism were preoccupied with scientific-technological thought and derived their epistemological and ontological orientations from the natural sciences.

These limitations alienated Mannheim from positivism; restrictions of a different kind led him to reject 'formal apriorism', a second position inhabited by those bourgeois and social democratic theorists whose investigations were guided by the various types of neo-Kantianism. Formal apriorism, or the philosophy of formal validity, limited the sociology of knowledge perspective to examinations of the material substratum in which the formal elements of thought, such as the categories, and formal values, such as democracy, are actualized. Studies of this type avoided all questions concerning changes in the cognitive and value spheres since they had the ultimate purpose of protecting the timeless validity of these spheres from the anarchic flux of their socio-historical origins.

The system of formal apriorism was subject to severe strains caused by its advocates' fanatic devotion to the principle of the separation of 'form' and 'matter'. In the case of the third sociology of knowledge position, that is, 'material apriorism' or modern phenomenology, the crack in the system was caused by its principal architect's devotion to the separation of mind and life; Max Scheler's dualistic conception of the world was anciently rooted in Platonic Idealism and unfolded via the phenomenological distinction between meaning and being to his bipolar sociology of knowledge which contended that 'essential knowledge' was fundamentally different from 'factual knowledge'. Among modern phenomenologists, then, Scheler emerged as the leading exponent of an objectivist, absolutist theory of values asserting that truths of timeless validity, or concrete, material values, could be grasped in acts of 'essential intuition'.

Scheler's basic contention repelled Mannheim who was rapidly developing serious interest in a sociological approach permitting the intellectual thrust through the phenomenological surface of ontic differences and into the substantial core of socio-historical reality. Mannheim, therefore, decided to launch his own work in the sociology of knowledge from the remaining fourth center of methodological and conceptual systematization which he saw represented by historicism. Much like Troeltsch and Lukács, he assumed that the theoretical advance into the battle scene of modern social life could only be accomplished by the active, engaged intellectual type. With the support of historicist principles, then, Mannheim tried to develop a sociology of knowledge capable of finding the correlation between intellectual standpoints and social standpoints.[6] At the close of his first systematic discussion of the sociology of knowledge, Mannheim felt sufficient confidence to define the discipline as a field of inquiry that 'explores the functional dependence of each intellectual standpoint on the differentiated social group reality standing behind it, and which sets itself the task of retracing the evolution of the various standpoints'.[7]

The interpretation of intellectual phenomena and political ideologies

Mannheim's explorations in the sociology of knowledge began with an interpretation of ideas as functions of social positions; in 1926, Mannheim tried to further clarify this approach with his essay on 'The ideological and the sociological interpretation of intellectual phenomena'. Drawing on Marx's contributions to the development of explanatory methodology and Max Weber's typology of meanings, Mannheim presented a complex scheme for the differentiation of various interpretations of the meanings of cultural phenomena.

The distinction between intrinsic (ideological) interpretation and extrinsic (sociological) interpretation is of special importance for the further development of the sociology of knowledge. The traditional intrinsic approach to intellectual phenomena does not permit the observer to make any assumptions other than those prescribed by these phenomena; he is forced to remain 'within' their direct field of influence. The intrinsic interpretation of a social theory, for example, does not reveal its ideological dimensions, but merely elucidates the theory as theory. The intrinsic attitude to ideas is, therefore, itself ideological; it imprisons the observer in the same darkness of unexamined assumptions engulfing the producer of the theory.

The enlightened pre-theoretical attitude to the same social theory enables the observer to suspend the entire array of its assumptions and to reveal the theory as ideology. The observer, who is capable of placing himself 'outside' another theorist's direct field of influence practices extrinsic interpretation. This new form of interpretation reveals the ideological dimension of observed intellectual phenomena, but is itself not ideological, but sociological.

The intrinsic (ideological) interpreter of intellectual phenomena sees ideas as ideas; the extrinsic (sociological) interpreter reveals ideas as ideologies. The achievement of extrinsic interpretation depends on the observer's ability to discover ultimate existential contexts in reference to which intellectual phenomena are functionalized. Contemporary extrinsic interpretation functionalizes ideas on economically, psychically, or socially conceived levels which act as configurations of existentially conditioned relationships permitting the concretization and rule of particular ideas.[8]

The sociology of knowledge is a type of extrinsic interpretation which functionalizes ideas on a socially conceived level. Mannheim tried to demonstrate the effectiveness of this method in his essay on 'Conservative thought', first published in 1927, which correlated the emergence and impact of a conservative style of thought with the social groups acting as 'carriers' of conservatism.

In the main Mannheim examined German conservatism during the first half of the nineteenth century which stood under the impact of the French Revolution. His sociological interpretation revealed the dominant conservative theories of this time as ideologies serving the interests and aspirations of social groups that opposed the scientific-industrial-capitalistic order and bourgeois society. After its differentiation from mere traditionalism, conservatism arose as a conscious reaction to the advance of capitalism and the ascendancy of the middle class. This development took place in a class society, that is, in a social reality in which change occurred 'through the medium of class conflict'.[9]

The conservative ideology stressed the qualitative character and concreteness of personal relationships which had allegedly fused the members of medieval society into an organic community; conservative ideologists shared common ground with Marx when they attacked the capitalist-bourgeois order as the material expression of a quantitative, rationalistic thought style which buried the reality of the world beneath generalized, abstract relations, thereby reducing the human being, as well, to an abstractly experienced calculable magnitude. The Marxist revolutionaries sought to overcome bourgeois capitalism by ushering in the future; the conservative reactionaries, conversely, meant to stop the advance of the new mechanistic society by restoring the lost life styles of pre-capitalistic forms of social organization.

The Marxist ideology was inevitably bound to the dimension of the future since it found its social carrier in a class that had no roots in the past and no place in the present; outside of its own negation, that is, capitalism, the proletariat had no tradition behind it; herded together in factories, it 'developed from an inchoate mass into a completely new class with its own traditions'.[10]

The conservative ideology was wedded to the past, because its social carrier consisted of groups that were alienated from the capitalistic process of rationalization and abstraction. Lacking in futuristic imagination and existing on the periphery of present society, the landed aristocracy, small peasant proprietors, and small bourgeois owners and artisans lived in the romantic landscape of a marginal social order, where the older traditions of pre-capitalist social relations were kept alive.[11]

The problem of generations and the rules of cultural competition

Mannheim's analysis of conservatism had the general purpose of revealing the social factor in the development of conflicting styles of thought; this search for the social factor also informed his subsequent study of 'The problem of generations', first published in 1928–9.

To begin with Mannheim rejects extant generation theories which have failed to advance analysis of the generational phenomenon beyond the basic stratum of biological data; the dominant naturalistic, quantifying approach does not achieve more than direct correlations between waves of decisive year classes of birth, set at intervals of thirty years, and waves of cultural changes. The direct observation of the effect of biological data bars the sociological understanding of the generational phenomenon, which can only be achieved by a type of analysis that reveals how biological factors are reflected through the medium of socio-cultural forces.

Generational analysis at the decisive level of the social and cultural structure presupposes conceptual differentiations among three generational groupings. First, the *generation location* ascribes to individuals belonging to the same age group a common experiential location in the social and historical process. Guided by Marx's conception of class, Mannheim argues that both classes and generations receive their unity in the first place from the objective fact of 'social location'. An individual's location in a social class or biological generation does not necessarily lead to the kind of personal interaction characterizing 'concrete groups', but it circumscribes his life chances with regard to wealth and power and modes of feeling, thought, and action. Second, the *generation as actuality* releases the latent potential inherent in generation location by orienting similarly located contemporaries toward each other in conflicting attempts at the interpretation and shaping of ideas and forms of action surrounding the unfolding of a common destiny. Third, the *generation unit* comprises individuals who share common attitudes and common principles of intellectual interpretation and action with regard to the socio-cultural process. Under present circumstances, youth, for example, representing the generation as actuality, is divisible into several generation units set apart from one another by, let us say, conservative, liberal, and radical responses to the socio-cultural process.

The appearance of diverse generation units in the contemporary 'youth culture' may well be linked to another general principle in Mannheim's analytical scheme. Mannheim claimed that new generation units only realize the potentialities inherent in a generation location under conditions of accelerated social and cultural change. The need for fast changes in basic attitudes ruptures the process of cultural transmission, creates a generation gap, and motivates new generation units to form a novel 'generation style' which is sharply set off from the life style of older members of society.

Alerted by Marx's understanding of the phenomenon of the crossing of class lines, Mannheim, furthermore, recognized that older people who are marginal to their own generation may act as forerunners of a new generation style. Just as renegade bourgeois intellectuals contributed to the evolving class ideology of the proletariat, so older individuals, we may argue, first shaped and practiced the attitudinal nucleus upon which configurations such as the youthful 'counter culture' are based. On a more general level Mannheim maintained that individuals belonging to earlier or later age groups may be attracted to certain practices particular to an 'alien' generation unit, especially, if these are favored by the trend of the times.[12]

The published lecture 'Competition as a cultural phenomenon', first delivered in September, 1928, at the Sixth Congress of German Sociologists in Zurich, again serves as proof of the applicability of the extrinsic interpretation that guides research in the sociology of knowledge. To begin with, Mannheim suggests that competition, far from being limited to economic action, co-determines the formal and substantive development of all cultural products. This basic assumption was not well received by the mandarins of German sociology; Alfred Weber dismissed Mannheim's approach as a rehash of historical materialism, while Werner Sombart defended Mannheim's paper on the grounds that it opposed Marxist determinism. In the course of this discussion Mannheim agreed with Sombart, acknowledging the ontic reality of the mind sphere; Sombart's failure to distinguish the simplified determinism of vulgar Marxism from genuine Marxism was not challenged.[13]

The sociology of knowledge generally assumes that mental life is determined by the major social processes; for the more specific purpose at hand, Mannheim delimits the field of investigation with the concept of 'sociology of the mind'.[14] Within this narrower framework the phenomenon of generations and the social process of competition function as key determinants of a special type of intellectual development which Mannheim identifies as the 'dialectical' form of change in mental activity.

Commonsense everyday thought, political thought, and thought in the social and cultural sciences are – in contrast to knowledge in the exact natural sciences – special types of thought which Mannheim characterizes as 'existentially-determined'. He, therefore, proposes to show that competition co-determines the formation of existentially-determined thought.

Informed by Martin Heidegger's analysis of the 'public interpretation of reality' (*das Man* or 'They'), Mannheim maintains that every element of existentially-determined knowledge is 'rooted in and carried by the desire for power and recognition of particular social groups who want to make their interpretation of the world the universal one'.[15] Moreover, competition for the establishment of the publicly dominant interpretation of reality is not a mere academic game, but reflects the competition of groups for dominant positions in the social structure.

Mannheim's analysis has roots in Marxian and Nietzschean reflections; Marx's view of intellectual production was informed by the basic assumption that the ideas of the ruling class are the ruling ideas of each age. In Marx's paradigm the class which acts as the ruling material force of society represents, at the same time, the ruling intellectual force of society. Nietzsche interpreted the origin of knowledge, even of language, as an expression of the power of rulers, who take possession of all objects and events by 'sealing them off' with sounds and names.[16]

Mannheim moved beyond partisan positions and doctrinaire philosophy, when he approached the problem of intellectual dominance via a sociological linkage of four social processes with four pure types of thinking. The first type of thinking is represented by the sanctional customs and usages of 'traditional folk wisdom'. This 'primitive' thought style is brought to dominance by the 'consensus of opinion' resulting from static social relationships which permit individuals and groups to merge in a process of 'spontaneous co-operation'. Second, the 'ecclesiastical-official' world interpretation predominates when a privileged group, such as a church, achieves a monopoly position in the social structure. Third, 'multipolar-rationalistic' conceptions of reality correspond to 'atomistic competition' which involves diverse groups, each trying to superimpose special world interpretations on other groups. Based on the anti-authoritarian, presuppositionless model of Cartesian rationalism this thought style is as fragmented as the areas of reality informing intellectual activity. In Western intellectual history multipolar rationalism emerged as a consequence of the dissolution of the medieval order; after the French Revolution it matured in the competitive climate of a secular society permitting the interplay of numerous groups including the nobility, the patriciate, the upper bourgeoisie, and the middle and lower classes. Fourth, 'doctrinal currents', such as liberalism, conservatism, and socialism, came to dominate the 'public interpretation of reality', as soon as atomistic competition gave way to the process of 'concentration' which has a dual function. On one hand, the fourth type of competition *fuses* spatially segregated groups of structurally analogous position, such as the working classes of different countries, and, on the other hand, it *polarizes* hostile groups in such a way that all partial antagonisms coalesce 'into decisive major intellectual currents and counter-currents combating one another'.[17]

As a dynamic thinker Mannheim could not bring himself to accept the static situation which he saw emerging in the evolution of thought; he, therefore, maintained that contemporary social processes do not only bring about polarization, but also 'syntheses'. Informed by Werner Sombart's law of 'competition on the basis of achievement', he pointed out that also in the region of mental production competing groups will take over from their opponents any intellectual element promising cognitive gain. Moreover, Mannheim assumed that these lesser, inter-group syntheses are accompanied by the larger effort to mediate the most pressing social tensions in a major synthesis. This overall synthesis may never materialize, but the intellectual and social energies invested on its behalf leave behind a common fund of experience and knowledge, a latter-day, pragmatic *consensus ex post*, that has the potential of providing an entire historical community with a unified intellectual perspective.[18]

Mannheim's attempts to correlate cognitive perspectives and world interpretations with social structure and process are rooted in French Enlightenment philosophy, Marxist social theory, and in the classical sociological tradition. At the outset, Saint-Simon pointed to the remarkable correspondence between the ideas of men and their forms of social organization; specifically, in *L'Industrie* (1816–18), he noted the links between theological knowledge and military despotism, scientific knowledge and industrialism. Then, Comte interpreted the evolution of mentality with regard to social evolution; he claimed that there are overlapping correspondences between the theological state of mind and primitive social organization, the dominance of metaphysics and feudalism, positivist science and industrial society.[19] The Saint-Simonians, as well, developed a theory of the social determination of knowledge; their analyses of different kinds of mental products, including aesthetics, historiography, law, literature, economics, science, and theology indicated that knowledge was intimately related to specific forms of social organization.[20] The larger part of Spencer's book, *The Study of Sociology* (1873), is given over to detailed analyses of the numerous social and psychic factors which influence intellectual activity, especially with regard to the hindrance of scientific interpretations of society. In France, Durkheim and members of his school described the interaction between primitive social structure, religious behavior, and the origin of basic logical categories; they, thereby, cast further light on the interdependent relations between social structure and social consciousness.[21] Max Weber's first study of the relationships between religion and socio-economic life, 'The Protestant ethic and the spirit of capitalism', was published in the *Archiv für Socialwissenschaft und Sozialpolitik* for 1904–5; in this early essay Weber stressed the contention that mental products, especially ethical and religious conceptions, played a major role in the development of modern capitalist society. The disastrous course of German politics during the First World War, however, sharpened Weber's growing awareness of the powerful influence which material interests exert on the career of ideas. His later sociological studies of religions, therefore, increasingly view mental conceptions from the basis of the social structure; in his analysis of *The Religion of China*, Weber chooses economic reality for his point of departure.[22] Max Scheler employed the criterion of artificiality to distinguish different types of knowledge; beginning with types of knowledge that are least artificial, he established a progression ranging from myth and legend through religion and philosophical-metaphysical knowledge to scientific-technological knowledge. The rate of change increases with degree of artificiality: while myth, legend, and religious knowledge change very slowly, positive science and technology undergo very fast alterations.[23]

In opposition to the positivists' unilinear conception of progress, which rendered historically earlier types of knowledge obsolete, Scheler viewed myth, religion, metaphysics, philosophy, and science as independently co-existing world interpretations corresponding to qualitatively different human needs for spiritual and intellectual orientation. Mannheim, as well, refused to accept scientific-technological knowledge as the only surviving prototype of all thinking and completely agreed with Scheler's contention that various types of knowledge, including metaphysics, must interact to provide modern men with interpretations of the intellectual and socio-historical world. Mannheim's typology of intellectual activity recognizes that in each society there are predominant patterns of reality construction, but never renounces the assumption that several types of thought co-exist and blend together.[24]

The lecture on 'Competition as a cultural phenomenon' concluded Mannheim's efforts on behalf of the development and application of basic concepts; at this point he was ready to face up to the need for a more systematic presentation of his sociology of knowledge. This systematization was achieved mainly by two of his remaining publications in Germany: the book, *Ideologie und Utopie*, and the article, 'Wissenssoziologie'.

4 The establishment of the sociology of knowledge

Mannheim's radical sociology of knowledge, as ultimately developed in *Ideologie und Utopie* (1929) and 'Wissenssoziologie' (1931), is rooted in a total conception of historicism which assumes that all mental products are part and parcel of an ongoing process of historical development. The radical nature of Mannheim's dynamic interpretation of mental activity stems largely from his claim that socio-cultural change represents a ceaseless force affecting not only the forms, but also the contents of intellectual production.

In *Ideologie und Utopie* (*Ideology and Utopia*), sociology in general and the sociology of knowledge in particular emerge as sciences that are central to the consciousness of twentieth-century men, since they make it possible to locate social processes and problems in the changing contexts of human life and experience. The social grounding of observed events helps us overcome the fragmented pseudo-reality created by disparate, isolated data; it, moreover, enables us to understand the existential meaning of historical and social processes.[1]

Toward the existential determination of knowledge

In his establishment of the sociology of knowledge as a central science Mannheim retains the basic distinction of two approaches to mental products. In 'Wissenssoziologie' ('The sociology of knowledge'), Mannheim reminds his readers that the sociology of knowledge derives its analytical strength from the method of extrinsic interpretation (sociological analysis) and that it differs, in this respect, from more traditional disciplines which rely on the method of immanent interpretation (pure theoretical analysis).[2] The method of *immanent interpretation* brings about the understanding of the content of mental products, but does not penetrate beyond the theoretical context. The method of *extrinsic interpretation*, on the other hand, takes the understanding of 'manifestations' for its point of departure and, consequently, brings the content of mental products into view as the manifestation of an underlying complex of reality forces (the absolute stratum).

Mannheim's method reflects the influence of Max Weber's efforts in Part III of *Wirtschaft und Gesellschaft*, which have the purpose of revealing the social conditions that are requisite to the genesis of basic ethical concepts such as sin, duty, and transgression.[3] In Part I of the English edition of *Ideology and Utopia* (1936), which introduces the topic to English-speaking audiences, Mannheim also acknowledges the importance of Wilhelm Dilthey's contributions to the method of understanding.[4]

Dilthey's *Lebensphilosophie* breaks with Hegel's conception of an inspirited universe and claims that the interpretative principle of the world is not inherent in it; on the contrary, the world can only be understood from the 'outside', from the vantage point of life. In contrast to Hegel, Dilthey reduces mental products (objective spirit) to the subjective-mental structure of human life. In Dilthey's philosophy, objective spirit is merely a concept indicating that a mental manifestation has been projected from the inner world of the creative subject into the objective outer world of historical reality. Significantly, Dilthey implies that such manifestations can be more adequately understood after they have found their way into the outside world. The key to the understanding of objective spirit (mental products) is provided by Dilthey's famous formula: Experience – Expression – Understanding. The human and social sciences must operate with this method, working back from the understanding of objective expressions to the underlying subjective, socially conditioned, experiences of living men.[5]

To begin with, Mannheim utilizes the distinction between intrinsic and extrinsic interpretation to locate the sociology of knowledge in the system of the sciences. The sociology of knowledge shares a position with other recently developed disciplines, such as cultural sociology and psychoanalysis, which contrasts with the stand taken by the traditional human sciences; the latter strive to reveal the immanent meaning of mental products by way of an intrinsic understanding of mind. The newer sciences, on the other hand, search for the extra-theoretical function served by mental products by way of an extrinsic understanding of the manifestations of existential relations. This novel research intention motivates sociologists of knowledge, for example, to interpret knowledge by understanding it as the manifestation of an ultimate reality represented by social process and structure. The sociology of knowledge, then, employs the method of extrinsic interpretation to functionally relate mental products to social reality as the absolute stratum.

Much like Dilthey, who proclaimed that thought cannot go behind life, that life is ultimate reality, Mannheim saw the new orientation represented by the sociology of knowledge as an inevitable scientific expression of modern existence. Contemporary men cannot go behind social reality, which is the vital center of all their experiences, and they must interpret all psychic-intellectual manifestations of life as dependent upon social positions and changing socio-economic orders.[6]

The interpretation of mental processes and products as functions of social life relies mainly on the notion of the social or 'existential determination of knowledge'. This concept is essentially of epistemological significance and does not suggest mechanical cause-effect sequences. Investigations of the social or existential determination of knowledge aim above all at an understanding of the meaning of structural interrelationships in the mental and social spheres. In the tradition of Max Weber, Mannheim deliberately leaves the exact nature of existential determination open to invite empirical studies of concrete correlations between existential situations and thought processes; only empirical research can reveal the strictness or variability of these correlations. In the language of Dilthey the existential determination of knowledge represents a 'category of understanding'.[7]

As a theory Mannheim's sociology of knowledge is primarily concerned with the existential determination of actual thinking. This theory equates reality with social existence and, consequently, assumes that social life possesses actual relevance (*Geltungsrelevanz*) for the meaning, content, validity, and structure of mental products. The methodological potential of the sociology of knowledge becomes effective whenever empirical research indicates that the content and form of a mental product are dependent on a specific social context. Max Scheler's sociology of knowledge assumed that the existential factors in the social process merely possessed genetic or factual relevance since they conditioned only the origin or factual development of ideas. Mannheim's radical theory goes beyond Scheler's moderate position and claims that, presently, social life centered around socio-economic orders does not only condition the temporal realization of ideas, that it does not only possess factual relevance (*Faktizitätsrelevanz*), but that it influences the form, structure, and content of mental products.[8]

Individual thinkers perform the function of 'mediating' the influence of social existence upon knowledge; these cognitive agents have specific locations in social space and historical time; consequently, their selection and interpretation of data reflects the particular 'standpoint' which they occupy in society. This implies that the objects of cognition are never accessible to men as total configurations; rather, individual thinkers can only perceive those partial aspects of cognitive objects that are consonant with their socio-historical standpoints of thinking.[9] The assumption of an existential determination of knowledge leads, then, to the companion claim that the situational factors in the social process penetrate into the particular 'perspective' circumscribing the content, structure, and direction of concrete thought processes.

The socio-historical location or 'standpoint' occupied by a thinking individual conditions his particular perspective or outlook which, in turn, penetrates into the products of his thought. Mannheim conceptualizes this situation with the term perspective context (*Aspektstruktur*), which describes how a cognitive agent approaches the subject matter of his investigation, which of its elements he grasps, and the manner in which he constructs a perspective context in the process of thinking. Thought in the humanities and social sciences is rooted in meta-empirical world view presuppositions and can, therefore, only be formulated within the limits established by particular perspective contexts. The problems and conceptual constructions arising in the process of socio-historical experience are irrelevant only in the case of clear-cut mathematical propositions – types of knowledge which are not conditioned by the existential situation of the knowing subject.

On this basis and within these limits Mannheim formulates the major assumption of his radical sociology of knowledge: the socio-existentially determined standpoint of thinking penetrates into the perspective context; from there it extends into the content of a mental product and leaves its imprint on the entire thought result since it exerts a decisive influence even upon the categorical apparatus.[10]

The location of the knowing subject in social space and historical time determines what aspect of reality is accessible to him, how he conceptualizes his experience of that reality within the confines of his perspective, and the manner in which the basic categories of thought function to order the raw data of cognition. Impressions and constructions of reality vary according to the differential location of knowing subjects in socio-historical reality.

Mannheim's arguments amount to a reinterpretation of Kant's universal, *a priori* view of the role which the categories play in the cognitive process; in this respect Mannheim's approach is similar to Durkheim's stand on the social origin of the categories. Moreover, both Mannheim and Durkheim are open to criticism for their failures to distinguish between materially determined general concepts which are changeable, and pure, formal concepts, such as the categories, that are without concrete content and, therefore, incapable of undergoing alterations.[11]

The sociology of knowledge relates mental products to the socio-existential standpoint of the producer; this relational process has the additional function of 'particularizing' or restricting the validity of mental products to the limited scope of a particular, socially conditioned perspective. In Mannheim's theory the existential connections of knowledge are not merely of an individual nature; rather they assume their greatest significance as collective social processes. The major thrust of his sociology of knowledge is in the direction of group behavior; in their thinking individuals largely share orientations that are prescribed by the collective interests and purposes of groups which afford them membership.[12]

In the sociology of knowledge perspective the assertions of individual thinkers appear, therefore, as expressions of an underlying, collective thought style, or as reflections of a larger world view context which is socio-existentially determined. In the course of empirical research a given mental product is 'imputed' to a particular central world view, such as conservatism. The world view is constructed as an ideal type and actual imputations must be carried out in full awareness of the problematic interaction of ideal, real, and mixed types. This procedure leads to the final technique of 'sociological imputation' which derives mental products, such as conservative ideas, from the structural and behavioral characteristics of social groups utilizing a central world view, such as conservatism, as a vehicle of ideational expression.

Sociological imputations also necessitate investigations of the pertinent social structure at large, such as US society, to determine its changing influence upon a particular world view and the groups that function as the social carriers of that world view. In this manner the various stages of the method of imputation build up an interpretative paradigm affording tenancy to individual thought products and the collective contexts to which they are related. The method of imputation enables empirical researchers to place concrete thought products in the context of a central world view which is, then, related to a configuration of group life, providing thinking individuals with their existential basis.[13]

Social conflict and ideological struggle

Mannheim's methodological reflections were carried out in a social environment, where the interaction of groups proceeded mainly along the lines of conflict; conservatism, liberalism, and socialism were the initial world views serving as vehicles of ideational expression for the conflicting socio-political goals pursued by fighting groups. The divisive force of inter-group conflict escalated social warfare and led to the proliferation of intellectual combat along new lines of confrontation including such world views as Communism, National Socialism, and National Bolshevism; the latter often served as a 'half-way house' for the cross traffic between Communism and National Socialism. Most National Bolshevists accepted various components of Leninism as the ideological vehicle for anti-capitalist national liberation movements. The philosopher and political activist Ernst Niekisch, for example, passed through the National Bolshevist world view on his way from Social Democracy to Communism. En route from nihilism to technicism, the novelist Ernst Jünger had his flirtations with National Bolshevist youth.[14]

Mannheim knew that social conflict and class struggle are forces that do not respect the imaginary boundary between theory and practice. In his estimate social and political theorists are not mere observers of social conflict, but participants whose interests and values anchor them to a special, partisan perspective. Political and social processes strongly influence the investigator's choice of a research problem and his decision to operationalize it by means of a particular approach; the socio-political undertow cuts through the intellectual seascape with such force that different thought styles are brought to the surface. These styles of thought are set apart by differences in logical structure and fundamental cognitive norms, including the categories. Mannheim's attempt at an empirical corroboration of these assumptions is represented by his work on the 'Prospects of scientific politics', which forms part of *Ideology and Utopia*. Here he analyzes the traditional and developing currents which are mainly responsible for the formation of the socio-political force field of Weimar Germany. He focuses on five ideal types represented by (1) bureaucratic conservatism, (2) conservative historicism, (3) liberal-democratic thought, (4) socialist-communist conceptions, and (5) fascism.[15]

The conflict of thought styles reflects on the intellectual level that opposing groups are fighting for the establishment of divergent economic systems and social orders. The destruction of medieval society was accomplished by bourgeois groups that not only espoused new values, but actively struggled for the instauration of a novel economic system. On the intellectual level the developing bourgeois thought style annihilated, therefore, the feudal paradigm of world interpretation as thoroughly as bourgeois forms of social and economic organization destroyed the socio-economic arrangements of feudalism on the societal level. Contemporary types of class struggle proceed on these two levels as well: proletarian groups desire to replace the bourgeois thought style with their own mode of world interpretation to establish the inescapable logic and reality-adequacy of their attempts at the establishment of proletarian forms of socio-economic organization.[16]

The intellectual and socio-economic conflicts surrounding the French Revolution of 1789 escalated political struggle to a novel niveau, marked by both increasing bitterness and sophistication. The development of ideological consciousness began in earnest with the French philosophers whose thought contributed to the revolution. In 1801, Destutt de Tracy used the concept of ideology to characterize his 'science of ideas'. He collided with Napoleon Bonaparte, who employed 'ideology' pejoratively to attack the alleged political threat posed by troublesome, 'foolish' intellectuals. In a decisive move beyond the notion of thought styles Mannheim adopts the concept of ideology, product of revolution and counter-revolution, to give adequate expression to modern varieties of group conflict which involve the interrelated dimensions of intellectual, social, economic, and political combat.[17]

To begin with, Mannheim differentiates the 'particular' from the 'total' conception of ideology. The particular conception of ideology limits the operation of distrust to a circumscribed set of ideas and assumptions propagated by the theorists and functionaries of groups which the ideological analyst considers hostile. The ideological analyst debunks this particular complex of mental products as the outgrowth of efforts to mask facts and processes which the opponent does not wish to be accurately known. The construction of an ideological façade is usually inspired by political and socio-economic interests which are best pursued in the shadows of a disguised reality. The particular conception of ideology recognizes that reality may be distorted in a number of ways: such distortions may take the form of conscious lies or they may become manifest as half-conscious disguises; furthermore, the deception of others may be replaced by self-deception. The limited nature of the particular conception of ideology is, furthermore, demonstrated by its characteristic focus on the *content* of certain ideas and the interpretation of ideological deception as a merely psychic and, above all, remediable process. Operating on the psychological level the particular conception of ideology never fully transcends individual thought processes and can only conceive of group phenomena as mere products of the integration of individual experiences. This variant of ideological analysis was, therefore, successful in the encounter with loosely integrated groups, such as eighteenth-century French court cliques, whose individual members had only a vague sense of the similarity of their interests. The psychic-individualistic tendencies inherent in the particular conception of ideology, however, rendered this type of analysis obsolete, as soon as naked material needs and powerful world view solidarities contributed to the emergence of strongly integrated groups, such as Socialist working-class parties, whose members had a vague sense of their individual interests, but a pronounced feeling for the collective purposes of their groups. During the later part of the nineteenth and the early part of the twentieth century the sense of proletarian solidarity was even stronger than the individual interest in life and liberty; in their struggle with the armed protectors of bourgeois-capitalist interests many workers readily faced death and imprisonment.[18]

The particular conception of ideology corresponds to the theory of 'prejudices' developed by French Enlightenment philosophers, such as Voltaire, Holbach, and Helvétius. These philosophers assumed that Baconian idols, material interests, and priestly deceit coalesce into a sphere of prejudice distorting cognitive processes. As ideological analysts they claimed that their adversaries, especially the priests, aristocratic court cliques, and their bourgeois satellites, exploited their knowledge and political influence to further their economic interests at the expense of the people. This type of ideological analysis, then, indicted particular individuals, assembled in loosely integrated groups, as deliberate liars who falsified socio-economic and political processes on behalf of their special interests. Significantly, however, the philosophers interpreted ideological distortion as a psychological, remediable process; they retained the assumption that men as cognitive agents were basically capable of reality-adequate knowledge and advertised their own role as therapists. The therapy of enlightening education was credited with the power of freeing the people from the shackles of ignorance and superstition, forged by their ideological adversaries. The philosophers' epistemological and social optimism was reflected in Helvétius's programmatic statement: 'L'éducation peut tout'.[19]

Mannheim realized that the transition from the particular to the total conception of ideology occurred in Marxian thought.[20] The influence of the French philosophers persuaded Marx to debunk all holy missions as reflections of material interests, pursued by their holy spokesmen.[21] Frequently, Marx employed the particular conception of ideology to express, in this manner, the opinion that ruling classes produce ideas to disguise social processes, the true recognition of which would be detrimental to their interests. The comprehensive dynamics of Hegelian logic, however, enabled Marx to penetrate into the sphere of the total conception of ideology which assumes the existence of a completely distorted mind, falsifying all phenomena that come within its cognitive range. Marx illustrated the effects of total ideological analysis when he explained Kant's ethics as a crazy mirror image of the bizarre socio-economic and political conditions reigning in Germany at the close of the eighteenth century.[22]

According to Mannheim the total conception of ideology critically invades the entire world view of an adversary: the ideological analyst relates an opponent's total world view and his entire conceptual apparatus to his socio-existential situation and interprets all of his mental products as functions of the collective life in which he participates. Total ideological analysis exchanges the psychological for the theoretical ('noological') level since this approach interprets the content, the form, the perspective, and the conceptual structure of thought styles as functions of the social conditions determining intellectual production. Ideologies are no longer interpreted as subjective, deliberate disguises concealing particular interests, but as the superstructural reflections of objective socio-economic conditions.[23]

The particular, psychological concept of ideology never brings the logic and method of science into doubt; by contrast total ideological analysis tries to annihilate not only specific ideas, but along with them the intellectual foundations supporting them. Total ideological analysis penetrates into the cognitive sphere, discredits the entire structure of the opponent's consciousness, and subverts the validity of his theories by revealing them as mere functions of his inescapable social situation.

It was Marx who first interpreted ideas as mere reflections of their producer's position in the 'process of production', of his class position. Marx, the representative of the working class, accused the entire mind of being ideological; at the same time, he limited the destructive effects of ideological analysis by attacking only the bourgeoisie. He exempted the working class from the charge of ideology, since he believed in the correspondence of proletarian interests and ideas with the real life-process of history. Marx's concept of ideology sensed in the opponent's entire behavior an unreliability that he interpreted as a function of the social situation in which the enemy found himself; therefore, his concept of ideology was total. But, Marx's conception of ideology was at the same time 'special' since its operation was limited to the examination of bourgeois mental production.

Under the impression of the 'socially disorganized' and intellectually fragmented situation of Weimar Germany, Mannheim felt compelled to widen Marx's *total* and *special* conception of ideology into his own *total* and *general* formulation of ideology, which claims that social conditions determine the mental products of *all* groups including the one affording membership to the ideological analyst. The ideas of Marxist intellectuals are, therefore, just as much of an ideological reflection of their proletarian social basis as the thought products of bourgeois theorists are the ideological echo of their liberal-capitalist existence.

Mannheim implies that the Marxists failed to advance ideological analysis beyond the level of partisan intellectual warfare and credits his general formulation of ideology with the features of a progressive instrument capable of transforming 'simple' ideological theory into a penetrating sociology of knowledge.[24]

The fire from the Left

The Marxists remained unimpressed by Mannheim's 'courageous' advancement of the theory of ideology which they debunked as a storm in the teacup of bourgeois social science. To begin with, neither Marx nor his followers had any interest in ideological analysis as such; their major commitment was to the class struggle and the revolutionary transformation of society. The theory of ideology, therefore, was important only as long as it remained part of revolutionary social theory. Furthermore, as Marx had made abundantly clear, ideological or false consciousness was not a perennial, inescapable intellectual condition, but merely a mental symptom indicating the presence of social ills in need of the cure of proletarian world revolution. Fully developed bourgeois-capitalist societies, in particular, inevitably create and become dependent upon socio-economic processes, such as division of labor, capital accumulation, commodity production, trade, and class conflict, which reduce human beings and their experiential world to things. In bourgeois-capitalist society the reification of this object world, which is non-human, hence alien and false, indicates the operation of a reified and, therefore, alienated, false consciousness incapable of grasping either the contradictions underlying its own existence or the true nature of human relations. Marxist ideological analysis is inseparable from historical materialism, since the process divorcing the idea of man from the reality of man has an economic basis to be found in the involuntary division of labor leading to forced labor and private property. In the process of capitalist production society split into warring classes and the state emerged as the organized expression of the will of the propertied upper class. Upon the loss of their freedom men developed false consciousness which is the consciousness of individuals in alienation. False consciousness leads men to create ideologies or systems of beliefs and ideas which are object-inadequate and, therefore, without effect upon reality. The beliefs and ideas produced by a false consciousness act merely upon man's imagination.

While Mannheim sees ideology as a general aspect of the human condition, Marx views ideological or false consciousness as a temporary madness that distorts reality by transforming the material world into a mere idea and mere ideas into material entities. For Marx ideology means that the fancies of the human brain take on bodily form, that a world of 'ghosts' materializes in the mind. Marx opposes the insanity engendered by false consciousness with his materialist social theory which reveals ideas as the 'mental reflection', or the 'symptom' of the material relations of production dominating an inhuman, hence, false social order.[25]

As a consequence of his revolutionary optimism Marx never doubted the possibility of staring down the ideological cobwebs dimming human vision in the bourgeois-capitalist house of intellect. The strategic futuristic advantages which the Marxist imagination attaches to the worker's social status and role extend into the intellectual realm. Consequently, thought processes that are grounded in the proletarian experience have the best chance for penetrating the ideological syndrome and for reaching the sane sphere of reality-adequate knowledge.

The universal significance of the proletariat results from the universal importance of its misery; representing a complete loss of humanity, it is only by way of a complete redemption of humanity that the proletariat can redeem itself. The goals and interests of the proletariat coincide with those of society in general, since a truly human existence for all can only be achieved once the proletariat abolishes itself along with the entire society that created the proletariat as its 'notorious crime'.[26]

In the Marxist view, then, the proletariat is capable of grasping the essence of capitalism and of the historical development leading to its destruction, since it occupies a social position in capitalistic society, where the inhuman reality of this doomed order is directly experienced. As Lukács pointed out in 1923, the class-conscious proletarian comprehends the struggle surrounding him and the truth of the future which he creates and which will be fully revealed to him at the moment of revolution. In the instant of revolutionary decision consciousness will be dialectically transformed into action, and theory into practice; the revolution, therefore, brings proletarian philosophy, science, and class-consciousness to their full levels of logical adequacy and, significantly, terminates the rule of ideology in the intellectual realm.[27]

Since Mannheim did not share the Marxists' belief in the revolutionary transformation of the social structure, he could not accept their companion assumption that ideology would dissolve along with the social conditions that had created it. On the other hand, Mannheim refused to draw the anarcho-nihilist conclusions which follow from the conception of total, general, interminable ideology; instead, he decided to soften the very conception of ideology by equating it with the notion that consciousness is somehow determined by vague elements originating in social existence. By replacing historical materialism with a sociological history of thought Mannheim loses a clearly defined conception of social existence; instead social existence takes on the features of an amalgam of 'extra-theoretical factors of the most diverse sort'.[28]

Mannheim's tendency to deflect the socio-critical thrust of ideological analysis was attacked by Max Horkheimer of the *Institut für*

Sozialforschung in Frankfurt shortly after the publication of *Ideologie und Utopie*.[29] Reviewers with affinity to Social Democratic officialdom were rather shocked by Mannheim's 'radicalism', but Horkheimer and other members of the Frankfurt Institute, such as Theodor Adorno and Herbert Marcuse, rebuked him for his betrayal of Marxist *praxis*. Horkheimer reminded Mannheim that Marx's intention was, after all, the destruction of metaphysics and the transformation of philosophy into positive science and *praxis*; in Mannheim's sociology of knowledge Horkheimer detected merely philosophical intentions. His metaphysical search for the meaning of history was ultimately nothing but a retreat to the mad streak of idealism in Hegel's thought and the Christian theory of God.[30] The Marxists employed the concept of socio-existential determination to correlate specific theories with concrete social classes, separated by property relations; Mannheim, on the other hand, transformed socio-economic contradictions and conflicts into struggles between contradictory world views, thought styles, and ideas.[31]

More recently, Hans-Joachim Lieber and Peter Furth have defended Marx's conception of ideology against Mannheim's charge that it represents merely an instrument for partisan polemics and intellectual subversion: Marxist ideological analysis is above all the intellectual foundation supporting all attempts at social self-enlightenment.[32] Mannheim's sociology of knowledge, on the other hand, suffers from the lack of socio-economic conceptualizations and the attendant need to distill social standpoints from the *consciousness* of social groups. In the end Mannheim, therefore, relates knowledge to collective mental constructs and transforms the dependency of the mental superstructure upon the material substructure into the interplay between two mental spheres, represented by intellectual self-consciousness (knowledge) and social self-consciousness (society).[33]

The long march toward truth

Mannheim confronted neither the problems arising from his hazy conception of social existence nor the questions concerning the actual novelty of his assumption that knowledge is always determined by the knower's social position – an assumption that had no news value to the Marxists, who were, however, alarmed by Mannheim's attempts to neutralize the qualitative differences between bourgeois and proletarian modes of existence. Instead, Mannheim added two further distinctions to his paradigm of ideological analysis by setting the *non-evaluative* general total conception of ideology apart from the *evaluative* conception.

On the non-evaluative level of total, general ideological analysis research reveals the changing interactions between mental products and their producers' socio-existential positions without concern for the correctness and validity of ideas. Mannheim claims that specific aspects of Weimar culture, such as social disorganization and intellectual conflict, have rendered the traditional, static, absolutist approach to ideas obsolete. On the other hand, he believes his non-evaluative ideological analysis to be congruent with the shifting social and intellectual situation of his transitional epoch. Mannheim's treatment of ideas does not intend to express disregard for truth; it merely wishes to express the conviction that the uncertainties of his time do not permit the acceptance of truth as a given, pre-established fact. Not unlike Hegel, he views truth as a process, as something to be discovered; contemporary researchers contribute to this search by providing approximate insights into the nature of social and intellectual phenomena which possess relevance for the discovery of true reality.

Mannheim claims, furthermore, that his rigorous attention to the socio-existential partiality of all intellectual positions does not lead to relativism, but to the novel perspective of 'relationism'. The assumption that the construction of knowledge is inescapably delimited by the researcher's situational perspective and research arrangement only justifies the charge of relativism, as long as criticism proceeds from an outmoded epistemological orientation that has its experiential basis in the older mathematical and physical science models which dominated thought before the advent of quantum theory, Heisenberg's principle of indeterminacy, and Einstein's theory of relativity. The static, absolutist norms of traditional epistemology demand the production of unperspectivistic thought results that are determined neither by the socio-existential position of the researcher nor by the experimental situation of the scientific observer; these norms are, however, irrelevant for modern physical science and the dynamic, changeable subject matter of the human and social sciences, rooted in the flux and flow of human life and history. An epistemology which demands disregard for the process of the human-existential derivation of thought promotes merely the accumulation of 'denatured' knowledge. The emerging dynamic, scientific theory of knowledge, however, accepts 'situational determination' as an inherent factor in knowledge and does not evoke the myth of an 'as such' sphere of absolute truth to dismiss it as the agent of norm-destroying relativism. From the vantage point of modern epistemology with its openness for the findings of contemporary physical and social scientists it is entirely conceivable to distinguish relativism from relationism which 'signifies merely that all of the elements of meaning in a given situation have reference to one another and derive their significance from this reciprocal interrelationship in a given frame of thought'.[34]

The sociologist of knowledge who applies the relational process to mental products does not merely reveal the presence of the relationship between these intellectual assertions and the socio-existential standpoints of those who assert them; he, simultaneously, subjects mental products and the perspective wherein they have arisen to a process of 'particularization'. This transition from the relational to the particularizing process results in the delimitation of mental products and intellectual perspectives with regard to their scope of comprehension and the extent of their validity. On the non-evaluative level of total and general ideological analysis the sociologist of knowledge, therefore, begins to transcend the mere description of empirical data that indicate the manner in which intellectual perspectives and mental products originate and develop in particular social situations. As soon as the sociologist of knowledge delimits the scope and validity of mental perspectives and the assertions arising within their boundaries he turns into a critic of specific meanings, values, and attitudes reflecting the social positions, collective interests, and strivings of identifiable social groups.

The inevitable transition from the relational to the particularizing process, then, leads to definite decisions concerning the powers of comprehension inherent in different social standpoints; such decisions, however, amount to evaluations of the greater or lesser reality-adequacy of the different modes of thought associated with the varying social positions.

As a consequence of these methodological, epistemological, and conceptual dynamics ideological analysis finally arrives on the evaluative level. The evaluative, total, and general conception of ideology enables the sociologist of knowledge to uncover the operation of 'false consciousness'. In the light of this type of analysis a theory, for example,[35]

> is wrong if in a given practical situation it uses concepts and categories which, if taken seriously, would prevent man from adjusting himself at that historical stage. Antiquated and inapplicable norms, modes of thought, and theories are likely to degenerate into ideologies whose function it is to conceal the actual meaning of conduct rather than to reveal it.

The rapid pace of social change which Mannheim witnessed in Weimar society persuaded him finally to conceptualize false consciousness as the expression of a cognitive lag. He claimed that the intellectual comprehension of social reality may lag behind the actual situation, thereby giving rise to knowledge which is ideological because of its propensity to hide the developing new aspects of reality beneath antiquated forms of perception. The search for reality may also be obstructed by utopian distortions which indicate the operation of forms of perception that are in advance of the actual situation. In this case the actual situation lags behind intellectual constructions of social reality. In either case mental structures fail to adequately comprehend a 'dynamic' reality. Consequently, Mannheim characterizes his final conception of ideology and utopia as evaluative and dynamic. 'It is evaluative because it presupposes certain judgments concerning the reality of ideas and structures of consciousness, and it is dynamic because these judgments are always measured by a reality which is in constant flux.'[36]

On the non-evaluative level of total and general ideological analysis Mannheim had countered the charge of relativism with his conceptualization of relationism and the associated reconstruction of epistemology. The evaluative, dynamic conception of total and general ideology could not help but sharpen the problem of relativism; on this analytical level Mannheim began to utilize the resources of philosophical pragmatism which were to play an increasingly significant role in the development of his sociology of planning. The evaluation of mental products as ideological concealments or utopian distortions of reality utilizes the pragmatic criterion of actual practice; evaluative ideological and utopian analysis, in other words, tests every idea by measuring its greater or lesser congruence with a reality that reveals itself in the living context of actual practice. The evaluative analyst of false consciousness has the task of distinguishing between ideas that are reality-adequate, hence true, and others that are not reality-adequate, therefore, false; he must contribute to the ongoing process 'of determining which of all the ideas current are really valid in a given situation'.[37]

Mannheim finds the pragmatic criterion for the determination of ideational validity by recourse to the practice of everyday life: ideas are true as long as they are congruent with the actual social situation of men, as long as they are successful in guiding the accommodation of human action to the changing context of group life.

This search for reality is the task of ideological and utopian analysis to be carried out in the force field of a dynamic sociology of knowledge. The rapid changes in contemporary social existence, which represents reality, however, have a dual effect: they complicate sociological analysis and facilitate the diffusion of false consciousness both in its ideological and utopian forms.

Mannheim's attempt to employ the Marxist concept of false consciousness in an 'ideologically' defused form reflects his desire to transcend the political boundaries of revolutionary historical materialism in the direction of a new type of evolutionary sociology. His rejection of both the revolutionary implications of Marxism and the reactionary practice of bourgeois social science, which is blind to the operation of false consciousness, further complicates his intellectual position in the uncharted no man's land between the two modes of interpretation dominating the imagination of his generation.

Marx's conception of false consciousness has its clear-cut empirical referent in bourgeois-capitalist society with its antagonistic class relationships. The false human relations of this society inevitably lead to the production of false consciousness. The need of this false society for intellectual distortion, concealment, and reification accelerates the diffusion of false consciousness throughout the social structure: ultimately false consciousness prevents all members of bourgeois-capitalist society from insight into the true character of their social order. The Marxist paradigm is equally unequivocal with regard to the potential destruction of false consciousness; the proletarian revolution will remove this distorted mental structure along with the contradictory, antagonistic social order which gave rise to it in the first place.

Mannheim's interpretation of false consciousness is unrelated to a specific social order; it, therefore, lacks the clear empirical reference point of Marxist analysis. False consciousness takes on the appearance of a general human predicament which functions to block 'comprehension of a reality which is the outcome of constant reorganization of the mental processes which make up our worlds'.[38] Equally vague and 'spiritualistic' is Mannheim's approach to the potential destruction of false consciousness; while Marx correlates intellectual change with the revolutionary transformation of society, Mannheim connects mental alterations with the complex dynamics of a largely imaginary historical process

5 Beyond ideology and utopia

With the evaluative, dynamic conception of ideology and utopia Mannheim had completed the thought structure of his radical sociology of knowledge which threatened to imprison all ideas, including his own, in the darkness of false consciousness as a total and general intellectual malaise. Equally unimpressed by nihilistic resignation and Marxist futurology, Mannheim searched for an historical process capable of carrying intellectual labors beyond the force field of ideology and utopia into the vicinity of reality-adequate, objective, and valid knowledge.

In Hegelian fashion Mannheim's problematic construction of this historical process proceeds from a conceptual basis and gains momentum as it advances along the borders of the metaphysics of history. Mannheim's search for the sphere of 'objectively' valid truth is documented by his essay on 'The prospects of scientific politics' which forms part of the book, *Ideology and Utopia*. In these reflections about the 'Relationship between social theory and political practice' Mannheim also identifies the dialectical interplay between analysis and synthesis, particularity and totality as his conceptual fundament.

Mannheim's belief in the potential elimination of false consciousness presupposes the assumption that the particularity of the different socio-existentially determined perspective contexts represents at the same time the basis for intellectual efforts striving to bring into view the totality of social and cultural life. Political and social life during the years of the Weimar Republic was dominated by partisan strife and society-wide conflict, involving numerous fragmentary forms of world interpretation, which functioned usually as expressions and justifications of the political and socio-economic purposes pursued by antagonistic groups. Strangely enough it was precisely this situation which inspired Mannheim's optimistic assumption that the contemporary observer was capable of insight not only into the partisan character of all political knowledge, but also into the particularity of each variety:[1]

> It has become incontrovertibly clear today that all knowledge which is either political or which involves a world-view, is inevitably partisan. The fragmentary character of all knowledge is clearly recognizable. But this implies the possibility of an integration of many mutually complementary points of view into a comprehensive whole.

In Mannheim's estimate Weimar culture, with its gliding of standpoints and intense intellectual conflicts, promised the elevation of at least some social sciences to the level of suprapartisan synthesis. 'The present structure of society makes possible a political science which will not be merely a party science, but a science of the whole. Political sociology, as the science which comprehends the whole political sphere, thus attains the stage of realization.'[2] Ironically, a few years later the Nazis brought German intellectual life to a grinding halt and transformed its remaining organizations into propaganda devices for the dissemination of a single, totalitarian point of view. Mannheim's optimistic prognosis of an impending synthesis of particular, but mutually complementary perspectives into an objective scientific entity remained unfulfilled; instead, in violation of all known principles of scientific and human discourse, there emerged a subjective, partisan world interpretation which achieved its preeminence by murdering its opponents and by outlawing all other perspectives.

The demise of the Periclean era

The proscription of creative activity formed part of the immediate program of Nazi oppression. Shortly after their assumption of power the Nazis ordered the Berlin newspaper *Die Nachtausgabe* to publish a 'first list' of forbidden authors. The black list, which appeared on April 23, 1933, outlawed all major writers including such Weimar luminaries as Bertolt Brecht, Max Brod, Alfred Döblin, Lion Feuchtwanger, Egon Erwin Kisch, Heinrich Mann, Thomas Mann, Theodor Plievier, Erich Maria Remarque, Arthur Schnitzler, Ernst Toller, Kurt Tucholsky, Arnold Zweig, and Stefan Zweig. This first list was followed by others and soon literate Germans realized that nearly eight hundred writers had disappeared from their cultural environment.[3]

The Nazi attack against German culture proceeded on all fronts of intellectual-artistic creativity; but like the later exhibitions of *entartete Kunst*, which were meant to demonstrate the evils of 'decadent art', the blacklisting of authors alerted the world to the astounding creative vitality of Weimar culture. People began to realize to what extent the artistic-intellectual community of Weimar Germany had contributed to the transformation of science, philosophy, literature, music, painting, the theater, motion pictures, and architecture into configurations of images expressing the dawn of a new consciousness. The Nazi policy of proscription could not fail to backfire since it included creative movements of international renown, such as expressionist painting, atonal music, Brechtian theater, Einsteinian physics, and *Bauhaus* architecture and design.[4]

On April 1, 1930, Mannheim succeeded to the chair of Franz Oppenheimer as Professor of Sociology and Political Economy at the University of Frankfurt am Main; at the same time he was appointed director of the *Soziologische Seminar* of Frankfurt University. In the twenties and early thirties the University of Frankfurt provided a congenial environment for many intellectuals of liberal and radical persuasion. Leftist Hegelians and Marxists were attracted by the *Institut für Sozialforschung* which had been formally affiliated with the University of Frankfurt since 1923. When the Institute began to function in 1924 its director, the socialist Carl Grünberg, underscored the revolutionary role of the research institute which was to teach students how to understand, criticize, and change social and political processes so that they could contribute to the victory of the new social order of socialism. In 1931, Max Horkheimer took the directorship and continued to emphasize the need for an understanding of the relations between economic reality and socio-cultural processes.[5] In 1931, the circle of the Frankfurt Institute began to express opinions in the *Zeitschrift für Sozialforschung*; in the pages of the new periodical and in the lecture rooms of the Institute there emerged the outlines of a new social science, sketched by men, such as Theodor Adorno, Erich Fromm, Max Horkheimer, Leo Loewenthal, Herbert Marcuse, and Franz Neumann.

Mannheim was not connected with the Institute for Social Research; according to Max Horkheimer 'his relations with the Institute were relatively friendly, especially in view of the growing National-Socialist movement, but we did not share his theories'.[6] At the University of Frankfurt, Mannheim was successful in his academic career and as 'a man of humor and a natural teacher with an appreciation of many things outside his field' he filled his lectures with enthusiastic students.[7]

Mannheim's Frankfurt years coincide with the declining period of the Weimar Republic. In 1929, Germany's prosperous economic development came to a grinding halt. The Great Depression, announced by the crash of the New York stock exchange in October, 1929, brought the German Reich to the brink of economic disaster:

by the end of 1932, nearly half of the German labor force was unemployed. Many jobless men provoked arrests, seeking shelter and food in prison – others swelled the ranks of the Red Front and, ominously, those of Hitler's Storm Troops. In the Reichstag elections of May, 1928, the Nazis had received a mere 3 per cent of valid votes, but in July, 1932, 37 per cent of the ballot went to Hitler's party. The budding dictator's propaganda machine – financed by big industrialists – exploited the additional economic problem of reparations payments to the Western Allies, which the Young Committee had finally set in such a way that the actual payments, including interest, were to total approximately twenty-nine billion dollars payable from 1929 to 1988.

The depression brought the beginning of the end for parliamentary government: on March 27, 1930, Weimar Germany's last Great Coalition broke up with the resignation of the Müller cabinet. The government of the Social Democratic chancellor Hermann Müller collapsed because of its inability to settle a dispute between the Social Democrats and the People's Party concerning the elimination of a serious deficit in the unemployment fund. The business-oriented People's Party called for a cut in unemployment benefits while the Social Democrats demanded new taxes on business. The crisis provided Hindenburg and Genral Kurt von Schleicher, head of the ministerial office in the ministry of defense, with the long-awaited opportunity for authoritarian government.

On March 28, 1930, President Hindenburg asked Heinrich Brüning, parliamentary leader of the Catholic Center party, to form a cabinet without firm party ties; two days later he appointed Brüning chancellor. The new government was weighted to the Right and included no Social Democrats. Brüning's deflationary policy and program of economic retrenchment found insufficient parliamentary support and his unpopular measures were carried out by means of the president's emergency powers under article 48 of the Weimar constitution. From the beginning the Social Democrat Rudolf Breitscheid implored the government not to use article 48: its employment, he warned, could only lead into the darkness of dictatorship.

These developments encouraged Hindenburg to drop all democratic pretenses and to show himself for what he was – a treacherous, reactionary Junker. The eighty-four-year-old president withdrew his support from Brüning, forcing his resignation on May 30; then Hindenburg sided openly with the large landowners and industrial magnates against the Social Democratic working masses that had supported him against the presidential candidates Hitler and Thälmann, thereby making possible the old field marshall's re-election on April 10, 1932. Hindenburg's betrayal of the democratic forces sealed the fate of the doomed republic which became subject to the dangerous cross-currents of partisan interests, represented by generals, cartel bosses, and East Elbian landlords, who shared an appreciation of the Nazis as an ill-mannered, but highly useful force counterbalancing the Socialist and Communist hordes. General von Schleicher confided in a letter: 'Indeed, if the Nazis did not exist, we should have had to invent them'. Under Schleicher's influence Hindenburg appointed Franz von Papen as chancellor on May 31, 1932; this ambitious, scheming Catholic aristocrat confronted the people with his 'cabinet of barons', a government consisting of military leaders, industrialists, and Junkers. Papen's non-party government had no popular support, but survived until November, 1932, propped up by the president and the army.

In 1932, German jails were crowded with close to 9,000 Leftist political prisoners. In the basements of their headquarters the Nazis tortured their enemies to death; in the streets Communists and Nazis fought pitched battles. Following the advice of his minister of defense, General von Schleicher, Papen lifted the ban which Brüning's government had imposed on the Nazi SA and SS. Hitler was given a free hand and the Reichstag elections of July 31, 1932, resulted in a triumph for 'Adolf Légalité' whose party became the largest in the country, polling over 13,700,000 votes with 230 seats in the Reichstag.

The Weimar Republic came to an end in the Byzantine power games which Papen, Schleicher, and Hitler played against a deadlocked parliament. The November elections of 1932 reduced the Nazi seats in the Reichstag to 196; only the Communists registered significant gains, polling close to six million votes with *100 seats*. The Social Democrats retained *121 seats* but deep-rooted programmatic differences between the two Marxist parties, as well as mutual blindness to the lethal nature of Nazi power prevented the formation of a Leftist coalition government. These differences would not interest the SS concentration camp guards who would later murder Communists and Socialists side by side.

Alarmed by the increase in the Communist vote and Hitler's drive for power, Schleicher forced Papen's resignation and took over the office of chancellor. On December 3, 1932, Schleicher's government began to operate in the hope of dividing the opposition on both the Right and the Left. Schleicher planned to reduce the Nazi threat by bringing Gregor Strasser's Left wing into his regime; he also intended to pacify the Social Democrats by inviting the participation of trade-union leaders. Hitler immediately reacted by removing Strasser from the office of party secretary; later, in the Nazi blood purge of June, 1934, he had Gregor Strasser murdered, along with Schleicher. The leaders of the Social Democratic Party opposed any form of cooperation with Schleicher and by January 6, 1933, they had succeeded in cutting all connections between organized labor and the chancellor.

On January 23, 1933, Schleicher admitted to Hindenburg that his strategy of forming a parliamentary majority had failed; he asked the president for an order dissolving the Reichstag linked with an indefinite and, therefore, unconstitutional postponement of the prescribed new elections. Hindenburg refused Schleicher's request, trusting in the success of secret negotiations involving Papen, Rightist leaders, and the detested, but unavoidable Hitler. On January 28, Schleicher and his entire cabinet resigned and Hindenburg asked Papen to 'clarify' the political situation. The nineteen Weimar governments were not noted for longevity: the average life-span of a cabinet was below nine months. With a duration of twenty-one months the Great Coalition of 1928 had survived the longest; with a duration of fifty-four days Schleicher's government was short-lived even by the standards of the Republic.

Papen wasted no time: with the support of Oskar von Hindenburg and Otto Meissner, he persuaded President Hindenburg to do what the old field marshall had so far considered inconceivable, namely, to appoint the 'Austrian corporal' Adolf Hitler chancellor of Germany. Hitler and the members of his proposed cabinet, which included von Papen as vice-chancellor, received their commissions from Hindenburg on the morning of January 30, 1933. On the evening of this demonic Monday, a confused eighty-five-year-old German president and an ecstatic Hitler gazed down on the stream of Nazi battalions, marching with flaming torches through the Wilhelmstrasse.

The Periclean era was over.

Germany sank into a satanic darkness from the depth of which there soon emerged a ceaseless stream of political refugees.[8]

The vision of the intellectuals

Unaware that the intellectual and social catastrophe of National Socialism was close at hand Mannheim proceeded on what appeared to be the long road leading beyond ideology and utopia.[9] In further pursuit of the dialectical relation between particularity and totality he argued that the diverse standpoints with their corresponding partial perspectives did not represent intellectual chaos, but mutually complementary parts of a comprehensive insight into the totality of the world.

Mannheim's conception of a total vision of reality has the major function of guiding intellectual labors toward an ultimate goal which will probably never be reached in its ideal totality. The intellectual, however, is called upon to synthesize from his current position as many partial perspectives as possible; in this activity he is to be directed by the desire to come as close as possible to a comprehensive understanding of the ideational and social cosmos. Informed by Troeltsch's conception of a 'contemporary cultural synthesis' Mannheim views the category of totality as a principle capable of introducing order, meaning, and relevance into empirical research. At the same time, he stresses the relative, provisional nature of the projected synthesis which is not equivalent to the reconstruction of a timeless, static absolute, but representative of ongoing intellectual efforts emanating from different, changing centers of systematization. Moreover, the synthesis is not a mere summation of disconnected partial truths, but rather the interpenetration and fusion of embracive thought styles. The synthesizing intellectual does not merely aim at an interpenetration of the contents of thought, but at a fusion involving the basis and categorical formal scope of thought. Only this movement toward the 'relative dynamic' synthesis, which must be reformulated from time to time, will enable contemporary thinkers to deal with the problems of modern society that are rapidly increasing both in number and complexity.

Successive attempts at the interpretation of the historical and social world form a meaningful context inasmuch as they are all directed toward the distant goal of a comprehensive world interpretation incorporating all partial perspectives. In Mannheim's metaphysics of history this movement toward intellectual synthesis represents a meaningful process unfolding beneath the surface of changing cognitive standpoints and contents of thought. 'A certain progress towards an absolute synthesis in the utopian sense may be noted in that each synthesis attempts to arrive at a wider perspective than the previous one, and that the later ones incorporate the results of those that have gone before.'[10]

At this point Mannheim had to identify the social agent capable of supporting the movement toward a total synthesis and the most adequate understanding of socio-cultural reality. Like Marx, he envisioned a social group whose members were wide-awake to contemporary socio-historical reality and equipped to separate the possible from the defunct and the premature. But unlike Marx, he argued that the experimental attitude and openness to the dynamics of social development could not be developed by members of a particular social class, but only by individuals belonging to a 'relatively classless stratum' that was not too strongly rooted in the social structure.

'This unanchored, *relatively* classless stratum is, to use Alfred Weber's terminology, the "socially unattached intelligentsia".'[11] The alleged cognitive advantage of the intellectuals is attributed to their lack of direct participation in the economic process. Unlike those who are more directly involved in the processes of material production, distribution, and acquisition, members of the intelligentsia have no clearly identifiable relationships with social classes. The social bond bestowing the characteristics of a group upon intellectuals is represented by education.

The social origin of the intelligentsia is interpreted in the manner of a spiritualistic sociology which attributes the reduction of social and economic differences to an 'educational heritage' shared by all educated individuals. Equally spiritualistic is Mannheim's view of the intellectuals' major social role which consists of the elevation of conflict from the material to the mental plane, or, the transformation of 'the conflict of interests into a conflict of ideas'.[12]

The intelligentsia recruits its members allegedly from all social classes and, thereby, comes to incorporate a multiplicity of perspectives which reflects the various social elements composing the structure of society. Intellectuals are not bound to specific interest groups and it is this detachment that permits them to 'float' above the existing social classes. In contrast to class-bound individuals, who are dominated by partisan and partial interests, members of the intelligentsia have the chance of moving into a position permitting the development of a comprehensive vision of social structure and process. The true intellectual may become the guarantor of the mental interests of all members of society, the watchman 'in what otherwise would be a pitch-black night'.[13]

Mannheim's spiritualistic sociology of the intelligentsia indicates an open rejection of Marx's revolutionary social theory. As part of an idealistic philosophy of history this theory is clearly designed to shift attention from the realities of the class struggle to the imaginary process of intellectual progress toward a society unified by reason and civility.

Ironically, Mannheim's suggestions appeared at a time when German universities were dominated by intellectuals who exhibited open allegiances to particular social classes and their partisan interests. The majority of university-based intellectuals continued to embrace the traditional mixture of reactionary conservatism and nationalism which had always served the political and socio-economic interests of the propertied and established classes. The historian Karl Dietrich Bracher has shown that most professors not only disliked the Weimar Republic, but that they actively supported the reactionary conservatism and chauvinism of the German National People's Party which represented the interests of large landowners and heavy industrialists. Since 1929, the year in which *Ideology and Utopia* was first published, the Nazis were gaining the support of more and more students and as a consequence academic life deteriorated under the onslaught of anti-Semitic brawls and attacks against republican and pacifistic instructors. By 1930, the National Socialists had won absolute majorities in the student governments (ASTA) of the universities of Erlangen, Greifswald, Breslau, Giessen, Rostock, Jena, Königsberg, and in the technical and veterinary academies of Berlin. In most of the remaining universities the Nazis received close to 50 per cent of the student vote.[14]

Excellent and innovative scholarly work originated in several of the institutes of the Weimar Republic which were independent from or only loosely connected with the established universities. The modernistic spirit of institute-based intellectuals and their scientific quest for reality frequently infuriated conservative university professors. But even the institutes fell short of the exacting criteria which Mannheim established for his 'socially unattached' intelligentsia. The historian Peter Gay has demonstrated that two of the famous Weimar institutes – the *Kulturhistorische Bibliothek Warburg* in Hamburg and the *Psychoanalytische Institut* in Berlin – remained entirely unpolitical. The *Deutsche Hochschule für Politik* in Berlin strove for interparty consensus, but only within the confines of bourgeois liberalism; consequently, Communists were barred from teaching at this political academy. The radical intellectuals at the Frankfurt *Institut für Sozialforschung* were partisans of Marxism; they conceived of their research function as revolutionary activity on behalf of the emerging socialist order.[15] In this climate of opinion there was no room for the notion of a socially unattached intelligentsia which could only be interpreted as counter-revolutionary.

Outside the universities and research institutes numerous free publicists and writers shaped what has been called 'the other Germany' – a witty, cosmopolitan, urban subculture in opposition to 'Hitler, Hugenberg, and that fish-cold academic type'.[16] The free literati of Weimar Germany relentlessly attacked the existing order and subjected all political parties to their biting criticism. With the exception of conservative and Right-wing ideologists most of the free publicists contributed to the weekly Berlin journal, the *Weltbühne*, edited in succession by Siegfried Jacobsohn, Kurt Tucholsky, and Carl von Ossietzky. Istvan Deak, the historian of the *Weltbühne*, has shown that the journal has both quantitative and qualitative significance; no less than seventy-five Weimar literati contributed regularly to this crusading publication and among them there were such personalities as Max Brod, Alfred Döblin, Lion Feuchtwanger, Erich Kästner, Egon Erwin Kisch, Arthur Koestler, Heinrich Mann, Erich Mühsam, Ernst Toller, and Arnold Zweig. Socially these writers were sufficiently detached from the German establishment to warrant membership in a 'free-floating intelligentsia'. Their political orientation, however, was anything but 'unattached' and implied faith in the movement of history towards a Socialist economy. In Weimar Germany these literati were customarily referred to as 'Left-wing intellectuals'. Deak has placed them somewhere between the Social Democrats and the Communists and the writer Leonhard Frank described their attitudes in a novel characteristically entitled *Heart on the Left*.[17]

In view of the German intellectual scene it is not surprising that Mannheim finds it difficult to correlate his conception of the 'socially unattached intelligentsia' with a concrete group. With regard to the question of group membership even his most precise definition retains a considerable element of caution: 'We are not referring here to those who bear the outward insignia of education, but to those few among them, who, consciously or unconsciously, are interested in something else than success in the competitive scheme that displaces the present one.'[18]

Mannheim's difficulties are not limited to the problem of locating the socially unattached intelligentsia in the existing order. He also admits that the comprehensive view to be achieved by this, as yet unconstituted, group is not synthesizable into a system in the present situation. None the less, he perceives in the historical process the emergence of 'a *consensus ex post* or an increasingly broader stratum of knowledge which is valid for all parties'.[19]

There are indications that Mannheim viewed Weimar Germany as another Periclean era.[20] This optimism motivates both his belief in the emergence of an intellectual élite capable of dynamic intellectual mediation and his assumption that the succession of relative, time-bound syntheses leaves in its wake a certain amount of unproblematic knowledge which accumulates into a *consensus ex post*. This growing fund of reality-adequate knowledge steadily enlarges the basis from which the intellectual cohort will launch its offensive against false consciousness and move beyond ideology and utopia toward the distant goal of society-wide consensus flowing from non-partisan thought.

In Mannheim's thinking there arose then the vision of the post-ideological society which was to become fashionable among members of the next generation of sociologists. Importantly, however, Mannheim distinguished between the overcoming of ideology and the loss of utopia. Ideologies merely serve to conceal reality on behalf of groups benefiting from the established social and intellectual order; the destruction of ideologies by means of enlightenment and rationalization, therefore, supports the movement toward a juster, more democratic society. The utopian mentality, however, is a motor force of social change which directs the activities of groups opposing the given order. The inequities present in any established social situation bring forth 'utopias which in turn break the bonds of the existing order, leaving it free to develop in the direction of the next order of existence'.[21]

While Mannheim looked forward to the 'decline of ideology' as the dawn of general social clarification, he feared that the complete loss of the utopian mentality would lead to a deadly 'matter-of-factness', robbing men of all creativity and vitality. 'The disappearance of utopia brings about a static state of affairs in which man himself becomes no more than a thing . . . with the relinquishment of utopias, man would lose his will to shape history and therewith his ability to understand it.'[22]

The fire from the Right

Despite his decision to combat false consciousness with a paradigm far removed from Marxism, Mannheim did not escape the wrath of bourgeois intellectuals. In 'Sociology and its limits', a critique of *Ideologie und Utopie*, Ernst Robert Curtius attacked Mannheim's sociology of knowledge in general and his dynamic relationism in particular as dangerous manifestations of nihilism and anti-idealism.[23] In his subsequent book, *German Spirit in Danger*, Curtius portrayed Mannheim's thinking as a 'typical' amalgamation of Marxist social theory with Jewish skepticism that conflicted with the necessary development of a unifying belief in 'Germany and the German mission'.[24]

Curtius's critique was one of the least impressive reactions to Mannheim's book; it is not without significance, therefore, that he was singled out as the recipient of a rebuttal. Apparently Mannheim was sufficiently interested in the impression he made on members of the bourgeois intellectual establishment to engage a conservative such as Curtius – a specialist in French culture – in a detailed debate. In 'Problems of sociology in Germany' – his defense of *Ideologie und Utopie* – Mannheim hastens to assure his bourgeois critic that he accepts the basic social and spiritual elements of the German tradition. The names which Mannheim evokes for his 'self-defense' are those of bourgeois intellectuals: Max Weber, Troeltsch, and Scheler, he claims, have inspired his work which is neither nihilistic nor anti-idealistic.[25]

With regard to the charge of nihilism Mannheim pleads innocent on two counts: first, dynamic relationism, which questions even the thinker's own position, is akin to Descartes's methodical doubt and not at all related to the thinking of some unshaven subversive; second, the sociology of knowledge merely diagnoses the contemporary existential and intellectual crisis, but does neither create it nor question its solubility.[26] Next, Mannheim declares his acceptance of metaphysics and ontology to clear himself of the charges of anti-idealism and sociologism; his character witness is none other than the anti-Republican philosopher Heidegger.[27]

In presenting his intellectual credentials to Curtius – a favorite of Bonn high society – Mannheim does not mention any Socialist theorists; indeed, Lukács and Marx are conspicuous for their absence from Mannheim's sketch of his intellectual antecedents. There is merely the dubious claim that German sociologists, especially Weber, Troeltsch, and Scheler, have fused the bourgeois and Socialist world views into a novel perspective, which is allegedly a radical critique of inherited absolutizations and a visionary expansion of 'soul' and 'consciousness'. The only reference to Marxism stresses, once again, the receptivity of bourgeois thinkers, such as Max Weber, who absorbed those Marxist elements that fitted their paradigms.[28]

Actually, most German academics remained hostile to Socialism and Marxism; the attitudes of Weber, Troeltsch, and Scheler ranged from highly selective affinity to open enmity. Max Weber's late flirtation with 'Socialism' was circumscribed by the nationalistic intention of attracting the workers to groups working toward the establishment of a powerful, unified German state. Ernst Troeltsch viewed the end of imperial Germany's rigid class society as a catastrophe which he bemoaned as the result of weakening faith in the history-making power of the 'spirit'. Max Scheler initially championed German nationalism and militarism; in the second part of the 1920s he supported the established bourgeois order and attacked the Marxists.[29]

Education and the democratization of society

In his next publication Mannheim developed an essentially Marxist thesis within the confines of a 'structural-functional' paradigm which permitted him to substitute social adjustment for social revolution. The essay 'On the nature of economic ambition and its significance for the social education of man' first appeared in 1930, but owed its major content to a lecture which Mannheim had delivered, in the fall of 1929, to participants in a political science training program, which convened at Bad Elster, under the auspices of the *Deutsche Vereinigung für staatswissenschaftliche Fortbildung*.

In this essay Mannheim investigates the manner in which economic factors influence the process of socialization. In his paradigm the psychic mechanism of ambition – the striving for economic success – represents the bridge connecting objective institutional with subjective psychical processes. In other words, economic ambition provides the interpretative scheme which registers the effect of the economic system on personality development. The social-psychological theoretical intent combines with an educational practical purpose. Mannheim claims that unsociological educational principles have so far prevented the analysis and control of social and economic influences on personality formation; consequently education has remained an abstract, artificial process adapting individuals to a vague 'life in general'. Meaningful existence and success in an industrial society, however, presuppose that individuals have been trained to master a specific socio-economic environment. The new approach of an 'industrial pedagogy' involves more than the planned development of needed skills and useful attitudes; even more important is the education of individuals capable of acting as change agents. The new, sociologically-oriented educational system envisioned by Mannheim, will, therefore, not merely adapt individuals to an existing developmental stage – it will also shape men 'capable of developing the existing form of society beyond itself to a further stage'.[30]

Mannheim's subsequent 'structural' analysis of *success* separates objective from subjective success; in the first case social acceptance is bestowed upon an achievement such as an invention or discovery, whereas in the latter case it is the achieving individual who gains social acceptance. Subjective success, which is central to the modern experience, is unstable when the achieving individual is rewarded with forms of recognition such as prestige or fame. Subjective success is relatively stable when the achieving individual is rewarded with fairly permanent opportunities to gain advantages in the spheres of political power, economic influence, or career life.

Next, Mannheim develops a structural analysis of *ambition* to support his claim that industrial capitalism conditions individuals to strive mainly for the more permanent and secure type of relatively stable subjective success. The rise of industrial capitalism to dominance has two additional salutary consequences. First, the competitive economic structure allows ambition to function as a means for the 'democratization' of society. Mannheim's equation of capitalism with democracy rests on the assumption that 'success in the economic sphere, measurable in money terms, is least subject to being monopolized by status groups, particularly so long as the nature of the economy is largely competitive rather than planned or controlled'.[31] Second, in a manner reminiscent of Durkheim's transition from mechanical to organic solidarity, Mannheim attributes to capitalistic economic development a significant growth of peaceful social interdependence. The pursuit of economic self-interest introduces a web of social control that renders individual behavior far more homogeneous, predictable, and rational than the historically older control mechanisms of military, political, or bureaucratic force. 'This growing interdependence of economic activity resulting from the natural working of individual self-interest, which is rapidly becoming a unifying factor of first importance in society, is also producing great changes in the social function . . . of the intellectual, spiritual, and cultural factors in our society.'[32] Earlier in this essay Mannheim announced his intention of expanding and substantiating the essentially Marxist thesis proclaiming the dependence of the subjective structure of human experience on the objective structure of social institutions; at this point he was bemused by the alleged failure of Marxist theorists to identify the mechanisms mediating the effects of alterations in the objective structure of the economy on changes in the cultural and spiritual spheres.[33] Regarding both Marxist social theory and Mannheim's initial formulation of ideological analysis it seems even stranger that the intervening train of thought leads him to a precocious establishment of the 'end of ideology' theme. The intensely ideological character of socio-economic and political conflict in late Weimar Germany hardly supports Mannheim's assumption that the unfolding of industrial capitalism causes the disappearance of traditionalized ideological responses. Even in the so-called 'post-industrial' Western world of today the thesis proclaiming the exhaustion and disappearance of ideological conflict has been severely criticized by social scientists who believe that ideology has re-emerged as the focal point of contemporary social conflict.[34]

Mannheim's post-ideological hypothesis is based on assumptions which are similar to those supporting the beliefs of classical social theorists in societal evolution and rational progress. Pre-capitalistic social systems (Spencer's 'militant society') rely on the social control mechanisms of military force and bureaucratic power, which are so centralized and rigid that large areas of everyday existence remain outside the radius of their effective operation. Pre-capitalistic societies are, therefore, in need of auxiliary means of social control to habituate the masses to forms of conduct that are regularized and predictable. These additional aids to social control are provided by ideologies that traditionalize behavior along the lines of moral and religious ideas. The transition to capitalism (Spencer's 'industrial society') opens the way to forms of social control relying in the main on the operation of rational self-interest which renders the actions of individuals increasingly predictable. With the accompanying growth of social interdependence and society-wide rationality the need for ideologies withers and disappears.

Neither the irrational spectacle surrounding the crash of the New York stock exchange in October, 1929, nor the intensification of ideological conflict during the Depression deterred Mannheim from proclaiming the continuing reduction of irrationalism and the eclipse of ideological factors in modern capitalistic societies. 'The effects of a stock-exchange panic . . . are now just as calculable as . . .

the direction and nature of irrational reactions of declassed groups in the process of social struggle.'[35] The widespread feeling of social solidarity generated by the industrial-capitalist system furthermore permits the remaining political and intellectual ideologists to operate in a climate of opinion suffused with freedom and tolerance. 'If the economic structure functions properly, it is possible to renounce all control over opinion and "ideas".'[36]

The integrated structure of the modern economic system is to a large extent a function of integrating, reciprocal psychic processes. In a language reminiscent of symbolic interactionism Mannheim describes the striving for economic success as a pathway making possible a partial, but significant understanding of the 'Other' as well as of the 'inner self'.[37]

In pursuit of the outlines of an educational theory adequate to the structural-functional characteristics of industrial-capitalist society, Mannheim realized the need for combining the social-psychological with the sociological dimension. On the basis of Max Weber's analysis of relations between incentives to economic activity and social class position Mannheim correlates typical economic motives with positions in the social hierarchy. In the lower social stratum of 'wage earners' necessity and habit are generally the only known incentives leading to economic activity. The middle stratum consists of the 'professional intelligentsia' which includes officials, engineers, and technicians; members of this group share a desire for recognition which mainly motivates them to work. At the top of the social hierarchy Mannheim places the 'capitalists' and 'managers' who are driven by such typical economic motives as the desires for luxury, power, and symbolic financial success. The specific position of an individual in the social hierarchy, therefore, largely determines his psychic capacities for the internalization of norms and the development of meaningful attitudes to work. These normative and psychic realities must guide educators who have the task of training students for economic activities the scope of which is essentially predetermined by the industrial-capitalist class system.[38]

To dispel the impression of economic fatalism Mannheim maintains 'that under certain circumstances men can also form their economic and social systems'.[39] Significantly, he does not spell out what kind of circumstances he has in mind and concludes by recommending an educational process geared to the established order as 'work in personality formation which one can pursue consciously in full freedom and responsibility'.[40]

Divergences between American and German sociology

On February 28, 1932, Mannheim delivered a lecture at a meeting of German sociologists which was published during the same year as *Contemporary Tasks of Sociology: A Teaching Program.*[41] In the somewhat confessional and defensive style of his late German publications, he informs his colleagues that he is at peace with the sociological enterprise which he views as a structure consisting of three equally valuable components. First, he recognizes the importance of 'general sociology' which reveals recurrent and general social forces; the first branch of sociology has a tripartite methodology represented by the ahistorical-axiomatic, the comparative-typological, and historico-idiographic approaches. Second, 'special sociologies' correlate the social process with major areas of intellectual activity such as language, knowledge, education, art, literature, religion, law, and the economy. Third, the 'sociology of culture' reveals both the experiential wealth residing in particular socio-cultural and historical situations and the overall interdependence of the institutional and social processes. The sociologist of culture activates research problems cutting across special disciplines and prevents practitioners of general sociology from losing touch with the fullness of life.[42]

In an attempt at self-criticism, Mannheim describes his earlier orientation as 'over-emphasized historicism', but proceeds by crediting himself with prolonged reflections which freed him from this methodological over-emphasis. Therefore, he is now in a position to appreciate the varied approaches to sociology and the significance of 'natural-scientific' and 'positivistic' research models.[43]

The interest in education links Mannheim's last lecture to a German audience with his preceding work 'On the nature of economic ambition and its significance for the social education of man'. The sociology of knowledge, which is represented as both ideological analysis and self-revision of thought, has above all an enlightening function; its major task is to teach individuals how to bear truth and reality.[44] Mannheim's call for mass enlightenment and education has consequences for the teaching of sociology in general which should above all present timely and urgent topics in a climate of value-free objectivity. These educational goals necessitate the addition of auxiliary fields such as 'sociography and statistics' and problem-oriented 'current studies' to the sociological teaching program, which has the potential of replacing classical cultural studies and of attaining the rank of industrial man's most adequate life orientation.[45]

'American sociology' is the last publication which Mannheim wrote in his capacity as professor at the University of Frankfurt.[46]

This review of an American 'case book' on methodology transcends the significance commonly associated with such writings. First, 'American sociology' is a bridge connecting his last German publication on the *Contemporary Tasks of Sociology* with 'German sociology (1918–1933)' – his first essay to originate in England.[47] Second, the decision of the editors of the *American Journal of Sociology* to start the review symposium on *Methods in Social Science* with Mannheim's contribution reflects his international acceptance as a scholar. Third, the review essay foreshadows the future direction of Mannheim's sociological work.

In his *Contemporary Tasks of Sociology*, Mannheim had argued for an extension of the empirical dimension in German sociology and the need for close contact with the practical problems of everyday life. The review of Rice's anthology provided him with an opportunity to pursue further these issues within a comparative perspective, taking into account basic differences in the American and German practice of sociology. On the positive side, Mannheim lauds the Americans for the comprehensiveness of their scientific teamwork – documented by the anthology – and chides his German colleagues for their exaggerated individualism and excessive striving for originality and personal uniqueness. The Americans score again with their practical approach which effectively relates each methodological issue to concrete social problems demanding immediate solutions and which also guarantees the authenticity of factual observations on the basis of ready documentary evidence. This direct approach contrasts soundly with the alleged tendency of German sociologists to forget the pressing necessities of everyday life in abstract searches for general methodological developments, divergences, and prerequisites.[48]

After this appraisal of meritorious characteristics Mannheim turns to a discussion of 'defective' traits of American sociology. First, he believes American sociology to suffer from a 'methodological asceticism' which suffocates the generation of constructive hypotheses and the growth of comprehensive theories concerning the functional interplay between parts and the whole and the totality of social problems and processes. American sociologists master a sophisticated methodological apparatus which permits them to produce outstanding treatments of social details; the absence of basic, integrative conceptions of social life, however, condemns single phenomena such as delinquency, crime, marginality, and poverty to remain marooned in an empty social space. At bottom this situation reflects misinterpretations of positivism which escalate the desire for security to the point of intellectual sterility. In this climate of opinion apostles of false positivism attempt either to prevent the application of theories or 'to know reality without having theories'.[49]

Second, American methodological asceticism is the symptom of an anti-philosophical bias which prevents the significant distinction between outmoded, uncontrolled speculation and the empirically grounded 'constructive imagination' that reveals the social structure. Foreshadowing Robert Merton's distinction between certain and important knowledge, Mannheim sees many American empiricists aiming 'in the first place at being exact, and only in the second place at conveying a knowledge of things'.[50] Knowledge of social reality demands more than flawless methods – it presupposes the kind of scientific inspiration which C. Wright Mills will later conceptualize as the 'sociological imagination' and which Mannheim calls the 'realistic imagination'. This 'comprehensive vision will put every fact in its place within the framework of a broad hypothesis embracing the whole of society'.[51]

Third, the American practice of 'isolating empiricism', which buries social reality beneath secondary details, mirrors a typical lack of commitment to issues of social and political importance.[52] In America sociological research is carried out in an atmosphere that is strangely removed from the group struggles for survival. 'It looks as if science had no social background; as if groups devoted to social research cultivated no exchange of ideas on matters social and political.'[53]

Fourth, the absence of the kind of perspective represented by the sociology of knowledge deprives American sociologists of insights into the correspondence between social and scientific evolution and of the critical 'self-control' stemming from an awareness of the partiality of all knowledge. Methodological analyses without historical and social roots cannot detect the distortions which occur in conceptualization and in 'the technique of questioning, the articulation and grouping of problems'.[54]

Mannheim's interest in the divergences between American and German sociology was not merely an expression of his theoretical concern for contrasting thought styles and their socio-existential roots; he foresaw the possibilities for interpenetration and mutual enrichment. American sociologists, he believed, could teach their German colleagues how to stay attuned to everyday problems and the demands of social existence; conversely American sociologists could learn from German scholars how to achieve a more comprehensive view of social reality. American sociology will be enriched, Mannheim concludes shortly before his departure for England, 'if its studies on questions of practical detail are alive to the great theoretical problems which pervade and co-ordinate with each other all the scattered empirical facts'.[55]

A few months after the publication of 'American sociology' Hitler's barbarous hordes rang down the curtain on German sociology; Mannheim did not live to see the realization of his specific expectations, but his own subsequent work on social planning, education, and power politics represents a sociological paradigm that combines a sense of practical urgency with an imaginative and comprehensive theoretical vision.

6 The sociology of social planning

Karl Mannheim left Germany shortly after the Nazis came to power. On May 11, 1933, the London School of Economics and Political Science invited him to deliver the Hobhouse Memorial Lecture for 1934. On May 16, the Director of the London School wrote to Mannheim suggesting that he might come to the School to undertake some postgraduate teaching and inviting him to discuss this possibility. This invitation was supported by Morris Ginsberg, the 'Dean' of British sociology, who had succeeded Leonhard Hobhouse to the Martin White Chair for Sociology in 1929; in the letter of May 16, 1933, Mannheim was also informed that Professor Ginsberg would be very pleased to offer him hospitality. By this time Mannheim was in Holland fulfilling lecturing engagements at the universities of Leiden, Amsterdam, Groningen, and Utrecht. On May 19, Mannheim wrote to the London School from Paris indicating that he would be happy to discuss the possibility of his working at the School; he also agreed to give the Hobhouse Memorial Lecture. Shortly thereafter Mannheim arrived in England to pursue the offer from the London School. On June 12, 1933, the Director of the School wrote to him 'c/o Professor Ginsberg' and offered him an initial appointment as a part-time member of the staff. At the beginning of the academic year 1933–4, that is, in October, 1933, Mannheim commenced his teaching as a lecturer in Sociology.[1]

In 'German sociology', his first publication written in London, Mannheim comments favorably on the even and continuous sociohistorical development of English society which permits a progressive evolution consisting mainly of 'the reforming and reconditioning of old institutions'.[2] The decision to shift his attention from the sociology of knowledge to studies of social planning and social reconstruction is, therefore, partially motivated by his exposure to a novel environment, where different opinions and social positions have allegedly not destroyed a generally shared universe of discourse with its communality of ideas, values, and symbols. In addition it is his firsthand experience of the German catastrophe that drives Mannheim with great urgency to apply the insights of sociology to the problem of social planning. On the practical side Mannheim's new role as a reformist social scientist is strengthened by the considerable access of English academicians to the media, politicians, administrators, and general audiences.

At the time of Mannheim's appointment the London School of Economics was directed by Sir William Beveridge, the British economist and administrator famed for his lifelong interest in the problem of unemployment, social insurance, and other social services. The outlines of the British Welfare State were worked out by Beveridge in the Second World War at the invitation of the government. Mannheim's new academic environment was, therefore, conducive to the development of plans for social reform. From 1937 to 1945, the British Labour Party was especially active in the formulation of its program for nationalization, social security, and education, as documented by *Labour's Immediate Programme* (1937), and *Let Us Face the Future* (1945).

Mannheim's decision to remain in England was voluntary as evidenced by his declining of several invitations from American universities; apparently Mannheim sensed the affinity between his burgeoning interest in social planning and those elements of British public opinion that were destined to be partially realized in the post-war Welfare State.

Requiem for a liberal-capitalist society

At the time of Mannheim's arrival Britain was still the center of a huge empire embracing about a quarter of the population of the globe. Five hundred million people lived under the imperial umbrella, but of these 430 million were subject colonials. From her far-flung colonies Britain obtained investment income, low-priced raw materials, and food. Furthermore, British industry had the benefit of tariff protection provided by the Imperial Preference system. Britain's privileged imperial position, however, was no match for the fury of the economic storms unleashed by the world crisis of capitalism.[3]

When Mannheim arrived in London in the spring of 1933 the British economy was in the severe grip of the Great Depression. At that time exports of British merchandise had sunk from the 1920 level of 1,334·5 million pounds to a record low of 368·0 million pounds. In 1920, registered unemployment in Great Britain had totaled less than one million; by the beginning of 1933 nearly three million men and women, representing 23 per cent of all insured workers, were jobless. In addition to these officially acknowledged unemployed there were many unknown others in uninsured categories, as well as those who had been removed from the register under the Anomalies Regulations.

From 1934 to 1937, the Conservative-led governments oversaw a slow and uneven process of recovery which heavily depended on armaments expenditure. In 1938, the economy deteriorated again and one British worker in eight was out of work. In the conservative political climate of the 1930s government intervention aimed above all at the maintenance of profits and the protection of big business interests by means of tariffs, import quotas, government contracts, and legislation favoring trusts and holding companies. These and other forms of legislation benefited the owners of large blocks of shares since dividends never fell much below 6 per cent. In parliament industrial interests were represented by the numerous Tory members who were directors of holding companies and trusts; successive prime ministers were provided by Baldwin's steel trust and the Chamberlain munitions firm.

The concentration of political power was accompanied by the monopolization of capital: in the 1930s 79 per cent of the wealth in private hands was owned by 5 per cent of the adult population, and 56 per cent was owned by the richest 1 per cent of that population.[4] The depression did not significantly lower the degrees of luxury and wealth enjoyed by the upper classes. The members of Society continued their interminable round of luncheons, dinners, and parties and their tables went on sparkling with heavy 'gold plate'.[5] The cheap labor supporting the social whirl came from the ranks of the oppressed; almost one-quarter of all working women were in private domestic service.

During the 1930s the brunt of immiserization was suffered by manual wage-earners, representing three-quarters of the working population. All workers were threatened by the processes of mechanization and job intensification which combined to lower the number of workers necessary for the production of a given output. After the loss of export markets traditional industries such as coalmining, iron and steel, textiles, and ship-building tried to maintain profits by means of reductions in productive capacity. The related strategy of monopolization led to the closing of many plants which were sacrificed to permit remaining works to produce at a profit. These developments transformed many of the traditional industrial regions into Distressed Areas and initiated a massive migration of younger workers to the South-East, the Midlands, and the South-West, where new science-based industries awaited cheap semi-skilled labor. Most of the new factories were established in Greater London and the workers had to pay for this principle of industrial location with higher tax rates, transportation costs, and exhausting hours in overcrowded trains, buses, and subways. The wages of all women workers were well below the minimum income necessary for the maintenance of health; the earnings of most adult male workers were so low that they stayed either below or barely above the subsistence level which Seebohm Rowntree defined as poverty in *The Human Needs of Labour*. The misery of these uprooted, lonely, economically insecure, and harassed workers was deepened by the introduction of relentless American speed-up, rate-cutting, and efficiency systems which led to an appalling rise of the toll of death and injury and the erosion of the workers' health and psychic well-being.

In the newer industries many employers exploited heavy unemployment and intense job competition to enforce anti-union policies. In the older industries, as well, large sections of employers attempted to destroy the trade-union movement. In the forefront of the attack against the workers were the mine-owners who had already shown their hand in the preceding decade. The coalminers had been locked out by the mine-owners in April, 1926 in the wake of a dispute over the reduction of wages and the lengthening of hours. In the following month the Trades Union Congress had come to the support of the miners by calling a General Strike. After a week the unions conceded their defeat and the miners were left to fight their own battle until they were starved back to work in November, 1926. The failure of the General Strike led to a decline of trade-union membership and the loss of labor militancy. After the defeat of organized labor in 1926 some trade-union leaders made it clear that they did not wish to be regarded as revolutionaries, but as partners in the stabilization of capitalist industry.[6] In 1935, Arthur Pugh, former chairman of the TUC, and Walter Citrine, secretary of the TUC, permitted the National Government to bestow knighthoods upon them, while the General Council of the Trades Union Congress busied itself with the banning of Communists from office.

In July, 1935, unemployment dropped below the two million mark and trade-union membership showed a slight increase, but labor leaders continued their cautious, conciliatory policies to avoid conflict with employers and capitalists. For the remainder of the decade the dominant leadership of labor acted on behalf of workers with steady jobs whose standard of living had begun to rise with the price fall of the 1930s. In the meantime Fascism was growing into a formidable power on the Continent and political labor began to view British capitalism as an ally in the fight against the workers' deadliest enemy. In 1939, British workers formed a united front against Nazi Germany and her Fascist satellites; most workers realized, then, that the time had come to defend the bad against the worst.

The lack of militancy in the official labor movement permitted

Conservative politicians and other upper-class spokesmen to propagate the idea that Britain was safe from an evil that Stanley Baldwin had labeled the 'insidious' doctrine of the class struggle.[7] In this climate of opinion Karl Mannheim, as well, arrived at a position from where power struggles and especially class antagonisms appeared to be less significant than co-operative efforts on behalf of the development of pragmatic social techniques.[8]

Beneath surface manifestations of national co-operation, however, there were strong undercurrents of radical dissent and bitter conflict between unemployed workers and the state authorities. As in Russia and Germany mutinous sailors dramatized the confrontation between workers and the governing class: on September 15, 1931, 12,000 sailors in the Royal Navy at Invergordon paralyzed the bulk of the Atlantic Fleet, refusing to sail under a new pay rate which reflected a cut of 25 per cent. The sailors' action was triggered not only by their unwillingness to sink below the bare minimum of subsistence, but also by their awareness that the cuts for the officers would be proportionately much smaller than those for the men of the Lower Deck.[9]

The mutinous sailors were sufficiently close to the hardware of power to convince the governing class of the need for compromise. The unarmed men and women of the industrial reserve army seemed less formidable; the state authorities, therefore, met expressions of discontent on the part of the unemployed with stern, repressive counteractions. Local 'hunger marches' which were organized by the National Unemployed Workers' Movement in the early 1930s were frequently broken up by baton charges of the police. In September, 1932, the police of Birkenhead battled demonstrators for four days; on October 27, 1932, many people were injured in London's Hyde Park where mounted police rode several baton charges against contingents of a national hunger march which came from Scotland and distant parts of England to present a petition against the means test that subjected many unemployed individuals to the indignities and hardships of the Poor Law.

In August, 1932, the police carried out numerous baton charges against the 150,000 striking weavers who closed the big Lancashire mills after their employers had announced wage cuts and the introduction of six-loom working. In the Nottinghamshire coalfield, where the mine-owners were intent on destroying the Miners' Federation, confrontations between strikers and police were the common feature of an industrial conflict lasting from 1926 to 1937.[10]

Trade unionists attempting to organize workers in the newer industries frequently had to cope with police action and arbitrary arrests. Inside the plant recruitment efforts were often hindered by the employer's repressive and punitive anti-union policy.[11] In London's East End confrontations between the police and massed workers concluded the rent strike movement against slum landlords which had pitched the exploited against their exploiters from the summer of 1938 to June, 1939.[12]

The hunger marches and strikes of the 1930s were last-ditch survival battles forced upon the pariahs of the working class by a group of hardened property owners whose more lunatic members escalated the general fascination with the mystique of law and order into specific expressions of admiration for the 'non-union' Germany of Adolf Hitler.[13] For the industrial reserve army the 1930s were times of semi-starvation. Seebohm Rowntree warned in his *Poverty and Progress* that malnutrition among the unemployed and the underpaid of York was so severe that its protraction was likely to cause permanent health damage.[14] More generally, Sir John Boyd Orr showed that half of the population of Britain was unable to afford a diet fully adequate for the maintenance of health.[15] The intense competition for the remaining jobs and the accompanying fear of unemployment motivated many workers to accept wages that were only slightly above unemployment allowances. This development was particularly pronounced in the Distressed Areas where poverty took on such nightmarish qualities that J. B. Priestley felt compelled to speak of it as an eternal 'bleak Sabbath' that transformed human faces into the hollow visages of captured soldiers.[16] Most demonstrations of working-class militancy originated in these satanic depths of hopeless immiserization.

The socio-economic problems and upheavals of the 1920s and 1930s shattered the dream of free enterprise so thoroughly that even members of the middle and upper classes began to explore social and economic alternatives to the *laissez-faire* dogma. More and more middle-class individuals opened their minds to socialist interpretations of the crisis of capitalism which were provided by several Left-wing periodicals and the Left Book Club, started by Victor Gollancz in May, 1936. The club's membership grew to about fifty thousand subscribers; many readers joined the discussion groups of the Left Book Club which increased in number to about 1,200 organizations.[17] The club's contingent of writers and speakers included upper-middle- and upper-class individuals revolting against the immoral impotence of a social system that had spawned them.

From the more elevated strata of British society came youthful rebels who infused small, but vociferous student movements at prestigious universities with radical energy. In 1934 – during Mannheim's second year at the London School of Economics – left-wing students actively propagated there the revolutionary ideology of the class struggle. Student activists also voiced their opposition to imperialism, war, and Fascism which they recognized as demented manifestations of decaying capitalism.

The collapse of the structure of traditional capitalist society motivated not only Leftists, but also Liberals and Young Conservatives to oppose the business-as-usual attitude of the ruling groups. Consequently, theories of social and economic planning were diffused across class lines, throughout society. The 1930s were bleak, bitter years for the masses in capitalist societies. The people of Britain, however, emerged from this dark decade and their subsequent life-and-death battle with the satanic forces of Fascism firmly resolved to hold future governments resonsible for the dignity and well-being of all citizens. This widespread sense of responsibility was destined to grow into the popular base supporting the modern structure of the Welfare State.

A theory for the reconstruction of man and society

On March 7, 1934, Mannheim made his first public statement on the serious dislocations in industrial-capitalist society and the resulting need for social planning.[18] A month later he followed up with an investigation of the impact of social disintegration upon cultural development.[19] In 1935, he confronted German-speaking audiences with a first book-length summation of his views on the nature of critical social transformations and the necessity of social reconstruction.[20]

Mannheim's first book on social planning is aptly entitled *Mensch und Gesellschaft im Zeitalter des Umbaus* (*Man and Society in an Age of Reconstruction*). In the introduction Mannheim establishes and clarifies his most basic assumption: contemporary Western democracies suffer from tensions created by two conflicting socio-economic practices. The uncontrolled co-existence of the principles of *laissez-faire* and planless regulation represents the major cause for these tensions which threaten to disintegrate Western society. The ideology of free enterprise capitalism, which is responsible for this societal crisis, presupposes that the antagonistic elements of a market society will continuously and automatically readjust themselves on new levels of equilibrium. The liberal system of *laissez-faire* economics, however, ceased to produce new forms of social equilibrium; instead it led to the perverted social arrangements of late industrial-capitalistic democracy. This social system has conditioned the masses to bow to the rule of monopolistic cliques and to suffer through periodic economic and social disasters.

People who have been conditioned to accept the prevailing order, can be reconditioned to reject it in favor of alternative arrangements. According to Mannheim human personality must be reconstructed to the extent of enabling individuals to think and act in ways conducive to the creation of a planned democracy.

Correlations of psychic, societal, and cultural problems further illuminate the extent and nature of the crisis of Western society. First, individuals experience psychic-mental dislocations which, in turn, contribute to the second process of societal disorganization. Third, distorted culture patterns reflect the alienated and anomic drift of the psychical and social processes.

Mannheim confronts the psychic and societal problems in the first chapter, entitled 'Rational and irrational elements in contemporary society'. His discussion evolves around three major assumptions. First, rational self-control and social control lag behind the rational mastery of scientific-technological development. This disparity in the development of human capabilities threatens the disintegration of contemporary society. Second, the problems originating in the established social structure determine the development of rationality, as well as the unfolding of human motivations and morality. Third, historically earlier societies were actually founded on the disproportionate distribution of rationality and moral force; they could, therefore, afford the split between a responsible ruling minority and the passive masses.[21]

Disparities in the development and distribution of rationality create irrational conditions which endanger the survival of industrial mass society. Two contemporary processes are mainly responsible for the incompatibility of irrationality with modern social life: the 'fundamental democratization of society' and the process of 'increasing interdependence'.

The fundamental democratization of society is an integral part of modern social structure; this process manifests the widespread desire of contemporary men to participate in policy-formation. As the process continues political participation is diffused across class lines and eventually people in all social strata will have their interests represented at the centers of power. Mannheim's analysis pays insufficient attention to counter-democratic processes such as co-optation, repression, and ideological manipulation which established ruling groups employ to divert and emasculate movements aiming at equitable redistributions of power and wealth. The thrust of his social criticism moves in a different direction; in the manner of Enlightenment philosophy he attacks the contradiction between fundamental democratization and irrationality. The expansion of political and social responsibilities is incompatible with the fact that newly mobilized groups are still influenced by the irrational thought-ways characteristic of their original state of ignorance.[22]

The process of increasing interdependence augments and tightens the interaction between the various social, political, economic, and cultural components of modern social structure. Contemporary social systems are especially vulnerable to irrational shocks since the interdependence of their parts escalates the effects of any malfunction to the level of chain reactions.[23]

The irrational tendencies in industrialized mass societies are perpetuated by the human type with the 'handcart mind' who symbolizes the disproportional development of man's capacities. Man with the handcart mind is representative of individuals who utilize novel technological means to satisfy primordial impulses. In a manner reminiscent of William F. Ogburn's cultural lag hypothesis Mannheim points to the discrepancy between rapid scientific-technological development and the retarded growth of human creativity in the area of values, norms, and social control. In the twentieth century men with the mentality of primitives employ advanced weapon systems to perpetuate a system of human relations that is as antiquated as handcarts and horse-drawn carriages. The ascendancy and rule of the National Socialists have shown that men with the handcart mind are quick to utilize the mass media to shape men in their own image; as a consequence contemporary primitives are capable of multiplying their own human type a million-fold.[24]

In industrialized mass societies Mannheim observes the accentuation of a special form of rationality and this process as well contributes to the dangerous growth of irrational tendencies. To begin with, modern men are rapidly losing the capacity to engage in 'substantially rational' acts of thought, which are the sole basis for an autonomous mastery of situations. Acts of thought which follow the rules of 'substantial rationality' intend existing phenomena and situations and provide meaningful insights into the interrelations of their components. As a consequence of industrial-technological development this type of rationality is superseded by 'functional rationality'. Functional acts of thought efficiently organize sequences of behavior toward specific goals and endow each behavioral element with a functional status and role. Series of actions are rationally coordinated as means to ends and, therefore, permit potential actors to calculate the behavioral requirements facilitating their adjustment to a given behavioral context. The direction of behavior by functional rationality is especially pronounced in the case of individuals seeking corporate or administrative careers since adjustment to pre-established, calculable career stages enforces their subordination to the outside requirements of a prefabricated 'life-plan'. The transition from substantial to functional rationality foreshadows to some extent David Riesman's assumption of an inevitable shift from 'inner-direction' to 'other-direction' and connects in a similar manner with contemporary forces of social change. Each advance in the industrial technological process adds to the functionally rational, calculable, nonautonomous areas of human action and forces individuals to make the necessary adjustments in their behavior.[25]

The second chapter of *Mensch und Gesellschaft im Zeitalter des Umbaus* deals with the 'Social causes of the contemporary crisis in culture'. In Mannheim's opinion the effects of the distintegration of modern society are not limited to psychic and social processes, but extend into the sphere of cultural development.

The conflict between liberal *laissez-faire* policies and the practice of planless regulation affects the production and consumption of cultural phenomena just as negatively as economic and social processes. In the socio-economic and political chaos of industrial capitalism culture deteriorates into cheap amusement; elsewhere intellectual-artistic creativity has been ossified by the deadly embrace of totalitarian mass society. The survival of cultural creativity depends, therefore, on the success of social scientific analyses designed to identify both the social causes of cultural disintegration and the techniques permitting the realization of the novel principle of substantially rational planning.

The roles of cultural production and distribution belong to the intelligentsia, that is, to groups operating outside the commercial and industrial spheres. Mannheim distinguishes several major types of 'intellectual élites': the political, the organizing, the scientific-cognitive, the artistic-aesthetic, and the moral-religious. These élites are most effective as long as they are in contact with an educated public capable of functioning as mediator between the élites and the masses. An educated public has continuous interest in the activities of creative élites and, thereby, protects them from the unpredictable, irrational fluctuations of fads that cater to the momentary cravings of sensation-hungry masses.

The contemporary process of massification threatens both the survival of the existing intelligentsia and the formation of new intellectual élites. To begin with, the drift into mass society destroys the culturally significant function of mediation performed by the educated public. The informed, concerned members of the public are rapidly losing ground to totally fluid masses which are manipulated by commercial opportunists, military adventurers and political demagogues. Massification, furthermore, leads to a simplification of academic training which swells the ranks of the intelligentsia. As the labor market becomes glutted with university-educated individuals more and more members of the intelligentsia sink into the proletariat. As a result of this process popular esteem for cultural élites and the products of their work begins to diminish. In summary, contemporary culture is seriously threatened in the most vital areas of production, distribution, acceptance, and effectiveness.

The deterioration of social and cultural processes in liberal-democratic, industrial-capitalist mass societies benefits forces working toward the establishment of dictatorships that cater to the special interests of an exclusive group. This threat to human freedom and dignity cannot be countered by a return to the socio-cultural conditions of élitist minority democracies. The only solution is represented by a system of planning capable of transferring creative initiative to the emerging world of organized mass democracy.[26]

In his third chapter, 'Thought at the level of planning', Mannheim claims that social and cultural reconstruction must begin with thorough transformations of human thought, will, and behavior. In the manner of John Dewey's pragmatic instrumentalism Mannheim defines thought as an instrument serving specific survival functions within the structural limits of particular environmental conditions.[27]

Mannheim distinguishes three basic stages in the development of thought to provide historical support for his assumption that new ways of thinking are brought into existence by corresponding alterations of the social order. Cognitive progress has led men from the 'chance discovery' type of reasoning (*finden*) to the stage of 'inventing' (*erfinden*) and promises their elevation to the level of 'planned thinking' (*planen*). The record of cognitive progress shows, therefore, that men have steadily increased their capacities for exact and rational ways of thought and indicates, furthermore, that they are about to develop a new pattern of thought permitting the construction of a multidimensional model of social change. This model, which can only be completed on the level of planned thinking, will transcend the isolating sphere of immediate problems and purposes by focusing on the interplay of large long-range processes.

Chance discovery is a form of rationality which dominates problem solving activities in early developmental stages. Young children and members of non-literate groups rely predominantly on the method of trial and error in their attempts to master environmental challenges and problems; they 'feel' their way to appropriate solutions which they 'find' rather accidentally after having failed in a series of attempted solutions. Furthermore, chance discovery is a thought style corresponding to a developmental stage in which problems posed by the physical environment, by nature, are experienced as the major threat to human survival.

The thought style of inventing guides problem-solving activities in more complex developmental stages and becomes dominant as soon as men are mainly threatened by unresolved social tensions and conflicts. This type of rationality matured as the social structure came to correspond to ideological orientations based on the principles of liberalism and free enterprise. In industrial-capitalist societies men learn to stress pragmatic solutions to discrete, immediate problems; consequently 'inventing' deteriorates into 'functional rationality' which permits only the mastery of technological processes, but provides neither control over long-range effects nor answers concerning the human meaning and metatechnical significance of thoughts and actions.

The contemporary situation calls, therefore, for the development of a new social thought style which will return to modern men the capacity for substantially rational acts of thought – a capacity they nearly lost under the dominance of capitalistic ruling groups. Substantial rationality will guide intellectual activity at the level of planned thinking. At this stage of development men will achieve the ability of mastering social processes. Thought at the level of planning enables men to grasp scientifically the manifold, interdependent connections in a social structure.

Mannheim's discussion of historical changes in thought styles has the purpose of supporting his basic assumption that social reconstruction presupposes the reconstruction of human thought and action. In his view each stage of social development corresponds to a specific type of intellectual activity and the planned society has its cognitive correlate in a thought style capable of revealing the functional interdependence of all social elements. The cognitive achievement of planned thinking makes possible the social action of planning whereby an historically evolved society is rebuilt into a structure permitting steadily improving forms of human regulation. ' "Planning" as a new stage of the development of thought and action is realized in so far as the previously vast arena of competition and the consequent process of selection are increasingly narrowed by regulatory intervention and the forces at work are consciously controlled.'[28]

In his initial approach Mannheim defines planning as the 'reconstruction of an historically developed society into a unity which is regulated more and more perfectly by mankind from certain central positions'.[29] This type of regulation demands from the planners insights into the operation of general social forces and an understanding of concrete developmental stages which provide the setting wherein unique factors coalesce into universal forces. In other words, the planners discover the central positions for their regulatory activities by analyzing the general aspects of the social structure in relation to unique, changing situations. Planned thinking does not permit accidental occurrences; therefore both general and unique phenomena must be grasped on the level of their essential functioning. Intellectual operations on this level are made possible by logical principles suggested by Francis Bacon and further developed by John Stuart Mill who calls them *principia media*. In Mannheim's methodology these *principia media* represent 'regularly recurring special laws, special relationships of a certain historical phase in a particular social setting'.[30]

On the level of planned thinking the understanding of social structure and process is aided by the *principia media* which mediate between unique social situations and general social forces. The employment of *principia media* leads to distinctions between, let us say, liberal competitive capitalism and oppressive monopoly capitalism; these historical stages of economic development must be distinguished from capitalism in general. The effects of unemployment on the social structure, for example, can only be understood as long as situational distinctions of this type temper the use of generalizations. At the stage of late capitalism the generally accepted correlation between enforced unemployment and rebelliousness no longer holds true:[31]

> Chronic or structural unemployment as we know it, for the most part creates apathy rather than rebellion in the minds of its victims. The primary reason for this is that modern unemployment destroys the 'life plan' of the individual. Under these circumstances rebellion and aggression lose their purpose and social direction.

The growth of working-class militancy during the depression, however, makes Mannheim's assertion even more questionable than the generalization it means to replace.

In Mannheim's paradigm the dynamics of social reconstruction are set in motion by planned transformations of human personality. To begin with, Mannheim rejects the notion that social planners are confronted by a given type of man; therefore, the ordering of society does not have to follow the 'dictates of an immutable human nature. What we do is rather to accept the older human type as it stands in the first place, and then try, by a wise strategy, to guide it while it is still in action.'[32] The new educational strategy has no interest in the formation of an 'ideal' personality in general; rather the planned stage of social development demands that educators shape men capable of coping with both the general tendencies of social life and the *principia media* of their specific social environments.

The tasks of social reconstruction and planned personality development are facilitated by some of the intellectual products of the old social order. Pragmatism, for example, aids the emergent planned society since this philosophy links thought with action. Although pragmatism is limited by the narrow horizon of the liberal society which spawned this intellectual orientation, it nevertheless contributes to the movement towards interdependent, situation-oriented thinking. The behaviorist psychologists are on the road to planning as well, since they show an active interest in the manipulation of the external conduct of the members of society. Behaviorism is even more severely limited than pragmatism since this intellectual orientation resembles the political practice of Fascism. Fascists manipulate the political world at a behaviorist level as demonstrated by their acceptance of 'an abstract ordering principle which changes man through the maximum combination of external coercion and suggestion with no wider aim than the regulation of outward behavior and the integration of the sentiments'.[33] The planners' interest in the transformation of the entire personality necessitates the advance from the surface sphere of external behavior to the deeper levels of mental-psychic existence. This advance is aided by the understanding method developed by Freud and other exponents of psychoanalysis. The limitations of psychoanalysis are those of the liberal-individualistic age in which this type of psychology arose. Typically psychoanalysts fail to realize that individual personalities cannot be reorganized without the reconstruction of the entire society. What psychoanalysis lacks is 'the sociological insight into the social mechanism which is indispensable for complete planning'.[34]

Mannheim intends to combine insights into concrete societies and their *principia media* with the viable contributions made by pragmatists, behaviorists, and psychoanalysts to achieve his ultimate purpose, 'which is the planned guidance of people's lives on a sociological basis, and with the aid of psychology'.[35] This methodological synthesis, which must remain open to changing needs and circumstances, permits the flexible use of both external and internal approaches to personality transformation. These developments finally lead to planned, interdependent thinking which is scientifically accurate and 'concrete, because it starts with the context of things, and it is into concrete *situations* that one integrates the otherwise disconnected elements of knowledge'.[36]

Techniques of social planning and the problem of human freedom

Mannheim pursues the problems of personality transformation in part III of *Man and Society in an Age of Reconstruction*. Apart from some revisions, this third part, entitled 'Crisis, dictatorship, war', corresponds to a lecture given at the London School of Economics; the material was first published in 1937 as a chapter in the anthology *Peaceful Change*.[37]

In this essay, added to the English version of his first work on social planning, Mannheim assumes a correlation connecting the disorganization of society with mental and behavioral forms of disintegration. For social planners this correlation signifies that efforts on behalf of the reorganization of personality structure must be accompanied by corresponding changes in the structure of society. In Mannheim's opinion human personality is eminently susceptible to reconstructive measures designed to recreate the basic attitudes and behaviors of men. In support of this position Mannheim draws attention to discussions involving behaviorists, endocrinologists, instinctivists, and psychoanalysts which permit 'the conclusion that, although inherited chromosomes, certain established nerve connections, and the gland system set limits to the changeability of the individual, there is nevertheless a great plasticity in man'.[38]

Under the influence of the military threat represented by Nazi Germany, Mannheim steers the discussion of the correlation between social and personal disorganization into a special direction. In his analysis he focuses on the social causes of psychic phenomena such as xenophobic hatred and the lust for war which he does not interpret as manifestations of speciate instincts, but as environmentally induced attitudes.

To begin with, liberal-capitalist society failed to create meaningful living conditions for the bulk of the population. In its late phase this type of society produced corrosive phenomena such as structural unemployment and chronic economic recessions which, in turn, gave birth to individual and collective neuroses and psychoses. The 'unorganized insecurity' of late liberal-capitalist society signally contributed to that plethora of alienating attitudes which includes self-doubt, self-hatred, other-directed hatred, suspicion, fear of life, scapegoating, and anti-Semitism.[39]

The experience of liberal-capitalist decadence prepares the masses for the next stage of social development: led by Fascist or Communist dictators they enter the social world of 'organized insecurity'. Mannheim's failure to distinguish Fascism from Communism leads him to the sweeping generalization that totalitarian rulers typically fail to eradicate the economic and social evils they inherited from their liberal-capitalistic predecessors; the dictators, therefore, provide the people with substitute goals and surrogate rewards.

Late monopolistic capitalism deteriorated into a social system which satisfied and enriched only a small group of owners and manipulators. The near-sighted egotism of plutocratic class rule came to limit social mobility and monetary success to such an extent that it eventually negated the very premises of liberal-capitalist society. The new totalitarian rulers, incapable as they are of genuine social reform, replace the striving for material and social success with such surrogates as national honor, party rank, and the various symbols and emblems which so lavishly decorate the otherwise dismal social world of organized insecurity.[40] The pressure generated by continuing social and psychic disintegration is now released through the safety valve of a foreign policy which replaces psychological self-mutilation with military actions against foreign populations. Dictators educate the masses for warfare to divert their attention from the continuation of the social tensions and injustices which originally motivated them to exchange their plutocratic rulers for totalitarian masters. 'Nationalist slogans call little people who love their homes and gardens to become heroes by killing other little people who love their homes and gardens.'[41] For the same reasons dictators rely heavily on scapegoating in their practice of domestic politics. Scapegoats, such as Jews, afford 'relief by providing an opportunity for once more externalizing the aggressive tendencies, an opportunity that is equally welcome to the frustrated in every class'.[42]

In Mannheim's opinion social planning provides Western democracies, such as England and the United States, with their only chance of avoiding totalitarian solutions to the problems created by the decay of liberal-capitalist social systems. Social planning, however, forms an integral part of totalitarian statecraft; Mannheim, therefore, devotes the entire fifth part of *Man and Society* to an elaboration of the concept 'planning for freedom'. This historical and comparative analysis has the purpose of demonstrating the vital difference between totalitarian 'planning for conformity' and democratic 'planning for freedom'.[43]

The realization of social planning depends in the main on the proper functioning of 'social techniques'. Heavily influenced by the work of American sociologists on social control Mannheim investigates the origin, functioning, and applicability of various social techniques. The application of the scientific-technical attitude to social life presupposes that new ways of personality formation prepare individuals for the novel patterns of interaction and performance evolved by the process of social planning. For the creation of a new human type planners rely on social techniques, such as adult education, schooling in collective responsibility, vocational guidance, education for leisure, group analysis, and clinical guidance.

In Mannheim's paradigm psychic reorientation must be accompanied by social reorganization. The economic chaos created by contemporary capitalism must be overcome by various social techniques including controls which permit the co-ordination of production and consumption. 'A planned society would direct investment, and by means of efficient advertisement, statistically controlled, would do everything in its power to guide the consumer's choice towards co-ordinated production.'[44] Planning not only necessitates control of the trade cycle and the regulation of financial and productive activities, but also calls for the transformation of liberal politics into social government. In the political sphere planning aims at the creation of a social service state which, by means of taxation, would try to achieve 'a growing equality in income and to transfer property from the rich to the poor'.[45] Redistributive social reforms must be accompanied by positive measures such as public works, the expansion of public utilities, the growth of social work, and, most importantly, the widening of social insurance against unemployment, sickness, and old age. These policies depend for their success on high levels of awareness among the masses; therefore, propaganda, advertising, broadcasting, and the organization of leisure must pass from the hands of profit-oriented corporations into those of the public service-oriented state.[46]

Mannheim viewed the emergence of the planned social service state as an evolutionary process, propelled by the motor force of human reason. He hoped that intelligent men would tire of the permanent state of emergency created by the socio-economic upheavals of monopoly capitalism; in this event they would quietly, but inexorably move toward a future social system capable of providing not just a privileged few, but all men with economic security and social justice. This movement would cut across extant social classes and the ideological barriers erected by Marxist devotees of the class struggle, because 'those who can promise security and greater justice will have the proletariat and after the recent negative experiences with Fascism, the middle classes and the reasonable elements among the organizing élites on their side'.[47]

As a social reformer Mannheim fails to take into account that huge concentrations of economic and political power have isolated existing élites from the people. Contemporary élites are mostly self-perpetuating groups, immune to democratic selection processes, and deaf to appeals to their good will. Mannheim is explicit in his discussion of private property in a corporate economy: he upholds the claims of private property and rejects the notion of expropriation.[48] On the other hand, he does not specify what groups are to obtain sufficient power in democratic societies to actualize his brand of social planning. Instead of providing a concrete analysis of the power-means of planning, he merely expresses the hope that the established élites may be won over to planning by so-called 'progressive groups'.[49] In Mannheim's paradigm the emergence of the new élite of social planners takes place in a curiously unpolitical atmosphere: supported by the 'rising classes' the planners will supposedly share power positions with acceptable remnants of the older ruling élites.[50] These assumptions permit Mannheim to skirt the issues of social and political conflict, but create a yawning gap which swallows several problematic questions: What is the composition of the rising classes? Who motivates them to rise? What are the power implications of their movement? What will persuade the rest of the former ruling class to go away?

While Mannheim obscures the problems of the power context of planning he spotlights education which emerges as the major factor in the formation and improvement of the new élite group of planners. He foresees a new educational process which will not only maintain high academic standards, but also broaden the quantity and participatory base of education. The planning function can only be entrusted to the ablest members of society and their rise to the top must be the result of a democratically open educational process which rewards intelligence and meritorious performance.[51] But again, Mannheim fails to recognize that education is not an objective process operating in a power vacuum. Established élites are not selected by anybody – they select themselves; élite control over education, furthermore, ensures that only members of the élite rise to the top and that unwanted individuals are kept out. English 'public' boarding schools, American 'prep schools', and the exclusive clubs in Ivy League colleges function to perpetuate the power and influence of established ruling élites. Where education really makes the difference social gate-keeping functions are paramount and learning becomes coincidental.[52]

Mannheim believes that modern political life has created new alliances which bridge economic divisions and dwarf the significance of power struggles and class antagonisms. As a sociologist Mannheim wishes above all to be pluralistic and he does not see social life as a panorama of conflict, but as a scene of equilibrium where the basic institutions of society undergo a continuous process of mutual adjustment.[53] In the course of this speculative process Mannheim convinces himself of the relative insignificance of class divisions and power factors; he feels, therefore, free to move in the direction of Saint-Simon's 'socialism', which renounced the hardware of revolution for soft 'spiritual' principles of social equilibration. As a planner Mannheim wishes to apply scientific knowledge to social life and to perform intelligent feats of social and psychic engineering. For its implementation this technocratic planning process depends to a large extent on the operation of benevolent, paternalistic principles.

In Mannheim's new world the intellectuals are neither revolutionaries nor ideologists, but members of a community of scientific planning experts who advise the ruling élites how to govern with wisdom and kindness. To begin with, Mannheim believes English society to be diffused with an 'objective kindness' and spirit of mutual co-operation. These attitudes which Mannheim sees rooted in Anglo-Saxon traditions have fostered the development of new social services combining material assistance with spiritual help. Even big business has allegedly softened commercial activities with the 'spirit of service'. Building on these foundations the planners will educate the people to organize social relationships around such core virtues as brotherly help, co-operation, and decency.[54] Finally, Mannheim expects from the ruling élites an eager readiness 'to avail themselves of any existing or potential knowledge as to the fairest and most efficient methods of conducting social affairs'.[55]

On the operational level Mannheim's planning conception displays an impressionistic softness which earned him the contempt of the Marxists. Mannheim's failure to formulate firm, convincing plans for the mastery of major conflicting problems has roots in his treatment of the theoretical level where his analysis focuses on planning as a type of thought. Planning, therefore, is not revolutionary social reconstruction carried out by new élites after their victory over the old ruling class. On the contrary, planning is a new *thought style* brought to dominance by a peaceful process of intellectual evolution and diffused throughout society by the power of reason: the reasonable members of all social classes may bathe beneath the light of the new consciousness which, like the sun, warms poor and rich alike. Social change, then, is not propelled by the dialectical conflicts of material interests, but moves gently to the changing rhythm of human consciousness. At bottom it is this translation of concrete dialectical *conflicts* into abstract evolutionary *concepts* which permits that peculiar bracketing of the realities of power – realities which to begin with determine the chances for the actualization of thought styles and forms of consciousness. While Mannheim's undialectical conception of planning transforms social conflicts into spiritualized behavioral divergences, his rationalistic notion of compromise perpetuates precisely the contradictions that effective planning should remove from society.

Mannheim knew that liberal-capitalist society was a hotbed of contradictions, but he, nevertheless, permitted himself to conceive of planning as 'sound thinking' which intellectual evolution diffused throughout society until it reached the 'ruling élites'.[56] Some of Mannheim's critics realized the political dangers inherent in his planning conception which, as Adorno warned, relied on reason to offer power to people who had it anyhow in the name of unreason.[57]

The conciliatory features of Mannheim's advocacy of planning did not protect him from the wrath of conservatives; he did not fail to anticipate this turn of events and in conclusion offered an impassioned appeal to elicit the understanding that his approach to planning was not a road to serfdom.

In 'Freedom on the level of planning' – the concluding part of the book – Mannheim returns to the question which expresses the most common form of resistance to social planning: 'Is not an ideally planned society a prison, a strait-jacket, even compared with the almost intolerable life led by many classes in an unplanned society?'[58]

The problem of human freedom is of signal importance for Mannheim's intellectual situation. In the first place, he must confront the problem as a key issue in the battle against popular apathy, suspicion, and resistance to change. Moreover, the question of liberty assumes decisive proportions for a thinker who combines the conviction that planning is inevitable with the belief that undemocratic, authoritarian planning is a disaster. At this point Mannheim must, therefore, demonstrate that planning and freedom are compatible.

Mannheim begins his defensive argument by rejecting as meaningless all attempts to discuss the concept of freedom in the intellectual vacuum represented by an abstract, generalizing approach. Freedom has no meaning unless the concept is related to concrete reality factors, such as specific historical situations, particular types of social structure, and given levels of social technique. The presence or absence of freedom, then, cannot be determined in the abstract; instead, concrete social settings bring forth specific types of freedom.

The sociological variations in the conception of freedom assume major significance in their correlation with the different stages in the development of social technique. The historical transition from one developmental stage to the next brings with it changes in social structure and alterations of the meaning of freedom.

The first stage in the evolution of social technique is dominated by the trial and error method of chance discovery; on this level men fight the tyranny of the forces of nature and experience freedom 'in direct action on and reaction to the stimuli of the surroundings'.[59] Conversely, freedom is diminished by everything that hinders primitive men in their haphazard attempts to change their physical environment; freedom disappears tragically when they are prevented from escaping the powers of nature. The development to the second stage of invention increasingly liberates men from the pressures of the physical environment: humans are now sufficiently free to evolve social techniques for the mastery of the social world. The social technique of invention corresponds to the social structure represented by liberal-capitalist society; on this level freedom becomes fragmented into liberties, just as the social structure dissolves into uncoordinated institutions. On this developmental level society consists of a growing number of isolated institutions which are permitted to function independently; now the supreme 'guarantee of freedom consists in playing off these institutions against each other'.[60]

Since capitalistic 'liberties' mainly benefit the rich, most people experience merely the anxiety and insecurity created by a maladjusted institutional configuration, an erratic trade cycle, and irrational forms of collective behavior. The attainment of the third stage of planning will, therefore, benefit the majority of the population which will be liberated from the destructive interplay of blind and uncoordinated *social* forces. On the level of planning a new type of freedom emerges: freedom now means regulation of the entire institutional configuration, based on a democratically chosen plan which guarantees the collective freedom of society. On the highest level of social evolution there can be no freedom without planning, but there must never be a plan without the safeguards of democratic consensus and parliamentary control.[61]

7 The values and the education of democratic men

During the Second World War Mannheim directed his theoretical efforts mainly at questions concerning the role of values and education in a democracy. He realized that Nazi Germany – a fanatical incarnation of the will to power – could not be defeated by guns alone; victory depended to a large extent on popular enthusiasm, the will to overcome, and informed commitment to democratic values. The collapse of the liberal-capitalist system during the 1930s, furthermore, necessitated a complete revision of democratic values and educational practices.

On the practical level Mannheim attempted to reach a large audience to spread awareness of the needed changes in orientation; he was especially interested in persuading educators and administrators of the urgent need for bold innovations in methods of socialization and public policy. Mannheim expressed his concern for the reconstruction of democratic society in a variety of lectures to reform-oriented groups; in co-operation with his publisher, Routledge & Kegan Paul, he established the 'International Library of Sociology and Social Reconstruction' which also appealed to a public of activist reformers.[1]

Sir Frederick Clarke, the director of the University of London Institute of Education, encouraged Mannheim's search for educational practices capable of shaping individuals for the complex social roles thrust upon them by modern society.

Since Mannheim believed that social planning should be based on a democratic consensus, he could not avoid the pursuit of ideals and values underlying that type of collective agreement about the ultimate purpose of social interaction. Liberal-capitalist society had spawned primary values such as rugged individualism, ruthless competition, and survival of the fittest which perpetuated the mystique of fear invented by Calvin and other high priests of repressive Protestantism.

These values had glorified the behavior of an exploitative minority; as far as the masses were concerned they merely served to hasten the disintegration of conduct into the fragmented actions of terrorized, disconnected individuals.

Mannheim's search for co-operative, communal, liberating values took place in the narrow space between the ideals of capitalists which he considered obsolete and the convictions of Socialists which he did not share. During his quest for new values Mannheim came under the influence of a peculiar group called the Moot which afforded membership to mainly religiously oriented and basically conservative men. As a member of this group Mannheim participated in meetings which were held four times a year for a weekend with the purpose of discussing the relevance of socio-cultural transformations for Christianity. The last chapter of the book *Diagnosis of Our Time* was first presented as a paper to the members of the Moot; in this paper, entitled 'Towards a new social philosophy: a challenge to Christian thinkers by a sociologist', Mannheim explored the possible role of religion in the planned democracy of the future.

Mannheim's search for new values ended with a curious turn toward the sphere of religious belief: this development is probably not unrelated to his participation in the activities of the Moot. This group consisted of writers, senior civil servants, and professors, but was dominated by Anglican theologians and clergymen such as Alec Vidler, then dean of Windsor Chapel, and Joseph Oldham who had established his reputation in Church of England affairs and related social reform activities. Among the prominent members of the Moot were J. Middleton Murry, the vatic literary pacifist, and the conservative literary intellectual T. S. Eliot who, in 1941, had called for religious education at the Anglican gathering at Malvern College.

Mannheim's wartime lectures and essays reflect an increasing optimism with regard to the possibility of social planning. As an advocate of planning Mannheim certainly did not occupy the position of an outsider: during the Second World War the conception of planning made significant inroads into British public opinion and policy decisions.

To begin with, many people shared the opinion of Tom Wintringham, inspirer of the Home Guard, who called the confrontation with Fascism a 'People's War'. A large number of individuals did not view this concept as a poetic phrase, but accepted it as the expression of a popular will to prevent the recurrence of the pattern of the last peace which had condemned millions of men to the terror of unemployment after their return from the horrors of war. Opinion leaders, such as the novelist J. B. Priestley whose Sunday night 'Postscripts' broadcasts attracted over 30 per cent of the population, contributed to the radicalization of public opinion. In his broadcast of July 21, 1940, Priestley attacked the sacred cow of the liberal-capitalist system: it was time, he argued, to value the ideal of 'community' more highly than the 'old-fashioned' idea of private property. It is true that Priestley's talks were eventually taken off the air, but there were other makers of public opinion who continued the process of revaluation.

In 1941, George Orwell attacked the 'rottenness' of the capitalist system and on July 1, 1940, *The Times* published a leader celebrating the dawn of a 'new order' based on economic planning for the sake of the equitable distribution of wealth and the realization of social justice. On September 19, 1942, another *Times* leader demanded government control of all monopolies as part of a democratic post-war policy. Meanwhile the war was creating by the millions the change agents for a new order: the indefatigable Priestley described the cadres of the Civil Defence services as 'militant citizens' and cohorts of a new democracy. On a larger scale the Liberal and Socialist Left interpreted the war as a universal battle between decent men and Fascist oppressors; in this perspective the European Resistance movements appeared as the political advance troops of a New Order, destined to replace the Old Order dominated by corrupt generals, industrialists, and aristocrats. In Britain the Left wing of the Labour party mounted vigorous attacks against capitalism and Aneurin Bevan gave expression to the restive mood of many rank and file members of the party when he warned that big business was getting ready to take over the state. Since the beginning of the war middle-of-the-road Liberals and Socialists had been clamoring for 'positive war aims' which amounted to demands for socialism at home and federalism abroad.

In wartime England organization and planning were the order of the day. Conservatives who were fearful of revolution acquiesced in planning measures which overrode their vested interests; others took their cue from Winston Churchill and accepted planning activities as temporary means to victory and the perpetuation of Britain's power. Some Liberals and most of the representatives of Labour thought that planning had come to stay as the guarantor of a new, just democracy. Left-wing liberals and unaligned socialists and radicals formed the '1941 Committee' which summed up its views in one of its publications entitled *Planning and Freedom*.

Early in the war the House of Commons had extended the Emergency Powers Act giving the government control over the lives of individuals and their property; in May 1940, Excess Profits Tax was raised to 100 per cent. In July 1940, the government decided to provide mothers and small children with free or inexpensive milk; Bevan's initiative led to the Essential Work Order which forced employers to win the consent of a Ministry of Labour National

Service officer before firing any worker. The government vastly extended rehabilitation services and the Disabled Persons Act of 1944 prescribed a quota of rehabilitated workers which employers had to hire. State-sponsored day nurseries were greatly expanded for the benefit of workers' children.

These pieces of legislation were not always effective: many businessmen continued to reap ill-gotten gains by evading Excess Profits Tax and the co-operation between government and industry often deteriorated into forms of racketeering favorable to private interests. But many advocates of planned democracy, such as Karl Mannheim, viewed these legislative developments as necessary first steps in the right direction.

Meanwhile organized labor was spearheading a movement toward more comprehensive and systematic forms of social legislation. In February, 1941, the TUC began to press the Minister of Health for an investigation of the ramshackle structure of health insurance which the custodians of the liberal-capitalist system had foisted on the British people. On June 10, 1941, Arthur Greenwood, the deputy leader of the Labour party, who had been assigned to planning for the post-war world, appointed a committee for the purpose of conducting a thorough survey of all existing social insurance schemes. With Sir William Beveridge as its chairman the committee made it clear that the needed rationalization and co-ordination of extant social insurance schemes had to be viewed as part of a larger effort aiming at nothing less than the elimination of poverty.

The 'Beveridge Report' – published on December 1, 1942 – found enthusiastic popular support. Informed Socialists realized that the Beveridge 'Plan' was a compromise between the forces of social progress and the defenders of capitalism, but the people of Britain viewed the proposed unitary scheme, covering every crisis of life from the cradle (maternity grants) to the grave (funeral grants) as something that gave meaning to their war efforts. The Beveridge Report popularized the idea that the provision of income security through fully develped social insurance was an attack on 'Want' spearheading the larger offensive against 'Disease', 'Ignorance', 'Squalor', and 'Idleness'.

The report, which called for the establishment of a new Ministry of Social Security, was endorsed by the National Council of Labour, representing the TUC and the Labour party; it also received support from the Liberal party, the British Council of Churches, and from most younger Conservatives. The private insurance companies mounted a campaign of slander and intimidation against the Beveridge plan. Since the report and subsequent publications demanded a complete National Health Service, financed by taxation, the wealthy leaders of the British Medical Association joined the frantic attack on the proposed social services. The cabinet reacted to the report's popular success with a display of embarrassment and indecision; despite the enthusiasm of the people and the Commons for the Beveridge Report, Churchill favored postponement of the necessary legislation: he, fatefully, misread the mood of the population.

War and social reform

With the publication of his chapter on 'Mass education and group analysis' in 1939 Mannheim began to concentrate on a series of investigations concerned with the functional significance of the institutions of education and religion and the social importance of values.[2] During the early war years Mannheim continued to lecture on these topics and in 1943 he published his accumulated output in a book entitled *Diagnosis of Our Time*.

This essay collection, which summarizes the major ideas of Mannheim's third phase, has a dual purpose: first, *Diagnosis of Our Time* popularizes the planning theme of *Man and Society in an Age of Reconstruction* and second, the new book calls attention to the needs for socially relevant education, a new system of democratic values, and religious forms of social cohesion. Under the impression of the Second World War, which pits the British people against fanatically determined enemies, Mannheim realizes that emotional and volitional forces must rally to the support of his hitherto predominantly rationalistic paradigm for social planning. Mannheim sees the processes of education, valuation, and religious expression in close connection with the human will and men's feelings and he, therefore, believes them to be capable of activating mass support for the planned construction of a fundamentally and militantly democratic society.

Mannheim's interest in education and valuation is of long standing, but his wartime essays represent original contributions to the sociology of education, the sociology of religion, and the sociology of values which stress the functional interdependence of these social forces.[3] Moreover, substantial morality, which is needed as a complement of substantial rationality, supposedly arises within the confines of this institutional configuration.

The essay collection has the additional, practical purpose of aiding members of various groups trying to gain insights into the crises afflicting modern industrial societies. The diagnostic intent is frequently combined with the pragmatic purpose of convincing audiences of the need for remedial action. In his lectures addressed to academic groups Mannheim underscores above all the need for active involvement in programs of social amelioration. Academicians in general are advised that it is no longer possible to tolerate the confusion of scientific objectivity with ethical and ideological neutrality; sociologists in particular are exhorted to offer not only the customary array of surveys and factual descriptions, but also significant analyses and definitions of the new direction of social development.[4]

The lead essay on the 'Diagnosis of our time' was first presented as a lecture in January, 1941 at a Conference of Federal Union at Oxford.[5] As in his *Man and Society in an Age of Reconstruction*, published during the preceding year, Mannheim emphasized the importance of the new social techniques in the unavoidable transition from *laissez-faire* liberalism to the planned society. On this occasion, however, Mannheim did not stress the technological efficiency of the techniques, but the ethical implications of their use.

On the ethical level the social techniques may be correlated with three social systems. First, liberal-capitalist society represents a social system which drifts without firm plan or recognizable purpose; hence, liberal-capitalist governments are incapable of adequately utilizing modern social techniques. Second, there are the 'new orders' expressing the resolute plans and clear-cut purposes of twentieth-century dictators. Dictatorial governments concentrate all available social techniques in a few hands and utilize them to the fullest extent to satisfy the interests of a small ruling minority. Third, there is the emergent social system of 'militant democracy' which permits parliamentary governments fully to utilize modern social techniques for the benefit of the entire population. By the standards of humanist, democratic ethics the full application of social techniques to social life may be considered as 'just' and 'good' only as long as it takes place within the framework of a militant democracy dedicated to the new ideal of planning for freedom.

The potential future society of militant democracy represents a 'Third Way' leading out of liberal-capitalist waste and inefficiency and away from the satanic efficiency of brutal dictators. The concept of the Third Way of social reform does not originate in Mannheim's thinking; on the contrary this notion has fascinated change-conscious conservative intellectuals at least since the times of Saint-Simon and Comte. In Saint-Simon's and Comte's positivist philosophy it was the third stage of intellectual development that promised the deliverance of mankind from reactionary injustice and revolutionary terrorism. The third stage of mental progress represented the triumph of science and permitted the rational conduct of politics and the scientific organization of society. Mannheim, therefore, echoes Comte's call for the union between the forces of progress and the forces of order. The liberation of mankind presupposes the success of this alliance: 'To-day all those forces which are determined to fight the forces of evil and oppression rally round the flag of progressive democracy, which is bound to plan the New Order of Freedom and Social Justice.'[6] In France it was Frédéric Le Play, a contemporary of Comte, who steered the cause of conservative social reform into the direction of empirical research. Le Play's approach to sociology and social reform influenced the English railway company director and financier Victor Branford who combined his commercial activities with an intellectual career dedicated to the establishment of scientific sociology and the instauration of a just, equitable society, conceptualized as the 'Third Alternative'. The forces of order and the forces of revolution had failed to improve social life; therefore, Branford placed his hopes for a viable society in the 'party of the Third Alternative', which would combine the ethical force of good will with the intellectual power of scientific knowledge to achieve improved social conditions by way of practical, concrete reformist activities.[7]

In 1942, the economist and sociologist Wilhelm Röpke used the concept of the Third Way (*dritter Weg*) in his book on the *Social Crisis of the Present*. In opposition to the Marxists, this German émigré claimed that human behavior was strongly influenced by emotions and values shared by all men regardless of their class positions or special interests. Röpke operated with the nebulous concept of 'economic humanism' to advertise the assertion that it was possible to take a Third Way between the extremes of capitalism and collectivism.[8]

In Mannheim's opinion the Third Way promises to deliver modern men from the contemporary social crisis by means of existing instruments of social reform whereby it becomes possible to avoid the disastrous road leading from revolution to dictatorship.[9] The latent tendencies of the Third Way represent social changes that may take place beyond the extremes of Fascism and Communism; the emergent solution of the Third Way, therefore, stands for 'the new pattern of planned society which, although using the techniques of planning, maintains its democratic control, and keeps those spheres of freedom and free initiative which are the genuine safeguards of culture and humanity'.[10]

The militant democracy, envisioned by Mannheim as the Third Way, represents a determined force in opposition to the new orders of dictatorial regimes. Contemporary dictators have misused the means of planning to bring about deadly forms of bureaucratic conformity and military uniformity. By contrast, the solution of the Third Way intends to realize the ideal of planning for freedom by maintaining the social world of democratic pluralism and free spheres for the exercise of individualistic value decisions. The conception of a militant democracy conflicts also with the old order established by the governing groups of liberal-capitalist society.

In contrast to liberal-capitalist society the Third Way of militant democracy represents the basic conviction that the democratic process is neither a formalistic shibboleth nor an ideological smokescreen concealing the machinations of special interest groups, but a living reality and genuine mechanism of popular rule. A militant democrat neither tolerates his avowed enemies nor retains a suicidal stance of objectivity in political confrontations. The ethos of liberal-capitalist society is competitive and assumes the moral efficacy of the 'survival of the fittest'. By contrast, the planned democratic order derives its ethical strength from the ideal of social justice which will be realized by various means of reform including 'taxation, control of investment . . . public works and the radical extension of social services'.[11]

Mannheim believes that militant democracy will first become a reality in England, where the war experience has led to trend-setting social reforms. The war economy has taught the British people several important lessons. They have learned that finance and business are public activities; they have also learned that the public interest may call for the control of private profiteering and the ownership of capital; people have come to realize that important investments and large-scale speculations must be part of comprehensive planning; in Britain people are beginning to understand that society is responsible for the compensation or retraining of the victims of social and technological change; people are also beginning to grasp that they have the right to demand heavy taxation for the few individuals who manage to reap excessive gains from social and technological alterations.[12]

In Mannheim's estimate the development toward democratic planning for freedom and social justice will continue after the end of the war; the will to reform will actually be strengthened by the economic and political insecurity of the post-war world. Everybody knows 'that from this war there is no way back to a laissez-faire order of society, that war as such is the maker of a silent revolution by preparing the road to a new type of planned order'.[13]

The sociology of values and the evolution of substantial morality

In 'The crisis in valuation', his major wartime statement of the modern value crisis, Mannheim is particularly explicit about the question of Marxism. To begin with, he rejects the Marxist approach which allegedly hinders the full understanding of the crisis in valuations; the Marxists, Mannheim claims, explain both the crisis of culture and the related value crisis by exclusive reference to economic and class factors. But an analytical framework which only holds the economic order and the social class structure responsible for the cultural and evaluative crisis is not conducive to comprehensive explanations of these contemporary problems. The Marxists claim that only the economy needs to be re-organized to remove the prevailing chaos in valuation. According to Mannheim 'no remedy of the chaos is possible without a sound economic order, but this is by no means enough, as there are a great many other social conditions which influence the process of value creation and dissemination'.[14]

Mannheim's sociology of values rejects Marxist economic determinism because it is too limited; at the same time this sociology discredits the perspective of religious and philosophical idealists because it is society-blind. The Marxists see the painful process of economic transition from capitalism to socialism as the cause of the value crisis; the idealists conversely interpret the crisis in values as the cause of the crisis of modern civilization. The Marxist paradigm suffers from its limitation to just one social factor; the idealist approach ignores social factors altogether and leads nowhere since it merely explains one spiritually conceived process as the effect of another spiritual process.

Mannheim's sociology of values is based on the assumption that there exists 'a coherent system of social and psychological activities which constitute the process of valuation; among them value creation, value dissemination, value reconciliation, value standardization, value assimilation are the most important, and there are definite social conditions which favor or upset the smooth working of the process of valuation'.[15] Mannheim, furthermore, asserts that the process of valuation in contemporary society has been disturbed by changes in at least eight social factors.

The first discernible dislocation occurs as a consequence of accelerated social development and the growth of mass society. Contemporary socialization is still dominated by an evaluative tradition which Charles Horton Cooley conceptualized as the world of primary ideals.[16] While individuals are trained to act in congruence with emotional and personal primary ideals such as love and brotherhood they have to survive in the unemotional and impersonal social context of a mass society rewarding ruthlessness and self-serving egocentricity. This discrepancy leads some individuals into ethical confusion and encourages others to disregard values altogether; consequently anomie and alienation take on the quality of permanence.

A second disturbance in the system of valuations arises from the fact that many norms are transferred from simple to complex social conditions without the necessary reforms. In the bygone days of small-scale industrial techniques the law of private property served the value of social justice since it protected the tools of independent craftsmen performing socially useful work. In the contemporary world of monopolistic big industry the norm of private property often acts as an instrument of social oppression: 'Here the very same principle of the private ownership of the means of production implies the right to the exploitation of the many by the few.'[17]

The third set of disturbances in the process of valuation originates in the altered meaning of values guiding human aspirations for aesthetic expression, meaningful work, and stimulating leisure. In the transition from pre-industrial to industrial society value emphasis has changed from qualitative to quantitative dimensions and the requirements of the mechanical process have come to be valued more highly than the needs of men. The pre-industrial craftsman frequently experienced aesthetic, productive, and recreational activities as a meaningful unity; the modern worker is forced to exist in separate spheres which are unrelated and without discernible meaning.

A fourth source of disturbance in the value system of liberal-capitalist society is represented by the various processes transforming structured society into a shapeless mass. In the spirit of Romantic Conservatism, Mannheim deplores the loss of social and regional lines of demarcation and the erosion of corresponding scales of valuation. The leisurely pace of pre-industrial social development allegedly permitted the mediation, assimilation and standardization of values whenever members of socially or regionally heterogeneous groups, such as aristocrats and burghers, interacted or fused. The proliferation of social interaction, communication, migration, and social mobility hinders the incorporation of values. The modern indivudal, therefore, stands bewildered and confused in an anarchic whirlpool of unreconciled, antagonistic evaluations: in this situation the value experience is robbed of all significance.

Mannheim's fifth argument, again, reflects the influence of Romantic Conservatism: the disappearance of God and the crumbling of tradition opened the door to the modern procession of confusing, arbitrary attempts at value justification. 'The Utilitarian justification of values by their usefulness or the belief in the uncontrollable inspiration of the Leader became as plausible as the belief in the law of the strongest.'[18] Value chaos prevails not only in the sphere of legitimation, but also in the areas of ethical influence and responsibility. The more diverse ethico-religious and political proselytizers compete for the allegiance of the masses, the more they neutralize all forms of ethical influence upon the population. Social class divisions in industrial society, furthermore, prevent the appearance of generally accepted personal representatives of authority. Consequently, responsibility is dispersed among equally suspect functionaries and in the end there remains nobody who can be held responsible.

A sixth predicament is brought about by the fact that the creation of values and institutional arrangements is dominated by those unconscious and traditional forces which William Graham Sumner conceptualized as the 'folkways'.[19] Democratic planning, however, is a deliberate process which depends on the rational creation and conscious appreciation of new values and institutional arrangements. Conscious and rational value creation and value guidance have the purpose of predicting and influencing social development; the linkage of valuation with rational deliberation and persuasion is attempted in some areas such as pastoral and social work. But society at large has so far failed to achieve this linkage and novel techniques of rational valuation are, therefore, upsetting 'the balance between conscious and unconscious forces operating in our society'.[20]

A seventh disturbance is created by the clash between regressive educational practices and the need for progressive valuations. The existing educational system creates inhibitions and suppresses the development of personal autonomy and intelligent judgment. Most individuals are not educated to develop their intellectual powers, but subjected to processes of imitation and emotional suggestion which train them for an unthinking acceptance of values and blind obedience. The educational practices prevailing in *laissez-faire* societies, therefore, fail to prepare people for life in a democratic order, founded upon the rational creation and conscious deliberation of its system of values and social control.

The eighth set of disturbances arises from the purposeless drifting of liberal-capitalist society which is caused by the lack of commonly accepted values and the complete absence of ethical and intellectual consistency. *Laissez-faire* societies have moral and political propaganda, but they have no values. *Laissez-faire* societies are dominated by political mandarins and economic oligarchs, whose self-serving machinations are so monstrous that they even undermine the effectiveness of their own propaganda. *Laissez-faire* societies are on the road to complete disintegration – a process which has been delayed by attempts at the moronization of the masses. In these societies all intellectual and ethical efforts are doomed to futility. In a social reality darkened by complete uncertainty the perfection of techniques in the spheres of education, social work, propaganda, child guidance, and psychotherapy becomes meaningless since there are no value standards providing these efforts with direction and continuity. 'Sooner or later everyone becomes neurotic, as it gradually becomes impossible to make a reasonable choice in the chaos of competing and unreconciled valuations.'[21]

Mannheim's critique of contemporary forms of valuation is accompanied by ameliorative suggestions. His recommendations initially follow a fairly obvious path: he advocates a reversal of existing procedures or proposes the addition of missing practices. (1) Values with origins in primary groups must be 'translated' into the conditions of urban, industrial societies; (2) some primary ideals, such as the notion of private property, are in need of 'complete reform'; (3) modern forms of work and leisure must be brought into contact with human value aspirations; (4) the drift of mass society toward evaluative anarchy must be reversed with the help of a 'gradual standardization' of fundamental values; (5) 'value reconciliation' and the 'focusing' of responsibility and authority upon visible agents must supplement value standardization; (6) 'conscious deliberation' has to replace irrational forces in the process of valuation; (7) a 'gradual re-education' of the entire personality is needed to balance the rational and irrational components of valuation; (8) the Third Way of planning for freedom must create areas of 'basic conformity' and 'continuity' so that mass society may be steered away from the dark horizon concealing chaos and dictatorship.[22]

Democratic planning, then, is a process which is not limited to the socio-economic and political spheres, but which extends into the area of valuations. Three major principles should guide a democratic value policy. First, democratic societies must overcome their *laissez-faire* attitudes to values: uninterest in valuations must be replaced by active involvement in evaluative processes designed to achieve ethical consensus and democratic forms of social progress. Second, the virtue of democratic self-discipline must be diffused across class lines to bring about the reconciliation of antagonistic valuations and the mutual assimilation of disparate values. The struggle for ethical consensus is inseparable from the fight for social justice. Remaining sources of discord should be studied empirically and organizations such as conciliation committees and courts of arbitration should become active in the mitigation of conflicts. Third, democratic value policy has to recognize that agreement about the mechanisms of social reform and basic valuations must be achieved to prevent the deterioration of liberal-capitalist societies into dictatorships. Survival depends on the ability of democratic men to co-ordinate basic values with social institutions so that the development of ethical consensus will not be left to chance. A conscious philosophy of values will focus democratic efforts and spawn the necessary instruments; some of the means for the realization of democratic value policy are available today and include social work, child guidance clinics, adult education, and juvenile courts.[23]

The success of democratic value policy will depend to a large extent on the efficacy of new forms of socialization designed to foster the development of substantial morality. Like Max Weber's 'ethics of responsibility' (*Verantwortungsethik*), substantial morality correlates normative behavior with social reality and the requirements of a rationally designed social order. Substantial morality, therefore, increases the range of predictable behavioral consequences and enables individuals to assume greater responsibility for the effects of their actions.[24] The norms of substantial morality are the result of conscious and rational experimentation and selection; therefore, they can only be enacted by people who have been educated to accept and assimilate values in a conscious and rational manner. It is no coincidence that the norms of substantial morality are usually opposed by individuals who are still entrapped in the irrational fogs of traditional, society-blind processes of valuation.[25]

The value grounds of everyday life

With the advance of positivism the sources of the ethical imagination began to dry up. During the second half of the nineteenth century Friedrich Nietzsche, Wilhelm Dilthey, and a shrinking band of historicists fought their rather lone battles against the moral entropy threatening the vitality of a civilization enthralled by the tin gods of science and technology. The social and cultural crises surrounding the events of the First World War helped to set the stage for the great value debate of the early twentieth century which unleashed the creative energies of Edmund Husserl, Max Scheler, and Nicolai Hartmann.

Following Scheler's example Hartmann styled his 'material' ethics in contradistinction to Kant's formalism. When Max Weber distinguished between the ethics of ultimate ends (*Gesinnungsethik*), expressed by Kantianism, and the ethics of responsibility (*Verantwortungsethik*), he, as well, asserted the impossibility of returning to Kant's ethical formalism. As a sociologist Weber placed his hopes in the ethics of responsibility representing a material, substantive ethics. He believed that only substantive ethical norms could guide the value decisions of modern men whose actions take place in highly complex social situations. In this climate of opinion Mannheim arrived at *his* demand for that substantial morality which orients valuation to constantly changing situations. Substantive morality emphasizes rational values and action in the context of freedom; this value system also rejects the normative expectations of 'abstract Idealism' which fail to take into account the social context of human behavior. Mannheim's ethical approach – later characterized as 'concrete idealism' – is informed by the conviction that it is necessary to rediscover the importance of the social context of value decisions.[26]

Despite its philosophical antecedents Mannheim's ethical approach remains under the action-oriented, pragmatic influence of change-conscious sociology. His sociology of values approaches all ethical problems at a niveau which F. Warren Rempel aptly defines as the tertiary level of 'concrete ethics'. Mannheim's practical attention to the social context of valuation is so pronounced that neither the primary level of axiological presuppositions, nor the secondary level of theoretical ethical presuppositions receives the benefits of systematic elaboration.[27]

The absence of systematically developed presuppositions for a theoretical ethics leads to a proliferation of concepts: at times the value experience is designated by terms such as valuation, ideal, goal, or social code and on other occasions by concepts such as value, virtue, sentiment, deeper purpose, or morality. Similarly the normative dimensions of behavior are conceptualized by means of interchangeably used terms, including code, regulation, rule, habits, and public norms. Furthermore, the value experience is not consistently distinguished from the normative aspects of social existence.[28]

These semantic problems indicate that Mannheim's major concern is not directed at the formulation of a theoretical ethics, but at the establishment of common values for everyday life in a planned society. The major thrust of his sociology of values is not theoretical, but practical since it serves the larger purposes of a reformist strategy designed to provide for freedom through social planning. In Mannheim's paradigm freedom implies the continued existence of certain traditions and the presence of social consensus. Like other social systems the planned society will depend for its survival on the operation of forces guaranteeing cohesion, order, and continuity. The sociologist of planning must assume the role of the sociologist of values, since the selection of planning methods and objectives must be guided by common values. The techniques of planning do not bring about social consensus – this prerequisite for social cohesion and order originates in the sphere of values. Without common values a plan merely operates to perpetuate the special interests of ruling groups.

On the practical level of his concrete ethics Mannheim unequivocally interprets norms and values as changing instruments facilitating the adjustment of individuals to the flux and flow of social life.[29] As a sociologist Mannheim shows little interest in norms and values as the intrinsic qualities of an object; in his estimate they derive their meaning from the social context in which they function. This 'contextualization' of values and norms presupposes a measure of popular awareness in social affairs that only sociological information and education can provide.[30] Mannheim retained this emphasis on the instrumental character of norms and values and the consciousness-raising function of sociology until the end of his life.[31]

Mannheim's dynamic sociology of values acknowledges that competition, conflict, and inequality create serious tensions in society and the human value experience. But the fusion of the sociology of values with the sociology of planning permits a solution to the problems of social and personal disintegration. In the value sphere the drift toward anomie and alienation may be halted with the help of the ultimate values of solidarity, collective responsibility, communitarian harmony, freedom, democracy, and respect for personality. Mannheim believes that 'the democratic form of planning will do everything to make planning compatible with these values'.[32]

Unlike Marxist theorists, Mannheim assumes that ultimate, humanist values depend for their realization upon evolutionary, reformist processes of social transformation. Socio-cultural changes and revaluations do not originate in the chaos of revolutions, but flow from processes powered by consensus and intellectual understanding.[33] Reformist alterations of social structure will invite the co-operation of established ruling groups that represent the traditional values of Western civilization. The society of the future needs the guidance of leading groups composed of old and new élites. 'Together they can help to rejuvenate the valuable elements in tradition, continuing them in the spirit of creative evolution.'[34] The reformist spirit of the Third Way prevents revolutionary ruptures in valuation and cultural tradition and encourages the development of solidarity and peace-loving co-operation.[35]

As in his preceding writings on social planning Mannheim skirts the conflict dimensions of his assertion that socially heterogeneous élites can share the privileged positions of power and influence; instead, he reaffirms his belief that the growth of social awareness and various wartime measures will lead to the instauration of a progressive democracy in England. 'It is perhaps not by chance that the craving for social awareness is awakening in this country exactly at a juncture when this transformation is taking place in reality.'[36]

In Mannheim's opinion English society is founded on the traditions of freedom, democracy, and spontaneous reform and, therefore, uniquely equipped to bring to life the ideal of 'planning for freedom'.[37] Moreover, he assumes that the experience of the Second World War provides the final push into the desired direction by making it clear to all the people that 'there is no way back to a laissez-faire order of society, that war as such is the maker of a silent revolution by preparing the road to a new type of planned order'.[38]

The society of the future must be based on a sound interplay of collective and individual needs to retain its vital dissimilarity from totalitarian models of conformity. A society capable of balancing the sense of collective responsibility with respect for personal independence will bring to life the novel ideal of 'democratic personalism'.[39] The roots for the dynamic equilibrium of individualization and socialization reach deeply into English tradition. The English people have long-standing respect for privacy and inwardness and the expressions of personal autonomy resulting from these means of individualization.[40] Traditional elements are also present in the basic virtues of collective life which must come to supplement the ethics of personal relationships.

The practical application of the ideal of democratic personalism will foster forms of socialization based on the value of judicious identification with others. The value grounds of everyday life in a democratically planned society include additional 'basic virtues such as decency, mutual help, honesty and social justice, which can be brought home through education and social influence'.[41] Some of the basic virtues will only function in industrial-urban society after having been 'translated' into the appropriate idiom. Primary ideals such as sympathy, love, and brotherhood can only be effective in the world of secondary group relationships after having found the abstract equivalents of political and legal equality.[42]

Mannheim's concern for those basic values capable of integrating groups does not reflect endeavors on behalf of a theoretical ethics, but efforts aimed at the just reconstruction of society. The new society does not only need expert knowledge of social techniques – the world of the future depends above all on a communitarian vision of shared goals and such insight originates on the level of daily co-operation for the common good.[43]

The sociology of education

New values are mainly created and expressed by individuals who confront established society as outsiders. Artists, poets, intellectuals, and members of oppressed groups are mostly marginal men – and so are young and youth-oriented people.[44] Like other individuals who live on the fringe of society young men and women have the potential for bringing new values to life. The change from a commercially-oriented, defensive democracy to a community-oriented, militant democracy is a process which depends for its success on the participation of the young. The latent resources of youth must, therefore, be released together with the energies of other future-oriented population segments so that society may be infused with new vitality. The vital and spiritual potentialities of the young can only be mobilized through policies which overcome the generation gap by allowing young individuals to participate fully in the tasks of social reconstruction. Only the creative, purposeful integration of youth into society will transform the reserves latent in the young into constructive function.

In traditional, capitalistic democracies condescending public attitudes and calcified educational procedures have largely neutralized the psychological resources of youth. The revitalization of society demands a break with these obstructive practices; they must be replaced by a democratic youth policy which will permit the growth of a nation-wide youth movement and the creation of a youth-oriented educational system.

The ethics of democratic personalism allow the formation of youthful personalities who can co-operate in groups to foster the common good without diminishing their sense of judgment and independence. In this way the young will neither be the lonely victims of alienation nor the regimented prisoners of fanaticism. In other words, the youth policy of the Third Way opposes both the atomistic individualism of liberal-capitalist society and the mechanical collectivism of totalitarian social systems.[45]

The success of democratic youth policy depends to a large extent on the co-operation of educators who view the school and the world as complementary categories. The 'integral concept' of education demands that the realities and requirements of life become part of the academic process of knowledge distribution. But, education is not only important as far as the young are concerned: in a planned democracy the educational process must not only be life-oriented, it must also go on for life. The liberal-capitalist order brought with it a society-blind, mechanical compartmentalization of education which must be overcome with the help of adult education and similar practices guided by the concepts of 'post-education' and 're-education'.[46]

People who recognize society as an educational agent will come to realize that the social sciences are agents of education. The behavioral and social sciences are significant because they provide practitioners of integral education with integrating methods and theories. These sciences, furthermore, provide insights which are useful for resolving both personality-centered and group-centered social problems.[47] The activities of sociologists are especially important: sociologists do not merely contribute to the creation of a new educational system; they also have the potential for raising the consciousness of the people to a level from which the intricate interplay of contemporary social forces becomes visible. Such awareness enables individuals to determine social situations fairly accurately. Undoubtedly this ability should greatly facilitate life in societies which are subject to continuous structural changes and severe social conflicts.

The capacity for arriving at adequate definitions of changing situations is especially important for members of intellectual, educational, and administrative élites. Optimally, educational reconstruction should raise the consciousness of all the people: 'fundamental democratization claims for everyone a share in real education'.[48] In the meantime, however, survival demands that 'at least the leaders of the nation, and among them the teachers, should be educated in a way which will enable them to understand the meaning of change'.[49]

The efforts which Mannheim expects from these élites are similar to those he once demanded from the so-called 'socially unattached' intellectuals: efforts aimed at an integration of diverse collective experiences for the purpose of synthesizing particularistic aspects of social life into a total awareness of the overall historical situation.[50]

In Mannheim's opinion the British educational system has so far suppressed the growth of social awareness. The problem has been brought about by an overemphasis on academic specialization. But this is not the only reason for the failure of educators to develop the ability for a comprehensive understanding of the situation: they have also been mistaken in confusing tolerance and objectivity with cowardly neutrality. Fearful of disturbing social consensus and solidarity the nation's teachers have, furthermore, stressed technical problems at the expense of vital issues.[51]

The time has come for changing the direction of educational processes: students must not only be taught special skills, but also how to survive in the changing situations and institutions of contemporary society; they must be alerted to the significance of commonly accepted basic virtues; they must be stimulated to grasp the importance of collective interests and needs. Relevant and reality-adequate education will bridge the stage of incipient planning with the future world of comprehensive democratic planning.[52]

On the concrete level of 'educational techniques' Mannheim recommends the method of group analysis which makes the catharsis of group interaction available to democratic forms of readjusting the masses to changing social conditions. Group analysis applies psychological and psychoanalytical methods of therapy to several individuals simultaneously. The emerging practice of group analysis is supported by sociologists and psychologists who are interested in helping people to adjust rationally and creatively to the requirements of changing environments. In contemporary social life individuals must continuously equilibrate their personal impulses with the collective needs of groups: the experience of group analysis helps people to develop an understanding of the mechanisms which maintain and restore the social equilibrium. As a social technique group analysis will be especially important in the planned society of the future in which 'collective adjustment will become as important as individual adjustment'.[53]

Several findings in psychological and sociological research seem to support the basic assumptions underlying the theory and practice of group analysis. At least since Thrasher's work on youth gangs we know that re-education and re-socialization are greatly facilitated by the dynamics of group interaction. Aichhorn has shown that the treatment of individual adjustment problems can only succeed as long as the neurotic constellation of groups, such as the family, is also dealt with. Group analysis has benefited from the suggestions of Fromm, Ichheiser, and Schilder who have made it clear that many individual neuroses have taproots in the subsoil of society.[54] Neuroses may be rooted in ideologies which are difficult to remove since they are surrounded by defense mechanisms instilled into the individual by group interaction. Since the obsessional effects of public ideologies are associated with group interaction they can only be dispelled by therapeutic adjustments appealing to the entire group of similarly afflicted individuals. These public ideologies not only distort the political outlook of individuals; they also twist their sexual, socio-economic, and professional behavior. The attack on public ideologies, therefore, demands large-scale measures of public enlightenment. This attack should be led by representatives of the new social services and educators who are capable of linking up the 'regeneration of man with the regeneration of society'.[55]

The new Christianity

The programs of conservative sociologists frequently end with efforts to resuscitate the irrational forces of religion. In France Comte and Durkheim praised the regulative power and unifying moral strength of religion; in England it was Benjamin Kidd – an ideological defender of British imperialism – who recommended group constraint and the suprarational sanctions of religion as mainsprings of social progress. In the end Mannheim, as well, came to believe that group survival depended on religion which alone could establish valuational consensus about the ultimate ends of social life.[56]

Life in a planned democracy must be guided by a new morality which takes into account the existence of society as a whole. Planning for freedom aims at a far-reaching integration of the community which can only succeed as long as the deepest resources of the human psyche are mobilized for the attack on the chaotic conditions permeating the entire liberal-capitalist system. Non-totalitarian comprehensive planning, in other words, implies not only redefinitions of crucial existential situations, but also the emotionalization of new issues.

The penetration of the religious spirit into society will result both in a spiritualization of human relations and the creation of a unifying purpose. In a planned democracy religious leaders will have the task of recommending fundamental virtues such as voluntary co-operation, social justice, and mutual aid leading to that 'basic conformity which gives stability and soundness to social life'.[57]

What Mannheim expects from religious leaders is ultimately a new world view capable of connecting actual behavior with models of satisfactory social institutions. Optimally the recommendations of the churches will grow into a coherent, 'consistent system similar to the Summa of St Thomas'.[58]

The planned democracy will, however, evolve as a Christian order only if the churches and their members are willing to undergo a process of regeneration in keeping with the emergent social transformation. Neither the behavioral nor the institutional manifestations of contemporary religion are adequate to the tasks of human and social reconstruction. The regeneration of Christianity must begin with a return to the 'genuine sources' of religious life.[59]

Mannheim assigns to the representatives of religion the task of an ultimate integration of all human activities. The movement of religion from the periphery to the center of society is, however, subject to several sociological conditions. First, the search for an authentic vision of existence and exemplary patterns of behavior can only be entrusted to religious leaders who simultaneously strive for freedom from superstition, intolerance, and authoritarianism. Religious and moral recommendations, in other words, must be offered to the people as the products of 'creative imagination'; they must never be forced upon the population as the dictatorial orders of a privileged élite. The second condition establishes tacit or explicit consensus as the sole mechanisms for achieving society-wide agreement on values. The striving for solidarity and common purpose must never deteriorate into a drift toward Christian clericalism and religious totalitarianism. Third, the striving for consensus must be limited to basic survival needs of society such as decency, co-operation, and social justice; more complex personal and intellectual issues must remain in the spheres of individual creed and free experimentation.[60] A fourth condition demands that Christian virtues must be 'translated' according to the circumstances of contemporary mass society. Only this sociological translation infuses the religious vision with relevance. Sociologists and modern theologians must approach moral issues scientifically to understand that human actions and valuations reflect adjustment problems encountered by individuals and groups.[61] Fifth, the regeneration of Christianity depends on successful forms of co-operation between clergymen and social scientists; it also presupposes a fusion of progressive thinking with religious ideas.[62] A sixth condition demands from Christians active involvement in the work of social transformation: in a democratically planned society ethical decisions do not remain limited to the parochial world of private relationships, but involve control of social structure at large. Planning for freedom necessitates a continuous testing of ethical principles in social situations: this evaluative process maintains the equilibrium between religious values and social organization.[63]

The regeneration of the religious experience depends above all on the co-operation of sociologists who must energize theological thought on the one side and contribute to the creation of new scales of valuation on the other. The alliance between theology and sociology presupposes complete intellectual freedom and the possibility to experiment with values in changing social situations. The art of social planning consists essentially of the ability to balance freedom of thought with a basic evaluative consensus.[64] Social planners must keep reinterpretations of basic principles within sane limits without losing flexible, experimental attitudes towards socio-cultural change. Like Comte, Mannheim would like to entrust this difficult task of equilibration to 'a body somehow similar to the priests' who would have to steer the ship of state between the Scylla of anarchy and the Charybdis of tyranny.[65]

Mannheim realized that an adequate modern religion would have to balance the archaic with the contemporary, the unconscious with the rational, and the personal with the collective. The demand for an equilibration of these polar types of human experience brings the real magnitude of the value problem to light. Valuations which merely regulate behavior to facilitate the adjustment of human conduct to changing situations point the way into the empty, spiritless world of mechanized labor and leisure; conversely values which merely glorify the archaic and irrational pull men back into the night of primitivism where superstitions burn with the sinister intensity of ancient masks. Caught between modernistic despiritualization and archaic mystification contemporary people must attempt a synthesis of the polar types of the human experience which permits a creative choice of adjustment possibilities in keeping with a meaningful world view. A regenerated Christianity has the potential for providing modern men with a unifying world view which is the basis for the needed synthesis: 'the Christian does not simply want to adjust himself to the world in general . . . but he wants to do so only in terms of an adjustment which . . . is in harmony with his basic experience of life.'[66] The religious focus makes it possible for modern men to interpret life from the center of a basic, 'paradigmatic' Christian experience.

Certain human experiences are so decisive and basic in their intensity that they have the power of revealing the meaning of life as an entirety. The pattern of these 'paradigmatic experiences' is so deeply impressed on the minds of men 'that they provide a mold into which further experiences flow. Thus once formed they lend shape to later experiences.'[67] Paradigmatic experiences are especially important for the maintenance of that fundamental religious sense which Christians must retain whenever they adjust their values and conduct to the changing modern environment. Purely pragmatic processes of adjustment which are not rooted in specific basic experiences merely increase efficiency and this leads to the question:

Efficiency for what? The pursuit of money, possessions, power, or prestige fails to answer this central question.

Life only takes on dramatic significance where it is guided by paradigmatic experiences which are intuitive, integrating mental processes operating at the deepest level of the psyche. Paradigmatic experiences are comparable to Jakob Burkhardt's 'primordial images' and St Augustine's and Carl Jung's 'archetypes'. Experiential prototypes such as the Saint, the Hero, the Repentant, and the Sage have guided men through the vast corridors of history. Under communal systems of social organization deeper common experiences were conveyed by celebrations of significant events such as birth, marriage, and death which punctuated the life-history of the individual with paradigmatic visions of the meaning of existence.[68]

Mannheim's theory of social planning intends to integrate a controlling vision of existence with intellectual mastery of the needs and potentialities of the contemporary world. Rational-scientific activity firmly anchors men in the present and prevents them from dropping out of the historical process. But it is the psychic force of paradigmatic vision – rising from the 'archaic depth' of the human mind – which fuels and directs the actions of men.[69] Paradigmatic experiences function in this theory mainly as experiential symbols which integrate efforts towards the construction of a cosmos of contemporaneous norms and values. Religion with its taproots in the ancient subsoil of archetypal visions of life has the powerful integrative potentials which a planned democracy will need. Religion promises to fuse primordial norms and values with a contemporaneous action paradigm into a cosmos of overarching significance which affords tenancy both to just social institutions and a cohesive world view illuminating the total meaning of human existence.

8 Political power and human freedom

On July 5, 1945, shortly after the defeat of Nazi Germany, a large number of English men and women indicated that their concern for human freedom outweighed their interest in power politics. On that day twenty-five million people went to the polls; when the ballot-boxes were opened on July 26, Churchill learned that over fifteen million citizens had voted against his government. In the new parliament Labour seats increased from 164 to 392; the Conservatives fell from 358 seats to 198.

Churchill's departure from the benches of the ministerial majority signified the end of Britain's imperial ambitions. The Labour leaders, especially on the Left, shared an insight with other representatives of international socialism: they knew that power politics and imperialist grandeur merely benefited numerically insignificant propertied ruling classes. The Labour government soon made preparations for the steady process of imperial withdrawal; at home the government began to marshall the remaining energies of a war-worn economy to face the desires of the working masses for adequate wages, full employment, and increased social services.

With the 1946 National Insurance Act and the accompanying National Health Service Act the Labour government successfully enacted the Beveridge Report; the government continued a massive legislative program and by 1949 it was clear that the British people had achieved the rudiments of a 'Welfare State'. The Labour government's nationalization program transferred run-down key industries such as coalmining and the railways to public ownership. The government took over the Bank of England and decided to run the airlines. In the course of 1948 the troubled utility industries producing gas and electricity were nationalized; the iron and steel nationalization Bill established a form of public ownership for the major units of this heavy industry.

The leaders of Labour failed to transform Britain into a Socialist country. They had widespread popular support for an all out attack on the capitalist system and the abolition of middle- and upper-class privileges. But, like the German Social Democrats, whom the demos had elevated to power after the First World War, they lacked the will for the radical transformation of society and began to operate within a 'mixed system'. The program of nationalization was limited to moribund industries which – with the exception of steel – no longer interested private capitalists; moreover, the powermongers of private enterprise could now blame their own failures on the Labour government that had inherited scores of run-down pits and plants. Meanwhile, private firms were free to exploit all money-making industries, including engineering and electronics; Labour even failed to take over jet engine production and other industries which had been developed almost exclusively by the tax payments of the community. In 1951, Churchill would return to replace Attlee as prime minister and his government would adapt Labour's welfare policies to provide the best service for the well-to-do.

During the war Mannheim had followed the London School of Economics to Cambridge; after the end of the aerial menace he had returned to London. He resigned from the London School, effective December 31, 1945, and succeeded Sir Fred Clarke to the chair of the sociology and philosophy of education in the Institute of Education at the University of London. Illness prevented him from accepting the chairmanship of the European section of the United Nations Educational, Scientific and Cultural Organization for which he had been designated a few weeks before his death. When Mannheim died during the evening of January 9, 1947, at the age of 53, he left several unpublished manuscripts in varying stages of completion.

At Julia Mannheim's invitation Adolph Lowe formed an editorial team, selected from Mannheim's former students and friends, for the purpose of making the author's unpublished writings available to the public. The first of the posthumous volumes was the unfinished work, *Freedom, Power, and Democratic Planning*, which appeared in 1950.

Diagnosis of the situation

Mannheim's book is more openly prescriptive than his preceding works on social planning; but, apart from this nuance and the more explicit handing of various details, *Freedom, Power, and Democratic Planning* is essentially a sequel to *Man and Society* and *Diagnosis of Our Time*.

Once again, Mannheim begins with a 'Diagnosis of the situation' claiming that the prevailing pattern of unguided development threatens contemporary society with social and spiritual disintegration.[1]

Mannheim distinguishes several major causes for the disintegration of contemporary society: rapid social change from primary to secondary group relations, concentration of social techniques in a few hands, and evolution of a 'power complex'.

The power complex sanctifies the exploitation of economically weakened majorities and the rule of monopolistic corporations which makes a farce of the notion of free competition and the ideal of private property.

The effects of social disintegration are manifold: self-regulating groups are replaced by urban masses; arbitrary dehumanizing forms of discipline take the place of need-oriented group controls; large organizations conflict with each other and the interests of society at large; different population segments are at war with each other; want, hatred, and fear dissolve human personalities; moral and religious commitments crumble and disappear into the void of the modern wasteland.

Social disintegration transforms structured society into an uprooted, powerless, apathetic mass whose members do not seek freedom and dignity but cheap thrills and empty amusement. Both 'The pessimistic view of Fascism' and 'The utopian hope of Marxism' appeared as reactions to social disintegration and succeeded by convincing the bewildered masses that totalitarian planning represented the only solution to the crisis. There is, however, an alternative response to disintegration which Mannheim propagates: democratic planning which, he believes, may be gradually evolved by the allegedly progressive policies of Western democracies.[2]

For modern people, then, it is no longer necessary to drift helplessly with the tides of history: they have at their disposal a variety of 'key' positions from which society can be controlled in its entirety. Passive attitudes to social change are not only unnecessary, but also undesirable because twentieth-century individuals are no longer free to wonder whether these key positions will be taken over; realistically they can only ask: Who will occupy these strategic points?

Mannheim assumes that the business bureaucrats who at present occupy the key positions in society will lose their power since their capitalist masters are rapidly fading into obsolescence. The breakdown of monopolistic capitalism opens the road to new élites: the key positions will either be seized by totalitarian groups or, as Mannheim hopes, they will be taken over by democratically elected groups capable of planning society in the spirit of humanism and freedom.

The resolution of social conflict

In the second part of the book, entitled 'Democratic planning and changing institutions', Mannheim attempts to conceptualize some of the shifts in the meaning of power which would follow in the wake of the projected change of leaders.

To begin with, Mannheim attacks the traditional liberal-capitalist assertion that freedom is mainly threatened by governmental power. In preceding centuries the conflict between the monarchical state and civil-commercial society was very real, but in the twentieth century the freedom of the people is not only endangered by agents of the government. Individual liberties are curtailed by other powerful agencies as well, whose representatives arbitrarily go beyond their legitimate sphere of activity. Arrogant usurpations of power are as common among dominant bureaucrats in private industry and trade unions as they are in governmental bureaucracies. Moreover, in several capitalist countries the government acts as a partner in 'private' industry and business: 'Hence the old boundary lines between private and public enterprise no longer hold.'[3]

In view of these developments Mannheim believes that it has become necessary to develop a 'democratic theory of power'. According to this theory ruling groups and individuals must be prevented from wielding more power than their legitimate activities and functions require. Power which is used for socially recognized purposes is 'functional power'. Any exercise of power which transcends socially recognized purposes constitutes 'arbitrary power'.[4]

In keeping with his initial assumptions Mannheim does not limit his analysis to political power, but strives for a theory based on a comprehensive conception of power. He claims that power is present wherever overt or covert constraint is brought to bear upon the individual to induce prescribed behavior. In contemporary society power has many manifestations: there is the obvious, brutal power vested in the armed forces and the police; there are the administrative mandarins and masters of economic organizations; there are forms of power rooted in manipulation and persuasion which accompany the roles of educators, advertisers, commentators and reporters, as well as the activities of gurus in religion and entertainment.

Mannheim's theory does not stress the conflict between freedom and power, but underscores the need for alternative constraints. The abolition of capitalist controls is not as important as the replacement of ineffectual controls by new ones capable of resolving major issues such as the instauration of foresight, the restoration of efficiency, the elimination of waste, and the abolition of cyclical unemployment. Moreover, the new controls should accomplish their tasks 'without inhuman regimentation or needless interference with the normal aspirations of the citizenry'.[5]

Mannheim is mainly interested in a basic form of power which is controlled by institutional processes and which controls behavior in keeping with norms and rules. This 'canalized power' must be applied judiciously so that there occurs neither a drift from freedom into chaos nor a transition from regulation to tyranny. Mannheim pursues this problem of power equilibration by tracing its connection with numerous social processes ranging from personal to international relations. The intelligentsia must play a key role in the process of power equilibration by guiding and integrating community sentiments; the just and peaceful use of canalized power is only possible as long as the influence of intellectuals equals that of generals and businessmen. Emancipated intellectuals are needed on all levels of power so that their influence may benefit local and national governments, as well as the United Nations and the unified world authority which Mannheim projects against the horizon of the future.[6]

The subsequent analysis of capitalist and Communist ruling classes has the purpose of lending weight to Mannheim's warning that democratic planning for freedom is far more complex than either partial regulation or totalitarian planning for conformity.[7]

Democratic élites will have to accommodate polar types of experience such as unity and pluralism, consensus and disagreement, liberty and discipline, centralization and decentralization. Democratic planning, therefore, not only presupposes the adaptation of social institutions and the reformation of politics, but also calls for the creation of a novel human type guided by new values.[8] Democratic planning is a flexible approach to the control of society which can only succeed as long as the processes of education and valuation shape flexible democratic personalities whose individual goals coincide with those of the planners.

The theory and practice of social education

In keeping with this conception of planning Mannheim attempts to develop a theory of 'democratic personality' in the third part of the book, entitled 'New man – new values'.[9] The new human type is capable of 'integrative behavior' which harmoniously interrelates different existential levels such as politics and economic activity, work and leisure. Integrative behavior, furthermore, fosters the co-operative attitudes and people-oriented life styles which are prerequisites for the restoration of a genuine democratic community. The democratic personality lives on higher levels of awareness and human fulfilment than either the programmed follower of totalitarian leaders or the alienated subject of capitalist masters.

The creation of a new man presupposes novel forms of socialization and pedagogy which Mannheim conceptualizes as 'social education'. The new educators will work in close co-operation with social scientists who share their interest in the co-ordination of human behavior with social institutions. The theory and practice of social education recognize the significant influence of the social and cultural environment upon personality formation. Successful socialization depends to a considerable extent on an individual's chances for participation in group situations of increasing complexity. The planners must, therefore, restore the vitality of the family, the neighborhood, and other primary groups which prepare individuals for their involvement with large, complex organizations. The larger social world of secondary groups must be made more meaningful through various forms of planned intervention and educational strategies which proceed from the basic intention of creating equal start chances for all the people, eliminating unfair economic and political practices, and discouraging excessive striving for power and prestige.

The creation and maintenance of the new order does depend not only on the reformation of educational and social processes. The subject of all these efforts – the new man – must also live up to novel expectations. The democratic personality must at all times retain enthusiasm for co-operation with others; democratic interaction must take place in the spirit of freedom and ensure that power and coercion are only used under the control of equals as a last resort; the democratic attitude must be one of tolerance and openness to diverse opinions. Tolerant people increase their ability to learn and never lose their capacity to participate creatively in the process of becoming. The democratic personality will combine a capacity for constructive social criticism with a mature sense of responsibility for the welfare of the society which affords him tenancy. The individual members of the new social order will experience accelerated social and cultural change and the impact of lively democratic criticism; they must, therefore, possess a marked degree of psychic-mental self-confidence. The democratic personality must be free from anxieties about the loss of status or identity.

Mannheim's ideal of 'democratic personalism', then, has two aspects: 'Socialization . . . should never go so far as to stifle individualization, the emancipation of the "I". Individualization, on the other hand, should never proceed so far as to induce social chaos.'[10] The creation and survival of the democratic personality depends on the success of an educational process that judiciously blends ego-security with social rootedness.

The practice of social education promises to transform everything in society into an educational factor. In view of this projected development Mannheim cannot avoid the question concerning the new function of formal education. Mannheim approaches this question by paraphrasing a concept used by W. Lloyd Warner and his colleagues: the school functions as a 'transitional society' by preparing young people for the roles they may play in the adult world of secondary group interaction.[11] Furthermore, the school may perform its special task by preparing a basis for social life consisting of interrelated educational experiences which balance everyday realities with formal learning processes. In pursuit of this goal the school will lose its exclusive youth-orientation and assume relevance for the entire social process. This transformation which will bring to life the conception that man is 'forever learning' is in the take-off stage: several modern societies provide opportunities for continued learning which include university extension courses and the more basic educational facilities 'from the nursery through primary, secondary, vocational, and adult educational institutions'.[12]

In co-operation with youth organizations and 'community centers' the school will provide opportunities for the discussion and interpretation of the democratic way of life. On the highest level adult education should be carried out by a 'people's university'. This educational facility has the dual purpose of bringing forth new élites and strengthening the intellectual integration of all social strata.

The policy of the new social order aims at a democratization of education that maintains high standards of performance. These goals can only be reached through comprehensive planning of the educational system, including universities, and the regulation of vocational and professional activities. The planners must protect the existence of an independent intelligentsia which is the major safeguard against cultural monotony and a declining intellectual *niveau*. Similar care must be taken to maintain the productive diversity of cultural and intellectual groups.

A planned democracy must also overcome the division between work and leisure to achieve meaningful interrelations between two spheres of human activity providing equally valuable opportunities for self-expression and creativity.[13] The planners will have to restructure the order of priorities in the world of work by replacing the excessive emphasis on pecuniary rewards with other gratifications such as esteem for workmanship and the social usefulness of labor. Simultaneously they must abolish the dominance of entertainment and leisure industries which have diminished the creative potential of relaxation and play. The planners will have to replace profit-oriented leisure manipulators with well-financed public organizations designed to provide a wide range of meaningful forms of enjoyment and relaxation. Modern orientations such as Herbert Read's concept of 'art as a way of life' for all the people indicate ways in which 'leisure may be integrated into the democratic plan like work and education. A type of mind should mature that is eager to expand, yet ready and willing to curb itself in the face of demands of the community.'[14]

The problem of social solidarity

In a planned democracy the relation between freedom and discipline takes on special significance.[15] Mannheim favors a system that offers individuals as much free choice as possible; he also defends the right of self-expression in small groups and private relationships. Moreover, he believes that large organizations must be allowed to develop freely. On the other hand, the planners should be given the power to prevent the growth of monopolistic organizations and other groups representing special interests. The controls curbing self-serving groups must, however, be voted into existence and their legitimacy must rest on constitutional grounds. In addition to formal controls the restraining influence of self-discipline should come into play: under democratic planning groups would be expected to realize the same measure of self-restraint and moderation that would govern personal relations.

In other areas such as consumption and occupational choice freedom and discipline will not be determined by the interests of the rich, but by the common good. In a democratically planned society everybody will receive a just share of the national wealth and educational opportunities. Intelligent forms of occupational guidance will correlate individual abilities with social needs. Guided by such considerations the central planners will bring into play various means of implementation including educational campaigns, low-cost public housing, subsidized consumption, consumer credit, price privileges, rationing, and price controls.

In essence Mannheim believes that in a planned society freedom 'should not be judged in terms of the absence or presence of bureaucracy and regulation, but in terms of the common good and the best use of individual potentialities'.[16]

In the last, unfinished chapter of the book Mannheim returns to the concluding topic of his work, *Diagnosis of Our Time*: he stresses the integrating function of a progressive religion as a valuable component not only in the development of the 'democratic personality', but in the entire transition to a dynamically planned society.

The need for social cohesion and integration should motivate contemporary planners to utilize religious forces which may provide society with stability and continuity. On the other hand, the strategist of reform must make sure that 'religion is not allowed to become, as in the case of the reactionary, a bulwark of vested interests, but rather a force to help to bring about change and, in the process, regenerate man and society'.[17]

An undogmatic force making for cultural continuity and integration is especially important because of two major intellectual influences which promote disintegrating processes. On the one side, the hypothetical and critical spirit of modern science dissolves the world into fragmented bundles of probabilities; on the other side, irresponsible political *condottieri* lure the insecure masses into barren systems of 'organized thought' which threaten to annihilate the spirit of inquiry. This conflict between the scientific dismemberment of reality and the arbitrary stabilization of world interpretation results in the 'delocalization of the mind'. This process began when individuals were severed from the secure, traditional thoughtways of small communities and commenced to drift into the cold seascape of modern civilization. The delocalization of the mind is a process which removes the individual from the shelter of communal existence and thrusts him into 'a world in which all emotional signs and meanings that had previously lent direction to his wishes and activities become meaningless'.[18]

The mental balance of contemporary men is upset by additional processes such as 'debunking' and the unmasking of ideologies. Professional thought jugglers increase the fundamental uncertainty of modern existence: they exploit psychological and sociological insights and advanced methods of mass communication for the profit-oriented manipulation of mental-psychic processes. In the service of ruling groups these virtuosi of persuasion cloud the imagination of the people with ideologies and thought clichés which benefit the material and political interests of the power élite. The mandarins of the entertainment and advertising industries amass fortunes through the strategic deployment of phony folksiness, the personal appeal, the human touch: they owe their material success to the cynical exploitation of uprooted people who are homesick for emotional intimacy and communal experiences. These manipulative practices paralyze efforts to separate the real from the fabricated, the truth from the lie: in the end they reduce human consciousness to a permanent state of hysterical insecurity and hopeless negativism.

For their long march away from insecurity and anxiety the people will need 'collective guidance'. The collective guidance envisioned by Mannheim will have to combine sociological insight into the nature and causes of social change with the spiritual power to integrate people. The functions of interpretation and integration are to be entrusted to a progressive religion: 'In the old days religion was a stabilizer; today we turn to it again for assistance in the transition. That means that our religious leaders must keep up with the changing order, building their world outlook and policy upon deeper insight and intellectual comprehension.'[19]

Mannheim's analysis of contemporary society, which is often powerful and penetrating, ends in the misty regions of an imaginary religious revival. His peculiar decision to delegate a leading role to the largely discredited and thoroughly powerless churches, however, reflects more general shortcomings of his intellectual and political orientation. Throughout the work Mannheim's prescriptions remain within the boundaries of that 'general view' he announced in the preface.[20] This self-assigned limitation permits Mannheim to prescribe an abundance of general goals and general means with regard to social planning – it also allows him to produce a plethora of generalities hiding both the concrete problems of planning and his lack of political commitment. In the manner of Romantic Conservatives Mannheim expresses his dislike for both corporate capitalists and Socialists; he shows concern for the philosophical question: Who plans the planners? But, he fails to confront the political question: Who shall actually do the planning?

Mannheim's tendency to postpone discussions of the technical aspects of planning reflects his unwillingness to face the power implications of large-scale alterations in social structure. In his last work on planning Mannheim makes it quite clear that he does not favor radical economic changes; he looks forward to a 'Mixed System' promoting economic stability. Therefore, he admonishes the major economic contestants to search for compromise solutions: capital and labor should exercise self-restraint and sound judgment to avoid radical economic transformations in their search for stability and progress.[21] Mannheim favors industrial democracy, but suggests that 'central authorities', whose constitution remains an ominous mystery, should make vital decisions by determining 'what share workers should have in the management of industry'.[22] Mannheim fails to specify the nature and extent of working-class power in managerial decisions just as he ignores the realities of the power struggle between capital and labor in his call for compromise solutions.

Mannheim runs into difficulties not only with regard to the question: Who plans the means of social reconstruction? Even more serious problems surround the companion query: Who plans the goals of social change? As a young sociologist Mannheim demonstrated that general concepts such as liberty have no meaning unless they are related to specific social groups and their aspirations and social philosophies.[23] Mannheim's last discussion of social planning offers many general goals ranging from order, stability, and integration to creativity, justice, and freedom; but now he fails to relate these general concepts to specific social groups and his planning goals remain, therefore, beyond the realm of unambiguous definition. For the late Mannheim education is a social technique aiming at a 'planned attack on the self' and the recreation of man in the image of 'democratic personality'. But, again, he does not ascribe this godlike function to any known social group.

For the allocation of ultimate decisions and final responsibilities Mannheim initially turned to such shadowy corporate entities as 'intervening authorities', 'democratic planners', 'central authorities', and the 'new leadership'. In this ghostly world he did not shrink from formulations addressed to imaginary beings: 'A planned society should make up its mind about ultimate issues'.[24] In the end he moved into the direction of Auguste Comte's right-wing utopia and suggested the establishment of an 'Order' capable of providing planned democracies with top-level decisions and mediations. The members of this 'supreme tribunal' should be selected from the most prominent and esteemed representatives of the different social groups. 'As in a religious order, admission should require such rigorous commitments from members that the highest devotion and disinterestedness would be secured.'[25]

Political sociology and the problem of power

In *Freedom, Power, and Democratic Planning*, Mannheim essentially retains the paradigm for social planning as developed in the third phase of his intellectual development. But in this posthumous volume there emerge the outlines of a critical sociology of power conceived as the necessary presupposition for a realistic political sociology. Political sociology and especially the sociology of power, then, represent the central concerns of Mannheim's fourth phase which began in 1945 with the conclusion of the Second World War and ended abruptly in 1947 as a consequence of his untimely death.

Freedom, Power, and Democratic Planning derives its significance mainly from the fact that it is a theoretical reflection of the international political situation taking shape after the Second World War. Mannheim views the phenomenon of power and the 'power complex' as the most serious threats to the stability of the post-war world. The unfolding of industrial capitalism was accompanied by the growth of a neurotic power complex: the malfunctions and crises of late monopoly capitalism have escalated this power complex into a form of collective possession which destroys the international political equilibrium as well as the mental and psychic security of individuals.[26]

Mannheim's analysis of the power complex proceeds on two levels. First, he attacks the undue concentration of power in the hands of small élites which have arrogated to themselves remarkable degrees of immunity from public opinion and the popular will. In the Western world the dangerous concentration of power results from the interplay of interests pursued by monopoly capitalists and business-oriented politicians and military leaders. In the East the élitist manipulation of power is occasioned by the dictatorial development of Communist governmental processes. Second, Mannheim criticizes the ominous division of the post-war world into two primary power centers, which creates the potential for the Third World War.[27] For the post-war world Mannheim predicts in 1946 that the major powers will strive for economic, political, and cultural hegemony among clusters of weaker nations: their competition is likely to establish a novel pattern of regional consciousness and solidarity: 'The main world regions will probably be polarized between an Anglo-Saxon orbit and a Russian orbit.'[28]

These observations motivated Mannheim to indicate the need for a 'democratic theory of power'.[29] The survival of democratic social systems depends ultimately on the democratic control of power in all its forms which range from military, political, and economic to intellectual and opinion-making power. As a first step Mannheim recommends the establishment of democratic control positions to prevent power abuses. This development necessitates, furthermore, the integration of master positions into a 'unified world authority' which will have to co-ordinate secondary power centers. The planners of this process will have to be especially alert during the final stage of top level integration to prevent any abuse of power at the level of global supervision.[30]

Mannheim realized that the development of coherent international policies presupposed corresponding adjustments of national political processes. The roles of national governments as well had to be transformed to such an extent that they could combine their original function of social integration with the new task of planning for freedom.[31]

The new international order envisioned by Mannheim is based on the co-operation of nation states dedicated to the principle of 'preventive planning'. Peaceful international co-operation can only be successful as long as the participating governments maintain peace at home by means of democratic policies supporting the functions of the modern 'social service state'.

The practice of preventive planning involves the social service state in all areas of social life. In a social service state means of communication such as radio networks are publicly owned and managed so that the population may be informed of the needs of a changing society. State-supported education performs the more basic function of creating general awareness of the need for preventive planning and international co-operation. Transportation, electricity, gas and other public utilities are managed by public authorities. The social service state ensures a decent standard of living for the unemployed, the immature, and the old. Governments which practice preventive planning ease the burden of illness by providing adequate health insurance and public-health services; they also use administrative, financial, and legal devices for the prevention of epidemics and the advancement of medical research and training.

The policy of preventive planning has power implications of its own. According to Mannheim such a policy can only be made effective by a strong central power capable of co-ordinating the multitude of essential planning measures. Ultimate decision-making power must be in the hands of a 'co-ordinating planning body' whose members will not only resolve conflicts of opinion among experts, but also judge the compatibility of specific measures with the basic policy of democratic planning. The effective operation of this planning body presupposes the centralization of political authority.

As soon as authority is granted to a central government freedom must be safeguarded by means of democratic controls operating through established parliamentary channels and new supplementary devices: 'The threat to freedom does not come from a government which is "ours", which we have elected and which we can remove, but from oligarchies without public responsibility. Public accountability of administration and rotation in office are key provisions of democratic government to be guarded jealously.'[32]

The balance of power

Mannheim does not fail to indicate the need for countervailing power to offset the influence of centralized organizations. In his model the co-ordinating planning body has the additional responsibility of limiting centralization to the essential issues of basic policy formulation. Wherever justified the central authorities should allocate decision-making power to local authorities in order to strengthen the countervailing power of local self-government. The movement toward local self-government would not only encourage self-help and individual initiative, but would also encourage the people to develop a sense of identification with their government and its plan. The dialogue between central and local authorities would furthermore bridge the gap between the abstractions of large-scale planning and the workaday realities experienced by individual citizens. In Mannheim's model of a planned society the two-way flow of communication between central authorities and the people has the ultimate purpose of eliminating the separation of government from the community which has plagued industrial society for so long.

The balance between central state interference and local self-determination must be maintained in the economic sphere which has the most significant effect on the lives of contemporary people. The planning measures of the government have the overall purpose of protecting the 'public interest' against industrial and commercial power combinations which usually establish arbitrary policies of undue restriction of output, market outlets, resources, and which generally work against the welfare of the people in their parochial pursuit of artificially rising prices and profit maximization. The role of the central authorities is not limited to the control of arbitrary monopolies: the lawful interference of the government is needed in other areas of broad-range significance such as maintenance of full resource utilization, production, and employment. The goal of economic stabilization demands additional efforts from the central planners: they must adjust the interest rate, control investment, extend public enterprise, halt the waste of resources, redistribute wealth and income through taxation, strengthen mass consumption, expand social services, eliminate the traditional business cycle, prevent mass unemployment, stabilize income, and alleviate mass poverty.

The countervailing power of local self-determination is represented by the practice of 'industrial democracy' as far as the workers are concerned. By participating in the day-by-day management of their plant the workers may protect themselves against the dangers of overcentralization. Mannheim's model of democratic planning, however, has no room for radical economic transformation: with few exceptions all industries are to remain in private hands. The sense of private ownership must remain intact to protect the business community from excessive forms of centralization. Mannheim's 'mixed system' of economic activity intends to keep alive 'pioneer adventure' and initiative which thrive on the combination of private ownership with the managerial role. 'Private property may well have a lasting educational significance for industrial leadership, and a planned society should deliberately foster small-scale enterprise as a training ground for such leadership, as well as another protection against overbureaucratization.'[33]

In a planned democracy controlling measures are not limited to the economy, but must be applied to all institutions which show tendencies toward undue forms of power concentration.

The armed forces represent the most dangerous source of concentrated power. The development of sophisticated weapons systems has elevated small units of military specialists to positions of ultimate power. The technological developments leading to nuclear warfare and long-range missiles have brought with them increased chances for the usurpation of power by a military oligarchy. Democratic planners must therefore devise means which guarantee that military power is transferred to a people's army organized preferably along the lines of a 'national militia' consisting of 'civilian soldiers' which represent the interests of the common people.[34]

In a similar way democratic controls of the civil service must be developed to prevent administrative corruption and undue concentrations of bureaucratic power. The planners must make sure that social scientifically trained recruits from different social levels are amalgamated in a public service capable of adjusting to the changing needs and interests of society. They must also direct administrative agencies to give regular, full reports addressed not merely to policy makers but to all the people.[35]

Planning for freedom demands attention to the role of the mass media which possess enormous power with regard to the flow of information and the shaping of public opinion. Society will remain unbalanced as long as small, privileged groups are allowed to misuse the powerful apparatus of the mass media for the 'dissemination of their ideas while the less privileged are deprived of similar means of expression'.[36] The liberation of the mass media from their dependence on powerful, monopolistic interests may be initiated by the planned transfer of control to a body of elected public trustees representing all major social groups with their different views. Power considerations demand that these public trustees remain under parliamentary control.

The planned democracy must facilitate discussions of varying views and opinions. But adherence to the principle of free expression should neither hinder the planners from developing a core of democratic educational policy, nor prevent them from the deliberate use of propaganda on behalf of the morality of the democratic process. The planners should furthermore focus attention on the factory as the primary cell for the formation of democratic opinion. Other important nuclei in forming opinion are represented by such existing democratic organizations as trade unions, chambers of commerce, and county councils. Community and town planning strategies should be used to restore other important cells for the formation of opinion including the workshop, neighborhood groups, and the family.[37]

All efforts to control the growing power centers of modern society must at all times remain subject to the overriding principle of minimal interference with the people's freedom. All forms of regulation should protect as much as possible spontaneous organizational and institutional processes. All controls must reflect popular consensus and democratic methods of realization: their alteration must be publicly supervised. For the future Mannheim envisions the merging of agencies for public regulation into an integrated 'Vigilance Committee' which will have the task of watching 'over the expansion of power centers as well as the preventive measures themselves lest they become as autocratic as the institution they seek to check'.[38]

9 Retrospect and prospect

Seminal thinkers tend to leave behind unanswered questions and unsolved problems. The completion of a theoretical edifice is a particularly difficult enterprise when the original contribution is so complex, virtuosic, and encyclopedic that it prevents the formation of a school of fairly like-minded followers.

In Mannheim's case it was not only the unique character of his work which hindered the emergence of an influential group of partisans: the migrations which historical circumstances forced upon him shortened his span of effectiveness in the three intellectual scenarios which his participation enriched.

Steadily increasing specialization has fragmented the social sciences to such an extent that only a strong movement toward their reintegration can restore their meaning, vitality, and social relevance. Apart from the significance of Mannheim's segmental contributions it is precisely at this juncture that his work assumes overarching importance: in an age fascinated by the minutiae of specialized research and the striving for boundary maintenance he kept alive the spirit of co-operation between the various humanistic and social sciences.

Unity in diversity

Throughout his career Mannheim remained attuned to the realities of a world experiencing rapid transformations: consequently his thinking underwent the significant changes which have been conceptualized as four phases of his intellectual development involving relationist socio-cultural theory, instrumental planning theory, the reinterpretation of the functions of institutions and values, and the redefinition of military-political reality.

At each stage of development, however, Mannheim's work was inspired by an existential concern for the cultural and social crises of twentieth-century societies. This abiding concern not only permitted him to utilize numerous kindred intellectual resources, including Hegelian philosophy, *Lebensphilosophie*, and Weberian sociology, but also connected him with major types of contemporary analysis such as Marxism, phenomenology, depth psychology, and existentialism.

As a macro-level sociologist Mannheim never lost the ability to grasp social phenomena as totalities deriving their dynamic unity from the changing complementarity of conflicting social relationships. His capacity to understand interrelated social phenomena as wholes remained constant because of his unwavering commitment to structural analysis. At each stage of development his vision was empowered by the concept of structure which revealed the meaning of phenomena as wholes.[1]

The existential concern for socio-cultural crises and the interest in structural analysis represent prominent links connecting the different stages of Mannheim's sociological work. Pragmatism is an additional point of reference which has the similar function of establishing unity in diversity. His sociology of knowledge evolved along pragmatic lines which converged in *Ideology and Utopia*, where the relationship of thinking to action was investigated with radical thoroughness. In Germany Mannheim's pragmatic orientation was akin to Marx and Nietzsche; in England he developed an approach which incorporated elements of William James's and John Dewey's pragmatism.[2] His sociology of planning continued the pragmatic search for the linkage of thought with action: in essence it was the purpose of this sociology to join desirable ends with available means. Social planning was a pragmatic enterprise which depended for its success on the linkage of the thinking of technical experts with the action of political deciders.

Mannheim's lifelong interest in education and the role of intellectuals formed an integral part of his pragmatic orientation: it was, after all, the creative and educative mission of the intelligentsia to work toward the linkage of thinking to action and the co-operation between planning experts and politicians. Education furthermore was an instrument designed to cut through the walls of apathy so that the needed support of the people would become available to intellectual and social innovators.

The problem of social change

Mannheim's sociology of knowledge concluded with the pragmatic assertion that ideas were true as long as they met two essential criteria: congruence with the actual social situation of men and capacity to pilot the accommodation of human action to the changing context of group life. In his sociology of knowledge Mannheim, then, announced the need for the discovery of an historical process capable of carrying the potentially holistic view of the intellectuals beyond the restrictive fields of ideology and utopia into the area of reality-adequate knowledge.

The social realities of Weimar Germany prevented the achievement of a synthesis of particular, but mutually complementary perspectives into an objective scientific entity. But in England Mannheim regained the confidence that intellectual efforts could re-establish an holistic view through the rational mastery of human irrationality and the planned guidance of social change in keeping with a scientific understanding of the patterned complexities of social processes. In this respect the sociology of planning continued the search for order and progress, sanity and innovation which had lured Mannheim into the intricate network of the sociology of knowledge.

In Germany Mannheim had found it difficult to verify empirically the existence of a body of synthesizing intellectuals: in England he did not resolve the problematic relationship between intellectual planners and established groups whose interests were endangered by the planners' search for a new social order. Mannheim claimed for his 'redistributive society' the right to control the aspirations of individuals and groups which obstructed the democratically evolved plan.[3] But instead of exploring the complexities of changing power relations he merely asserted that strong democratizing trends were at work in Great Britain and in the United States. He claimed, furthermore, that these alleged trends were bringing new, innovative leaders to the forefront. His model of a 'mixed economy' also suffered from the evasion of the power question: the model revealed neither the balance between private and public enterprise, nor the precise means effecting the change from the private to the public sector.

Under the influence of assorted Christian humanists, including T. S. Eliot, he temporarily abandoned the power problem in favor of less controversial *principia media* of social change: education and religion. In the democratization of educational opportunity Mannheim discovered a vehicle of peaceful change. For similar reasons he recommended alterations in the content and practice of education: the teachers of the nation were expected to foster social rationality and insight as well as the diffusion of the planning mentality throughout society. A lengthy process of education emerged as the major strategy in the battle against the opponents of constructive social change. In religion Mannheim saw unifying forces which were capable of infusing the new society with an abiding sense of purpose and solidarity.

Ideas and delusions

Change-conscious intellectuals have favored education as a means of social reconstruction at least since the time of Helvétius who popularized the notion that: 'L'éducation peut tout.'[4] The French philosopher's faith in the omnipotence of education rested on the companion assumption that he was witness to a radical and revolutionary transformation of the existing social order. Mannheim's theory made no allowances for revolutionary social change; consequently his discussion of education floated above the decisive realm of socio-economic and political power. His educational theory failed to explore the traditional upper-class domination of schools and universities and hardly explained why the representatives of the old order should hand the reins of education to men committed to the ideal of fundamental democratization.

Mannheim's extravagant hopes with regard to the democratization of education were based on his faith in the omnipotence of ideas and the power of their producers. He was convinced that ideas were finally creating communal solidarity and that intellectuals had moved into a key position in the power process which rivaled the vantage points occupied by business leaders and military chiefs.[5]

Religious ideas came to play an especially significant role in Mannheim's social theory since he credited them with outstanding power in the creation and maintenance of communal solidarity. The integration of human personality and society was greatly aided by dramatic archetypes working through religious tradition. Mannheim devoted attention to the discussion of religious archetypes such as the Saint, the Virgo, and the Good Shepherd, but failed to explore the role of Socialist archetypes which had sustained European workers on the bitter road leading from the realities of the class struggle to the emerging world of the social service state.[6] In Germany the toil and misery of the working class had attracted the attention of several leading artists: the most compassionate portrayals of the proletarian experience were created by Käthe Kollwitz, the wife of a physician who chose to practice in the slums of Berlin. Her graphic work was dominated by the figures of a mother, a child, and death which she first displayed in 1898 in a set of prints inspired by Gerhart Hauptmann's naturalistic drama *The Weavers*. In Weimar Germany her proletarian posters became familiar sights. The monumental simplicity of her style gave birth to the archetypes of proletarian existence: the starving child, the welfare mother, the unemployed worker, the war cripple, the political prisoner.

While Mannheim was eloquent with regard to religious archetypes and spiritual solidarity he said little about proletarian archetypes and working-class solidarity. This reticence obscured the very process of social change which his later sociology tried to describe: in his portrayal the social service state appeared rather mysteriously as the product of British democracy and Christian goodwill, rather than as the fruit of long and determined struggles on the part of organized labor. Mannheim's works on planning and social reconstruction provided extensive comments on the significance of religious forces, but shed no light on the role of the Labour party and the activities of other working-class organizations in the process of social transformation. As a political sociologist he did not transcend the conventional liberal interpretation of the 'Russian experiment' and managed to ignore the significant contributions of European Social Democracy to the liberation of the workers.[7]

Failing to explore the kinship between the initial thrust of his ideas and the intentions of Socialist labor Mannheim became marooned on an empty stage awaiting ghostly visitors from a largely imaginary past and hallucinatory present. In this scenario the makers of the American constitution emerged as the 'fathers' of planning for freedom.[8] With regard to the present he placed great hopes in the mechanisms of British and American democracy; especially the American two-party system appeared to him as ready-made tool for the implementation of 'preventive' planning.[9] The ruling groups of contemporary capitalist societies were credited with nothing less than the willingness to balance the social order through voluntary co-operation and far-sighted compromise with the working masses.[10]

In his search for allies among the ruling groups Mannheim repudiated radical economic changes and divorced himself from political movements seeking to nationalize large-scale industries.[11] On the other side, he made it clear that he did not view powerful conservative groups as enemies, but rather as components of the democratic process.[12]

The renewed search for alternatives

After the Second World War most Western sociologists moved into an intellectual territory that shared no boundaries with the social scientific domain of Karl Mannheim. The dominant concerns of sociologists included speculations about a social structure that was taken for granted, but excluded critical diagnostic efforts. The interest in quantitative methods burgeoned while qualitative studies fell into disrepute. The vogue of statistical descriptions of the given order discouraged the search for alternatives. A spreading fear of value judgments and their political consequences paralyzed the further development of sociological approaches in need of normative foundations. The observation and measurement of the behavior of individuals and small groups became popular while macro-level social analysis faded into the background.

In this climate of opinion Mannheim's sociology of knowledge received the sparse attention customarily reserved for exotic phenomena. His futuristic sociology of planning was incomprehensible to a sociological profession which had become rooted in the established order of the present. Planning studies passed into the hands of economists and specialized professionals who had no interest in the pursuit of society-wide objectives since they were content with the discovery of narrow decision-making mechanisms and small, short-term adjustments within an unquestioned structural context.

In the late 1950s C. Wright Mills broke the first windows in the ivory tower of establishment sociology.[13] A few years later the entire structure was threatened by the flames of the student revolt. These events and the general loss of confidence in the viability of the established social order motivated younger cadres of sociologists to return to areas of inquiry where social diagnosis and criticism, society-wide analysis and normative recommendation, futuristic exploration and the discovery of alternatives ranked high on the list of priorities.[14]

The 1960s and 1970s brought rapid and violent changes which nearly tore apart the liberal-capitalist structure of Western society. They also stimulated the search for new ways of sociological research and analysis. The New Sociology emerged to satisfy the need for problem-conscious, relevant, society-wide probing and future-oriented social criticism.

The new generation of social scientists has demonstrated that the independent and courageous use of the tools of social analysis not only permits significant insights into many social developments, but that it also provides the larger, coherent outlook which lets us live both in and above the immediacy of social existence. The growing commitment of the new generation of social scientists to free and fearless social analysis numbers among the lasting contributions which the 'campus revolt' has made to Western culture. The forays of change-conscious intellectuals into the labyrinths of power and privilege are of special importance to the growing number of people who are enraged by the deterioration in the quality of life – people who no longer ask 'what do we have?' but demand to know 'where are we going?'

As a consequence of these developments and because of the intellectual orientation of the New Sociologists the sociology of knowledge was again propelled into a position of centrality. The rediscovery of Mannheim's sociology of planning, however, was hindered by the distrust of technology and bureaucracy which formed part of the new intellectual attitude.

Contempt for the conventional scientific world view dates back to

Nietzsche and Heidegger who debunked formal logic and science as expressions of narrow philistine ostentatiousness and rigidity: this attitude inspired a counter philosophy celebrating the freedom of unattached thinkers and poets and their ability to cleanse the world from the commonplaceness and indifference with which a merely logical intelligence had soiled it. The attack on scientific-industrial, politico-military, and legal-bureaucratic constructions of reality was renewed by a phalanx of alienated intellectuals including Norman O. Brown and Herbert Marcuse, Paul Goodman and Timothy Leary, Allen Ginsberg and Alan Watts. The intellectual-artistic expressions of discontent with late twentieth-century life stirred the imagination of young people who were profoundly alienated from the generation of their parents. The combination of radical intelligence and youthful vitality gradually created a counter culture which threatened the foundations of technocracy.

In the wake of these developments the search for a central, omniscient intelligence and stabilizing rationality became as disreputable as the striving for bureaucratic guidance and hierarchical relationships. New person-centered life styles appeared in order to accommodate the quest for the discovery of selfhood and existential meaning. A growing faith in the values of spontaneous understanding and autonomous decisions undermined the credibility of large scale plans, administrative procedures, and superimposed interpretations of reality.[15] In their search for credibility, trust, mutual learning, and communal experience the cohorts of the counter culture had no use for the authoritative professionalism of a scientific-technological priesthood serving the interests of ruling political, military, and economic élites. In this light all specialists, experts, and master minds became equally suspect as bad magicians vying for the attention of the mandarins of exploitative privilege.

Repression, co-optation, and commercialization on the one side, despair, dissension, and confusion of purpose on the other have emasculated the counter culture to the extent of changing the rules of critical dialogue. The readmission of alternative proposals for meaningful socio-cultural change promises to facilitate the rediscovery of macro-level approaches such as Mannheim's non-partisan sociology of planning.

In 1973, John Friedmann, the Director of Urban Planning at the University of California at Los Angeles, presented a theory of transactive planning which combines an understanding of Mannheimian contributions with the awareness that a new style of planning must be in harmony with the changes in consciousness wrought by the counter culture.[16]

Several key elements of Friedmann's 'transactive style of planning' are in tune with revisions of the social order demanded by partisans of the counter culture. To begin with, transactive planning has the purpose of transcending the closed circle of experts and penetrating the formal roles which customarily conceal the living human beings existing behind them. Furthermore, the hierarchical relation between experts and the recipients of expertise is to be replaced by a problem-conscious dialogue between equal partners: at decisive points for social intervention interpersonal communication will fuse the processed knowledge of planning specialists with the personal knowledge their clients derive from everyday experience. The equalitarian connection of processed knowledge with personal knowledge leads to a process of 'mutual learning' which, in turn, infuses systems of societal guidance with the capacity for experimentation and self-correction. Finally, the specter of a central directorate is exorcised by the novel idea of a 'cellular structure'. The new approach requires networks of communication linking task-oriented, open working groups which will co-operate with other cells whenever the occasion warrants such interaction. The structural principle of 'cellular' organization promises to tap the psychic energies of participatory democracy, which are central to the counter culture, without losing the motor force of science and technology which is of signal importance for social development.

Friedmann acknowledges that contemporary theories of societal guidance and planning have their roots in Karl Mannheim's pioneering explorations into these processes.[17] Moreover, Mannheimian themes and concepts inform the general structure of his argument. Basically Friedmann conceives of planning as a process which links systematic knowledge with organized action.[18] His approach, as well, is inspired by the conviction that serious crises of social organization, knowing, and valuation impose new obligations upon intellectuals and all responsible members of society. There is a pressing need for relevant, normative knowledge which alone can illuminate the matrix of ongoing social processes and human actions. Ultimately Friedmann envisions a 'learning society' which will be guided in its development by the structural principle of cellular organization. But, like Mannheim, he assumes that this futuristic reconstruction of society presupposes a thorough re-education of man.[19]

The waning of the twentieth century is marked by political circumstances which are as fluctuating as the forces that overshadowed its cataclysmic beginnings. But this conflictual historical period has also generated various attacks on existential meaninglessness and socio-cultural paralysis – may the rediscovery of Karl Mannheim as a member of this humanist assault force augur the more complete success of future ventures.

10 Bibliographical guide to the sociology of knowledge, ideological analysis, and social planning

The bibliographical guide, which forms an integral part of this volume because of its organization and substance, consists of eleven major sections and the six subdivisions of the last section on social planning:

- I Books and monographs by Karl Mannheim
- II Mannheim's posthumously published works
- III Articles, chapters, papers, and reviews by Karl Mannheim
- IV Books on Karl Mannheim's sociology
- V Articles, chapters, papers, and reviews on Karl Mannheim's sociology
- VI Books on the sociology of knowledge
- VII Books with relevance for the sociology of knowledge
- VIII Articles, chapters, papers, and reviews concerning the sociology of knowledge
- IX Selected publications on ideology and utopia
- X Selected publications on élites and intellectuals
- XI Selected publications on social planning
  - 1 Background and general aspects
  - 2 Housing and urban renewal planning
  - 3 Land use planning and new communities
  - 4 Participatory, social, and social welfare planning
  - 5 Planning for community facilities: health, education, recreation
  - 6 Transportation planning

The initial five sections of the bibliography are directly related to Mannheim's sociology; their chronological and substantive organization aims at rapid and thorough orientation.

Sections six, seven, and eight include a wide range of material on the sociology of knowledge in general, beginning with the earliest publications in this area of sociological specialization. Again, for the purpose of rapid orientation, books in 'hard core' sociology of knowledge (section six) are distinguished from the more voluminous area of kindred works (section seven).

Sections nine and ten provide bibliographical information on topics such as ideological analysis and the social role of élites and intellectuals which occupy a prominent position, both in Mannheim's sociology and the work of other sociologists of knowledge.

The final section presents selected publications from the vast and expanding field of social planning to which Mannheim contributed significantly during his later career; section eleven includes material pertinent to the state of social planning during Mannheim's time, as well as writings typifying contemporary approaches to planning.

Books and monographs by Karl Mannheim

1 *Lélek és Kultura* (programmatic lecture delivered at the University of Budapest, 1917), Budapest: Gyula Benkö, 1918. Trans. by Ernest Manheim and reprinted as 'Seele und Kultur' in *Wissenssoziologie*, pp. 66–84 (see 26).

2 *Die Strukturanalyse der Erkenntnistheorie* (*Kant-Studien*, Ergänzungsheft no. 57), Berlin: Reuther & Reichard, 1922. Reprinted in *Wissenssoziologie*, pp. 166–245 (see 26). Trans. by Edith Schwarzschild and Paul Kecskemeti and reprinted as 'Structural analysis of epistemology' in *Essays on Sociology and Social Psychology*, pp. 15–73 (see 20).

3 *Ideologie und Utopie*, Bonn: Friedrich Cohen, 1929. Enlarged and trans. as *Ideology and Utopia* (see 7).

4 *Die Gegenwartsaufgaben der Soziologie: Ihre Lehrgestalt*, Tübingen: J. C. B. Mohr (Paul Siebeck), 1932.

5 *Rational and Irrational Elements in Contemporary Society* (Hobhouse Memorial Lecture, delivered on March 7, 1934 at Bedford College, University of London), London: Oxford University Press, 1934. Enlarged version reprinted in *Man and Society in an Age of Reconstruction*, pp. 38–75 (see 10).

6 *Mensch und Gesellschaft im Zeitalter des Umbaus*, Leiden: A. W. Sijthoff's Uitgeversmaatschappij N. V., 1935. Revised, enlarged and trans. as *Man and Society in an Age of Reconstruction* (see 10).

7 *Ideology and Utopia: An Introduction to the Sociology of Knowledge* (trans. by Louis Wirth and Edward Shils, Preface by Louis Wirth), London: Routledge & Kegan Paul; New York: Harcourt, Brace & World; 1936 (see 3). Paperback edition as a Harvest Book.

8 *Idéologie et utopie* (trans. by Pauline Rollet, Preface by Louis Wirth), Paris: Marcel Rivière, 1936. French edition of *Ideology and Utopia* (see 7).

9 *El hombre y la sociedad en la época de crisis* (trans. by F. Ayala), Madrid: Librería de Porrúa Hermanos y Compañía, 1936. Spanish edition of *Mensch und Gesellschaft* (see 6).

10 *Man and Society in an Age of Reconstruction: Studies in Modern Social Structure* (trans. by Edward Shils), London: Routledge & Kegan Paul; New York: Harcourt, Brace & World, 1940 (see 6). Paperback edition as a Harvest Book.

11 *Ideología y utopia: introducción a la sociología del conocimiento*

(versión española de Salvador Echavarria), Mexico City: Fondo de Cultura Económica, 1941. Spanish translation of *Ideology and Utopia* (see 7).

12 *Libertad y planificación social* (versión española de Rubén Landa), Mexico City: Fondo de Cultura Económica, 1942. Spanish translation of *Man and Society* (see 10).

13 *Diagnosis of Our Time: Wartime Essays of a Sociologist*, London: Kegan Paul Trench, Trubner, 1943; New York: Oxford University Press, 1944.

14 *Diagnóstico de nuestro tiempo* (versión española de José Medina Echavarría), Mexico City: Fondo de Cultura Económica, 1944. Spanish translation of *Diagnosis of Our Time* (see 13).

Mannheim's posthumously published works

15 *Freedom, Power, and Democratic Planning* (ed. by Ernest K. Bramsted and Hans Gerth, Foreword by Adolph Lowe), New York: Oxford University Press, 1950; London: Routledge & Kegan Paul, 1951.

16 *Freiheit und geplante Demokratie* (trans. by Peter Müller and Anna Müller-Krefting), Cologne-Opladen: Westdeutscher Verlag, 1970. German edition of *Freedom, Power, and Democratic Planning* (see 15).

17 *Diagnose unserer Zeit* (trans. by Fritz Blum), Zürich: Europa-Verlag, 1951. German edition of *Diagnosis of Our Time* (see 13).

18 *Ideologie und Utopie* (trans. by Heinz Maus), 3rd enlarged edition, Frankfurt: Schulte-Bulmke, 1952. German edition of *Ideology and Utopia* (see 7).

19 *Essays on the Sociology of Knowledge* (ed. and trans. by Paul Kecskemeti, editorial Note by Adolph Lowe, Introduction by Paul Kecskemeti), London: Routledge & Kegan Paul; New York: Oxford University Press, 1952.

20 *Essays on Sociology and Social Psychology* (ed. by Paul Kecskemeti, editorial Note by Adolph Lowe, Introduction by Paul Kecskemeti), London: Routledge & Kegan Paul; New York: Oxford University Press, 1953.

21 *Essays on the Sociology of Culture* (ed. by Ernest Manheim in co-operation with Paul Kecskemeti, editorial Note by Adolph Lowe, Introduction by Ernest Manheim), London: Routledge & Kegan Paul; New York: Oxford University Press, 1956.

22 *Systematic Sociology: An Introduction to the Study of Society* (ed. by J. S. Erös and W. A. C. Stewart), London: Routledge & Kegan Paul; New York: Oxford University Press, 1957. Paperback edition as an Evergreen Book.

23 *Mensch und Gesellschaft im Zeitalter des Umbaus* (trans. from the English edition by Ruprecht Paqué), Darmstadt: Wissenschaftliche Buchgesellschaft, 1958. German edition of *Man and Society* (see 10).

24 *Sociologia sistematica* (trans. by Franco Leonardi), Milan: Edizione

communità, 1960. Italian translation of *Systematic Sociology* (see 22).

25 *An Introduction to the Sociology of Education*, by Karl Mannheim and W. A. C. Stewart, London: Routledge & Kegan Paul; New York: Humanities Press, 1962. Issued as a Humanities Paperback.

26 *Wissenssoziologie: Auswahl aus dem Werk* (ed. and with an Introduction by Kurt H. Wolff), Berlin and Neuwied: Hermann Luchterhand Verlag, 1964.

27 *From Karl Mannheim* (ed. with an Introduction by Kurt H. Wolff), New York: Oxford University Press, 1971. Page references are to the Oxford University Press paperback edition.

Articles, chapters, papers, and reviews by Karl Mannheim

28 Review of 'Georg Lukács, *Die Theorie des Romans: Ein geschichtsphilosophischer Versuch über die Formen der grossen Epik*', *Logos*, vol. IX, no. 2 (1920–1), pp. 298–302. Reprinted in *Wissenssoziologie*, pp. 85–90 (see 26). Trans. by Kurt H. Wolff and reprinted as 'A review of Georg Lukács' theory of the novel', in *From Karl Mannheim*, pp. 3–7 (see 27).

29 'Beiträge zur Theorie der Weltanschauungs – Interpretation', *Jahrbuch für Kunstgeschichte*, vol. I (XV), no. 4 (1921–2), pp. 236–74. Reprinted in *Wissenssoziologie*, pp. 91–154 (see 26). Reprinted as 'On the interpretation of Weltanschauung', in *Essays on the Sociology of Knowledge*, pp. 33–83 (see 19; also reprinted in 27).

30 'Zum Problem einer Klassifikation der Wissenschaften', *Archiv für Sozialwissenschaft und Sozialpolitik*, vol. 50, no. 1 (1922), pp. 230–7. Reprinted in *Wissenssoziologie*, pp. 155–65 (see 26).

31 'Historismus', *Archiv für Sozialwissenschaft und Sozialpolitik*, vol. 52, no. 1 (June, 1924), pp. 1–60. Reprinted in *Wissenssoziologie*, pp. 246–307 (see 26). Reprinted as 'Historicism', in *Essays on the Sociology of Knowledge*, pp. 84–133 (see 19).

32 'Das Problem einer Soziologie des Wissens', *Archiv für Sozialwissenschaft und Sozialpolitik*, vol. 53, no. 3 (April, 1925), pp. 577–652. Reprinted in *Wissenssoziologie*, pp. 308–87 (see 26). Reprinted as 'The problem of a sociology of knowledge', in *Essays on the Sociology of Knowledge*, pp. 134–90 (see 19; also reprinted in 27).

33 'Ideologische und soziologische Interpretation der geistigen Gebilde', *Jahrbuch für Soziologie*, vol. II (ed. by Gottfried Salomon), Karlsruhe: G. Braun, 1926, pp. 424–40. Reprinted in *Wissenssoziologie*, pp. 388–407 (see 26). Trans. by Kurt H. Wolff and reprinted as 'The ideological and the sociological interpretation of intellectual phenomena', in *From Karl Mannheim*, pp. 116–131 (see 27).

34 'Das konservative Denken: Soziologische Beiträge zum Werden des politisch-historischen Denkens in Deutschland', *Archiv für Sozialwissenschaft und Sozialpolitik*, vol. 57, nos 1–2 (1927), pp. 68–142,

470–95. Reprinted in *Wissenssoziologie*, pp. 408–508 (see 26). Trans. by Karl Mannheim and Paul Kecskemeti and reprinted as 'Conservative thought', in *Essays on Sociology and Social Psychology*, pp. 74–164 (see 20; also reprinted in 27).

35 'Das Problem der Generationen', *Kölner Vierteljahrshefte für Soziologie*, vol. VII, nos 2–3 (1928–9), pp. 157–85, 309–30. Reprinted in *Wissenssoziologie*, pp. 509–65 (see 26). Reprinted as 'The problem of generations', in *Essays on the Sociology of Knowledge*, pp. 276–322 (see 19).

36 'Die Bedeutung der Konkurrenz im Gebiete des Geistigen', *Verhandlungen des sechsten deutschen Soziologentages vom 17. bis 19. September 1928 in Zürich*, Tübingen: J. C. B. Mohr (Paul Siebeck), 1929, pp. 35–83. Reprinted in *Wissenssoziologie*, pp. 566–613 (see 26). Reprinted as 'Competition as a cultural phenomenon', in *Essays on the Sociology of Knowledge*, pp. 191–229 (see 19; also reprinted in 27).

37 'Zur Problematik der Soziologie in Deutschland', *Neue Schweizer Rundschau*, vol. 22, nos 36–7 (November, 1929), pp. 820–9. Reprinted in *Wissenssoziologie*, pp. 614–24 (see 26). Trans. by Kurt H. Wolff and reprinted as 'Problems of sociology in Germany', in *From Karl Mannheim*, pp. 262–70 (see 27).

38 'Über das Wesen und die Bedeutung des wirtschaftlichen Erfolgsstrebens: Ein Beitrag zur Wirtschaftssoziologie', *Archiv für Sozialwissenschaft und Sozialpolitik*, vol. 63, no. 3 (1930), pp. 449–512. Reprinted in *Wissenssoziologie*, pp. 625–87 (see 26). Reprinted as 'On the nature of economic ambition and its significance for the social education of man', in *Essays on the Sociology of Knowledge*, pp. 230–75 (see 19).

39 'Wissenssoziologie', in *Handwörterbuch der Soziologie* (ed. by Alfred Vierkant), Stuttgart: Ferdinand Enke, 1931, pp. 659–80. Reprinted as 'The sociology of knowledge', in *Ideology and Utopia*, pp. 237–80 (see 7).

40 Review of 'Stuart A. Rice (editor), *Methods in Social Science*, Chicago: University of Chicago Press, 1931', *American Journal of Sociology*, vol. 38, no. 2 (September, 1932), pp. 273–82. Reprinted as 'American sociology', in *Essays on Sociology and Social Psychology*, pp. 185–94 (see 20).

41 'German sociology (1918–1933)', *Politica*, vol. I (February, 1934), pp. 12–33. Reprinted in *Essays on Sociology and Social Psychology*, pp. 209–28 (see 20).

42 'The crisis of culture in the era of mass-democracies and autarchies', *Sociological Review*, vol. XXVI, no. 2 (April, 1934), pp. 105–29. Enlarged and reprinted as 'Social causes of the contemporary crisis in culture', in *Man and Society in an Age of Reconstruction*, pp. 78–114 (see 10).

43 'Troeltsch, Ernst', *Encyclopaedia of the Social Sciences* (ed. by Edwin R. A. Seligman and Alvin Johnson), vol. XV, New York: Macmillan, 1935, p. 106.

44 'Utopia', *Encyclopaedia of the Social Sciences* (ed. by Edwin R. A.

Seligman and Alvin Johnson), vol. XV, New York: Macmillan, 1935, pp. 200–3.

45 'The place of sociology', Paper presented at a conference held under the auspices of the Institute of Sociology and World University Service, British Committee, London, 1936. Reprinted in *Essays on Sociology and Social Psychology*, pp. 195–208 (see 20).

46 'A few concrete examples concerning the sociological nature of human valuations: with some theoretical remarks on the difference between the psychological and the sociological approach', Paper presented at a conference held under the auspices of the Institute of Sociology and World University Service, London, September, 1936. Reprinted in J. E. Dugdale (ed.), *Further Papers on the Social Sciences, Their Relations in Theory and Teaching*, London: LePlay House Press, 1937, pp. 171–91. Reprinted in *Essays on Sociology and Social Psychology*, pp. 231–42 (see 20).

47 Untitled. *Prager Presse*, March 28, 1937. Trans. by Kurt H. Wolff and reprinted as 'Mannheim's answer to a newspaper poll', in *From Karl Mannheim*, pp. cv–cvi (see 27).

48 'Les sciences sociales et la sociologie', in *Les convergences des sciences sociales et l'esprit international* (Introduction by C. Bouglé), Paris: Centre d'Études de Politique Étrangère, 1937, pp. 208–24. French version of 'The place of sociology' (see 45).

49 'Present trends in the building of society' (trans. by H. Lewis), in Cattell, R. B., Cohen, J. I., and Travers, R. M. W. (eds), *Human Affairs*, London: Macmillan, 1937, pp. 278–300. Enlarged and reprinted as 'Planning for freedom' in *Man and Society in an Age of Reconstruction*, pp. 238–366 (see 10).

50 'Zur Diagnose unserer Zeit', *Mass und Wert*, vol. I (September–October, 1937), pp. 100–21. Trans. by Kurt H. Wolff and reprinted as 'On the diagnosis of our time', in *From Karl Mannheim*, pp. 350–66 (see 27).

51 'The psychological aspect', in Manning C. A. W. (ed.), *Peaceful Change: An International Problem*, London: Macmillan, and New York: Macmillan, 1937, pp. 101–32. Revised, enlarged, and reprinted as 'Crisis, dictatorship, war', in *Man and Society in an Age of Reconstruction*, pp. 117–43 (see 10).

52 'Adult education and the social sciences', *Tutors' Bulletin of Adult Education*, 2nd series, no. 20 (February, 1938), pp. 27–34.

53 'The age of planning', Lecture delivered at Manchester College, Oxford, 1938. Reprinted in *Essays on Sociology and Social Psychology*, pp. 255–66 (see 20).

54 'The structure of personality in the light of modern psychology', Lecture delivered at Manchester College, Oxford, 1938. Reprinted in *Essays on Sociology and Social Psychology*, pp. 267–78 (see 20).

55 'The impact of social processes on the formation of personality in the light of modern sociology', Lecture delivered at Manchester College, Oxford, 1938. Reprinted in *Essays on Sociology and Social Psychology*, pp. 279–93 (see 20).

56 'Limits of the sociological approach to personality and the emergence of the new democratic idea of planning', Lecture delivered

at Manchester College, Oxford, 1938. Reprinted in *Essays on Sociology and Social Psychology*, pp. 294–310 (see 20).

57 'Mass education and group analysis', in Cohen, J. I. and Travers, R. M. W. (eds), *Educating for Democracy*, London: Macmillan, 1939, pp. 329–64. Reprinted in *Diagnosis of Our Time*, pp. 73–94 (see 13).

58 'On war-conditioned changes in our psychic economy', *Internationale Zeitschrift für Psychoanalyse und Imago*, vol. 25, no. 314 (1940). Reprinted in *Essays on Sociology and Social Psychology*, pp. 243–51 (see 20).

59 'Diagnosis of our time', Lecture delivered at a Conference of Federal Union at Oxford, January, 1941. Reprinted in *Diagnosis of Our Time*, pp. 1–11 (see 13).

60 'The problem of youth in modern society', Opening Address to the New Education Fellowship Conference at Oxford, April, 1941. Reprinted in *Diagnosis of Our Time*, pp. 31–53 (see 13).

61 'Education, sociology and the problem of social awareness', Lecture delivered at the University of Nottingham, May, 1941. Reprinted in *Diagnosis of Our Time*, pp. 54–72 (see 13; also reprinted in 27).

62 'Nazi group strategy', BBC Overseas broadcast, 1941; *Listener* (June 19, 1941). Reprinted in *Diagnosis of Our Time*, pp. 95–9 (see 13).

63 'The crisis in valuation', Lecture delivered at Cambridge under the auspices of the London School of Economics (University of London), January, 1942. Reprinted in *Diagnosis of Our Time*, pp. 12–30 (see 13).

64 'Sociology and education', Lecture delivered to a conference organized by the Institute of Sociology at Oxford, 1943. Revised and reprinted as 'Sociology for the educator and the sociology of education', in *An Introduction to the Sociology of Education*, pp. 143–55 (see 25).

65 'Democratic planning and the new science of society', in Brumwell, J. R. M. (ed.), *This Changing World*, London: George Routledge, 1944, pp. 71–82.

66 'The meaning of popularisation in a mass society', *Christian News-Letter*, Supplement to no. 227 (February 7, 1945), pp. 7–12.

67 'The function of the refugee', *New English Weekly*, vol. 27, no. 1 (April 19, 1945), pp. 5–6.

Books on Karl Mannheim's sociology

68 BARTOLOMEI, GIANGAETANO, *L'unità del sapere in Karl Mannheim* (*Sociologia del sapere ed epistemologia*), Padua: CEDAM, 1968.

69 CORRADINI, DOMENICO, *Karl Mannheim*, Milan: Giuffrè, 1967.

70 FISHER, MARGARET BARROW, *Leadership and Intelligence*, New York: Bureau of Publications, Teacher's College, Columbia University, 1954.

71 KETTLER, DAVID, *Marxismus und Kultur: Mannheim und Lukács in den ungarischen Revolutionen 1918/19*, Berlin: Luchterhand Verlag, 1967.

72 MAQUET, JACQUES J., *The Sociology of Knowledge; Its Structure and Its Relation to the Philosophy of Knowledge: A Critical Analysis of the Systems of Karl Mannheim and Pitirim A. Sorokin* (trans. by John F. Locke), Boston: Beacon Press, 1951.

73 MONTSERRAT, MIRA, *Política e irracionalidad: la tipología de las mentalidades políticas en Karl Mannheim*, Buenos Aires: Editorial Pleamar, 1970.

74 NEUSÜSS, ARNHELM, *Utopisches Bewusstsein und freischwebende Intelligenz: Zur Wissenssoziologie Karl Mannheims*, Meisenheim am Glan: A. Hain, 1968.

75 NYBERG, PAUL, 'The Educational Implications of Karl Mannheim's Sociology', unpublished thesis for Ed.D. of Harvard University, 1957.

76 REMMLING, GUNTER W., *Wissenssoziologie und Gesellschaftsplanung: Das Werk Karl Mannheims*, Dortmund: Verlag Friedrich Wilhelm Ruhfus, 1968.

77 REMPEL, F. WARREN, *The Role of Value in Karl Mannheim's Sociology of Knowledge*, The Hague: Mouton, 1965.

78 RÜSCHEMEYER, DIETRICH, 'Probleme der Wissenssoziologie: Eine Kritik der Arbeiten K. Mannheims und M. Schelers und eine Erweiterung der wissenssoziologischen Fragestellung durchgeführt am Beispiel der Kleingruppenforschung', unpublished doctoral thesis, Cologne, 1958.

79 SCHOECK, HELMUT, 'Karl Mannheim als Wissenssoziologe', unpublished doctoral thesis, Tübingen, 1948.

80 STEWART, WILLIAM A. C., *Karl Mannheim on Education and Social Thought*, London: Harrap, 1967.

81 WYLIE, JOYCE FYFE, *Karl Mannheim's Social Theory and Concept of Education*, Ann Arbor: University Microfilms, 1956.

Articles, chapters, papers, and reviews on Karl Mannheim's sociology

82 ADORNO, THEODOR W., 'Über Mannheims Wissenssoziologie', *Aufklärung*, II (1953), pp. 224–36.

83 ALBINI, JOSEPH L., 'Crisis or reconstruction: Mannheim's alternatives for the Western democracies', *Sociological Focus*, vol. 3, no. 3 (Spring, 1970), pp. 63–71.

84 ASCOLI, MAX, 'On Mannheim's ideology and utopia', *Social Research*, vol. 5, no. 1 (February, 1938), pp. 101–6.

85 BAILEY, ROBERT B., 'Rationality reconsidered', in BAILEY, ROBERT B., *Sociology Faces Pessimism*, The Hague: Martinus Nijhoff, 1958.

86 BASH, HARRY H., 'Determinism and avoidability in socio-historical analysis', *Ethics*, vol. 74, no. 3 (April, 1964), pp. 186–200.

87 BEERLING, R. F., 'Mannheim en de Ideology', *Mens en Maatschappij*, vol. 39, no. 4 (July–August, 1964), pp. 255–69.

88 BOGARDUS, EMORY S., 'Mannheim and social reconstruction', *Sociology and Social Research*, vol. 32 (September–October, 1947), pp. 548–57.

89 BOGARDUS, EMORY S., 'Mental processes and democracy', *Sociology*

and Social Research, vol. 41, no. 2 (November–December, 1956), pp. 127–32.

90 BOGARDUS, EMORY S., 'Mannheim and systematic sociology', *Sociology and Social Research*, vol. 43, no. 3 (January–February, 1959), pp. 213–17.

91 BOSKOFF, ALVIN, 'Karl Mannheim: theories of social manipulation in transitional society', in BOSKOFF, ALVIN, *Theory in American Sociology; Major Sources and Applications*, New York: Thomas Y. Crowell, 1969, pp. 159–81.

92 BRAMSTEDT, ERNEST K. and GERTH, HANS, 'A note on the work of Karl Mannheim', in *Freedom, Power, and Democratic Planning*, pp. vii–xv (see 15).

93 CECILIO DE LORA, S. M., 'Mannheim y Toynbee en relación a la situación de cambio social', *Revista Internacional de Sociología*, vol. 19, no. 76 (1961), pp. 467–70.

94 CHILD, ARTHUR, 'The problem of imputation in the sociology of knowledge', *Ethics*, vol. 51, no. 2 (January, 1941), pp. 200–19.

95 COOMBS, ROBERT H., 'Karl Mannheim, epistemology and the sociology of knowledge', *Sociological Quarterly*, vol. 7, no. 2 (Spring, 1966), pp. 229–33.

96 COSER, LEWIS A., 'Karl Mannheim 1893–1947', in COSER, LEWIS A., *Masters of Sociological Thought: Ideas in Historical and Social Context*, New York: Harcourt Brace Jovanovich, 1971, pp. 429–463.

97 EISERMANN, GOTTFRIED, 'Ideologie und Utopie: Aus Anlass der dritten Auflage von Karl Mannheims Buch', *Kölner Zeitschrift für Soziologie und Sozialpsychologie*, vol. 5, no. 4 (1953), pp. 526–534.

98 EPPSTEIN, PAUL, 'Mannheim: Die Fragestellung nach der Wirklichkeit im historischen Materialismus', *Archiv für Sozialwissenschaft und Sozialpolitik*, vol. 60 (1928), pp. 449–69.

99 ERÖS, J. S. and STEWART, W. A. C., 'Editorial Preface' to *Systematic Sociology*, pp. xi–xxx (see 22).

100 FARBERMAN, HARVEY A., 'Mannheim, Cooley, and Mead: toward a social theory of mentality', *Sociological Quarterly*, vol. 11, no. 1 (Winter, 1970), pp. 3–13. Reprinted in *Towards the Sociology of Knowledge*, pp. 261–72 (see 184).

101 FLOUD, JEAN, 'Karl Mannheim (1893–1947)' in RAISON, TIMOTHY (ed.), *The Founding Fathers of Social Science*, Baltimore, Maryland: Penguin, 1969, pp. 204–13.

102 GLUCK, SAMUEL E., 'The epistemology of Mannheim's sociology of knowledge', *Methodos*, vol. 6, no. 23 (1954), pp. 225–34.

103 HARTUNG, FRANK E., 'Problems of the sociology of knowledge', *Philosophy of Science*, vol. 19, no. 1 (January, 1952), pp. 17–32.

104 HINSHAW, VIRGIL G., JR, 'The epistemological relevance of Mannheim's sociology of knowledge', *Journal of Philosophy*, vol. 40, no. 3 (February 4, 1943), pp. 57–72. Reprinted in *Towards the Sociology of Knowledge*, pp. 229–44 (see 184).

105 HORKHEIMER, MAX, 'Ein neuer Ideologiebegriff?', *Archiv für die*

Geschichte des Sozialismus und der Arbeiterbewegung, vol. XV (1930), pp. 33–56.

106 HOSSFELD, PAUL, 'Historismus und Wissenssoziologie bei Karl Mannheim', *Sociologia Internationalis*, vol. III, no. 2 (1965), pp. 230–8.

107 HUGHES, H. STUART, 'The role of the intellectuals: Mann, Benda, Mannheim', in HUGHES, H. STUART, *Consciousness and Society: The Reorientation of European Social Thought 1890–1930*, Vintage Books, New York: Alfred A. Knopf & Random House, 1958, pp. 404–31.

108 KAHN, PAUL, 'Idéologie et sociologie de la connaissance dans l'oeuvre de K. Mannheim', *Cahiers Internationaux de Sociologie*, vol. 8, nos 1–2 (1950), pp. 147–68.

109 KECSKEMETI, PAUL, 'Introduction' to *Essays on the Sociology of Knowledge*, pp. 1–32 (see 19).

110 KECSKEMETI, PAUL, 'Introduction' to *Essays on Sociology and Social Psychology*, pp. 1–11 (see 20).

111 KETTLER, DAVID, 'Sociology of knowledge and moral philosophy: the place of traditional problems in the formation of Mannheim's thought', *Political Science Quarterly*, vol. LXXXII, no. 3 (September, 1967), pp. 399–426.

112 LAVINE, THELMA Z., 'Karl Mannheim and contemporary functionalism', *Philosophy and Phenomenological Research*, vol. 25, no. 4 (June, 1965), pp. 560–71. Reprinted in *Towards the Sociology of Knowledge*, pp. 245–57 (see 184).

113 LENK, KURT, 'Karl Mannheim', in *Handwörterbuch der Sozialwissenschaften* (ed. by E. von Beckerath *et al.*), vol. 7, Stuttgart, Tübingen, Göttingen: G. Fischer, Mohr, Vandenhoeck & Ruprecht, 1960.

114 LEWALTER, ERNST, 'Wissenssoziologie und Marxismus: Eine Auseinandersetzung mit Karl Mannheims Ideologie und Utopie von Marxistischer Position aus', *Archiv für Sozialwissenschaft und Sozialpolitik*, vol. 64, no. 1 (April, 1930), pp. 63–121.

115 LIEBER, HANS-JOACHIM, 'Sein und Erkennen: Zur philosophischen Problematik der Wissenssoziologie bei Karl Mannheim', *Zeitschrift für philosophische Forschung*, vol. 3, no. 2 (1948), pp. 249–64.

116 MANHEIM, ERNEST, 'Karl Mannheim, 1893–1947', *American Journal of Sociology*, vol. LII, no. 6 (May, 1947), pp. 471–4.

117 MANHEIM, ERNEST, 'Introduction' to *Essays on the Sociology of Culture*, pp. 1–13 (see 21).

118 MARCUSE, HERBERT, 'Zur Wahrheitsproblematik der soziologischen Methode: Karl Mannheims Ideologie und Utopie', *Die Gesellschaft*, vol. 6 (October, 1929), pp. 356–69.

119 MARTIN, ALFRED VON, 'Soziologie als Resignation und Mission', *Neue Schweizer Rundschau*, vol. 1 (1930).

120 MARTINDALE, DON, 'Karl Mannheim', in MARTINDALE, DON, *The Nature and Types of Sociological Theory*, Boston: Houghton Mifflin, 1960, pp. 414–18.

121 MERTON, ROBERT K., 'Karl Mannheim and the sociology of know-

ledge', *Journal of Liberal Religion*, vol. 2 (December, 1941), pp. 125–47.

122 MERTON, ROBERT K., 'Karl Mannheim and the sociology of knowledge', in MERTON, ROBERT K., *Social Theory and Social Structure*, Chicago: Free Press, 1957, pp. 489–508.

123 MILLS, C. WRIGHT, Review of 'Karl Mannheim, *Man and Society in an Age of Reconstruction*', *American Sociological Review*, vol. V, no. 6 (December, 1940), pp. 965–9.

124 REMMLING, GUNTER W., 'Kann Freiheit geplant werden? Zum zehnten Todestag von Karl Mannheim', *Frankfurter Neue Presse* (January 9, 1957), p. 9.

125 REMMLING, GUNTER W., 'Karl Mannheim 1893 bis 1947', *Archiv für Rechts- und Sozialphilosophie*, vol. XLIII, no. 2 (May, 1957), pp. 271–85.

126 REMMLING, GUNTER W., 'Menschenformung im Zeitalter der zweiten industriellen Revolution: Karl Mannheims Beitrag zur modernen Strukturpädagogik', *Kölner Zeitschrift für Soziologie und Sozialpsychologie*, vol. 9, no. 3 (1957), pp. 371–96.

127 REMMLING, GUNTER W., 'Kommt die Kultur noch mit? Die Soziologen und die technische Vorherrschaft', *Deutsche Stimmen*, no. 33 (1957), p. 10.

128 REMMLING, GUNTER W., 'Zur Soziologie der Macht: Der Beitrag Karl Mannheims zur politischen Soziologie', *Kölner Zeitschrift für Soziologie und Sozialpsychologie*, vol. 12, no. 1 (1960), pp. 53–64.

129 REMMLING, GUNTER W., 'Karl Mannheim: revision of an intellectual portrait', *Social Forces*, vol. 40, no. 1 (October, 1961), pp. 23–30.

130 REMMLING, GUNTER W., 'Das Unbehagen an der Gesellschaft: Karl Mannheims Beitrag zur Theorie der Gesellschaftsplanung', *Soziale Welt*, vol. 14, no. 3/4 (1963), pp. 241–63.

131 REMMLING, GUNTER W., 'The radical sociology of knowledge and beyond', in *Road to Suspicion*, pp. 40–9 (see 182).

132 REMMLING, GUNTER W., 'The significance and development of Karl Mannheim's sociology', read to the Upstate New York Sociological Society, November 7, 1969, Albany, New York. Reprinted in *Towards the Sociology of Knowledge*, pp. 217–28 (see 184).

133 REMMLING, GUNTER W., 'Mannheim, Karl', in *Basic Sociology*, pp. 333–4 (see 362).

134 REMMLING, GUNTER W., 'Philosophical parameters of Karl Mannheim's sociology of knowledge', *Sociological Quarterly*, vol. 12, no. 4 (Autumn, 1971), pp. 531–47.

135 ROBINSON, DANIEL S., 'Karl Mannheim's sociological philosophy', *Personalist*, vol. 29, no. 2 (April, 1948), pp. 137–48.

136 SALOMON, ALBERT, 'Karl Mannheim, 1893–1947', *Social Research*, vol. 14, no. 3 (September, 1947), pp. 350–64.

137 SANTUCCI, ANTONIO, 'Forme e significati dell'utopia in Karl Mannheim', *Filosofia e Sociologia*, vol. 3 (1954), pp. 238–48.

138 SANTUCCI, ANTONIO, 'Karl Mannheim e la sociologia americana', *Filosofia e Sociologia*, vol. 4 (1955), pp. 1027–51.

139 SARAN, A. K., 'Sociology of knowledge and traditional thought', *Sociological Bulletin*, vol. 13, no. 2 (September, 1964), pp. 36–48.

140 SCHELTING, ALEXANDER VON, Review of 'Karl Mannheim's *Ideologie und Utopie*', *American Sociological Review*, vol. 1, no. 4 (August, 1936), pp. 664–74.

141 SCHOECK, HELMUT, 'Die Zeitlichkeit bei Karl Mannheim', *Archiv für Rechts- und Sozialphilosophie*, vol. 38, no. 2 (1949/50), pp. 371–82.

142 SCHOEK, HELMUT, 'Der sozialökonomische Aspekt in der Wissenssoziologie Karl Mannheims', *Zeitschrift für die gesamte Staatswissenschaft*, vol. 106, no. 1 (1950), pp. 34–45.

143 SHILS, EDWARD, 'Mannheim, Karl', *International Encyclopedia of the Social Sciences*, vol. 9, New York: Macmillan, and Free Press, 1968, pp. 557–62.

144 SIMIRENKO, ALEX, 'Mannheim's generational analysis and acculturation', *British Journal of Sociology*, vol. 17, no. 3 (September, 1966), pp. 292–9. Reprinted in *Towards the Sociology of Knowledge*, pp. 331–8 (see 184).

145 SJOBERG, GIDEON and CAIN, LEONARD D., 'Negative values and social action', *Alpha Kappa Deltan*, vol. 29, no. 1 (Winter, 1959), pp. 63–70.

146 SPEIER, HANS, Review of '*Ideologie und Utopie*, by Karl Mannheim', *American Journal of Sociology*, vol. 43, no. 1 (July, 1937), pp. 155–66.

147 STERN, GÜNTHER, 'Über die sogenannte "Seinsverbundenheit" des Bewusstseins', *Archiv für Sozialwissenschaft und Sozialpolitik*, vol. 64, no. 3 (1930), pp. 492–509.

148 STEWART, W. A. C., 'Introduction' to *An Introduction to the Sociology of Education*, pp. vii–xvii (see 25).

149 TIMASHEFF, NICHOLAS S., 'Mannheim: social structure and meaning', in TIMASHEFF, NICHOLAS S., *Sociological Theory: Its Nature and Growth*, 3rd edition, New York: Random House, 1967, pp. 306–8.

150 TONSOR, STEPHEN J., 'Gnostics, romantics, and conservatives', *Social Research*, vol. 35, no. 4 (Winter, 1968), pp. 616–34.

151 TOURAINE, ALAIN, Review of 'Mannheim: *Essays on the Sociology of Knowledge*', *L'Année Sociologique*, 3rd series (1952), pp. 251–6.

152 TREVES, RENATO, 'Karl Mannheim', *Rivista di Filosofia*, vol. 39, no. 2 (1948), pp. 165–72.

153 WAGNER, HELMUT R., 'Mannheim's historicism', *Social Research*, vol. 19, no. 3 (September, 1952), pp. 300–21.

154 WAGNER, HELMUT R., 'The scope of Mannheim's thinking', *Social Research*, vol. 20, no. 1 (Spring, 1953), pp. 100–9.

155 WATKINS, J. W. N., 'Massification', *Spectator*, vol. 197, no. 6687 (August 24, 1956), pp. 258–9.

156 WIESE, LEOPOLD VON, 'Karl Mannheim (1893–1947)', *Kölner Zeitschrift für Soziologie und Sozialpsychologie*, vol. 1 (1948–9), pp. 98–100.

157 WILENSKY, HAROLD L., 'Orderly careers and social participation: The impact of work history on social integration in the middle class', *American Sociological Review*, vol. 26, no. 4 (August, 1961), pp. 521–39.

158 WIRTH, LOUIS, 'Preface' to *Ideology and Utopia*, pp. i-xxxi (see 7).

159 WIRTH, LOUIS, 'Karl Mannheim, 1893–1947', *American Sociological Review*, vol. 12, no. 3 (June, 1947), pp. 356–7.

160 WOLFF, KURT H., 'Karl Mannheim in seinen Abhandlungen bis 1933', Introduction to *Wissenssoziologie*, pp. 11–65 (see 26).

161 WOLFF, KURT H., 'A reading of Karl Mannheim', Introduction to *From Karl Mannheim*, pp. xi–cxxiii (see 27).

162 ZEITLIN, IRVING M., 'Karl Mannheim (1893–1947)', in ZEITLIN, IRVING M., *Ideology and the Development of Sociological Theory*, Englewood Cliffs, New Jersey: Prentice-Hall, 1968, pp. 281–319.

Books on the sociology of knowledge

163 ANSART, PIERRE, *et al.*, *Contributions à la sociologie de la connaissance*, Paris: Éditions Anthropos, 1967.

164 BERGER, PETER L. and LUCKMANN, THOMAS, *The Social Construction of Reality: A Treatise in the Sociology of Knowledge*, Garden City, New York: Doubleday, 1966.

165 CHILD, ARTHUR, 'The Problems of the Sociology of Knowledge: A Critical and Philosophical Study', unpublished Ph.D. dissertation, Berkeley: University of California, 1938.

166 CURTIS, JAMES E. and PETRAS, JOHN W. (eds), *The Sociology of Knowledge*, New York: Praeger, 1970.

167 DEGRÉ, GÉRARD L., *Society and Ideology: An Inquiry into the Sociology of Knowledge*, New York: Columbia University Bookstore, 1943.

168 DURKHEIM, ÉMILE and MAUSS, MARCEL, *Primitive Classification* (trans. by Rodney Needham from 'De quelques formes primitives de classification', *L'Année Sociologique* (1903)), University of Chicago Press, 1963.

169 GADOUREK, IVAN, *Kennissociologie: Een Korte Inleiding*, The Hague: Servire, 1955.

170 GRÜNWALD, ERNST, *Das Problem der Soziologie des Wissens: Versuch einer kritischen Darstellung der wissenssoziologischen Theorien*, Wien and Leipzig: Wilhelm Braumüller, 1934, and Hildesheim: G. Olms, 1967.

171 GURVITCH, GEORGES, *Initiation aux recherches sur la sociologie de la connaissance*, Paris: Tournier & Constans, 1948.

172 HAMILTON, PETER, *Knowledge and Social Structure: An Introduction to the Classical Argument in the Sociology of Knowledge*, London and Boston: Routledge & Kegan Paul, 1974.

173 HOLZNER, BURKART, *Reality Construction in Society*, Cambridge, Massachusetts: Schenkman, 1968.

174 HOROWITZ, IRVING LOUIS, *Philosophy, Science, and the Sociology of Knowledge*, Springfield, Illinois: Charles C. Thomas, 1961.

175 HOROWITZ, IRVING LOUIS (ed.), *Historia y elementos de la sociología del conocimiento*, Buenos Aires: University of Buenos Aires Press, 1964.

176 KURUCZ, JENÖ, *Falsches Bewusstsein und Geronnener Geist: Ein*

Beitrag zur Theorie und Anwendung der Wissenssoziologie, Cologne: Grote, 1970.

177 LENK, KURT, *Von der Ohnmacht des Geistes: Kritische Darstellung der Spätphilosophie Max Schelers*, Tübingen: Hopfer, 1959.

178 LENK, KURT (ed.), *Ideologie: Ideologiekritik und Wissenssoziologie*, Berlin and Neuwied: Luchterhand Verlag, 1961.

179 LIEBER, HANS-JOACHIM, *Wissen und Gesellschaft: Die Probleme der Wissenssoziologie*, Tübingen: Max Niemeyer Verlag, 1952.

180 MAQUET, JACQUES J., *The Sociology of Knowledge; Its Structure and Its Relation to the Philosophy of Knowledge: A Critical Analysis of the Systems of Karl Mannheim and Pitirim A. Sorokin* (trans. by John F. Locke), Boston: Beacon Press, 1951.

181 NEISSER, HANS, *On the Sociology of Knowledge: An Essay*, New York: James H. Heinemann, 1965.

182 REMMLING, GUNTER W., *Road to Suspicion: A Study of Modern Mentality and the Sociology of Knowledge*, New York: Appleton-Century-Crofts, 1967; Englewood Cliffs, New Jersey: Prentice-Hall, 1974.

183 REMMLING, GUNTER W., *Wissenssoziologie und Gesellschaftsplanung: Das Werk Karl Mannheims*, Dortmund: Verlag Friedrich Wilhelm Ruhfus, 1968.

184 REMMLING, GUNTER W. (ed.), *Towards the Sociology of Knowledge: Origin and Development of a Sociological Thought Style*, London: Routledge & Kegan Paul, and New York: Humanities Press, 1973.

185 ROTHACKER, ERICH, *Max Schelers Durchbruch in die Wirklichkeit*, Bonn: Bouvier, 1949.

186 SCHAAF, JULIUS JAKOB, *Über Wissen und Selbstbewusstsein*, Stuttgart: Schmiedel, 1947.

187 SCHAAF, JULIUS JAKOB, *Grundprinzipien der Wissenssoziologie*, Hamburg: Felix Meiner, 1956.

188 SCHELER, MAX FERDINAND (ed.), *Versuche zu einer Soziologie des Wissens*, Munich, Leipzig: Duncker & Humblot, 1924.

189 SCHELER, MAX FERDINAND, *Die Formen des Wissens und die Bildung*, Bonn: Cohen, 1925.

190 SCHELER, MAX FERDINAND, *Die Wissensformen und die Gesellschaft*, Leipzig: Der Neue Geist Verlag, 1926.

191 SCHELTING, ALEXANDER VON, *Max Webers Wissenschaftslehre: Das logische Problem der historischen Kulturerkenntnis; die Grenzen der Soziologie des Wissens*, Tübingen: J. C. B. Mohr (Paul Siebeck), 1934.

192 SOROKIN, PITIRIM A., *Social and Cultural Dynamics*, vol. II: *Fluctuation of Systems of Truth, Ethics, and Law*, New York: American Book Company, 1937.

193 SPROTT, W. J. H., *Science and Social Action*, London: Watts, 1954.

194 STARK, WERNER, *The Sociology of Knowledge: An Essay in Aid of a Deeper Understanding of the History of Ideas*, London: Routledge & Kegan Paul, 1958.

195 STARK, WERNER, *Montesquieu: Pioneer of the Sociology of Knowledge*, London: Routledge & Kegan Paul, 1960.

196 TREVES, RENATO, *Politica della cultura e sociologia della conoscenza: Spirito critico e spirito dogmatico*, Milan: Nuvoletti, 1954.

197 WHORF, BENJAMIN L., *Language, Thought, and Society* (ed. by John B. Carroll), New York: John Wiley, 1956.

198 WOLFF, KURT H., 'La sociologia del sapere', unpublished doctoral thesis, Florence, 1935.

199 WOLFF, KURT H., *Versuch zu einer Wissenssoziologie*, Berlin and Neuwied: Luchterhand Verlag, 1968.

200 ZNANIECKI, FLORIAN, *The Social Role of the Man of Knowledge*, New York: Columbia University Press, 1940.

Books with relevance for the sociology of knowledge

201 ABELL, W., *The Collective Dream in Art: A Psycho-historical Theory of Culture Based on Relations between Arts, Psychology, and the Social Sciences*, Cambridge, Massachusetts: Harvard University Press, 1957.

202 ADLER, MAX, *Das Soziologische in Kants Erkenntniskritik: Ein Beitrag zur Auseinandersetzung zwischen Naturalismus und Kritizismus*, Wien: Verlag der Wiener Volksbuchhandlung, 1924.

203 ADLER, MAX, *Kant und der Marxismus; Gesammelte Aufsätze zur Erkenntniskritik und Theorie des Sozialen*, Berlin: S. Laub, 1925.

204 ADORNO, THEODOR W. and HORKHEIMER, MAX, *Dialektik der Aufklärung*, Amsterdam: Querido Verlag, 1947.

205 ALTICK, R. D., *The English Common Reader: A Social History of the Mass Reading Public, 1800–1900*, University of Chicago Press, 1957.

206 ANTAL, F., *Florentine Painting and Its Social Background*, London: Routledge & Kegan Paul, 1947.

207 ANTONI, CARLO, *From History to Sociology: The Transition in German Historical Thinking* (trans. by Hayden V. White), Detroit: Wayne State University Press, 1959.

208 BACON, FRANCIS, *Novum Organum*, New York: Colonial Press, 1900.

209 BAIER, H. (ed.), *Studenten in Opposition: Beiträge zur Soziologie der deutschen Hochschule*, Gütersloh: Bertelsmann, 1969.

210 BARBER, BERNARD, *Science and the Social Order*, Chicago: Free Press, 1952.

211 BARBER, BERNARD and HIRSCH, WALTER, *The Sociology of Science*, New York: Free Press, 1962.

212 BARITZ, L., *The Servants of Power: A History of the Use of Social Science in American Industry*, Middletown, Connecticut: Wesleyan University Press, 1960.

213 BARKER, J. E., *Diderot's Treatment of the Christian Religion in the Encyclopédie*, New York: King's Crown Press, 1941.

214 BAUER, GERHARD, *'Geschichtlichkeit': Wege und Irrwege eines Begriffs*, Berlin: Walter de Gruyter, 1963.

215 BAUER, RAYMOND A., *The New Man in Soviet Psychology*, Cambridge, Massachusetts: Harvard University Press, 1952.

216 BAUMGARTEN, A., *Bemerkungen zur Erkenntnistheorie des dialektischen und historischen Materialismus*, Berlin: Akademie Verlag, 1957.

217 BECK, HUBERT PARK, *Men Who Control Universities: The Economic and Social Composition of Governing Boards of Thirty Leading American Universities*, New York: King's Crown Press, 1947.

218 BENICHOU, P., *Morales du grand siècle*, Paris: Gallimard, 1948.

219 BERELSON, BERNARD, *Content Analysis in Communication Research*, Chicago: Free Press, 1952.

220 BERNAL, JOHN DESMOND, *The Social Function of Science*, New York: Macmillan, 1939.

221 BERNAL, JOHN DESMOND, *Science and Industry in the Nineteenth Century*, London: Routledge & Kegan Paul, 1953.

222 BODENSTEIN, WALTER, *Neige des Historismus: Ernst Troeltschs Entwicklungsgang*, Gütersloh: Bertelsmann, 1959.

223 BOGDANOV, ALEXANDER A., *Die Entwicklungsformen der Gesellschaft und die Wissenschaft* (trans. by I. Dursky), Berlin: Nike Verlag, 1924.

224 BORKENAU, FRANZ, *Der Übergang vom feudalen zum bürgerlichen Weltbild: Studien zur Geschichte der Philosophie der Manufakturperiode*, Paris: F. Alcan, 1934.

225 BOUGLÉ, CELESTIN, *The Evolution of Values* (trans. by Helen S. Sellars), New York: Holt, Rinehart & Winston, 1926.

226 BRAMSON, LEON, *The Political Context of Sociology*, Princeton, New Jersey: Princeton University Press, 1961.

227 BROWN, NORMAN O., *Life against Death: The Psycho-analytical Meaning of History*, Middletown, Connecticut: Wesleyan University Press, 1959.

228 BUSCH, ALEXANDER, *Die Geschichte des Privatdozenten: Eine soziologische Studie zur grossbetrieblichen Entwicklung der deutschen Universitäten*, Stuttgart: F. Enke, 1959.

229 BUTTERFIELD, H., *The Origins of Modern Science, 1300–1800*, London: G. Bell, 1949.

230 CASSIRER, ERNST, *The Philosophy of Symbolic Forms*, 3 vols (trans. by Ralph Mannheim), New Haven: Yale University Press, 1953–1957.

231 CASSIRER, ERNST, *The Philosophy of the Enlightenment* (trans. by F. C. A. Koelln and J. P. Pettegrove), Boston: Beacon Press, 1955.

232 CHILDE, VERE GORDON, *Society and Knowledge*, New York: Harper, 1956.

233 COHEN, M., *Pour une sociologie du langage*, Paris: Albin Michel, 1956.

234 CROWTHER, JAMES GERALD, *The Social Relations of Science*, New York: Macmillan, 1941.

235 DAVIS, ALLISON, *Social-Class Influences upon Learning*, Cambridge, Massachusetts: Harvard University Press, 1948.

236 DAWSON, R., *The Chinese Chameleon: An Analysis of European Conceptions of Chinese Civilization*, New York: Oxford University Press, 1967.

237 DEGRÉ, GÉRARD L., *Science as a Social Institution*, Garden City, New York: Doubleday, 1955.

238 DEWEY, JOHN, *The Quest for Certainty*, New York: Minton, Balch, 1929.

239 DILTHEY, WILHELM, *Die Jugendgeschichte Hegels und andere Abhandlungen zur Geschichte des deutschen Idealismus, Gesammelte Schriften*, vol. IV, Leipzig and Berlin: B. G. Teubner, 1921.

240 DILTHEY, WILHELM, *Einleitung in die Geisteswissenschaften: Versuch einer Grundlegung für das Studium der Gesellschaft und der Geschichte, Gesammelte Schriften*, vol. I, Stuttgart: B. G. Teubner, 1923.

241 DILTHEY, WILHELM, *Die Geistige Welt: Einleitung in die Philosophie des Lebens, Gesammelte Schriften*, vol. V, Leipzig and Berlin: B. G. Teubner, 1924.

242 DILTHEY, WILHELM, *Studien zur Geschichte des deutschen Geistes, Gesammelte Schriften*, vol. III, Leipzig and Berlin, B. G. Teubner, 1927.

243 DILTHEY, WILHELM, *Der Aufbau der geschichtlichen Welt in den Geisteswissenschaften, Gesammelte Schriften*, vol. VII, Leipzig and Berlin: B. G. Teubner, 1927.

244 DILTHEY, WILHELM, *Weltanschauungslehre: Abhandlungen zur Philosophie der Philosophe, Gesammelte Schriften*, vol. VIII, Leipzig and Berlin: B. G. Teubner, 1931.

245 DILTHEY, WILHELM, *The Essence of Philosophy* (trans. by Stephen A. Emery and William T. Emery), Chapel Hill: University of North Carolina Press, 1954.

246 DOUGLAS, JACK D. (ed.), *Understanding Everyday Life: Toward the Reconstruction of Sociological Knowledge*, Chicago: Aldine, 1970.

247 DUNCAN, HUGH DALZIEL, *Language and Literature in Society: A Sociological Essay on Theory and Method in the Interpretation of Linguistic Symbols, with a Bibliographical Guide to the Sociology of Literature*, University of Chicago Press, 1953.

248 DUNCAN, HUGH DALZIEL, *Communication and Social Order*, New York: Oxford University Press, 1968.

249 DUPUY, MAURICE, *La philosophie de Max Scheler: Son évolution et son unité*, 2 vols, Paris: Presses Universitaires de France, 1959.

250 DURKHEIM, ÉMILE, *The Elementary Forms of the Religious Life: A Study in Religious Sociology* (trans. by Joseph W. Swain), London: Allen & Unwin, 1915.

251 EISERMANN, GOTTFRIED, *Die Grundlagen des Historismus in der deutschen Nationalökonomie*, Stuttgart: F. Enke, 1956.

252 ERIKSON, E. H., *Young Man Luther: A Study in Psycho-analysis and History*, New York: W. W. Norton, 1958.

253 FEBVRE, L., *Au coeur religieux du XVIe siècle*, Paris: Sevpen, 1957.

254 FESTINGER, LEON, *A Theory of Cognitive Dissonance*, Evanston, Illinois: Row, Peterson, 1957.

255 FEUER, L., *Spinoza and the Rise of Liberalism*, Boston: Beacon Press, 1958.

256 FREIDSON, ELIOT, *Profession of Medicine: A Study of the Sociology of Applied Knowledge*, New York: Dodd, Mead, 1970.

257 FREUD, SIGMUND, *Civilization and Its Discontents* (trans. by Joan Riviere), New York: Jonathan Cape & Harrison Smith, 1930.

258 FREYER, HANS, *Soziologie als Wirklichkeitswissenschaft*, Leipzig and Berlin: B. G. Teubner, 1930.

259 FREYER, HANS, *Über das Dominantwerden technischer Kategorien in der Lebenswelt der industriellen Gesellschaft*, Wiesbaden: F. Stein, 1960.

260 GELDSETZER, LUTZ, *Die Ideenlehre Jakob Wegelins*, Meisenheim am Glan: Hain, 1963.

261 GERTH, HANS H., *Die sozialgeschichtliche Lage der bürgerlichen Intelligenz um die Wende des 18. Jahrhunderts: Ein Beitrag zur Soziologie des deutschen Frühliberalismus*, Berlin: V.D.I.-Verlag, 1935.

262 GRANET, MARCEL, *Chinese Civilization* (trans. by K. E. Innes and M. R. Brailsford), New York: Alfred A. Knopf, 1930.

263 GRANET, MARCEL, *La pensée chinoise*, Paris: La Renaissance du Livre, 1934.

264 GRANET, MARCEL, *Études sociologiques sur la Chine*, Paris: Presses Universitaires de France, 1953.

265 GROETHUYSEN, BERNHARD, *Die Entstehung der bürgerlichen Welt- und Lebensanschauung in Frankreich*, Halle/Salle: M. Niemeyer Verlag, 1927.

266 GURVITCH, GEORGES, *Les tendances actuelles de la philosophie allemande: E. Husserl, M. Scheler, E. Lask, N. Hartmann, M. Heidegger*, Paris: J. Vrin, 1930.

267 GURVITCH, GEORGES, *Dialectique et sociologie*, Paris: Flammarion 1962.

268 GURVITCH, GEORGES, *Les cadres sociaux de la connaissance*, Paris: Presses Universitaires de France, 1966.

269 HALBWACHS, MAURICE, *Les cadres sociaux de la mémoire*, Paris: F. Alcan, 1925.

270 HALBWACHS, MAURICE, *La topographie légendaire des Évangiles en Terre Sainte: étude de mémoire collective*, Paris: Presses Universitaires de France, 1941.

271 HALL, E. W., *Modern Science and Human Values: A Study in the History of Ideas*, Princeton, New Jersey: D. Van Nostrand, 1956.

272 HAUSER, ARNOLD, *The Social History of Art*, 2 vols, New York: Alfred A. Knopf, 1951.

273 HEGEL, G. W. F., *Science of Logic*, 2 vols (trans. by W. H. Johnston and L. G. Struthers), New York: Macmillan, 1929.

274 HEGEL, G. W. F., *Phenomenology of Mind* (trans. by J. B. Baillie), London: Oxford University Press, 1931.

275 HEGEL, G. W. F., *The Philosophy of History* (trans. by J. Sibree), New York: Wiley, 1944.

276 HEGEL, G. W. F., *Philosophy of Right* (trans. by T. M. Knox), London: Oxford University Press, 1945.

277 HEGEL, G. W. F., *Reason in History: A General Introduction to the Philosophy of History* (trans. with an introduction by Robert S. Hartman), New York: Liberal Arts Press, 1954.

278 HEGEL, G. W. F., *Lectures on the History of Philosophy*, 3 vols (trans. by E. S. Haldane), London: Routledge & Kegan Paul, 1955.

279 HELVÉTIUS, CLAUDE ADRIEN, *De l'homme*, vol. I., London: Société Typographique, 1774.

280 HELVÉTIUS, CLAUDE ADRIEN, *De l'esprit*, Paris: Durand, 1776.

281 HERTZ, F., *The Development of the German Public Mind: A Social History of German Political Sentiments, Aspirations and Ideas; The Middle Ages, The Reformation*, London: Allen & Unwin, 1957.

282 HERZBERG, GÜNTHER, *Der Zeitgeist: Kritik-Problematik-Entwurf*, Meisenheim am Glan: Hain, 1960.

283 HEUSSI, KARL, *Die Krisis des Historismus*, Tübingen: J. C. B. Mohr, 1932.

284 HINTZE, OTTO, *Soziologie und Geschichte, Gesammelte Abhandlungen*, vol. II, Göttingen: Vandenhoeck & Ruprecht, 1963.

285 HIRSCH, WALTER, *Scientists in American Society*, New York: Random House, 1968.

286 HODGES, H. A., *Wilhelm Dilthey: An Introduction*, London: Kegan Paul, Trench, Trubner, 1944.

287 HODGES, H. A., *The Philosophy of Wilhelm Dilthey*, London: Routledge & Kegan Paul, 1952.

288 HOLBACH, PAUL HENRI THIRY, *Système de la nature*, part one, London, 1770.

289 HOLBACH, PAUL HENRI THIRY, *Essai sur les préjugés*, London: M. M. Rey, 1777.

290 HOLBACH, PAUL HENRI THIRY, *Letters to Eugenia: On the Absurd, Contradictory, and Demoralizing Dogmas and Mysteries of the Christian Religion* (trans. by H. D. Robinson), New York: H. M. Duhecquet, 1823.

291 HOLBACH, PAUL HENRI THIRY, *Good Sense: Or, Natural Ideas Opposed to Supernatural* (trans. by H. D. Robinson), Boston: J. P. Mendum, 1856.

292 HOLTON, G. (ed.), *Science and the Modern Mind: A Symposium*, Boston: Beacon Press, 1958.

293 HOOK, SIDNEY, *Towards the Understanding of Karl Marx: A Revolutionary Interpretation*, New York: John Day, 1933.

294 HORKHEIMER, MAX, *The Eclipse of Reason*, New York: Oxford University Press, 1947.

295 HUGHES, H. STUART, *Consciousness and Society: The Reorientation of European Social Thought 1890–1930*, New York: Alfred A. Knopf, 1958.

296 HUMBOLDT, WILHELM VON, *Über die Aufgabe des Geschichtsschreibers, Abhandlungen der Königlichen Akademie der Wissenschaft zu Berlin: Historisch-Philologische Klasse, 1820–1821*, Berlin: B. Behrs Verlag, 1822.

297 HUSSERL, EDMUND, *Logische Untersuchungen*, vol. I, Halle: Max Niemeyer Verlag, 1913.

298 HUSSERL, EDMUND, *Ideas: General Introduction to Pure Phenomenology* (trans. by W. R. Boyce Gibson), New York: Macmillan, 1952.

299 JASPERS, KARL, *Reason and Existence*, New York: Noonday Press, 1955.

300 JONAS, F., *Sozialphilosophie der industriellen Arbeitswelt*, Stuttgart: F. Enke, 1960.

301 KECSKEMETI, PAUL, *Meaning, Communication and Value*, University of Chicago Press, 1952.

302 KLUBACK, WILLIAM, *Wilhelm Dilthey's Philosophy of History*, New York: Columbia University Press, 1956.

303 KOHN-BRAMSTEDT, ERNST, *Aristocracy and the Middle-Classes in Germany: Social Types in German Literature 1830–1900*, London: P. S. King, 1937.

304 KRAUCH, H. (ed.), *Forschungsplanung: Eine Studie über Ziele und Strukturen amerikanischer Forschungsinstitute*, Munich: Oldenbourg, 1966.

305 KRIEGER, L., *The German Idea of Freedom: History of a Political Tradition*, Boston: Beacon Press, 1957.

306 KRYSMANSKI, HANS-JÜRGEN, *Soziales System und Wissenschaft*, Gütersloh: Bertelsmann, 1967.

307 LACROIX, JEAN, *Marxisme, existentialisme, personnalisme, présence de l'éternité dans le temps*, Paris: Presses Universitaires de France, 1950.

308 LANDSHUT, SIEGFRIED, *Kritik der Soziologie und andere Schriften zur Politik*, Neuwied: Luchterhand Verlag, 1968.

309 LAZARSFELD, PAUL F. and KATZ, E., *Personal Influence: The Part Played by People in the Flow of Mass Communications*, Chicago: Free Press, 1955.

310 LEE, O., *Existence and Inquiry: A Study of Thought in the Modern World*, University of Chicago Press, 1949.

311 LEIBFRIED, S. (ed.), *Wider die Untertanenfabrik: Handbuch zur Demokratisierung der Hochschule*, Cologne: Pahl-Rugenstein, 1967.

312 LIEBFRIED, S., *Die angepasste Universität: Zur Situation der Hochschulen in der Bundesrepublik und in den USA*, Frankfurt: Suhrkamp Verlag, 1968.

313 LÉVY-BRUHL, LUCIEN, *Primitive Mentality* (trans. by Lilian A. Clare), London: George Allen & Unwin, 1923.

314 LÉVY-BRUHL, LUCIEN, *L'expérience mystique et les symboles chez les primitifs*, Paris: F. Alcan, 1938.

315 LÉVY-BRUHL, LUCIEN, *Les carnets de Lucien Lévy-Bruhl*, Paris: Presses Universitaires de France, 1949.

316 LEWIS, MORRIS MICHAEL, *The Importance of Illiteracy*, London: G. Harrap, 1953.

317 LILGE, FRIEDRICH, *The Abuse of Learning: The Failure of the German University*, New York: Macmillan, 1948.

318 LITT, THEODOR, *Technisches Denken und menschliche Bildung*, Heidelberg: Quelle & Meyer, 1957.

319 LÓPEZ CAMARA, F., *La génesis de la conciencia liberal en México*, Mexico City: Colegio de México, 1954.

320 LOWENTHAL, LEO, *Literature and the Image of Man: Sociological Studies in the European Drama and Novel, 1600–1900*, Boston: Beacon Press, 1957.

321 LÖWITH, KARL, *From Hegel to Nietzsche: The Revolution in Nineteenth-Century Thought* (trans. by David E. Green), New York: Holt, Rinehart & Winston, 1964.

322 LUKÁCS, GEORG, *Geschichte und Klassenbewusstsein: Studien über marxistische Dialektik*, Berlin: Der Malik-Verlag, 1923.

323 LUKÁCS, GEORG, *Karl Marx and Friedrich Engels als Literaturhistoriker*, Berlin: Aufbau-Verlag, 1948.

324 LUKÁCS, GEORG, *Existentialisme ou marxisme?* (trans. by E. Kelemen), Paris: Nagel, 1948.

325 LUKÁCS, GEORG, *Der junge Hegel: Über die Beziehungen von Dialektik und Ökonomie*, Zürich and Wien: Europa-Verlag, 1948.

326 LUKÁCS, GEORG, *Die Zerstörung der Vernunft*, Berlin: Aufbau-Verlag, 1954.

327 LUKÁCS, GEORG, *History and Class Consciousness: Studies in Marxist Dialectics* (trans. by Rodney Livingstone), Cambridge, Massachusetts: MIT Press, 1971.

328 MACHLUP, FRITZ, *The Production and Distribution of Knowledge in the United States*, Princeton University Press, 1962.

329 MACKENZIE, DAN, *The Infancy of Medicine: An Inquiry into the Influence of Folklore upon the Evolution of Scientific Medicine*, London: Macmillan, 1927.

330 MCLUHAN, MARSHALL, *Understanding Media: The Extensions of Man*, New York: McGraw-Hill, 1964.

331 MANDELBAUM, MAURICE, *The Problem of Historical Knowledge: An Answer to Relativism*, New York: Liveright, 1938.

332 MANDELBAUM, MAURICE, *The Phenomenology of Moral Experience*, Chicago: Free Press, 1955.

333 MAO TSE-TUNG, *Über die Praxis: Über den Zusammenhang von Erkenntnis und Praxis, von Wissen und Handeln*, Berlin: Dietz Verlag, 1952.

334 MARCUSE, HERBERT, *Reason and Revolution: Hegel and the Rise of Social Theory*, New York: Oxford University Press, 1941.

335 MARCUSE, HERBERT, *Eros and Civilization: A Philosophical Inquiry into Freud*, Boston: Beacon Press, 1955.

336 MARTIN, ALFRED VON, *Sociology of the Renaissance* (trans. by W. L. Luetkens), London: Routledge & Kegan Paul, 1944.

337 MARTIN, ALFRED VON, *Geist und Gesellschaft*, Frankfurt am Main: Knecht, 1948.

338 MARX, KARL, *A Contribution to the Critique of Political Economy* (trans. from the 2nd German edition by N. I. Stone), Chicago: Charles H. Kerr, 1904.

339 MARX, KARL, *Economic and Philosophic Manuscripts of 1844* (trans. by M. Milligan), Moscow: Foreign Languages Publishing House, 1957.

340 MEAD, GEORGE HERBERT, *Mind, Self, and Society: From the Standpoint of a Social Behaviorist* (ed. by Charles W. Morris), University of Chicago Press, 1934.

341 MEERLOO, J. A. M., *The Rape of the Mind*, Cleveland and New York: World Publishing, 1956.

342 MEIJER, J. M., *Knowledge and Revolution*, Amsterdam: Assen, 1955.

343 MILLER, PERRY, *The New England Mind: The Seventeenth Century*, New York: Macmillan, 1939.

344 MUELLER, J. H., *The American Symphony Orchestra: A Social History of Musical Taste*, Indiana University Press, 1951.

345 NIETZSCHE, FRIEDRICH, *The Use and Abuse of History* (trans. by Adrian Collins), New York: Liberal Arts Press, 1957.

346 NISBET, ROBERT A., *The Quest for Community: A Study in the Ethics of Freedom and Order*, New York: Oxford University Press, 1953.

347 NORTHROP, FILMER STUART CUCKOW, *Cross-Cultural Understanding: Epistemology in Anthropology*, New York: Harper & Row, 1964.

348 NÜRNBERGER, R., *Die Politisierung des französischen Protestantismus*, Tübingen: J. C. B. Mohr (Paul Siebeck), 1948.

349 PARETO, VILFREDO, *The Mind and Society* (*Trattato di Sociologia Generale*; trans. by A. Livingston), New York: Harcourt, Brace & Company, 1935.

350 PARSONS, TALCOTT, *The Social System*, Chicago: Free Press, 1951.

351 PIAGET, JEAN, *La représentation du monde chez l'enfant*, Paris: F. Alcan, 1926.

352 PIAGET, JEAN, *La construction du réel chez l'enfant*, Paris, Neuchâtel: Delachaux & Niestlé, 1937.

353 PIAGET, JEAN, *Introduction à l'épistemologie génétique*, vol. III, Paris: Presses Universitaires de France, 1950.

354 PLESSNER, HELMUTH, *Zwischen Philosophie und Gesellschaft*, Berne: Francke Verlag, 1953.

355 PLESSNER, HELMUTH, *Die verspätete Nation: Über die politische Verführbarkeit bürgerlichen Geistes*, Stuttgart: Kohlhammer Verlag, 1959.

356 POLANYI, MICHAEL, *Personal Knowledge*, New York: Harper & Row, 1964.

357 POPITZ, H., *Der entfremdete Mensch: Zeitkritik und Geschichtsphilosophie des jungen Marx*, Basle: Verlag Recht & Gesellschaft, 1953.

358 POPPER, K. R., *The Poverty of Historicism*, Boston: Beacon Press, 1957.

359 RAUP, ROBERT BRUCE, *Education and Organised Interests in America*, New York: G. P. Putnam, 1936.

360 REISER, O. L., *The Integration of Human Knowledge: A Study of the Formal Foundations and the Social Implications of Unified Science*, Boston: P. Sargent, 1958.

361 REMMLING, GUNTER W. *et al.*, *Die Universität im Urteil ihrer Studenten*, Bonn: Verband Deutscher Studentenwerke, 1954.

362 REMMLING, GUNTER W. and CAMPBELL, ROBERT B., *Basic Sociology: An Introduction to the Study of Society*, Totowa, New Jersey: Littlefield, Adams, 1970.

363 REYNOLDS, LARRY T. and REYNOLDS, JANICE M. (eds), *The Sociology of Sociology: Analysis and Criticism of the Thought, Research, and Ethical Folkways of Sociology and Its Practitioners*, New York: David McKay, 1970.

364 RIDEOUT, W. B., *The Radical Novel in the United States, 1900–1954*, Cambridge, Massachusetts: Harvard University Press, 1956.

365 ROBIN, LÉON, *La pensée grecque et les origines de l'esprit scientifique*, Paris: La Renaissance du Livre, 1923.

366 ROUSTAN, M., *The Pioneers of the French Revolution* (trans. by F. Whyte, ed. by H. J. Laski), Boston: Little, Brown, 1926.

367 ROY, G. FRANCIS, *The Rhetoric of Science*, University of Minnesota Press, 1961.

368 SAPIR, EDWARD, *Selected Writings in Language, Culture, and Personality* (ed. by David B. Mandelbaum), Berkeley: University of California Press, 1949.

369 SARTRE, JEAN-PAUL, *Antisemite and Jew* (trans. by George J. Becker), New York: Schocken, 1948.

370 SCHELER, MAX, *Schriften zur Soziologie und Weltanschauungslehre*, 4 vols, Leipzig: Der Neue Geist Verlag, 1923–4.

371 SCHLESINGER, R., *Soviet Legal Theory: Its Social Background and Development*, London: Kegan Paul, Trench, Trubner, 1945.

372 SCHMIDT, GUSTAV, *Deutscher Historismus und der Übergang zur parlamentarischen Demokratie: Untersuchungen zu den politischen Gedanken von Meinecke, Troeltsch, Max Weber*, Lübeck and Hamburg: Mathiesen, 1964.

373 SCHOECK, HELMUT, *Die Soziologie und die Gesellschaften: Problemsicht und Problemlösung vom Beginn bis zur Gegenwart*, Freiburg: Alber, 1964.

374 SCHÜCKING, LEVIN LUDWIG, *The Sociology of the Literary Taste* (trans. by E. W. Dickes), London: Kegan Paul, Trench, Trubner, 1944.

375 SCHUTZ, ALFRED, *The Problem of Social Reality* (ed. and introduced by Maurice Natanson), *Collected Papers*, vol. I, The Hague: Martinus Nijhoff, 1962.

376 SCHUTZ, ALFRED, *Studies in Social Theory* (ed. and introduced by Arvid Brodersen), *Collected Papers*, vol. II, The Hague: Martinus Nijhoff, 1964.

377 SEIDEL, ALFRED, *Bewusstsein als Verhängnis* (posthumously ed. by Hans Prinzhorn), Bonn: Verlag Friedrich Cohen, 1927.

378 SHILS, EDWARD A., *The Torment of Secrecy*, Chicago: Free Press, 1956.

379 SIBLEY, ELBRIDGE, *The Education of Sociologists in the United States*, New York: Russell Sage Foundation, 1963.

380 SILBERMANN, ALPHONS, *Musik, Rundfunk und Hörer: Die soziologischen Aspekte der Musik am Rundfunk*, Cologne: Westdeutscher Verlag, 1959.

381 SIMMEL, GEORG, *Die Probleme der Geschichtsphilosophie: Eine erkenntnistheoretische Studie*, Leipzig: Duncker & Humblot, 1892.

382 SIMMEL, GEORG, *Philosophie des Geldes*, Leipzig: Duncker & Humblot, 1900.

383 SIMMEL, GEORG, *Das Problem der historischen Zeit*, Berlin: Reuther & Reichard, 1916.

384 SIMMEL, GEORG, *Vom Wesen des historischen Verstehens*, Berlin: Mittler, 1918.

385 SPAEMANN, R., *Der Ursprung der Soziologie aus dem Geist der*

Restauration: Studien über L.G.A. de Bonald, Munich: Kösel, 1959.

386 SPEIER, HANS, *Social Order and the Risks of War: Papers in Political Sociology*, New York: W. Stewart, 1952.

387 SPIEGELBERG, HERBERT, *The Phenomenological Movement: A Historical Introduction*, 2 vols, The Hague: Martinus Nijhoff, 1960.

388 SOROKIN, PITIRIM A., *Socio-cultural Causality, Space, Time: A Study of Referential Principles of Sociology and Social Science*, Durham, North Carolina: Duke University Press, 1943.

389 SPENCER, HERBERT, *The Study of Sociology*, Ann Arbor Paperbacks, Ann Arbor: University of Michigan Press, 1961.

390 SPRANGER, EDUARD, *Das humanistische und das politische Bildungsideal im heutigen Deutschland*, Berlin: Mittler, 1916.

391 SPRANGER, EDUARD, *Der Sinn der Voraussetzungslosigkeit in den Geisteswissenschaften*, Berlin: Walter de Gruyter, 1929.

392 STAUDE, JOHN RAPHAEL, *Max Scheler: An Intellectual Portrait*, New York: Free Press, 1967.

393 STEGER, H. A., *Die Universitäten in der gesellschaftlichen Entwicklung Latein-Amerikas*, 2 vols, Gütersloh: Bertelsmann, 1967.

394 STEIN, MAURICE and VIDICH, ARTHUR (eds), *Sociology on Trial*, Englewood Cliffs, New Jersey: Prentice-Hall, 1963.

395 STEINER, F., *Taboo*, London: Cohen & West, 1956.

396 STERN, BERNHARD JOSEPH, *Social Factors in Medical Progress*, New York: Columbia University Press, and London: P. S. King, 1927.

397 STORER, NORMAN, *The Social System of Science*, New York: Holt, Rinehart & Winston, 1966.

398 SZENDE, PAUL, *Verhüllung und Enthüllung*, Leipzig: Cl. Hirschfeld, 1922.

399 TAWNEY, RICHARD HENRY, *Religion and the Rise of Capitalism*, New York: Harcourt, Brace & Company, 1926.

400 TAYLOR, STANLEY, *Conceptions of Institutions and the Theory of Knowledge*, New York: Bookman Associates, 1956.

401 TIRYAKIAN, E. A., *Sociologism and Existentialism*, Englewood Cliffs, New Jersey: Prentice-Hall, 1962.

402 TOPAZIO, VIRGIL W., *D'Holbach's Moral Philosophy, Its Background and Development*, Geneva: Institut et Musée Voltaire, 1956.

403 TOPITSCH, ERNST, *Vom Ursprung und Ende der Metaphysik*, Vienna: Springer, 1958.

404 TOPITSCH, ERNST, *Die Freiheit der Wissenschaft und der Politische Auftrag der Universität*, Neuwied: Luchterhand Verlag, 1968.

405 TRILLING, LIONEL, *Freud and the Crisis of Our Culture*, Boston: Beacon Press, 1955.

406 TROELTSCH, ERNST, *Der Historismus und seine Probleme, Gesammelte Werke*, vol. III, Tübingen: J. C. B. Mohr, 1922.

407 TROELTSCH, ERNST, *Der Historismus und seine Überwindung*, Berlin: R. Heise, 1924.

408 TROELTSCH, ERNST, *The Social Teachings of the Christian Churches* (trans. by Olive Wyon), 2 vols, New York: Macmillan, 1931.

409 VAIHINGER, HANS, *The Philosophy of 'As If'* (trans. by C. K. Ogden), London: Kegan Paul, Trench, Trubner, 1924.

410 VEBLEN, THORSTEIN, *The Higher Learning in America: A Memorandum on the Conduct of Universities by Businessmen*, New York: B. W. Huebsch, 1918.

411 WARYNSKI, STANISLAW, *Die Wissenschaft von der Gesellschaft: Umriss einer Methodenlehre der dialektischen Soziologie* (trans. by Kazimierz Malecki), Berne: A. Francke, 1944.

412 WEBER, ALFRED, *Ideen zur Staats- und Kultursoziologie*, Karlsruhe: G. Braun, 1927.

413 WEBER, ALFRED, *Kulturgeschichte als Kultursoziologie*, Leiden: A. W. Sijthoff's Uitgeversmaatschappij, 1935.

414 WEBER, ALFRED, *Prinzipien der Geschichts- und Kultursoziologie*, Munich: R. Piper, 1951.

415 WEBER, MAX, *Gesammelte Aufsätze zur Religionssoziologie*, 3 vols, Tübingen: J. C. B. Mohr, 1920–1.

416 WEBER, MAX, *Gesammelte Aufsätze zur Wissenschaftslehre*, Tübingen: J. C. B. Mohr, 1922.

417 WEBER, MAX, *The Protestant Ethic and the Spirit of Capitalism* (trans. by Talcott Parsons), London: George Allen & Unwin, 1930, and New York: Charles Scribner, 1958.

418 WEBER, MAX, *The Hindu Social System* (trans. by Hans H. Gerth and Don Martindale), Chicago: Free Press, 1950.

419 WEBER, MAX *The Religion of China: Confucianism and Taoism* (trans. by Hans H. Gerth), Chicago: Free Press, 1951.

420 WEBER, MAX, *Ancient Judaism* (trans. and ed. by Hans H. Gerth and Don Martindale), Chicago: Free Press, 1952.

421 WEBER, MAX, *The Rational and Social Foundations of Music* (trans. and ed. by D. Martindale, J. Riedel and G. Neuwirth), Carbondale: Southern Illinois University Press, 1958.

422 WEIL, HANS, *Die Entstehung des deutschen Bildungsprinzips*, Bonn: F. Cohen, 1930.

423 WESTFALL, RICHARD S., *Science and Religion in Seventeenth Century England*, New Haven: Yale University Press, 1958.

424 WETTER, G. A., *Dialectical Materialism: A Historical and Systematic Survey of Philosophy in the Soviet Union* (trans. by P. Heath from the 4th German edition), London: Routledge & Kegan Paul, 1958.

425 WIESE, LEOPOLD VON, *Das Soziale im Leben und Denken*, Cologne/Opladen: Westdeutscher Verlag, 1956.

426 WILLENER, ALFRED, *Images de la société et classes sociales: une étude de la perception et des représentations des différences sociales*, Berne: Imprimerie Stämpfli, 1957.

427 WINDELBAND, WILHELM, *Die Erneuerung des Hegelianismus*, Heidelberg: C. Winter, 1910.

428 WISH, H., *The American Historian: A Social-Intellectual History of the Writing of the American Past*, New York: Oxford University Press, 1960.

429 ZIMAN, JOHN M., *Public Knowledge: An Essay Concerning the Social Dimension of Science*, Cambridge, Massachusetts: Harvard University Press, 1968.

430 ZNANIECKI, FLORIAN, *The Cultural Sciences: Their Origin and Development*, Urbana: University of Illinois Press, 1952.

Articles, chapters, papers, and reviews concerning the sociology of knowledge

431 ADLER, FRANZ, 'A quantitative study in the sociology of knowledge', *American Sociological Review*, vol. 19, no. 1 (February, 1954), pp. 42–8. Reprinted in REMMLING, GUNTER W. (ed.), *Towards the Sociology of Knowledge*, pp. 317–28 (see 184).

432 ADLER, FRANZ, 'The sociology of knowledge since 1918', *Midwest Sociologist*, vol. VII, no. 1 (Spring, 1955), pp. 3–12.

433 ADLER, FRANZ, 'The range of sociology of knowledge', in BECKER, HOWARD and BOSKOFF, ALVIN (eds), *Modern Sociological Theory in Continuity and Change*, New York: Dryden Press, 1957, pp. 398–423.

434 ALDER, MAX, 'Soziologie und Erkenntniskritik', *Jahrbuch für Soziologie*, vol. I (1925), pp. 4–34.

435 ADORNO, THEODOR W., 'Das Bewusstsein der Wissenssoziologie', in ADORNO, THEODOR W., *Prismen: Kulturkritik und Gesellschaft*, Berlin and Frankfurt: Suhrkamp Verlag, 1955, pp. 32–50.

436 ALBERT, HANS, 'Zur Logik der Sozialwissenschaften: Die These der Seinsgebundenheit und die Methode der kritischen Prüfung', *European Journal of Sociology*, vol. V (1964), pp. 241–54.

437 ANDRZEJEWSKI, S., 'Are ideas social forces?', *American Sociological Review*, vol. 14 (December, 1949), pp. 758–64.

438 ANSBACHER, HEINZ L., 'The significance of the socio-economic status of the patients of Freud and of Adler', *American Journal of Psychotherapy*, vol. 13 (April, 1959), pp. 376–82.

439 ARON, RAYMOND, 'American society and its sociology', *American Behavioral Scientist*, vol. IV, no. 3 (November, 1960), pp. 33–4.

440 ASHMORE, JEROME, 'Three aspects of Weltanschauung', *Sociological Quarterly*, vol. 7, no. 2 (Spring, 1966), pp. 215–28.

441 BAAR, CARL, 'Max Weber and the process of social understanding', *Sociology and Social Research*, vol. 51, no. 3 (April, 1967), pp. 337–46.

442 BAHRDT, H. P., KRAUCH, H., and RITTEL, H., 'Die wissenschaftliche Arbeit in Gruppen', *Kölner Zeitschrift für Soziologie und Sozialpsychologie*, vol. 12, no. 1 (1960), pp. 1–40.

443 BARBER, BERNARD, 'Sociology of knowledge and science, 1945–1955', in ZETTERBERG, HANS L. (ed.), *Sociology in the United States of America: A Trend Report*, Paris: UNESCO, 1956.

444 BART, PAULINE, 'The role of the sociologist on public issues: an exercise in the sociology of knowledge', *American Sociologist*, vol. 5, no. 4 (November, 1970), pp. 339–44.

445 BASTIDE, ROGER, 'Les cadres sociaux de l'anthropologie culturelle américaine', *Cahiers Internationaux de Sociologie*, vol. 26, no. 1 (1959), pp. 15–26.

446 BECK, LEWIS W., 'Psychology and the norms of knowledge', *Philosophy and Phenomenological Research*, vol. 14, no. 4 (June, 1954), pp. 494–506.

447 BECKER, HOWARD, 'Befuddled Germany: a glimpse of Max Scheler', *American Sociological Review*, vol. VIII, no. 2 (April, 1943), pp. 207–11.

448 BECKER, HOWARD and DAHLKE, HELMUT OTTO, 'Max Scheler's sociology of knowledge', *Philosophy and Phenomenological Research*, vol. II, no. 3 (March, 1942), pp. 310–22. Reprinted in REMMLING, GUNTER W. (ed.), *Towards the Sociology of Knowledge*, pp. 202–14 (see 184).

449 BEN-DAVID, JOSEPH, 'Scientific productivity and academic organization in nineteenth century medicine', *American Sociological Review*, vol. 25, no. 6 (December, 1960), pp. 828–43.

450 BEN-DAVID, JOSEPH and COLLINS, RANDALL, 'Social factors in the origins of a new science: the case of psychology', *American Sociological Review*, vol. 31, no. 4 (August, 1966), pp. 451–65.

451 BENJAMIN, WALTER, 'Zum gegenwärtigen gesellschaftlichen Standort des französischen Schriftstellers', *Zeitschrift für Sozialforschung*, vol. 3 (1934), pp. 54–77.

452 BENJAMIN, WALTER, 'Probleme der Sprachsoziologie', *Zeitschrift für Sozialforschung*, vol. 4 (1935), pp. 248–68.

453 BERGER, BRIGITTE, 'Vilfredo Pareto and the sociology of knowledge', *Social Research*, vol. 34, no. 2 (Summer, 1967), pp. 265–81.

454 BERGER, PETER L., 'Towards a sociological understanding of psychoanalysis', *Social Research*, vol. 32, no. 1 (Spring, 1965), pp. 26–41.

455 BERGER, PETER L., 'Identity as a problem in the sociology of knowledge', *European Journal of Sociology*, vol. 7, no. 1 (1966), pp. 105–15. Reprinted in REMMLING, GUNTER W. (ed.), *Towards the Sociology of Knowledge*, pp. 273–84 (see 184).

456 BERGER, PETER L., 'Zur Soziologie kognitiver Minderheiten', *Internationale Dialog Zeitschrift*, vol. 2, no. 2 (April, 1969), pp. 127–32.

457 BERGER, PETER and KELLNER, HANSFRIED, 'Marriage and the construction of reality: an exercise in the microsociology of knowledge', in DREITZEL, HANS PETER (ed.), *Recent Sociology No. 2: Patterns of Communicative Behavior*, New York: Macmillan, 1970, pp. 50–72.

458 BERGER, PETER and LUCKMANN, THOMAS, 'Sociology of religion and sociology of knowledge', *Sociology and Social Research*, vol. 47, no. 4 (July, 1963), pp. 417–27.

459 BERGER, PETER L. and PULLBERG, STANLEY, 'Reification and the sociological critique of consciousness', *History and Theory*, vol. IV, no. 2 (1965), pp. 196–211.

460 BERGMANN, WILM, 'Zur wissenssoziologischen Analyse kirchlicher Phänomene', *Internationale Dialog Zeitschrift*, vol. 2, no. 2 (April, 1969), pp. 156–62.

461 BIANCA, OMERO, 'Intorno alla sociologia della conoscenza', *Quaderni di Sociologia*, vol. 3, no. 2 (1952), pp. 103–16.

462 BINTON, JAMES, 'Effects of newspaper reading on knowledge and attitude', *Journalism Quarterly*, vol. 38, no. 2 (Spring, 1961), pp. 187–95.

463 BLUM, FRED H., 'Some contributions of dynamic psychology to the sociology of knowledge', *Transactions of the Fourth World Congress of Sociology*, vol. IV, Louvain: International Sociological Association, 1959, pp. 67ff.

464 BOAS, MARIE, 'Quelques aspects sociaux de la chimie au xviiie siècle',

Revue D'Histoire des Sciences, vol. 10, no. 2 (April–June, 1957), pp. 132–47.

465 BORKENAU, FRANZ, 'Zur Soziologie des mechanistischen Weltbildes', *Zeitschrift für Sozialforschung*, vol. 1 (1932), pp. 311–35.

466 BOTTOMORE, T. B., 'Some reflections on the sociology of knowledge', *British Journal of Sociology*, vol. 7, no. 1 (March, 1956), pp. 52–8.

467 BOULDING, KENNETH E., 'The public image and the sociology of knowledge', in BOULDING, KENNETH E., *The Image: Knowledge in Life and Society*, Ann Arbor: University of Michigan Press, 1961, pp. 64–81.

468 BOULDING, KENNETH E., 'Economics of knowledge and the knowledge of economics', *American Economic Review; Papers and Proceedings*, vol. 56, no. 1 (May, 1966), pp. 1–13.

469 BOURDIERE, PIERRE and PASSERON, JEAN-CLAUDE, 'Sociology and philosophy in France since 1945: death and resurrection of a philosophy without subject', *Social Research*, vol. 34, no. 1 (Spring, 1967), pp. 162–212.

470 BRANDE, LEE, 'Die Verstehende Soziologie: a new look at an old problem', *Sociology and Social Research*, vol. 50, no. 2 (January, 1966), pp. 230–5.

471 BREYSIG, KURT, 'Das geistige Schaffen als Gegenstand der Gesellschaftslehre', in *Verhandlungen des siebenten deutschen Soziologentages 1930, Berlin*, Tübingen: J. C. B. Mohr, 1931, pp. 156–69.

472 CASSIRER, ERNST, ' "Mind" and "Life" in contemporary philosophy', in *The Philosophy of Ernst Cassirer* (ed. by Paul Schilpp), New York: Tudor, 1949, pp. 855–80.

473 CAZENEUVE, JEAN and NAMER, GERARD, 'Sociologie de la connaissance', *L'Année Sociologique*, vol. 19 (1968), pp. 253–66.

474 CHACON, VAMIREH, 'Sociologia marxista e sociologia do conhecimento', *Sociologia*, vol. 20, no. 2 (May, 1958), pp. 248–54.

475 CHALL, LEO P., 'The sociology of knowledge', in ROUCEK, JOSEPH S. (ed.), *Contemporary Sociology*, New York: Philosophical Library, 1958, pp. 286–303.

476 CHALMERS, DAVID, 'From robber barons to industrial statesmen: standard oil and the business historians', *American Journal of Economics and Sociology*, vol. 20, no. 1 (October, 1960), pp. 47–58.

477 CHANCE, ERIKA, ARNOLD, JACK and TYRRELL, SYBIL, 'Professional background and themes used in clinical case description', *Human Relations*, vol. XV, no. 1 (February, 1962), pp. 53–61.

478 CHAUDHURY, P. J., 'Knowledge of the empirical world', *Philosophy and Phenomenological Research*, vol. 13, no. 4 (June, 1953), pp. 542–5.

479 CHILD, ARTHUR, 'The problem of imputation in the sociology of knowledge', *Ethics*, vol. 51, no. 2 (January, 1941), pp. 200–19.

480 CHILD, ARTHUR, 'The theoretical possibility of the sociology of knowledge', *Ethics*, vol. 51, no. 4 (July, 1941), pp. 392–418. Reprinted in REMMLING, GUNTER W. (ed.), *Towards the Sociology of Knowledge*, pp. 81–101 (see 184).

481 CHILD, ARTHUR, 'The existential determination of thought', *Ethics*, vol. 52, no. 2 (January, 1942), pp. 153–85.

482 CHILD, ARTHUR, 'The problem of imputation resolved', *Ethics*, vol. 54, no. 2 (January, 1944), pp. 96–109.

483 CHILD, ARTHUR, 'On the theory of the categories', *Philosophy and Phenomenological Research*, vol. VII (December, 1946), pp. 316–335.

484 CHILD, ARTHUR, 'The problem of truth in the sociology of knowledge', *Ethics*, vol. 58, no. 1 (October, 1947), pp. 18–34.

485 CHILD, JOHN, 'British management thought as a case study within the sociology of knowledge', *Sociological Review*, new series, vol. 16 (July, 1968), pp. 217–39.

486 CLARK, TERRY N., KORNBLUM, WILLIAM, BLOOM, HAROLD and TOBIAS, SUSAN, 'Discipline, method, community structure, and decision-making: the role and limitations of the sociology of knowledge', *American Sociologist*, vol. 3, no. 3 (August, 1968), pp. 214–17.

487 CLINARD, MARSHALL B. and ELDER, JOSEPH W., 'Sociology in India: a study in the sociology of knowledge', *American Sociological Review*, vol. 30, no. 4 (August, 1965), pp. 581–7.

488 COLE, STEPHEN and COLE, JONATHAN R., 'Scientific output and recognition: a study in the operation of the reward system in science', *American Sociological Review*, vol. 32, no. 3 (June, 1967), pp. 377–90.

489 CONSENTINI, FRANCESCO, 'Die "Erkenntnissoziologie" auf dem Kongress zu Heidelberg', *Verhandlungen des 4. deutschen Soziologentages 1924 in Heidelberg*, Tübingen: J. C. B. Mohr, 1925, pp. 238ff.

490 COOLEY, CHARLES HORTON, 'The roots of social knowledge', in COOLEY, CHARLES HORTON, *Sociological Theory and Social Research* (with an introduction and notes by Robert Cooley Angell), New York: H. Holt, 1930, pp. 287–312.

491 COSER, LEWIS A. and ROSENBERG, BERNARD, 'Sociology of knowledge', in COSER, LEWIS A. and ROSENBERG, BERNARD, *Sociological Theory*, New York: Macmillan, 1964, pp. 667–84.

492 CRANE, DIANA, 'Scientists at major and minor universities: a study of productivity and recognition', *American Sociological Review*, vol. 30, no. 5 (October, 1965), pp. 699–714.

493 CRANE, DIANA, 'The gatekeepers of science: some factors affecting the selection of articles for scientific journals', *American Sociologist*, vol. 2, no. 4 (November, 1967), pp. 195–201.

494 CRITTENDEN, BRIAN S., 'Durkheim: sociology of knowledge and educational theory', *Studies in Philosophy and Education*, vol. IV, no. 2 (Fall, 1965), pp. 207–54.

495 CURRIE, IAN D., 'The Sapir-Whorf hypothesis: A problem in the sociology of knowledge', *Berkeley Journal of Sociology*, vol. 11, no. 1 (1966), pp. 14–31.

496 CURTIS, JAMES E. and PETRAS, JOHN W., 'Community power, power studies, and the sociology of knowledge', *Human Organization*, vol. 29 (Fall, 1970), pp. 204–18.

497 CURTIUS, ERNST ROBERT, 'Die Soziologie und ihre Grenzen', *Neue Schweizer Rundschau*, vol. 22 (October, 1929), pp. 727–36.

498 CUVILLIER, ARMAND, 'Sociologie de la connaissance et idéologie

économique', *Cahiers Internationaux de Sociologie*, vol. 11 (1951), pp. 80–111.

499 DAHLKE, H. OTTO, 'The sociology of knowledge', in BARNES, HARRY ELMER, BECKER, HOWARD and BECKER, FRANCES B. (eds), *Contemporary Social Theory*, New York: D. Appleton-Century, 1940, pp. 64–87.

500 DANZIGER, K., 'Ideology and utopia in South Africa: A methodological contribution to the sociology of knowledge', *British Journal of Sociology*, vol. 14, no. 1 (March, 1963), pp. 59–76. Reprinted in REMMLING, GUNTER W. (ed.), *Towards the Sociology of Knowledge*, pp. 360–78 (see 184).

501 DEGRÉ, GÉRARD L., 'The sociology of knowledge and the problem of truth', *Journal of the History of Ideas*, vol. II, no. 1 (January, 1941), pp. 110–15.

502 DEUTSCHER, IRWIN, 'Looking backward: case studies on the progress of methodology in sociological research', *American Sociologist*, vol. 4, no. 1 (February, 1969), pp. 35–41.

503 DEVEREUX, GEORGE, 'Cultural thought models in primitive and modern psychiatric theories', *Psychiatry*, vol. 21, no. 4 (November, 1958), pp. 359–74.

504 DREITZEL, HANS PETER, 'Wissenssoziologie', *Pädagogisches Lexikon* (ed. by Hans H. Groothoff and Martin Stallmann), Stuttgart: Kreuz-Verlag, 1961.

505 DREITZEL, HANS PETER, 'Selbstbildnis und Gesellschaftsbild: Wissenssoziologische Überlegungen zum Image-Begriff', *European Journal of Sociology*, vol. III, no. 2 (1962), pp. 181–228.

506 DUPRÉEL, EUGÈNE, 'La sociologie et les problèmes de la connaissance', *Revue de l'Institut de Sociologie* (March–May, 1925), pp. 161–83.

507 DURKHEIM, ÉMILE, 'Sociologie religieuse et théorie de la connaissance', *Revue de Métaphysique et de Morale*, vol. 17, no. 6 (November, 1909), pp. 733–58.

508 DURKHEIM, ÉMILE and BOUGLÉ, CÉLESTIN, 'Les conditions sociologiques de la connaissance', *L'Année Sociologique*, vol. 11, no. 1 (1906–9), pp. 41–8.

509 DURKHEIM, ÉMILE and MAUSS, MARCEL, 'De quelques formes primitives de classification: Contribution à l'étude des représentations collectives', *L'Année Sociologique*, vol. 6, no. 1 (1901–2), pp. 1–72.

510 EISERMANN, GOTTFRIED, 'Die soziologischen Beziehungen der Tiefenpsychologie', in *Gegenwartsprobleme der Soziologie*, Potsdam: Akademische Verlagsgesellschaft Athenaion, 1949, pp. 203–30.

511 EISERMANN, GOTTFRIED, 'La sociologie de la connaissance et la théorie économique', *Cahiers Internationaux de Sociologie*, vol. 28, no. 1 (January–June, 1955), pp. 17–34.

512 EISERMANN, GOTTFRIED, 'Vilfredo Pareto als Wissenssoziologe', *Kyklos*, vol. 15, no. 2 (1962), pp. 427–64.

513 EISERMANN, GOTTFRIED, 'Wissenssoziologie', in EISERMANN, GOTTFRIED (ed.), *Die Lehre von der Gesellschaft*, Stuttgart: F. Enke Verlag, 1969, pp. 481–535.

514 ELEUTHEROPULOS, A., 'Sozialpsychologie und Wissenssoziologie',

Zeitschrift für Völkerpsychologie und Soziologie, vol. 3, no. 2 (1927), pp. 197–215.

515 ELLIS, J. and DAVIES, R. W., 'The crisis in Soviet linguistics', *Soviet Studies*, vol. 2, no. 3 (1951), pp. 209–64.

516 ERASMUS, C. J., 'Obviating the functions of functionalism', *Social Forces*, vol. 45 (March, 1967), pp. 319–28.

517 FALK, WERNER, 'The sociological interpretation of political ideas', *Sociological Review*, vol. 26, no. 3 (July, 1934), pp. 268–87.

518 FARBER, MARVIN, 'Max Scheler on the place of man in the cosmos', *Philosophy and Phenomenological Research*, vol. 14, no. 3 (March, 1954), pp. 393–9.

519 FAUL, ERWIN, 'Wissenssoziologie', in WEBER, ALFRED (ed.), *Einführung in die Soziologie*, Munich: R. Piper, 1955, pp. 358–90.

520 FECHNER, ERICH, 'Der Begriff des kapitalistischen Geistes und das Schelersche Gesetz vom Zusammenhang der historischen Wirkfaktoren', *Archiv für Sozialwissenschaft und Sozialpolitik*, vol. LXIII (May, 1930), pp. 93–120.

521 FEJTO, F., 'Georges Lukács entre le dogmatisme et le revisionisme', *Esprit*, vol. XXIX, no. 2 (February, 1961), pp. 249–60.

522 FEUER, LEWIS S., 'The sociology of philosophical ideas', *Pacific Sociological Review*, vol. 1, no. 2 (1958), pp. 77–80.

523 FILIASI, CARCANO PAOLO, 'Il contributo della sociologia della conoscenza all'analisi della crisi', in *Scritti di sociologia e politica in onore di Luigi Sturzo*, vol. 2, Bologna: Nicola Zanichelli, 1953, pp. 193–206.

524 FISCHER, GEORGE, 'Current Soviet work in sociology: a note on the sociology of knowledge', *American Sociologist*, vol. 1, no. 3 (May, 1966), pp. 127–32.

525 FONTAINE, WILLIAM T., ' "Social determination" in the writings of Negro scholars', *American Journal of Sociology*, vol. 49, no. 4 (January, 1944), pp. 302–15.

526 FOYER CULTUREL INTERNATIONAL DE CERISY-LA-SALLE, 'Colloque sur la sociologie de la connaissance', *Revue Française de Sociologie*, vol. II, no. 4 (1961), pp. 321–2.

527 FRANK, PHILIPP, 'The logical and sociological aspects of science', *Proceedings of the American Academy of Arts and Sciences*, vol. 80, no. 1 (1951), pp. 16–30.

528 FRANKLIN, RAYMOND, 'The French socio-economic environment in the eighteenth century and its relation to the physiocrats', *American Journal of Economics and Sociology*, vol. XXI, no. 3 (July, 1962), pp. 299–306.

529 FREYER, HANS, 'Ammerkungen über das Problem der Ideologie und über Wissenssoziologie', in FREYER, HANS, *Soziologie als Wirklichkeitswissenschaft: Logische Grundlegung des Systems der Soziologie*, Leipzig and Berlin: B. G. Teubner, 1930.

530 FRIEDENBERG, EDGAR Z., 'Truth: upper, middle and lower', *Commentary*, vol. 30, no. 6 (1960), pp. 516–23.

531 FROMM, ERICH, 'Die gesellschaftliche Bedingtheit der psychoanalytischen Therapie', *Zeitschrift für Sozialforschung*, vol. 4 (1935), pp. 365–96.

532 GARFINKEL, HAROLD, 'Common sense knowledge of social structures: the documentary method of interpretation in lay and professional fact finding', in SCHER, JORDAN M. (ed.), *Theories of the Mind*, New York: Free Press, 1962, pp. 689–712. Reprinted in GARFINKEL, HAROLD, *Studies in Ethnomethodology*, Englewood Cliffs, New Jersey: Prentice-Hall, 1967, pp. 76–103.

533 GEIGER, THEODOR, 'Bemerkungen zur Soziologie des Denkens', *Archiv für Rechts- und Sozialphilosophie*, vol. 45, no. 1 (1959), pp. 22–53.

534 GENOVESE, EUGENE D., 'Influence of the Black Power movement on historical scholarship: reflections of a white historian', *Daedalus*, vol. 99, no. 2 (1970), pp. 473–94.

535 GHURZE, G. S., 'Vidyās: Indian contribution to sociology of knowledge', *Sociological Bulletin*, vol. 6, no. 2 (September, 1957), pp. 29–70.

536 GHURZE, G. S., 'Aristotle and Bacon: pre-Comtian occidental contribution to sociology of knowledge', *Sociological Bulletin*, vol. 6, no. 2 (September, 1957), pp. 71–82.

537 GLASER, BARNEY and STRAUSS, ANSELM, 'Discovery of substantive theory: a basic strategy underlying qualitative research', *American Behavioral Scientist*, vol. VIII, no. 6 (February, 1965), pp. 5–12.

538 GOLDSCHMIDT, W., 'Ethics and the structure of society: an ethnological contribution to the sociology of knowledge', *American Anthropologist*, vol. 54, no. 4 (1951), pp. 506–24.

539 GREINACHER, NORBERT, 'Wissenssoziologie und Religion', *Internationale Dialog Zeitschrift*, vol. 2, no. 2 (April, 1969), pp. 97–101.

540 GREINACHER, NORBERT, 'Das Weltverständnis der katholischen Theologie in wissenssoziologischer Sicht', *Internationale Dialog Zeitschrift*, vol. 2, no. 2 (April, 1969), pp. 113–26.

541 GROSSMANN, HENRYK, 'Die gesellschaftlichen Grundlagen der mechanistischen Philosophie und die Manufaktur', *Zeitschrift für Sozialforschung*, vol. 4 (1935), pp. 161–229.

542 GRÜNWALD, ERNST, 'Systematic analyses' (trans. by Rainer Koehne), in CURTIS, JAMES E. and PETRAS, JOHN W. (eds), *The Sociology of Knowledge*, pp. 187–236 (see 166).

543 GRÜNWALD, ERNST, 'The sociology of knowledge and epistemology' (trans. by Rainer Koehne), in CURTIS, JAMES E. and PETRAS, JOHN W. (eds), *The Sociology of Knowledge*, pp. 237–43 (see 166).

544 GURVITCH, GEORGES, 'Sociologie de la connaissance et psychologie collective', *L'Année Sociologique*, vol. I (1948), pp. 463–86.

545 GURVITCH, GEORGES, 'Structures sociales et systèmes de connaissances', in *La notion de structure et structure de la connaissance*, Paris: A. Michel, 1957, pp. 291–342.

546 GURVITCH, GEORGES, 'Le problème de la sociologie de la connaissance', *Revue Philosophique*, vol. 147, no. 4 (1957), pp. 494–502.

547 GURVITCH, GEORGES, 'Wissenssoziologie', in EISERMANN, G. (ed.), *Die Lehre von der Gesellschaft: Ein Lehrbuch der Soziologie*, Stuttgart: F. Enke Verlag, 1958, pp. 408–51.

548 GURVITCH, GEORGES, 'Les cadres sociaux de la connaissance soci-

ologique', *Cahiers Internationaux de Sociologie*, vol. 26 (1959), pp. 165–72.

549 GURVITCH, GEORGES, 'Problèmes de la sociologie de la connaissance', in GURVITCH, G., *Traité de sociologie*, vol. 2, Paris: Presses Universitaires de France, 1960, pp. 103–36.

550 GURWITSCH, ARON, 'The common-sense world as social reality: a discourse on Alfred Schutz', *Social Research*, vol. 29, no. 1 (Spring, 1962), pp. 50–72.

551 HABER, A., 'Cognitive lag', *Social Research*, vol. 32, no. 1 (Spring, 1965), pp. 42–70.

552 HARTUNG, FRANK E., 'Problems of the sociology of knowledge', *Philosophy of Science*, vol. 19, no. 1 (January, 1952), pp. 17–32.

553 HASHAGEN, JUSTUS, 'Ausserwissenschaftliche Einflüsse auf die neuere Geschichtswissenschaft', in *Versuche zu einer Soziologie des Wissens*, pp. 233–55 (see 188).

554 HEBERLE, RUDOLPH, 'Alfred Weber's theory of historical sociology', *Sociology and Social Research*, vol. 44, no. 6 (July–August, 1960), pp. 387–93.

555 HEGENBERG, LEONIDAS, 'Duas posicoes em face da sociologia do conhecimento', *Sociologia*, vol. 19, no. 1 (February, 1957), pp. 36–43.

556 HEGENBERG, LEONIDAS, 'História das idéias e sociologia do conhecimento', *Sociologia*, vol. 19, no. 2 (May, 1957), pp. 133–8.

557 HEGENBERG, LEONIDAS, 'A razão na ciència e a sociologia do conhecimento', *Sociologia*, vol. 19, no. 3 (August, 1957), pp. 204–9.

558 HERRERO, CLAIR M. T. and VICTOROFF, D., 'Sociologie de la connaissance', *L'Année Sociologique*, vol. 16 (1965), pp. 132–6.

559 HILDAHL, SPENCER H., 'A note on a note on the sociology of knowledge', *Sociological Quarterly*, vol. 11, no. 3 (Summer, 1970), pp. 405–15.

560 HINSHAW, VIRGIL G., JR, 'The pragmatist theory of truth', *Philosophy of Science*, vol. 11, no. 2 (April, 1944), pp. 82–92.

561 HINSHAW, VIRGIL G., JR, 'Epistemological relativism and the sociology of knowledge', *Philosophy of Science*, vol. 15, no. 1 (January, 1948), pp. 4–10.

562 HODGES, DONALD CLARK, 'The class significance of ethical traditions', *American Journal of Economics and Sociology*, vol. XX, no. 3 (April, 1961), pp. 241–53.

563 HONIGSHEIM, PAUL, 'Soziologie der Scholastik', in *Versuche zu einer Soziologie des Wissens*, pp. 302–7 (see 188).

564 HONIGSHEIM, PAUL, 'Soziologie des realistischen und des nominalistischen Denkens', in *Versuche zu einer Soziologie des Wissens*, pp. 308–22 (see 188).

565 HONIGSHEIM, PAUL, 'Soziologie der Mystik', in *Versuche zu einer Soziologie des Wissens*, pp. 323–46 (see 188).

566 HONIGSHEIM, PAUL, 'Max Scheler als Sozialphilosoph', *Kölner Vierteljahrshefte für Soziologie und Sozialwissenschaften*, vol. VIII, no. 3 (1929), pp. 94–108.

567 HOROWITZ, IRVING L., 'Science, criticism, and the sociology of

knowledge', *Philosophy and Phenomenological Research*, vol. 21, no. 2 (December, 1960), pp. 173–86.

568 HOROWITZ, IRVING L., 'A formalization of the sociology of knowledge', *Behavioral Science*, vol. 9, no. 1 (January, 1964), pp. 45–55. Reprinted in HOROWITZ, IRVING L., *Professing Sociology: Studies in the Life Cycle of Social Science*, Chicago: Aldine, 1968, pp. 65–79.

569 HUTCHISON, T. W., 'Insularity and cosmopolitanism in economic ideas, 1870–1914', *American Economic Review*, vol. 45, no. 1 (May, 1955), pp. 1–16.

570 IGGERS, GEORG G., 'Elements of a sociology of ideas in the Saint-Simonian philosophy of history', *Sociological Quarterly*, vol. 1, no. 4 (October, 1960), pp. 217–25. Reprinted in REMMLING, GUNTER W. (ed.), *Towards the Sociology of Knowledge*, pp. 60–7 (see 184).

571 JERUSALEM, WILHELM J., 'Soziologie des Erkennens', *Die Zukunft*, vol. 67 (May, 1909), pp. 236–46.

572 JERUSALEM, WILHELM J., 'Soziologie des Erkennens. (Bemerkungen zu Max Schelers Aufsatz "Die positivistische Geschichtsphilosophie des Wissens und die Aufgabe einer Soziologie der Erkenntnis")', *Kölner Vierteljahrshefte für Soziologie und Sozialwissenschaften*, vol. I, no. 3 (1921), pp. 28–34.

573 JERUSALEM, WILHELM J., 'Die soziologische Bedingtheit des Denkens und der Denkformen', in *Versuche zu einer Soziologie des Wissens*, pp. 182–207 (see 188).

574 JORDAN, ROBERT WELSH, 'Husserl's phenomenology as an historical science', *Social Research*, vol. 35, no. 2 (Summer, 1968), pp. 245–59.

575 KHORUTS, L. E., 'A critique of the idealistic conception of ideology in the "sociology of knowledge" ', *Soviet Review*, vol. 6, no. 1 (Spring, 1965), pp. 60–6.

576 KILZER, ERNEST and ROSS, EVA, 'The sociology of knowledge', *American Catholic Sociological Review*, vol. 14, no. 4 (1953), pp. 230–3.

577 KÖNIG, RENÉ, 'Zur Soziologie der zwanziger Jahre', in REINISCH, LEONHARD (ed.), *Die Zeit ohne Eigenschaften: Eine Bilanz der zwanziger Jahre*, Stuttgart: Kohlhammer, 1961.

578 KRACAUER, S., 'Die Gruppe als Ideenträger', *Archiv für Sozialwissenschaft und Sozialpolitik*, vol. 19 (1922), pp. 594–622.

579 KRIESBERG, LOUIS, 'The retail furrier: concepts of security and success', *American Journal of Sociology*, vol. LVII, no. 5 (March, 1952), pp. 478–85.

580 KRUGER, MARLIS, 'Sociology of knowledge and social theory', *Berkeley Journal of Sociology*, vol. 14 (1969), pp. 152–63.

581 LANDSBERG, PAUL LUDWIG, 'Zur Soziologie der Erkenntnistheorie', *Schmollers Jahrbuch für Gesetzgebung, Verwaltung und Volkswirtschaft*, vol. 55, no. 2 (1931), pp. 772ff.

582 LAVINE, THELMA Z., 'Sociological analysis of cognitive norms', *Journal of Philosophy*, vol. 39 (June, 1942), pp. 342–56.

583 LAVINE, THELMA Z., 'Naturalism and the sociological analysis of

knowledge', in KRIKORIAN, YERVANT H. (ed.), *Naturalism and the Human Spirit*, New York: Columbia University Press, 1944, pp. 184ff.

584 LEFEBVRE, HENRI, 'Les cadres sociaux de la sociologie marxiste', *Cahiers Internationaux de Sociologie*, vol. 26 (1959), pp. 81–102.

585 LENK, KURT, 'Das tragische Bewusstsein in der deutschen Soziologie der zwanziger Jahre', *Frankfurter Hefte*, vol. XVIII (May, 1963), pp. 313–20.

586 LENK, KURT, 'Marx, Bernstein und die Wissenssoziologie', *Politische Vierteljahrsschrift*, vol. 6 (1965), pp. 132–44.

587 LIEBER, HANS-JOACHIM, 'Zur Problematik der Wissenssoziologie bei Max Scheler', *Philosophische Studien*, vol. I, no. 1 (1949), pp. 62–90.

588 LIEBER, HANS-JOACHIM, 'Wissenssoziologie', *Wörterbuch der Soziologie* (ed. by Wilhelm Bernsdorf and Friedrich Bülow), Stuttgart: F. Enke, 1955.

589 LIEBER, HANS-JOACHIM, 'Wissenssoziologie', in LIEBER, H.-J., *Philosophie, Soziologie, Gesellschaft*, Berlin: Walter de Gruyter, 1965, pp. 82–105.

590 LIEBER, HANS-JOACHIM and FURTH, PETER, 'Wissenssoziologie', *Handwörterbuch der Sozialwissenschaften* (ed. by E. von Beckerath), vol. 12, Stuttgart-Tübingen-Göttingen: G. Fischer, Mohr, Vandenhoeck & Ruprecht, 1965.

591 LIEBERMAN, LEONARD, 'The debate over race: a study in the sociology of knowledge', *Phylon*, vol. 29, no. 2 (Summer, 1968), pp. 127–41. Reprinted in *The Sociology of Sociology*, pp. 388–405 (see 363).

592 LIGHT, IVAN H., 'The social construction of uncertainty', *Berkeley Journal of Sociology*, vol. 14 (1969), pp. 189–99.

593 LINS, MARIO, 'The sociology of knowledge: aspects of its problematics', *Revue Internationale de Sociologie*, vol. 1, nos 2–3 (1958), pp. 3–10.

594 LUCHTENBERG, PAUL, 'Übertragungsformen des Wissens', in *Versuche zu einer Soziologie des Wissens*, pp. 151–81 (see 188).

595 LUKÁCS, GEORG, 'Théorie Léninienne de la connaissance et les problèmes de la philosophie moderne', in *Existentialisme ou Marxisme?*, Paris: Éditions Nagel, 1948.

596 MCKEE, JAMES B., 'Some observations on the self-consciousness of sociologists', *Ohio Valley Sociologist*, vol. XXXII (Summer, 1967), pp. 1–16. Reprinted in CURTIS, JAMES E. and PETRAS, JOHN W. (eds), *The Sociology of Knowledge*, pp. 531–44 (see 166).

597 MCKINNEY, JOHN C., 'George H. Mead and the philosophy of science', *Philosophy of Science*, vol. 22, no. 4 (October, 1955), pp. 264–71.

598 MCKINNEY, JOHN C., 'The contribution of George H. Mead to the sociology of knowledge', *Social Forces*, vol. 34, no. 2 (December, 1955), pp. 144–9.

599 MANDIC, OLEG, 'The Marxist school of sociology: what is sociology in a Marxist sense?', *Social Research*, vol. 34, no. 3 (Autumn, 1967), pp. 435–52.

600 MANIS, JEROME G., 'Some academic influences upon publication productivity', *Social Forces*, vol. 29 (March, 1951), pp. 267–72.

601 MANIS, JEROME G., 'The sociology of knowledge and community mental health research', *Social Problems*, vol. 15, no. 4 (Spring, 1968), pp. 488–501.

602 MAQUET, JACQUES J., 'Some anthropological contributions to the sociology of knowledge', *Social Sciences Information*, vol. I, no. 3 (October, 1962), pp. 5–20.

603 MARTIN, DAVID, 'The sociology of knowledge and the nature of social knowledge', *British Journal of Sociology*, vol. 19, no. 3 (September, 1968), pp. 334–42. Reprinted in REMMLING, GUNTER W. (ed.), *Towards the Sociology of Knowledge*, pp. 308–16 (see 184).

604 MATZNER, JUTTA, 'Der Begriff der Charaktermaske bei Karl Marx', *Soziale Welt*, vol. 15 (1964), pp. 130–9.

605 MAUCORPS, P.-H. and BASSOUL, RENÉ, 'Jeux de miroirs et sociologies de la connaissance d'autrui', *Cahiers Internationaux de Sociologie*, vol. XXXII (January–June, 1962), pp. 43–60.

606 MERTON, ROBERT K., 'Puritanism, pietism and science', *Sociological Review*, vol. 28, no. 1 (January, 1936), pp. 1–30.

607 MERTON, ROBERT K., 'The sociology of knowledge', *Isis*, vol. 27, no. 75 (November, 1937), pp. 493–503.

608 MERTON, ROBERT K., 'Science, technology and society in seventeenth century England', *Osiris*, vol. 4, no. 2 (1938), pp. 360–632.

609 MERTON, ROBERT K., Review of F. Znaniecki's 'The social role of the man of knowledge', *American Sociological Review*, vol. 6, no. 1 (February, 1941), pp. 111–15.

610 MERTON, ROBERT K., 'The sociology of knowledge', in GURVITCH, G. and MOORE, W. E. (eds), *Twentieth Century Sociology*, New York: Philosophical Library, 1945, pp. 366–405.

611 MERTON, ROBERT K., 'A paradigm for the study of the sociology of knowledge', in LAZARSFELD, PAUL F. and ROSENBERG, MORRIS (eds), *The Language of Social Research*, Chicago: Free Press, 1955, pp. 498–511.

612 MERTON, ROBERT K., 'Wissenssoziologie and mass communications research', in MERTON, ROBERT K., *Social Theory and Social Structure*, Chicago: Free Press, 1957, pp. 440–55.

613 MERTON, ROBERT K., 'The Sociology of Knowledge', in *Socia Theory and Social Structure*, pp. 456–588 (see 612).

614 MERTON, ROBERT K., 'Social conflict over styles of sociological work', in *Transactions of the Fourth World Congress of Sociology*, vol. III, Louvain: International Sociological Association, 1959, pp. 21–44. Reprinted in CURTIS, JAMES E. and PETRAS, JOHN W. (eds), *The Sociology of Knowledge*, pp. 507–30 (see 166).

615 MERTON, ROBERT K., 'Priorities in scientific discovery' in BARBER, B. and HIRSCH, W. (eds), *The Sociology of Science*, New York: Free Press, 1962.

616 MERTON, ROBERT K., 'Resistance to the systematic study of multiple discoveries in science', *European Journal of Sociology*, Vol. IV (1963), pp. 237–82.

617 MEYER, HOWARD N., 'Overcoming the White man's history', *Massachusetts Review*, vol. 7, no. 3 (Summer, 1966), pp. 569–78.

618 MILLIKAN, MAX F., 'Inquiry and policy: the relation of knowledge to action', in LERNER, DANIEL (ed.), *The Human Meaning of the Social Sciences*, New York: Meridian, 1959, pp. 158–80.

619 MILLS, C. WRIGHT, 'Methodological consequences of the sociology of knowledge', *American Journal of Sociology*, vol. 46, no. 3 (November, 1940), pp. 316–30.

620 MILLS, C. WRIGHT, 'On knowledge and power', *Dissent*, vol. II, no. 3 (Summer, 1955), pp. 201–12.

621 MITTENZWEY, KUNO, 'Zur Soziologie der psychoanalytischen Erkenntnis', in *Versuche zu einer Soziologie des Wissens*, pp. 365–75 (see 188).

622 MITZMAN, ARTHUR, 'Anti-progress: a study in the romantic roots of German sociology', *Social Research*, vol. 33, no. 1 (Spring, 1966), pp. 65–85.

623 MÜLLER-FRIENFELS, RICHARD, 'Die Wissensformen und die Gesellschaft', *Kölner Vierteljahrshefte für Soziologie und Sozialwissenschaften*, vol. VI (1925), pp. 190–4.

624 NASH, DENNISON, 'The ethnologist as stranger: an essay in the sociology of knowledge', *Southwestern Journal of Anthropology*, vol. XIX (Summer, 1963), pp. 149–67. Reprinted in CURTIS, JAMES E. and PETRAS, JOHN W. (eds), *The Sociology of Knowledge*, pp. 468–487 (see 166).

625 NASH, RONALD H., 'The structure of St Augustine's theory of knowledge', *Gordon Review*, vol. 8 (1964), pp. 25–34.

626 NATANSON, MAURICE, 'Alfred Schutz on social reality and social science', *Social Research*, vol. 35, no. 2 (Summer, 1968), pp. 217–44.

627 NETTLER, GWYNNE, 'A test for the sociology of knowledge', *American Sociological Review*, vol. 10, no. 3 (June, 1945), pp. 393–9.

628 NOTESTEIN, ROBERT B., 'William Graham Sumner: an essay in the sociology of knowledge', *American Journal of Economics and Sociology*, vol. 18, no. 4 (July, 1959), pp. 397–413.

629 ORTEGA Y GASSET, JOSÉ, 'Max Scheler', *Neue Schweizer Rundschau*, vol. XXXIV (October, 1928), pp. 725–9.

630 PALMORE, ERDMAN, 'Sociologists' class origins and political ideologies', *Sociology and Social Research*, vol. 47, no. 1 (October, 1962), pp. 45–50.

631 PARK, ROBERT E., 'News as a form of knowledge: a chapter in the sociology of knowledge', *American Journal of Sociology*, vol. 45, no. 5 (March, 1940), pp. 669–86.

632 PARSONS, TALCOTT, Review of 'Alexander von Schelting's *Max Webers Wissenschaftslehre*', *American Sociological Review*, vol. 1, no. 4 (August, 1936), pp. 675–81.

633 PARSONS, TALCOTT, 'The role of ideas in social action', *American Sociological Review*, vol. 3, no. 5 (October, 1938), pp. 652–64.

634 PARSONS, TALCOTT, 'An approach to the sociology of knowledge', in *Transactions of the Fourth World Congress of Sociology*, vol. IV, Louvain: International Sociological Association, 1959, pp. 25–49.

Reprinted in CURTIS, JAMES E. and PETRAS, JOHN W. (eds), *The Sociology of Knowledge*, pp. 282–306 (see 166).

635 PARSONS, TALCOTT, 'Definitions of health and illness in the light of American values and social structure', in JACO, E. GARTLY (ed.), *Patients, Physicians and Illness*, New York: Free Press, 1963, pp. 165–87.

636 PERELMAN, C., 'Sociologie de la connaissance et philosophie de la connaissance', *Revue Internationale de Philosophie*, vol. 4, no. 13 (1950), pp. 309–17.

637 PETERSEN, WILLIAM, 'The classification of subnations in Hawaii: an essay in the sociology of knowledge', *American Sociological Review*, vol. 34, no. 6 (December, 1969), pp. 863–77.

638 PLESSNER, HELMUT, 'Zur Soziologie der modernen Forschung und ihrer Organisation', in *Versuche zu einer Soziologie des Wissens*, pp. 407–25 (see 188).

639 PLESSNER, HELMUT, 'Max Scheler', *Handwörterbuch der Sozialwissenschaften* (ed. by E. von Beckerath), vol. 9, Stuttgart-Tübingen-Göttingen: G. Fischer, Mohr, Vandenhoeck & Ruprecht, 1956, pp. 115–17.

640 PLESSNER, HELMUT, 'Zur Lage der Geisteswissenschaften in der industriellen Gesellschaft', *Schweizer Monatshefte*, vol. 38, no. 8 (1958), pp. 647–56.

641 POLSBY, NELSON W., ' "Pluralism" in the study of community power, or Erklärung before Verklärung in Wissenssoziologie', *American Sociologist*, vol. 4, no. 2 (May, 1969), pp. 118–22.

642 POWELL, ELWIN H., 'Beyond utopia: the "beat generation" as a challenge for the sociology of knowledge', in ROSE, ARNOLD M. (ed.), *Human Behavior and Social Processes*, Boston: Houghton Mifflin, 1962, pp. 360–77.

643 PRALL, D. W., 'Sorokin and the dangerous science', *Harvard Guardian* (November, 1937), pp. 8–13.

644 PRICE, J. L., 'Use of new knowledge in organizations', *Human Organization*, vol. 23 (Fall, 1964), pp. 224–34.

645 PROESLER, HANS, 'Chladenius als Wegebereiter der Wissenssoziologie', *Kölner Zeitschrift für Soziologie und Sozialpsychologie*, vol. 6, nos 3–4 (1954), pp. 617–22.

646 PROESLER, HANS, 'Zur Genesis der wissenssoziologischen Problemstellung', *Kölner Zeitschrift für Soziologie und Sozialpsychologie*, vol. XII, no. 1 (1960), pp. 41–52.

647 PROSEN, ANTHONY J., 'The essence of the sociology of knowledge: a discussion of the stark thesis', *Sociological Analysis*, vol. 27, no. 1 (Spring, 1966), pp. 9–18.

648 REMMLING, GUNTER W., 'Die Freizeit-Industrie', *Rhein-Neckar-Zeitung* (April 30/May 1, 1957), p. 10.

649 REMMLING, GUNTER W., 'Umrisse der neuen Soziallandschaft', *Neue Zürcher Nachrichten*, vol. 53, no. 111 (May 13, 1957), p. 2.

650 REMMLING, GUNTER W., 'Mensch mit der Schubkarrenseele', *Der Tag* (September 1, 1957), p. 5.

651 REMMLING, GUNTER W., 'The age of suspicion: a history of the sociology of knowledge in two Continents', Read to the Fifty-

Fifth Annual Meeting of the American Sociological Association, August 29, 1960, New York City.

652 REMMLING, GUNTER W., 'Religion und Politik: Eine Untersuchung am Schnittpunkt von Religionssoziologie und politischer Soziologie', *Zeitschrift für die gesamte Staatswissenschaft*, vol. 117, no. 1 (May, 1961), pp. 166–74.

653 REMMLING, GUNTER W., 'Religion or religiousness? Genesis and present state of a critical theme in American religious sociology', Read to the Fifty-Seventh Annual Meeting of the American Sociological Association, August 30, 1962, Washington, DC.

654 REMMLING, GUNTER W., 'Die Religion der einsamen Masse: Eine Analyse der religionssoziologischen Perspektive in den Vereinigten Staaten', *Kölner Zeitschrift für Soziologie und Sozialpsychologie*, vol. 16, no. 4 (1964), pp. 742–56.

655 REMMLING, GUNTER W., 'Max Scheler: quest for a Catholic sociology of knowledge', in *Road to Suspicion*, pp. 32–9 (see 182).

656 REMMLING, GUNTER W., 'Edmund Gustav Albrecht Husserl: A Suspension of Belief', in *Road to Suspicion*, pp. 85–92 (see 182).

657 REMMLING, GUNTER W., 'Historicism: the oceanic sense for life', in *Road to Suspicion*, pp. 95–104 (see 182).

658 REMMLING, GUNTER W., Review of '*Max Scheler: An Intellectual Portrait*, by John Raphael Staude, New York: Free Press, 1967', *Social Forces*, vol. 46, no. 4 (June, 1968), p. 553.

659 REMMLING, GUNTER W., 'The intellectual heritage of sociology', in *Basic Sociology*, pp. 25–57 (see 362).

660 REMMLING, GUNTER W., Review of '*Values in Conflict: Christianity, Marxism, Psychoanalysis, Existentialism*, edited by Victor Comerchero, New York: Appleton-Century-Crofts, 1970', *Social Forces*, vol. 49, no. 3 (March, 1971), pp. 499–500.

661 REMMLING, GUNTER W., 'Philosophical parameters of Karl Mannheim's sociology of knowledge', *Sociological Quarterly*, vol. 12, no. 4 (Autumn, 1971), pp. 531–47.

662 REMMLING, GUNTER W., 'Existence and thought', in REMMLING, GUNTER W. (ed.), *Towards the Sociology of Knowledge*, pp. 3–43 (see 184).

663 REMMLING, GUNTER W., 'Francis Bacon and the French Enlightenment philosophers', in REMMLING, GUNTER W. (ed.), *Towards the Sociology of Knowledge*, pp. 47–59 (see 184).

664 REMMLING, GUNTER W., 'Marxism and Marxist sociology of knowledge', in REMMLING, GUNTER W. (ed.), *Towards the Sociology of Knowledge*, pp. 135–52 (see 184).

665 REMMLING, GUNTER W., 'The sociology of knowledge in the French tradition', in REMMLING, GUNTER W. (ed.), *Towards the Sociology of Knowledge*, pp. 155–66 (see 184).

666 REMMLING, GUNTER W., MAIER, GEORG and REMMLING, ELBA VALDIVIA, 'Social classes in Ecuador: a study of the ideological distortion of social reality', in REMMLING, GUNTER W. (ed.), *Towards the Sociology of Knowledge*, pp. 379–96 (see 184).

667 REYNOLDS, LARRY T., VAUGHAN, TED R., REYNOLDS, JANICE M. and WARSHAY, LEON H., 'The "self" in symbolic interaction theory:

an examination of the social sources of conceptual diversity', in *The Sociology of Sociology*, pp. 422–38 (see 363).

668 RICKMANN, H. D., 'The reaction against positivism and Dilthey's concept of understanding', *British Journal of Sociology*, vol. 11, no. 4 (December, 1960), pp. 307–17.

669 ROSENMAYR, LEOPOLD, 'Max Scheler, Karl Mannheim und die Zukunft der Wissenssoziologie', in SILBERMANN, ALPHONS (ed.), *Militanter Humanismus: Von den Aufgaben der modernen Soziologie*, Frankfurt: S. Fischer, 1966, pp. 200ff.

670 ROTHACKER, ERICH, 'Bausteine zur Kultursoziologie', in *Gegenwartsprobleme der Soziologie*, Potsdam: Akademische Verlagsgesellschaft Athenaion, 1949, pp. 79–99.

671 ROUCEK, JOSEPH S., 'La ideología como elemento componente en la sociología del conocimiento', *Revista Mexicana de Sociología*, vol. 18, no. 1 (January–April, 1956), pp. 37–50.

672 ROUCEK, JOSEPH S., 'Ideology as an aspect of the sociology of knowledge', *Sociologia*, vol. 22, no. 4 (December, 1960), pp. 385–96.

673 RYTINA, JOAN HUBER and LOOMIS, CHARLES P., 'Marxist dialectic and pragmatism: power as knowledge', *American Sociological Review*, vol. 35, no. 2 (April, 1970), pp. 308–18.

674 SARAN, AWADH KISHORE, 'Sociology of knowledge and traditional thought', part I, *Sociological Bulletin*, vol. 13, no. 1 (March, 1964), pp. 33–46.

675 SARAN, AWADH KISHORE, 'Sociology of knowledge and traditional thought', *Sociological Bulletin*, vol. 14, no. 1 (March, 1965), pp. 41–58.

676 SCHAFF, ADAM, 'L'objectivité de la connaissance à la lumière de la sociologie de la connaissance et de l'analyse du langage', *Social Science Information*, vol. 7, no. 2 (April, 1968), pp. 103–30.

677 SCHAFF, ADAM, 'Marxisme et sociologie de la connaissance', *L'Homme et la Société*, vol. 10 (October–December, 1968), pp. 117–46.

678 SCHAUB, EDWARD L., 'A sociological theory of knowledge', *Philosophical Review*, vol. 29, no. 4 (July, 1920), pp. 319–39. Reprinted in REMMLING, GUNTER W. (ed.), *Towards the Sociology of Knowledge*, pp. 167–83 (see 184).

679 SCHELER, MAX, 'Die positivistische Geschichtsphilosophie und die Aufgaben einer Soziologie der Erkenntnis', *Kölner Vierteljahrshefte für Soziologie und Sozialwissenschaften*, vol. I, no. 1 (January, 1921), pp. 22–31.

680 SCHELER, MAX, 'Zu W. Jerusalems Bemerkungen', *Kölner Vierteljahrshefte für Soziologie und Sozialwissenschaften*, vol. I, no. 3 (April, 1921), pp. 35–9.

681 SCHELER, MAX, 'Weltanschauungslehre, Soziologie und Weltanschauungssetzung', *Kölner Vierteljahrshefte für Soziologie und Sozialwissenschaften*, vol. II, no. 1 (January, 1922), pp. 18–33.

682 SCHELER, MAX, 'Probleme einer Soziologie des Wissens', in *Versuche zu einer Soziologie des Wissens*, pp. 5–146 (see 188).

683 SCHELER, MAX, 'Wissenschaft und soziale Struktur', in *Verhand-*

lungen des vierten deutschen Soziologentages 1924 in Heidelberg, Tübingen: J. C. B. Mohr, 1925, pp. 118–212.

684 SCHELER, MAX, 'On the positivistic philosophy of the history of knowledge and its law of three stages' (trans. by Rainer Koehne), in CURTIS, JAMES E. and PETRAS, JOHN W. (eds), *The Sociology of Knowledge*, pp. 161–9 (see 166).

685 SCHELER, MAX, 'The sociology of knowledge: formal problems' (trans. by Rainer Koehne), in CURTIS, JAMES E. and PETRAS, JOHN W. (eds), *The Sociology of Knowledge*, pp. 170–86 (see 166).

686 SCHELTING, ALEXANDER VON, 'Zum Streit um die Wissenssoziologie', *Archiv für Sozialwissenschaft und Sozialpolitik*, vol. 62, no. 1 (1929), pp. 1–66.

687 SCHILPP, PAUL A., 'The formal problems of Scheler's "sociology of knowledge" ', *Philosophical Review*, vol. 36, no. 2 (March, 1927), pp. 101–20.

688 SCHILPP, PAUL A., 'Max Scheler 1874–1928', *Philosophical Review*, vol. 38, no. 6 (November, 1929), pp. 574–88.

689 SCHOECK, HELMUT, 'Die Wissenssoziologie und ihre Entwicklung', in SCHOECK, HELMUT, *Soziologie: Geschichte ihrer Probleme*, Munich: Karl Alber, 1952, pp. 1–17.

690 SCHUTZ, ALFRED, 'On multiple realities', *Philosophy and Phenomenological Research*, vol. 5, no. 4 (June, 1945), pp. 533–76. Reprinted in *Collected Papers*, vol. I, pp. 207–59 (see 375).

691 SCHUTZ, ALFRED, 'The well-informed citizen: an essay on the social distribution of knowledge', *Social Research*, vol. 13, no. 4 (December, 1946), pp. 463–78. Reprinted in *Collected Papers*, vol. II, pp. 120–34 (see 376).

692 SCHUTZ, ALFRED, 'Common-sense and scientific interpretation of human action', *Philosophy and Phenomenological Research*, vol. 14, no. 1 (September, 1953), pp. 1–37. Reprinted in *Collected Papers*, vol. I, pp. 3–47 (see 375).

693 SCHUTZ, ALFRED, 'Max Scheler', in MERLEAU-PONTY, MAURICE (ed.), *Les philosophes célèbres*, Paris: Lucien Mazenod, 1956, pp. 330–5.

694 SCHUTZ, ALFRED, 'Tiresias, or our knowledge of future events', *Social Research*, vol. 26, no. 1 (Spring, 1959), pp. 71–89. Reprinted in *Collected Papers*, vol. II, pp. 277–93 (see 376).

695 SCHUTZ, ALFRED, 'The social world and the theory of social action', *Social Research*, vol. 27, no. 2 (Summer, 1960), pp. 203–22. Reprinted in *Collected Papers*, vol. II, pp. 3–19 (see 376).

696 SEEMAN, MELVIN, 'Intellectual perspective and adjustment to minority status', *Social Problems*, vol. 3, no. 3 (January, 1956), pp. 142–53.

697 SELVIN, HANNAN C., 'A critique of tests of significance in survey research', *American Sociological Review*, vol. 22, no. 5 (October, 1957), pp. 519–27.

698 SHASKOLSKY, LEON, 'The development of sociological theory in America: a sociology of knowledge interpretation', *Ohio Valley Sociologist*, vol. 32, no. 3 (Spring, 1967), pp. 11–35. Reprinted in *The Sociology of Sociology*, pp. 6–30 (see 363).

699 SHIBUTANI, TAMOTSU, 'Reference groups and social control', in ROSE, ARNOLD M. (ed.), *Human Behavior and Social Processes: An*

Interactionist Approach, Boston: Houghton Mifflin, 1962, pp. 128–47.

700 SILBERMANN, A., 'Definition of the sociology of art', *International Social Science Journal*, vol. 20, no. 4 (1968), pp. 567–88.

701 SIMPSON, RICHARD D., 'Pitirim Sorokin and his sociology', *Social Forces*, vol. 32, no. 2 (December, 1953), pp. 120–31.

702 SJOBERG, GIDEON, 'Operationalism and social research', in GROSS, LLEWELLYN (ed.), *Symposium on Sociological Theory*, New York: Harper & Row, 1959, pp. 603–27.

703 SMALL, ALBION W., Review of 'Scheler's *Versuche zu einer Soziologie des Wissens*', *American Journal of Sociology*, vol. 31, no. 2 (September, 1925), pp. 262–4.

704 SMITH, WILLIAM C., 'The rural mind: a study in occupational attitude', *American Journal of Sociology*, vol. 32, no. 5 (March, 1927), pp. 771–86.

705 SNYDER, ROBERT G., 'Knowledge, power and the university: notes on the impotence of the intellectual', *Maxwell Review*, vol. VI, no. 2 (Spring, 1970), pp. 51–71. Reprinted in REMMLING, GUNTER W. (ed.), *Towards the Sociology of Knowledge*, pp. 339–59 (see 184).

706 SOROKIN, PITIRIM A. and MERTON, ROBERT K., 'The course of Arabian intellectual development 700–1300 A.D.: a study in method', *Isis*, vol. 22, no. 64 (February, 1935), pp. 516–24.

707 SOROKIN, PITIRIM A. and MERTON, ROBERT K., 'Social time: a methodological and functional analysis', *American Journal of Sociology*, vol. 42, no. 5 (March, 1937), pp. 615–29.

708 SPECHT, KARL GUSTAV, 'Aufgaben und Möglichkeiten der Kultursoziologie', *Soziale Welt*, vol. 9, nos 3–4 (1958), pp. 202–10.

709 SPEIER, HANS, Review of 'E. Grünwald's *Das Problem einer Soziologie des Wissens*', *American Sociological Review*, vol. 1, no. 4 (August, 1936), pp. 681–2.

710 SPEIER, HANS, 'The social determination of ideas', *Social Research*, vol. 5, no. 2 (May, 1938), pp. 182–205. Reprinted as chapter 8 in SPEIER, HANS, *Social Order and the Risks of War*, Cambridge, Massachusetts: MIT, 1965.

711 SPEIER, HANS, 'The sociological ideas of P. A. Sorokin: an integralist sociology', in BARNES, HARRY ELMER (ed.), *An Introduction to the History of Sociology*, University of Chicago Press, 1948, pp. 884–901.

712 STANLEY, MANFRED, 'The structures of doubt', in REMMLING, GUNTER W. (ed.), *Towards the Sociology of Knowledge*, pp. 397–452 (see 184).

713 STARK, WERNER, 'Towards a theory of social knowledge', *Revue Internationale de Philosophie*, vol. 4, no. 13 (1950), pp. 287–308.

714 STARK, WERNER, 'Die idealistische Geschichtsauffassung und die Wissenssoziologie', *Archiv für Rechts- und Sozialphilosophie*, vol. 46 (1960), pp. 355–74.

715 STARK, WERNER, 'The conservative tradition in the sociology of knowledge', *Kyklos*, vol. 13, no. 1 (1960), pp. 90–100. Reprinted in REMMLING, GUNTER W. (ed.), *Towards the Sociology of Knowledge*, pp. 68–77 (see 184).

716 STARK, WERNER, 'Die Einheit der Sozialwissenschaften im Lichte der Wissenssoziologie', *Archiv für Rechts- und Sozialphilosophie*, vol. 48 (1962), pp. 525–38.

717 STARK, WERNER, 'The sociology of knowledge: a guide to truth', *Indiana Sociological Bulletin*, vol. 4, no. 1 (October, 1966), pp. 3–6.

718 STERN, GÜNTHER, 'Über sogenannte "Seinsverbundenheit" des Bewusstseins', *Archiv für Sozialwissenschaft und Sozialpolitik*, vol. 64, no. 3 (1930), pp. 492–509.

719 STOLTENBERG, H. L., 'Kundnehmen und Kundgeben', in *Versuche zu einer Soziologie des Wissens*, pp. 208–18 (see 188).

720 SYKES, GRESHAM M., 'The differential distribution of community knowledge', *Social Forces*, vol. 29, no. 4 (December, 1950), pp. 376–82.

721 SZENDE, PAUL, 'Eine soziologische Theorie der Abstraktion', *Archiv für Sozialwissenschaft und Sozialpolitik*, vol. 50 (1923), pp. 407–85.

722 TICHENOR, P. J., KONOHUE, G. A. and OLIEN, C. N., 'Mass media flow and differential growth in knowledge', *Public Opinion Quarterly*, vol. 34, no. 2 (Summer, 1970), pp. 159–70.

723 TIRYAKIAN, EDWARD A., 'Existential phenomenology and the sociological tradition', *American Sociological Review*, vol. 30, no. 5 (October, 1965), pp. 674–88. Reprinted in REMMLING, GUNTER W. (ed.), *Towards the Sociology of Knowledge*, pp. 285–307 (see 184).

724 TIRYAKIAN, EDWARD A., 'A problem for the sociology of knowledge', *European Journal of Sociology*, vol. 7, no. 2 (1966), pp. 331–6.

725 TOCH, HANS, *et al.*, 'Effects of the cancer scares: the residue of news impact', *Journalism Quarterly*, vol. 38, no. 1 (Winter, 1961), pp. 25–34.

726 TOPITSCH, ERNST, 'The sociology of existentialism', *Partisan Review*, vol. 21, no. 3 (1954), pp. 289–304.

727 TOULEMONT, RENÉ, Review of 'J. Maquet, *Sociologie de la connaissance*', *L'Année Sociologique*, 3rd series (1952), pp. 256–8.

728 TREVES, RENATO, 'Sociologia della conoscenza e politica della cultura', *Filosofia e Sociologia* (1954), pp. 137–44.

729 TUCHTFELDT, EGON, Zur heutigen Problemstellung der Wissenssoziologie', *Zeitschrift für die gesamte Staatswissenschaft*, vol. 107, no. 4 (1951), pp. 723–31.

730 VINCENT, C. E., 'The sociology of knowledge in critiques of family sociology', *Research Studies of State College of Washington*, vol. 21, no. 3 (1953), pp. 252–7.

731 WALLERSTEIN, I., 'Élites in French speaking West Africa: the social basis of ideas', *Journal of Modern African Studies*, vol. 3, no. 1 (May, 1965), pp. 1–33.

732 WALTER, BENJAMIN, 'The sociology of knowledge and the problem of objectivity', in GROSS, L. (ed.), *Sociological Theory: Inquiries and Paradigms*, New York: Harper & Row, 1967.

733 WALTON, JOHN, 'Discipline, method and community power: a note on the sociology of knowledge', *American Sociological Review*, vol. 31, no. 5 (October, 1966), pp. 684–9.

734 WANDERER, JULES J., 'Academic origins of contributors to *American*

Sociological Review, 1955–65', *American Sociologist*, vol. 1, no. 5 (November, 1966), pp. 241–3.

735 WANDERER, JULES J., 'An empirical study in the sociology of knowledge', *Sociological Inquiry*, vol. XXXIX, no. 1 (Winter, 1969), pp. 19–26. Reprinted in CURTIS, JAMES E. and PETRAS, JOHN W. (eds), *The Sociology of Knowledge*, pp. 422–33 (see 166).

736 WEBB, EUGENE J. and SALANCIK, JERRY R., 'Notes on the sociology of knowledge', *Journalism Quarterly*, vol. 42, no. 4 (Autumn, 1965), pp. 591–6.

737 WEBER, ALFRED, 'Der soziologische Kulturbegriff', in *Verhandlungen des zweiten Soziologentages 1912 in Berlin*, Tübingen: J. C. B. Mohr (Paul Siebeck), 1913, pp. 1–20.

738 WEBER, MAX, 'Die "Objektivität" sozialwissenschaftlicher und sozialpolitischer Erkenntnis', *Archiv für Sozialwissenschaft und Sozialpolitik*, vol. 19 (1904), pp. 22–87.

739 WEIGERT, ANDREW J., 'The immoral rhetoric of scientific sociology', *American Sociologist*, vol. 5, no. 2 (May, 1970), pp. 111–19.

740 WEILLER, JEAN, 'Les cadres sociaux de la pensée économique contemporaine', *Cahiers Internationaux de Sociologie*, vol. 26 (1959), pp. 103–18.

741 WELLEK, ALBERT, 'The impact of the German immigration on the development of American psychology', *Journal of the History of the Behavioral Sciences*, vol. 4, no. 3 (July, 1968), pp. 207–29.

742 WIATR, JERZY J., 'Sociology – Marxism – reality', *Social Research*, vol. 34, no. 3 (Autumn, 1967), pp. 416–24.

743 WIESE, LEOPOLD VON, 'Einsamkeit und Geselligkeit als Bedingungen der Mehrung des Wissens', in *Versuche zu einer Soziologie des Wissens*, pp. 218–29 (see 188).

744 WITTFOGEL, K. A., 'Wissen und Gesellschaft', *Unter dem Banner des Marxismus*, vol. 5 (1931).

745 WOLFF, KURT H., 'The sociology of knowledge: emphasis on an empirical attitude', *Philosophy of Science*, vol. 10, no. 2 (April, 1943), pp. 104–23.

746 WOLFF, KURT H., 'On the scientific relevance of "imputation"', *Ethics*, vol. 61, no. 1 (October, 1950), pp. 69–73.

747 WOLFF, KURT H., 'A preliminary inquiry into the sociology of knowledge from the standpoint of the study of man', in *Scritti di sociologia e politica in onore di Luigi Sturzo*, vol. 3, Bologna: Nicola Zanichelli, 1953, pp. 585–618.

748 WOLFF, KURT H., 'The sociology of knowledge and sociological theory', in GROSS, LLEWELLYN (ed.), *Symposium on Sociological Theory*, New York: Harper & Row, 1959, pp. 567–602.

749 WOLFF, KURT H., 'Ernst Grünwald and the sociology of knowledge: a collective venture in interpretation', *Journal of the History of the Behavioral Sciences*, vol. I, no. 2 (April, 1965), pp. 152–64.

750 WOLFF, KURT H., 'The sociology of knowledge in the United States of America', *Current Sociology*, vol. XV, no. 1 (1967), pp. 1–52.

751 WOLFF, KURT H., 'Wissenssoziologie', in *Wörterbuch der Soziologie* (ed. by W. Bernsdorf), 2nd edition, Stuttgart: F. Enke, 1969.

752 WORSLEY, P. M., 'Émile Durkheim's theory of knowledge', *Sociological Review*, vol. 4, no. 1 (July, 1956), pp. 47–62.

753 ZANER, RICHARD M., 'Theory of intersubjectivity: Alfred Schutz', *Social Research*, vol. 28, no. 1 (Spring, 1961), pp. 71–93.

754 ZILSEL, EDGAR, 'The sociological roots of science', *American Journal of Sociology*, vol. XLVII (January, 1942), pp. 544–62.

755 ZNANIECKI, FLORIAN, 'The present and the future of sociology of knowledge', in SPECHT, KARL (ed.), *Soziologische Forschung in unserer Zeit*, Cologne-Opladen: Westdeutscher Verlag, 1951, pp. 248–55.

756 ZOLTOWSKI, VICTOR, 'Les fonctions sociales du temps et de l'espace: contribution à la théorie expérimentale de la connaissance', *Revue D'Histoire Économique et Sociale*, vol. 26, no. 2 (1946–7), pp. 113–37.

757 ZUCKERMAN, HARRIET, 'Nobel laureates in science: patterns of productivity, collaboration and authorship', *American Sociological Review*, vol. 32, no. 3 (June, 1967), pp. 391–403.

Selected publications on ideology and utopia

758 ABENDROTH, WOLFGANG, *Sozialgeschichte der europäischen Arbeiterbewegung*, Frankfurt: Suhrkamp Verlag, 1965.

759 ABENDROTH, WOLFGANG (ed.), *Faschismus und Kapitalismus: Theorien über die sozialen Ursprünge und die Funktion des Faschismus*, 2nd edition, Frankfurt: Europäische Verlagsanstalt, 1967.

760 ADAMS, J. L., 'Religion and the ideologies', *Confluence*, vol. IV (April, 1955), pp. 72–84.

761 ADLER, GEORG, *Die Bedeutung der Illusionen für Politik und soziales Leben*, Jena: G. Fischer, 1904.

762 ADORNO, THEODOR W., *et al.*, *The Authoritarian Personality*, New York: Harper, 1950.

763 ADORNO, THEODOR W., 'Kulturkritik und Gesellschaft', in SPECHT, K. G. (ed.), *Soziologische Forschung in unserer Zeit*, Cologne-Opladen: Westdeutscher Verlag, 1951.

764 ADORNO, THEODOR W., 'Beiträge zur Ideologienlehre', *Kölner Zeitschrift für Soziologie und Sozialpsychologie*, vol. 6, nos 3–4 (1953–4), pp. 360–75.

765 ADORNO, THEODOR W., 'Ideologie', in ADORNO, T. W. and DIRKS, W. (eds), *Soziologische Exkurse*, Frankfurt: Europäische Verlagsanstalt, 1956.

766 ADORNO, THEODOR W., 'Soziologie und empirische Forschung', in ZIEGLER, K. (ed.), *Wesen und Wirklichkeit des Menschen*, Göttingen: Vandenhoeck & Ruprecht, 1957.

767 ADORNO, THEODOR W., 'Zum gegenwärtigen Stand der deutschen Soziologie', *Kölner Zeitschrift für Soziologie und Sozialpsychologie*, vol. 11, no. 2 (1959), pp. 257–80.

768 ADORNO, THEODOR W., *Jargon der Eigentlichkeit: Zur deutschen Ideologie*, Frankfurt: Suhrkamp Verlag, 1964.

769 AIKEN, HENRY D. (ed.), *The Age of Ideology*, New York: G. Braziller, 1957.

770 AIKEN, HENRY D., 'The revolt against ideology', *Commentary*, vol. XXXVII, no. 4 (April, 1964), pp. 29–39.
771 ALBERT, HANS, *Ökonomische Ideologie und politische Theorie: Das ökonomische Argument in der ordnungspolitischen Debatte*, Göttingen: Verlag Otto Schwartz, 1954.
772 ALBERT, HANS, 'Ideologische Elemente im ökonomischen Denken: Logische und ideologische Aspekte der Ideologienkritik', *Kyklos*, vol. X, no. 2 (1957), pp. 194–6.
773 APTER, DAVID (ed.), *Ideology and Discontent*, New York: Free Press, 1964.
774 ARENDT, HANNAH, 'Ideology and terror: a novel form of government', *Review of Politics*, vol. 15 (June, 1953), pp. 303–27.
775 ARIAN, ALAN, 'The role of ideology in determining behavior', *Sociological Review*, vol. 15, no. 1 (March, 1967), pp. 47–57.
776 ARMYTAGE, W., *Heavens Below: Utopian Experiments in England, 1560–1960*, London: Routledge & Kegan Paul, 1961.
777 ARNOLD, THURMAN W., *The Folklore of Capitalism*, New Haven: Yale University Press, 1937.
778 ARON, RAYMOND, 'L'idéologie', *Recherches Philosophiques*, vol. 6 (1936–7), pp. 65–84.
779 ARON, RAYMOND, 'The diffusion of ideologies', *Confluence*, vol. II, no. 1 (March, 1953), pp. 3–12.
780 ARON, RAYMOND, 'Sociologie allemande sans idéologie?', *European Journal of Sociology*, vol. I (1960), pp. 170ff.
781 ARON, RAYMOND, *The Industrial Society: Three Essays on Ideology and Development*, New York: Praeger, 1967.
782 AUBENQUE, PIERRE, 'Philosophie et idéologie', *Archives de Philosophie*, vol. 22, no. 4 (October–December, 1959), pp. 483–520.
783 BACON, FRANCIS, *Apothegms New and Old*, London: Barrett & Whittaker, 1626.
784 BACON, FRANCIS, *Sylva Sylvarum; or A natural historie. In ten centuries*, London: William Rawley, 1626.
785 BANERJEE, D. N., 'Political ideologies and political behavior', *Modern Review*, vol. XCII, no. 6 (December, 1952), pp. 444–50.
786 BARBER, ELINOR G., *The Bourgeoisie in 18th Century France*, Princeton University Press, 1955.
787 BARION, JAKOB, *Was ist Ideologie? Studie zu Begriff und Problematik*, Bonn: H. Bouvier, 1964.
788 BARION, JAKOB, *Ideologie, Wissenschaft, Philosophie*, Bonn: H. Bouvier, 1966.
789 BARTH, HANS, *Wahrheit und Ideologie*, Zürich: Manesse Verlag, 1945.
790 BARTH, HANS, *Masse und Mythos: Die ideologische Krise and der Wende zum 20. Jahrhundert und die Theorie der Gewalt – Georges Sorel*, Hamburg: Rowohlt Verlag, 1960.
791 BARTH, PAUL, 'Die ideologische Geschichtsauffassung', in BARTH, P., *Die Philosophie der Geschichte als Soziologie*, Leipzig: O. R. Reisland, 1922.
792 BASI, RAGHBIR S., 'Role of the "free enterprise" ideology in less-developed countries', *American Journal of Economics and Sociology*, vol. 26, no. 2 (April, 1967), pp. 173–87.

793 BASTIDE, ROGER, 'Mythes et utopies', *Cahiers Internationaux de Sociologie*, vol. VII, no. 28 (January–June, 1960), pp. 3–12.

794 BAUDRILLARD, JEAN, 'La genèse idéologique des besoins', *Cahiers Internationaux de Sociologie*, vol. 47 (1969), pp. 45–68.

795 BELL, DANIEL (ed.), *The New American Right*, New York: Criterion, 1955.

796 BELL, DANIEL, *The End of Ideology: On the Exhaustion of Political Ideas in the Fifties*, Chicago: Free Press, 1960.

797 BELL, DANIEL and AIKEN, HENRY DAVID, 'Ideology – a debate', *Commentary*, vol. 38, no. 4 (October, 1964), pp. 69–76.

798 BELLAMY, EDWARD, *Looking Backward, 2000–1887*, Chicago: Packard, 1946.

799 BENDIX, REINHARD, *Work and Authority in Industry: Ideologies of Management in the Course of Industrialisation*, New York: John Wiley, 1956.

800 BENDIX, REINHARD, 'A study of managerial ideologies', *Economic Development and Cultural Change*, vol. 5, no. 2 (January, 1957), pp. 118–28.

801 BENDIX, REINHARD, 'Industrialization, ideologies, and social structure', *American Sociological Review*, vol. XXIV, no. 5 (October, 1959), pp. 613–23.

802 BENDIX, REINHARD, 'The age of ideology: persistent and changing', in APTER, DAVID E. (ed.), *Ideology and Discontent*, New York: Free Press, 1964, pp. 294–327.

803 BERGER, PETER (ed.), *Marxism and Sociology: Views from Eastern Europe*, New York: Appleton-Century-Crofts, 1969.

804 BERGMANN, GUSTAV, 'Ideology', *Ethics*, vol. 61, no. 3 (April, 1951), pp. 205–18.

805 BERNDT, H., LORENZER, A. and HORN, K., *Architektur als Ideologie*, Frankfurt: Suhrkamp Verlag, 1968.

806 BERNERI, MARIE LOUISE, *Journey Through Utopia*, Boston: Beacon Press, 1951.

807 BESTOR, A. E., *Backwoods Utopias: The Sectarian and Owenite Phases of Communitarian Socialism in America, 1663–1829*, Philadelphia: University of Pennsylvania Press, 1950.

808 BETTELHEIM, CHARLES, 'Idéologie économique et réalité sociale', *Cahiers Internationaux de Sociologie*, vol. 4 (1948), pp. 119–134.

809 BETTELHEIM, CHARLES, *Initiation aux recherches sur les idéologies économiques et les réalités sociales*, Paris: Tournier & Constans, 1948.

810 BIRNBAUM, NORMAN, 'Ideologie', in GALLING, K. (ed.), *Religion in Geschichte und Gegenwart*, vol. III, Tübingen: J. C. B. Mohr (Paul Siebeck), 1959, pp. 567–72.

811 BIRNBAUM, NORMAN, 'The sociological study of ideology (1940–1960): a trend report and bibliography', *Current Sociology*, vol. IX, no. 2 (1960), pp. 91–172.

812 BLACKBURN, ROBIN, 'A brief guide to bourgeois ideology', in COCKBURN, ALEXANDER and BLACKBURN, ROBIN (eds), *Student Power*, Baltimore: Penguin, 1969.

813 BLOCH, ERNST, *Geist der Utopie*, Munich and Leipzig: Verlag Duncker & Humblot, 1918.

814 BLOCH, ERNST, *Freiheit und Ordnung: Abriss der Sozial-Utopien*, Berlin: Aurora Verlag, 1946.

815 BLUM, RICHARD, *et al.*, *Utopiates*, New York: Atherton Press, 1964.

816 BOGUSLAW, ROBERT, *The New Utopians: A Study of System Design and Social Change*, Englewood Cliffs, New Jersey: Prentice-Hall, 1965.

817 BOLLHAGEN, PETER, *Interesse und Gesellschaft*, Berlin: Deutscher Verlag der Wissenschaften, 1967.

818 BOORSTIN, DANIEL J., *The Image or What Happened to the American Dream*, New York: Atheneum, 1962.

819 BOTT, HERMANN, *Die Volksfeind-Ideologie: Zur Kritik rechtsradikaler Propaganda*, Stuttgart: Deutsche Verlagsanstalt, 1969.

820 BOULDING, KENNETH E., 'The role of ideology in the great transition', in BOULDING, KENNETH E., *The Meaning of the Twentieth Century: The Great Transition*, Harper Colophon edition, New York: Harper & Row, 1965, pp. 156–79.

821 BOWMAN, SYLVIA E., *Edward Bellamy Abroad: An American Prophet's Influence*, New York: Twayne, 1962.

822 BROWN, ROGER L., 'Some aspects of mass media ideologies', *Sociological Review*, monograph no. 13 (January, 1969), pp. 155–168.

823 BROWN, STEVEN R., 'Consistency and the persistence of ideology: some experimental results', *Public Opinion Quarterly*, vol. 34, no. 16 (Spring, 1970), pp. 60–8.

824 BRUNNER, OTTO, *Das Zeitalter der Ideologien*, Göttingen: Vandenhoeck & Ruprecht, 1956.

825 BRZEZINSKI, ZBIGNIEW, 'Communist ideology and power: from unity to diversity', *Journal of Politics*, vol. XIX, no. 4 (November, 1957), pp. 549–90.

826 BRZEZINSKI, ZBIGNIEW, *Ideology and Power in Soviet Politics*, New York: Praeger, 1962.

827 BUBER, MARTIN, *Paths in Utopia* (trans. by R. F. C. Hull), London: Routledge & Kegan Paul, 1949.

828 BUCHHOLZ, ERNST WOLFGANG, *Ideologie und latenter sozialer Konflikt*, Stuttgart: F. Enke, 1968.

829 BUNZEL, J. H., 'The general ideology of American small business', *Political Science Quarterly*, vol. LXX, no. 1 (March, 1955), pp. 87–102.

830 BURISCH, WOLFRAM, *Ideologie und Sachzwang: Die Entideologisierungsthese in neueren Gesellschaftstheorien*, Tübingen: Huth, 1967.

831 BURKS, R. V., 'Conception of ideology for historians', *Journal of the History of Ideas*, vol. X (April, 1959), pp. 183–98.

832 BUTLER, SAMUEL, *Erewhon: Or, Over the Range*, New York: E. P. Dutton, 1920.

833 BUTLER, SAMUEL, *Erewhon Revisited Twenty Years Later*, New York: E. P. Dutton, 1920.

834 CABET, ETIENNE, *Voyage en Icarie*, Paris: Bureau du Populaire, 1845.

835 CAILLIET, ÉMILE, *La tradition littéraire des idéologues*, Philadelphia: American Philosophical Society, 1943.

836 CAMPANELLA, T., 'Civitas solis, idea republicae Platonicae', in WHITE, F. R. (ed.), *Famous Utopias of the Renaissance*, New York: Packard, 1946.

837 CAMUS, ALBERT, *The Rebel*, New York: Alfred A. Knopf, 1956.

838 CANTRIL, H. A., 'Projective questions in the study of personality and ideology', in ADORNO, T. (ed.), *The Authoritarian Personality*, New York: Harper, 1950.

839 CHADWICK, H. M., *The Nationalities of Europe and the Growth of National Ideologies*, London: Cambridge University Press, 1945.

840 CHAMBRE, H., *Le Marxisme en Union Soviétique: idéologie et institutions, leur évolution de 1917 à nos jours*, Paris: Éditions du Seuil, 1955.

841 CHEVALLIER, J. J., 'Le XVIIIème siècle et la naissance des idéologies', *Res Publica*, vol. II, no. 3 (1960), pp. 194–204.

842 CHINOY, ELY, *Automobile Workers and the American Dream*, Garden City, New York: Doubleday, 1955.

843 CIORAN, E. M., *Histoire et utopie*, Paris: Gallimard, 1960.

844 COHEN, A. A., 'Religion as a secular ideology', *Partisan Review*, vol. XXIII (Fall, 1956), pp. 495–505.

845 COHN, NORMAN, *The Pursuit of The Millennium*, New York: Harper & Row, 1957.

846 CONNOLLY, WILLIAM E., *Political Science and Ideology*, New York: Atherton Press, 1967.

847 CONRAD-MARTIUS, HEDWIG, *Utopien der Menschenzüchtung: Der Sozialdarwinismus und seine Folgen*, Munich: Kösel-Verlag, 1955.

848 CUVILLIER, A., *Hommes et idéologies de 1840*, Paris: M. Rivière. 1957.

849 DAHRENDORF, RALF, 'Out of utopia: toward a reorganization of sociological analysis', *American Journal of Sociology*, vol. 64, no. 2 (September, 1958), pp. 115–27.

850 DAHRENDORF, RALF, 'Betrachtungen zu einigen Aspekten der gegenwärtigen deutschen Soziologie', *Kölner Zeitschrift für Soziologie und Sozialpsychologie*, vol. 11, no. 1 (1959), pp. 132–53.

851 DAHRENDORF, RALF, *Class and Conflict in Industrial Society*, Stanford University Press, 1959.

852 DAHRENDORF, RALF, 'Die drci Soziologien: zu Helmut Schelskys Ortsbestimmung der deutschen Soziologie', *Kölner Zeitschrift für Soziologie und Sozialpsychologie*, vol. 12, no. 1 (1960), pp. 120–33.

853 DAHRENDORF, RALF, 'European sociology and the American self-image', *European Journal of Sociology*, vol. II, no. 2 (1961), pp. 324–66.

854 DAHRENDORF, RALF, *Pfade aus Utopia: Arbeiten zur Theorie und Methode der Soziologie*, Munich: Piper-Paperbacks, 1967.

855 DANTZIG, D. V., 'The function of words in ideological conflicts', in MCKEON, RICHARD and ROKKAN, STEIN (eds), *Democracy in a World of Tensions*, University of Chicago Press, 1951.

856 DELEU, P., 'Idéologie, politique et polémologie', *Revue de l'Institut de Sociologie*, vol. 4 (1969), pp. 671–87.

857 DENINGER, W. T., 'Political power and ideological analysis', *Politico*, vol. XXVI, no. 2 (June, 1961), pp. 277–98.

858 DERMENGHEM, ÉMILE, *Thomas Morus et les utopistes de la Renaissance*, Paris: Plon, 1927.

859 DESROCHE, HENRI, 'Écriture et tradition de l'utopisme pratique', *Archives Internationales de Sociologie de la Coopération*, vol. 19 (January–June, 1966), pp. 3–18.

860 DESTUTT DE TRACY, ANTOINE LOUIS CLAUDE, *Éléments d'idéologie*, 4 vols, Paris: Courcier, 1825–7.

861 DIBBLE, VERNON K., 'Occupations and ideologies', *American Journal of Sociology*, vol. LXVIII (September, 1962), pp. 229–41.

862 DION, LEON, 'Political ideology as a tool of functional analysis in sociopolitical dynamics: an hypothesis', *Canadian Journal of Economics*, vol. XXV (February, 1959), pp. 47–59.

863 DION, LEON, 'Le libéralisme du "statu quo"; L'idéologie protectrice', *Recherches Sociographiques*, vol. I, no. 4 (October–December, 1960), pp. 435–65.

864 DODD, ANNA BOWMAN, *The Republic of the Future: Or Socialism a Reality*, New York: Cassell, 1887.

865 DOLBEARE, KENNETH M. and DOLBEARE, PATRICIA, *American Ideologies: The Competing Political Beliefs of the 1970's*, Chicago: Markham, 1971.

866 DUDOK, GERARD, *Sir Thomas More and His Utopia*, Amsterdam and Paris: A. H. Kruyt, 1923.

867 DUVEAU, GEORGES, 'Introduction à une sociologie de l'utopie', *Cahiers Internationaux de Sociologie*, vol. 9 (1950), pp. 17–41.

868 DUVEAU, GEORGES, 'La résurrection de l'utopie', *Cahiers Internationaux de Sociologie*, vol. 23 (1957), pp. 3–22.

869 DUVEAU, GEORGES, *Sociologie de l'utopie et autres 'essais'*, Paris: Presses Universitaires de France, 1961.

870 EHRENBERG, HANS, 'Ideologische und soziologische Methode: Ein Wort zur Sozialisierung der Denkart', *Archiv für Systematische Philosophie und Soziologie*, vol. XXX, no. 1 (1927), pp. 133–144.

871 EISERMANN, GOTTFRIED, 'Ideologie und Utopie: aus Anlass der dritten Auflage von Karl Mannheims Buch', *Kölner Zeitschrift für Soziologie und Sozialpsychologie*, vol. 5, no. 4 (1953), pp. 526–534.

872 EISERMANN, GOTTFRIED, 'Ideologie und Utopie', in EISERMANN, G., *Wirtschaft und Gesellschaft: Ausgewählte Abhandlungen*, Stuttgart: F. Enke, 1964, pp. 148–89.

873 EISERMANN, GOTTFRIED, 'Ideologia and Utopia', *Revue Internationale de Sociologie*, vol. 3, nos 1–3 (December, 1967), pp. 28–73.

874 ELLIOT, W. Y., 'Ideas and ideologies', *Confluence*, vol. 2, no. 3 (1953), pp. 127–41.

875 ELLUL, JACQUES, *The Technological Society*, New York: Alfred A. Knopf, 1964.

876 EMERY, LEON, 'L'université française et l'idéologie politique', *Contrat Social*, vol. 2, no. 1 (1958), pp. 1–8.

877 EMGE, CARL AUGUST, *Das Wesen der Ideologie*, Wiesbaden: F. Steiner, 1961.

878 ENGELMANN, HUGO, 'A systematic, dynamic analysis of right wing

ideology', *Indian Sociological Bulletin*, vol. 2, no. 4 (July, 1965), pp. 215–25.

879 ENGELS, FRIEDRICH, *Socialism: Utopian and Scientific*, London: Sonnenschein, 1892.

880 ENGELS, FRIEDRICH, *Herr Eugen Dühring's Revolution in Science* (*Anti-Dühring*), New York: International Publishers, 1939.

881 ENGELS, FRIEDRICH, *Ludwig Feuerbach and the Outcome of Classical German Philosophy*, New York: International Publishers, 1941.

882 EPPSTEIN, PAUL, 'Die Fragestellung nach der Wirklichkeit im historischen Materialismus', *Archiv für Sozialwissenschaft und Sozialpolitik*, vol. 60 (1928), pp. 449–507.

883 FALKE, RITA, 'Utopies d'hier et d'aujourd'hui', *Diogène*, no. 23 (July–September 1958), pp. 18–28.

884 FELDKELLER, PAUL, 'Die Rolle der "Ideologie" im Leben der Völker', *Sociologus*, vol. 3, no. 1 (1953), pp. 1–14.

885 FERBER, CHRISTIAN VON, *Arbeitsfreude: Wirklichkeit und Ideologie: Ein Beitrag zur Soziologie der Arbeit in der industriellen Gesellschaft*, Stuttgart: F. Enke, 1959.

886 FEUER, LEWIS, *The Conflict of Generations*, New York: Basic Books, 1969.

887 FEUERBACH, LUDWIG, *The Essence of Christianity* (trans. by George Eliot), New York: Harper, 1957.

888 FIJALKOWSKI, JÜRGEN, *Die Wendung zum Führerstaat: Die ideologischen Komponenten in der politischen Philosophie Carl Schmitts*, Cologne-Opladen: Westdeutscher Verlag, 1958.

889 FOGARTY, M. P., 'The rooting of ideologies', *Social Compass*, vol. 9, nos 1–2 (1962), pp. 109–24.

890 FORM, WILLIAM H. and RYTINA, JOAN, 'Ideological beliefs on the distribution of power in the United States', *American Sociological Review*, vol. 34, no. 1 (February, 1969), pp. 19–31.

891 FREYER, HANS, 'Das Problem der Utopie', *Deutsche Rundschau*, vol. 183 (1928), pp. 321–45.

892 FROMM, ERICH, *The Sane Society*, London: Routledge & Kegan Paul, 1956.

893 FUNG, THALIA and MONAL, ISABEL, 'Estructura agraria e ideología campesina', *Revista Mexicana de Sociología*, vol. 31, no. 4 (October–December, 1969), pp. 995–1018.

894 FUZ, J., *Welfare Economics in English Utopias from Francis Bacon to Adam Smith*, The Hague: M. Nijhoff, 1952.

895 GABEL, J., *Ideologie und Schizophrenie: Formen der Entfremdung* (trans. by H. Naumann), Frankfurt: S. Fischer, 1967.

896 GALANTIERE, L., 'Ideology and political warfare', *Confluence*, vol. II, no. 1 (March, 1953), pp. 43–54.

897 GALBRAITH, JOHN K., *The New Industrial State*, Boston: Houghton Mifflin, 1967.

898 GEIGER, THEODOR, 'Kritische Bemerkungen zum Begriffe der Ideologie', in EISERMANN, G. (ed.), *Gegenwartsprobleme der Soziologie*, Potsdam: Akademische Verlagsgesellschaft Athenaion, 1949, pp. 141–57. Reprinted in GEIGER, T., *Arbeiten zur*

Soziologie (ed. by Paul Trappe), Berlin and Neuwied: Luchterhand Verlag, 1962.

899 GEIGER, THEODOR JULIUS, *Ideologie und Wahrheit: Eine soziologische Kritik des Denkens*, Stuttgart: Humboldt-Verlag, 1953.

900 GEIGER, THEODOR, 'Ideologie', in *Handwörterbuch der Sozialwissenschaften*, vol. V, Stuttgart, Tübingen and Göttingen: Fischer–Mohr–Vandenhoeck & Ruprecht, 1956, pp. 179–84.

901 GEISMAR, LUDWIG L., 'Ideology and the adjustment of immigrants', *Jewish Social Studies*, vol. XXI, no. 3 (July, 1959), pp. 155–64.

902 GERMINO, DANTE, *Beyond Ideology: The Revival of Political Theory*, New York: Harper & Row, 1968.

903 GLASER, HERMANN, *Spiesser Ideologie: Von der Zerstörung des deutschen Geistes im 19. und 20. Jahrhundert*, Freiburg: Rombach Verlag, 1963.

904 GOLDMANN, L., *Le dieu caché: études sur la vision tragique dans les Pensées de Pascal et dans le théâtre de Racine*, Paris: Gallimard, 1955.

905 GOLFING, FRANCIS, 'Notes towards a utopia', *Partisan Review*, vol. 27, no. 3 (Summer, 1960), pp. 514–25.

906 GRAMSCI, A., *The Modern Prince and Other Writings* (trans. and ed. by L. Marks), London: Lawrence & Wishart, 1957.

907 GRAÑA, CÉSAR, *Modernity and Its Discontents*, New York: Harper Torchbooks, 1967.

908 GRIMES, A. P. and HORWITZ, R. H. (eds), *Modern Political Ideologies*, New York: Oxford University Press, 1959.

909 GROETHUYSEN, BERNHARD, 'Expérience sociale et idéologie: Fragment inédit sur l'esprit bourgeois', *Arguments*, vol. 4, no. 20 (1960), pp. 55–8.

910 GROSS, FELIKS (ed.), *European Ideologies: A Survey of Twentieth Century Political Ideas*, New York: Philosophical Library, 1948.

911 HABERMAS, JÜRGEN, *Technik und Wissenschaft als 'Ideologie'*, Frankfurt: Suhrkamp Verlag, 1968.

912 HABERMAS, JÜRGEN, *Erkenntnis und Interesse*, Frankfurt: Suhrkamp Verlag, 1968.

913 HACKER, ANDREW, 'In defence of utopia', *Ethics*, vol. 65, no. 2 (1955), pp. 135–8.

914 HACKER, ANDREW, *Political Theory, Philosophy, Ideology, Science*, New York: Macmillan, 1961.

915 HAHN, ERICH, 'Marxismus und Ideologie', *Deutsche Zeitschrift für Philosophie*, vol. 12 (1964), pp. 1171–90.

916 HAHN, ERICH, 'Ideologiekritik heute', *Deutsche Zeitschrift für Philosophie*, vol. 16 (1968), pp. 1494–503.

917 HALLER, BRUNO, 'Ideologie und Realitäten in Afrika', *Kölner Zeitschrift für Soziologie und Sozialpsychologie*, supplement 13 (1969), pp. 66–92.

918 HALLOWELL, JOHN H., *The Decline of Liberalism as an Ideology*, London: Kegan Paul, Trench, Trubner, 1946.

919 HALPERN, BEN, 'The impact of Israel on American Jewish ideologies', *Jewish Social Studies*, vol. 21, no. 1 (January, 1959), pp. 62–81.

920 HALPERN, BEN, 'Myth and ideology in modern usage', *History and Theory*, vol. 1 (1960), pp. 129–49.

921 HARRINGTON, JAMES, *The Oceana of James Harrington, and His Other Works*, London: Westminster Booksellers, 1700.

922 HARRIS, NIGEL, *Beliefs in Society: The Problem of Ideology*, London: Watts, 1968.

923 HAUG, WOLFGANG FRITZ, *Der hilflose Antifaschismus*, Frankfurt: Suhrkamp Verlag, 1967.

924 HAUPTMANN, GERHART JOHANN ROBERT, *The Island of the Great Mother; or, The Miracle of Ile des Dames: A Story from the Utopian Archipelago* (trans. by Willa and Edwin Muir), New York: B. W. Huebsch & Viking Press, 1925.

925 HAUSKNECHT, MURRAY, 'Values and mainstream sociology: some functions of ideology for theory', *American Behavioral Scientist*, vol. IX, no. 6 (1965–6), pp. 30–2.

926 HAYEK, F. A., *The Counter-Revolution of Science: Studies in the Abuse of Reason*, Chicago: Free Press, 1952.

927 HEINTEL, PETER, *System und Ideologie: Der Austromarxismus im Spiegel der Philosophie Max Adlers*, Vienna and Munich: Oldenbourg Verlag, 1967.

928 HEISE, WOLFGANG, *Aufbruch in die Illusion: Zur Kritik der bürgerlichen Philosophie in Deutschland*, Berlin: Deutscher Verlag der Wissenschaften, 1964.

929 HELMS, HANS GÜNTER, *Die Ideologie der anonymen Gesellschaft: Max Stirners 'Einziger' und der Fortschritt des demokratischen Selbstbewusstseins vom Vormärz bis zur Bundesrepublik*, Cologne: DuMont-Schauberg, 1966.

930 HERMAN, THELMA, 'Pragmatism: a study in middle-class ideology', *Social Forces*, vol. 22, no. 4 (May, 1944), pp. 405–10.

931 HERSCH, JEANNE, *Die Ideologien und die Wirklichkeit: Versuch einer politischen Orientierung* (trans. by Ernst von Schenck), Munich: R. Piper, 1957.

932 HERTZLER, JOYCE ORAMEL, *The History of Utopian Thought*, New York: Macmillan, and London: G. Allen & Unwin, 1923.

933 HIRSZOWITZ, MARIA, 'Ideologies and traditions', *International Social Science Journal*, vol. 18, no. 1 (1966), pp. 11–12.

934 HODGES, DONALD CLARK, 'The end of "the end of ideology" ', *American Journal of Economics and Sociology*, vol. 26, no. 2 (April, 1967), pp. 135–46.

935 HOFMANN, WERNER, *Universität, Ideologie, Gesellschaft: Beiträge zur Wissenschaftssoziologie*, Frankfurt: Suhrkamp Verlag, 1968.

936 HOGGART, R., *The Uses of Literacy*, London: Chatto & Windus, 1957.

937 HOLLOWAY, M., *Heavens on Earth: Utopian Communities in America, 1680–1880*, New York: Library Publishers, 1951.

938 HOLZ, H. H., *Utopie und Anarchismus: Zur Kritik der kritischen Theorie H. Marcuses*, Cologne: Pahl-Rugenstein-Verlag, 1968.

939 HÖLZLE, ERWIN, *Idee und Ideologie: Eine Zeitkritik aus universalhistorischer Sicht*, Berne and Munich: A. Francke Verlag, 1969.

940 HONIGMANN, JOHN J., 'Interpersonal relations and ideology in a

Northern Canadian community', *Social Forces*, vol. 35, no. 4 (May, 1957), pp. 365–70.

941 HOOGERWERF, A., 'Depolitisering en ontideologisering: Een theoretische analyse', *Acta Sociologica*, vol. 1, nos 1–4 (1965), pp. 21–35.

942 HORKHEIMER, MAX, 'Ideologie und Wertgebung', in *Soziologische Forschung in unserer Zeit*, Leopold von Wiese zum 75. Geburtstag, Cologne-Opladen: Westdeutscher Verlag, 1951, pp. 220–7.

943 HOROWITZ, IRVING LOUIS, *Radicalism and the Revolt Against Reason: The Social Theories of Georges Sorel*, London: Routledge & Kegan Paul, 1961.

944 HOROWITZ, IRVING LOUIS, 'Formalización de la teoría general de la ideología y la utopia', *Revista Mexicana de Sociología*, vol. 29 (January–April, 1962), pp. 87–100.

945 HORTON, JOHN, 'The dehumanization of anomie and alienation', *British Journal of Sociology*, vol. XV (December, 1964), pp. 283–300.

946 HORTON, JOHN, 'Order and conflict theories of social problems as competing ideologies', *American Journal of Sociology*, vol. LXXI (May, 1966), pp. 701–13.

947 HUBER, B., *Der Begriff des Interesses in den Sozialwissenschaften*, Winterthur: Keller, 1958.

948 HUDSON, G. F., 'Communist ideology in China', *International Affairs*, vol. 33, no. 2 (April, 1957), pp. 176–84.

949 HUELSMANN, HEINZ VON, 'Erkenntnis als Interesse', *Soziale Welt*, vol. 20, no. 2 (1969), pp. 199–213.

950 HUME, DAVID, *The Natural History of Religion*, London: Adam & Charles Black, 1956.

951 HUNTINGTON, SAMUEL P., 'Conservatism as an ideology', *American Political Science Review*, vol. 51, no. 2 (June, 1957), pp. 454–73.

952 HUXLEY, ALDOUS L., *Brave New World*, Garden City, New York: Doubleday, Doran, 1932.

953 HUXLEY, ALDOUS L., *Essays New and Old*, New York: H. W. Wilson, 1932.

954 IDEAL COMMONWEALTHS: More's *Utopia*, Bacon's *New Atlantis*, Campanella's *City of the Sun*, and Harrington's *Oceana*, New York: Colonial Press, 1901.

955 IDEAL EMPIRES AND REPUBLICS: Rousseau's *Social Contract*, More's *Utopia*, Bacon's *New Atlantis*, Campanella's *City of the Sun*, New York: Colonial Press, 1901.

956 JAKUBOWSKI, FRANZ, *Der ideologische Überbau in der materialistischen Geschichtsauffassung*, Frankfurt am Main: Verlag Neue Kritik, 1968.

957 JANOWITZ, MORRIS, 'Some observations on the ideology of professional psychologists', *American Psychologist*, vol. 9, no. 9 (September, 1954), pp. 528–38.

958 JASPERS, KARL, *Psychologie der Weltanschauungen*, Berlin: J. Springer, 1925.

959 JORDAN, ZBIGNIEW A., *Philosophy and Ideology: The Development of Philosophy and Marxism-Leninism in Poland Since the Second World War*, Dordrecht, Holland: D. Reidel, 1963.

960 JOUVENAL, BERTRAND DE, 'Utopia for practical purposes', *Daedalus*, vol. 94, no. 2 (Spring, 1965), pp. 437–53.

961 JUNG, CARL G., *Modern Man in Search of a Soul*, New York: Dover, 1934.

962 JURDANT, BAUDOIN, 'Vulgarisation scientifique et idéologie', *Communication*, vol. 14 (1969), pp. 150–61.

963 KATEB, GEORGE, *Utopia and Its Enemies*, New York: Free Press, 1963.

964 KELLEY, J. S., *Professional Public Relations and Political Power*, Baltimore: Johns Hopkins Press, 1956.

965 KELSEN, HANS, *Aufsätze zur Ideologiekritik* (ed. by F. Topitsch), Berlin and Neuwied: Luchterhand Verlag, 1964.

966 KENISTON, KENNETH, 'Alienation and the decline of utopia', *American Scholar*, vol. 29 (Spring, 1960), pp. 161–200.

967 KIRSHEN, H. B., 'The ideology of American labor', *Politico*, vol. XXV, no. 3 (September, 1960), pp. 581–95.

968 KLEINING, GERHARD, 'Angst als Ideologie', in WIESBROCK, HEINZ (ed.), *Die politische und gesellschaftliche Rolle der Angst*, Frankfurt: Europäische Verlagsanstalt, 1967, pp. 194ff.

969 KLUCKHOHN, CLYDE, 'Recurrent themes in myths and mythmaking', *Daedalus*, vol. 88, no. 2 (1959), pp. 268–79.

970 KNUTH, WERNER, *Ideen, Ideale, Ideologien: Vom Verhängnis ideologischen Denkens, ein Beitrag zu seiner Überwindung*, Hamburg: Holsten-Verlag, 1955.

971 KOFLER, LEO, *Der asketische Eros: Industriekultur und Ideologie*, Wien: Europa Verlag, 1967.

972 KOHN, HANS, *Political Ideologies of the Twentieth Century*, Torchbook edition, New York: Harper & Row, 1966.

973 KOLAKOWSKI, LESZEK, *Der Mensch ohne Alternative: Von der Möglichkeit und Unmöglichkeit, Marxist zu sein* (trans. by W. Bronska-Pampuch), Munich: R. Piper Verlag, 1960.

974 KORNHAUSER, WILLIAM, *The Politics of Mass Society*, Chicago: Free Press, 1959.

975 KRAUSE, ELLIOT A., 'Functions of a bureaucratic ideology: "citizen participation" ', *Social Problems*, vol. 16, no. 2 (Fall, 1968), pp. 129–42.

976 KRISTOL, IRVING, 'The ideology of economic aid', *Yale Review*, vol. 46, no. 4 (June, 1957), pp. 497–510.

977 KRYSMANSKI, HANS-JÜRGEN, 'Metrische Vorstellungen: Zur wissenssoziologischen Beschreibung modernen Bewusstseins', *Soziale Welt*, vol. 14, nos 3–4 (1963), pp. 297–310.

978 KRYSMANSKI, HANS-JÜRGEN, *Die utopische Methode: Eine literatur- und wissenssoziologische Untersuchung utopischer Romane des 20. Jahrhunderts*, Cologne-Opladen: Westdeutscher Verlag, 1963.

979 KÜHNL, REINHARD, *et al.*, *Die NPD: Struktur, Ideologie und Funktion einer neofaschistischen Partei*, Frankfurt: Suhrkamp Verlag, 1969.

980 LAEUEN, H., 'Polens Verhältnis zur Ideologie', *Osteuropa*, vol. XI, nos 7–8 (July–August, 1961), pp. 517–26.

981 LANE, DAVID, 'Ideology and sociology in the USSR', *British Journal of Sociology*, vol. 21, no. 1 (March, 1970), pp. 43–51.

982 LANE, ROBERT EDWARDS, *Political Ideology: Why the American Common Man Believes What He Does*, New York: Free Press, 1962.

983 LANE, ROBERT EDWARDS, 'The decline of politics and ideology in a knowledgeable society', *American Sociological Review*, vol. 31, no. 5 (October, 1966), pp. 649–62.

984 LAPALOMBARA, J., 'Decline of ideology: a dissent and an interpretation', *American Political Science Review*, vol. 60, no. 1 (March, 1966), pp. 5–16.

985 LASSWELL, HAROLD D., 'The relation of ideological intelligence to public policy', *Ethics*, vol. 53, no. 1 (October, 1942), pp. 25–34.

986 LASZLO, ERVIN, 'Dynamics of ideological change in Eastern Europe', *Inquiry*, vol. 9, no. 1 (Spring, 1966), pp. 47–72.

987 LEFEBVRE, H., *Critique de la vie quotidienne*, revised edition, Paris: L'Arche, 1958.

988 LENIN, V. I., *Materialism and Empirico-Criticism: Critical Comments on a Reactionary Philosophy*, Moscow: Foreign Languages Publishing House, 1947.

989 LENK, KURT, 'Soziologie und Ideologielehre: Bemerkungen zur Marxismusdiskussion in der deutschen Soziologie von Simmel bis Mannheim', *Kölner Zeitschrift für Soziologie und Sozialpsychologie*, vol. 13, no. 2 (1961), pp. 227–38.

990 LENK, KURT, 'Dialektik und Ideologie: Zum Ideologieproblem in der Philosophie Hegels', *Archiv für Rechts- und Sozialphilosophie*, vol. 49 (1963), pp. 303–18.

991 LENK, KURT, 'Gesellschaft und Ideologie', *Jahrbuch für Sozialwissenschaft*, vol. 15 (1964), pp. 62–81.

992 LENK, KURT, *Schriften zur Ideologie und Politik*, Berlin and Neuwied: Luchterhand Verlag, 1967.

993 LENK, KURT, 'Die These vom postideologischen Zeitalter', *Blätter für deutsche und internationale Politik*, vol. 13 (1968).

994 LERNER, MAX, *Ideas Are Weapons: The History and the Uses of Ideas*, New York: Viking Press, 1939.

995 LEVIN, M. B., *The Alienated Voter: Politics in Boston*, New York: Holt, Rinehart & Winston, 1960.

996 LEVINE, MORTON, 'Prehistoric art and ideology', *American Anthropologist*, vol. 59, no. 6 (December, 1957), pp. 949–64.

997 LEVINSON, DAVID J., 'The study of ethnocentric ideology', in ADORNO, THEODOR, *et al.* (eds), *The Authoritarian Personality*, New York: Harper, 1950.

998 LEWIS, JOHN, 'Idealism and ideologies', in LEWIS, JOHN, *Marxism and the Open Mind*, London: Routledge & Kegan Paul, 1957.

999 LICHTHEIM, GEORGE, 'The concept of ideology', *History and Theory*, vol. IV, no. 2 (1965), pp. 164–95.

1000 LIEBER, HANS-JOACHIM, 'Der Ideologiebegriff und die "Philosophie der Verdächtigung" ', *Schweizer Monatshefte*, vol. 31, no. 7 (1951).

1001 LIEBER, HANS-JOACHIM, 'Ideologienbildung und Ideologiekritik', *Moderne Welt*, vol. 3 (1961–2).

1002 LIEBER, HANS-JOACHIM, *Philosophie, Soziologie, Gesellschaft: Ge-*

sammelte Studien zum Ideologieproblem, Berlin: Walter de Gruyter, 1965.

1003 LIEBER, HANS-JOACHIM, *Ideologie und Aufklärung*, Berlin: Colloquium Verlag, 1966.

1004 LIPPE-WEISSENFELD, KURT BERNHARD, *Modern Ideologies and American Democracy: A Comparison*, San Francisco: Overseas Publishing Company, 1939.

1005 LIPSET, SEYMOUR MARTIN, 'The Activists', *Public Interest*, vol. 11 (Fall, 1958), pp. 39–51.

1006 LIPSET, SEYMOUR MARTIN, *Political Man: The Social Basis of Politics*, Garden City, New York: Doubleday, 1959.

1007 LOCKWOOD, T. D., 'A study of French socialist ideology', *Review of Politics*, no. 2 (April, 1959), pp. 402–16.

1008 LOEWENSTEIN, KARL, 'The role of ideologies in political change', *International Social Science Bulletin*, vol. V, no. 1 (1953), pp. 51–74.

1009 LOEWENSTEIN, KARL, 'Political systems, ideologies and institutions: the problem of their circulation', *Western Political Quarterly*, vol. VI, no. 4 (December, 1953), pp. 689–706.

1010 LOEWENSTEIN, KARL, 'Über die Verbreitung der politischen Ideologien', *Zeitschrift für Politik*, vol. 3, no. 3 (December, 1956), pp. 193–206.

1011 LORENZ, EMIL, *Der Politische Mythus*, Leipzig, Vienna, and Zürich: Internationaler Psychoanalytischer Verlag, 1923.

1012 LUDZ, PETER CHRISTIAN, 'Dialektik und Ideologie in der Philosophie Hegels: Ein Beitrag zur Phänomenologie des Ideologischen', *Archiv für Rechts- und Sozialphilosophie*, vol. 47 (1961), pp. 133–146.

1013 LUDZ, PETER CHRISTIAN, *Parteielite im Wandel: Funktionsaufbau, Sozialstruktur und Ideologie der SED-Führung*, Cologne-Opladen: Westdeutscher Verlag, 1967.

1014 LUKÁCS, GEORG, 'Marx und das Problem des ideologischen Verfalls', in LUKÁCS, GEORG, *Karl Marx und Friedrich Engels als Literaturhistoriker*, Berlin: Aufbau-Verlag, 1948.

1015 LUKÁCS, GEORG, *Schicksalswende: Beiträge zu einer neuen deutschen Ideologie*, Berlin: Aufbau-Verlag, 1948.

1016 LUKÁCS, GEORG, *Schriften zur Ideologie und Politik* (ed. by Peter C. Ludz), Berlin and Neuwied: Luchterhand Verlag, 1967.

1017 MCCLOSKY, HERBERT, 'Consensus and ideology in American politics', *American Political Science Review*, vol. LXVIII, no. 2 (June, 1964), pp. 361–82.

1018 MACDONAGH, E. C., 'Social myths in Soviet communism', *Sociology and Social Research*, vol. 36, no. 5 (1952), pp. 369–76.

1019 MACDONALD, H. MALCOM, 'The revival of conservative thought', *Journal of Politics*, vol. 19, no. 1 (February, 1957), pp. 66–80.

1020 MACEWAN, ARTHUR, 'Capitalist expansion, ideology, and intervention', in EDWARDS, RICHARD C., REICH, MICHAEL and WEISSKOPF, THOMAS E. (eds), *The Capitalist System: A Radical Analysis of American Society*, Englewood Cliffs, New Jersey: Prentice-Hall, 1972, pp. 409–20.

1021 MACK, RAYMOND W., 'Occupational ideology and the determinate role', *Social Forces*, vol. XXXVI, no. 1 (October, 1957), pp. 37–44.

1022 MACRAE, DONALD G., 'Class relationships and ideology', *Sociological Review*, vol. VI, no. 2 (December, 1958), pp. 261–72.

1023 MACRAE, DONALD G., *Ideology and Society: Papers in Sociology and Politics*, London: Heinemann, 1961, and New York: Free Press, 1962.

1024 MCWILLIAMS, CAREY, *A Mask for Privilege: Anti-Semitism in America*, Boston: Little, Brown, 1948.

1025 MAITRE, J., 'Le catholicisme d'extrême-droite et le croise ante subversive', *Revue Française de Sociologie*, vol. II, no. 2 (April–June, 1961), pp. 106–17.

1026 MALENBAUM, W. and STOLPER, W., 'Political ideology and economic progress', *World Politics*, vol. XII (April, 1960), pp. 413–21.

1027 MALEWSKI, A., 'Der empirische Gehalt der Theorie des historischen Materialismus', *Kölner Zeitschrift für Soziologie und Sozialpsychologie*, vol. 11, no. 2 (1959), pp. 281–305.

1028 MALINOWSKI, BRONISLAW, *Myth in Primitive Psychology*, New York: W. W. Norton, 1926.

1029 MANUEL, FRANK EDWARD, 'Toward a psychological history of utopias', *Daedalus*, vol. 94, no. 2 (April, 1965), pp. 293–322.

1030 MANUEL, FRANK EDWARD (ed.), *Utopias and Utopian Thought*, Boston: Houghton Mifflin, 1966.

1031 MANUEL, FRANK EDWARD (ed.), *French Utopias*, New York: Free Press, 1966.

1032 MAO TSE-TUNG, *On the Correct Handling of Contradictions Among the People*, New York: New Century, 1957.

1033 MARCUSE, HERBERT, *Soviet Marxism: A Critical Analysis*, New York: Columbia University Press, 1958.

1034 MARCUSE, HERBERT, *One Dimensional Man: Studies in the Ideology of Advanced Industrial Society*, Boston: Beacon Press, 1964.

1035 MARCUSE, HERBERT, *An Essay on Liberation*, Boston: Beacon Press, 1968.

1036 MARX, KARL, *The Poverty of Philosophy*, Moscow: Foreign Languages Publishing House, 1956.

1037 MARX, KARL and ENGELS, FRIEDRICH, *The German Ideology*, parts I and III (ed. with an introduction by R. Pascal), New York: International Publishers, 1939.

1038 MARX, KARL and ENGELS, FRIEDRICH, *The Holy Family, or Critique of Critical Critique*, Moscow: Foreign Languages Publishing House, 1956.

1039 MASSO, GILDO, *Education in Utopias*, New York: Teacher's College of Columbia University, 1927.

1040 MATOSSIAN, MARY, 'Ideologies of delayed industrialization: some tensions and ambiguities', *Economic Development and Cultural Change*, vol. 6, no. 3 (April, 1958), pp. 217–28.

1041 MATTELART, ARMAND, 'Une lecture idéologique de l'essai sur le principe de population', *L'Homme et la Société*, vol. 15 (January–March, 1970), pp. 183–219.

1042 MAUS, H., 'Bemerkungen zu Comte', *Kölner Zeitschrift für Soziologie und Sozialpsychologie*, vol. 5, no. 4 (1953), pp. 513–27.

1043 MAUS, H., 'Ideologen', in GALLING, K. (ed.), *Religion in Geschichte und Gegenwart*, vol. III, Tübingen: J. C. B. Mohr (Paul Siebeck), 1959, pp. 566–7.

1044 MAYER, HANS, *Karl Marx und das Elend des Geistes: Studien zur neueren deutschen Ideologie*, Meisenheim am Glan: A. Hain, 1948.

1045 MEIER, A., *Negro Thought in America, 1880–1915: Racial Ideologies in the Age of Booker T. Washington*, Ann Arbor: University of Michigan Press, 1963.

1046 MENA BRITO, BERNARDINO, *Maquinismo*, Mexico: Ediciones Botas, 1933.

1047 MERLEAU-PONTY, M., *Signes*, Paris: Gallimard, 1960.

1048 MILES, GERTRUDE ELIZABETH, 'The Abbé Morelly and His Contribution to Utopian Thought', unpublished dissertation, Syracuse, New York: Syracuse University, 1940.

1049 MILLS, C. WRIGHT, 'The professional ideology of social pathologists', *American Journal of Sociology*, vol. 49, no. 2 (September, 1943), pp. 165–80.

1050 MILLS, C. WRIGHT, *White Collar: The American Middle Classes*, New York: Oxford University Press, 1951.

1051 MILLS, C. WRIGHT, *The Power Élite*, New York: Oxford University Press, 1956.

1052 MILLS, C. WRIGHT, *The Sociological Imagination*, New York: Oxford University Press, 1959.

1053 MINAR, D. W., 'Ideology and political behavior', *Midwest Journal of Political Science*, vol. V, no. 4 (November, 1961), pp. 317–31.

1054 MOLNAR, THOMAS, *Utopia: The Perennial Heresy*, New York: Sheed & Ward, 1967.

1055 MOORE, WILBERT E., 'The utility of utopias', *American Sociologica. Review*, vol. 31, no. 6 (December, 1966), pp. 765–72.

1056 MORAZE, C., *Les bourgeois conquérants, XIXe. siècle*, Paris: Armand Colin, 1957.

1057 MORE, SIR THOMAS, SAINT, *The Most Pleasant, Fruitful, and Witty Work of the best state of a public weal, and of the new isle called Utopia*, 2 vols, London: Shakespeare Press, 1808.

1058 MORGAN, A. E., *Nowhere Was Somewhere*, Chapel Hill: University of North Carolina Press, 1946.

1059 MORGENTHAU, HANS J., *Scientific Man versus Power Politics*, University of Chicago Press, 1946.

1060 MORTON, ARTHUR LESLIE, *The English Utopia*, London: Lawrence & Wishart, 1952.

1061 MORTON, ARTHUR LESLIE, 'Utopias yesterday and today', *Science and Society*, vol. 17, no. 3 (1953), pp. 258–63.

1062 MOSCA, GAETANO, *The Ruling Class*, New York: McGraw-Hill, 1939.

1063 MOSKOS, CHARLES C., JR and BELL, WENDELL, 'Emerging nations and ideologies of American social scientists', *American Sociologist*, vol. 2, no. 2 (May, 1967), pp. 67–72.

1064 MOSSE, GEORGE L., *The Crisis of German Ideology*, New York: Grosset & Dunlap, 1964.

1065 MUKERJI, KRISHNA PRASANNA, *The Implications of the Ideology-Concept*, Bombay: Popular Book Depot, 1955.

1066 MUMFORD, LEWIS, *The Story of Utopias*, New York: Boni & Liveright, 1922.

1067 MUS, P., *Viet-Nam: sociologie d'une guerre*, Paris: Éditions du Seuil, 1952.

1068 MYRDAL, GUNNAR, *The Political Element in the Development of Economic Theory* (trans. by P. Streeten), London: Routledge & Kegan Paul, 1953.

1069 NAESS, ARNE, *et al.*, *Democracy, Ideology, and Objectivity: Studies in the Semantics and Cognitive Analysis of Ideological Controversy*, Oslo University Press, 1956.

1070 NAHRING, VLADIMIR C., 'Some observations on ideological groups', *American Journal of Sociology*, vol. 67, no. 4 (January, 1962), pp. 397–405.

1071 NAUMANN, WALTER, 'The writer in conflict with his age: a study in the ideology of Hermann Hesse', *Monatshefte*, vol. 46, no. 3, pp. 137–44.

1072 NEGLEY, GLENN ROBERT, *The Quest for Utopia*, New York: H. Schuman, 1952.

1073 NETTLER, GWYNN, 'Ideology and welfare policy', *Social Problems*, vol. 6, no. 3 (Winter, 1958–9), pp. 203–12.

1074 NEUSÜSS, ARNHELM, *Utopie: Begriff und Phänomen des Utopischen*, Berlin and Neuwied: Luchterhand Verlag, 1968.

1075 NIEKISCH, E., *Das Reich der niederen Dämonen*, Hamburg: Rowohlt, 1953.

1076 NISBET, ROBERT A., 'Conservatism and sociology', *American Journal of Sociology*, vol. 58, no. 2 (1952), pp. 167–75.

1077 NORTHROP, F. S. C. (ed.), *Ideological Differences and World Order: Studies in the Philosophy and Science of the World's Cultures*, New Haven: Yale University Press, 1949.

1078 OHRENSTEIN, R. A., 'Economic self-interest and social progress in Talmudic literature', *American Journal of Economics and Sociology*, vol. 29, no. 1 (January, 1970), pp. 59–69.

1079 ORTEGA Y GASSET, JOSÉ, *Vom Menschen als utopischem Wesen* (trans. by Gustav Kilpper and Gerhard Lepiorz), Stuttgart: Kilpper, 1952.

1080 PARRINGTON, VERNON LOUIS, *American Dreams: A Study of American Utopias*, Providence: Brown University, 1947.

1081 PARTRIDGE, P. H., 'Politics, philosophy, ideology', *Political Studies*, vol. IX, no. 3 (October, 1961), pp. 217–35.

1082 PETHYBRIDGE, ROGER, 'The assessment of ideological influences on East Europeans', *Public Opinion Quarterly*, vol. 31, no. 1 (Spring, 1967), pp. 38–50.

1083 PETRAS, JOHN, 'Ideology and the United States political scientists', *Science and Society*, vol. 29, no. 2 (Spring, 1965), pp. 192–216.

1084 PETTEE, G. S., 'Ideology in America', *Confluence*, vol. II, no. 2 (June, 1953), pp. 69–80.

1085 PICAVET, FRANÇOIS JOSEPH, *Les idéologues: essai sur l'histoire des idées et des théories scientifiques, philosophiques, religieuses en France depuis 1789*, Paris: F. Alcan, 1891.

1086 PINARD, MAURICE, 'Mass society and political movements: a new formulation', *American Journal of Sociology*, vol. 33 (May, 1968), pp. 682–90.

1087 PLATO, *The Republic* (trans. by Paul Shorey), Cambridge: Harvard University Press, and London: W. Heinemann, 1946.

1088 PLESSNER, HELMUT, 'Abwandlungen des Ideologiegedankens', *Kölner Vierteljahrshefte für Soziologie*, vol. 10 (1931), pp. 147–70.

1089 PLESSNER, HELMUTH, *Diesseits der Utopie: Ausgewählte Beiträge zur Kultursoziologie*, Dusseldorf: Diederichs, 1966.

1090 POPITZ, H., BAHRDT, H. P., JÜRES, E. A. and KESTING, H., *Das Gesellschaftsbild des Arbeiters: soziologische Untersuchungen in der Hüttenindustrie*, Tübingen: J. C. B. Mohr (Paul Siebeck), 1947.

1091 PRICE, RALPH B., 'Ideology and Indian planning', *American Journal of Economics and Sociology*, vol. 26, no. 1 (January, 1967), pp. 47–65.

1092 PYE, LUCIAN W., 'Personal identity and political ideology', *Behavioral Science*, vol. VI, no. 3 (July, 1961), pp. 205–21.

1093 REGNIER, ANDRÉ, 'Les surprises de l'idéologie: Heisenberg et Althusser', *L'Homme et la Société*, vol. 15 (January–March, 1970), pp. 241–54.

1094 REICH, W., *The Mass Psychology of Fascism*, New York: Orgone Institute Press, 1946.

1095 REIGROTZKI, ERICH, 'Die Utopialtität als wissenschaftliche Kategorie', in KARRENBERG, F. and ALBERT, H. (eds), *Sozialwissenschaft und Gesellschaftsgestaltung*, Berlin: Duncker & Humblot, 1963.

1096 REJAI, M., MASON, W. L. and BELLER, D. C., 'Political ideology: empirical relevance of the hypothesis of decline', *Ethics*, vol. 78, no. 4 (July, 1968), pp. 303–12.

1097 REMMLING, GUNTER W., 'Zum Problem der Entlarvung der Ideologien: Review of Hans Albert, *Ökonomische Ideologie und Politische Theorie: Das ökonomische Argument in der ordnungspolitischen Debatte*', *Zeitschrift für Politik*, vol. III, no. 4 (1956), pp. 356–9.

1098 REMMLING, GUNTER W., 'Die Interessenverbände in der westlichen Welt: Zur Frage der gesetzlichen Regelung des Verbändeeinflusses in einzelnen Ländern', *Zeitschrift für Politik*, vol. IV, no. 2 (1957), pp. 169–86.

1099 REMMLING, GUNTER W., 'Zur Soziologie der Macht: Der Beitrag Karl Mannheims zur politischen Soziologie', *Kölner Zeitschrift für Soziologie und Sozialpsychologie*, vol. 12, no. 1 (1960), pp. 53–64.

1100 REMMLING, GUNTER W., 'Immanuel Kant: the limitations of reason', in *Road to Suspicion*, pp. 53–62 (see 182).

1101 REMMLING, GUNTER W., 'Ideology: the twilight of ideas', in *Road to Suspicion*, pp. 105–17 (see 182).

1102 REMMLING, GUNTER W., 'Francis Bacon: the idols of the mind', in *Road to Suspicion*, pp. 118–27 (see 182).

1103 REMMLING, GUNTER W., 'Sigmund Freud: a tortuous epitaph for the mind', in *Road to Suspicion*, pp. 181–98 (see 182).

1104 REMMLING, GUNTER W., 'Die konstitutiven Begriffe und Prinzipien der Wissenssoziologie Mannheims', in *Wissenssoziologie und Gesellschaftsplanung*, pp. 22–36 (see 76).

1105 REMMLING, GUNTER W., 'Marxism and Marxist sociology of knowledge', in *Towards the Sociology of Knowledge*, pp. 135–52 (see 184).

1106 REMMLING, GUNTER W., MAIER, GEORG and REMMLING, ELBA VALDIVIA, 'Social classes in Ecuador: a study of the ideological distortion of social reality', in *Towards the Sociology of Knowledge*, pp. 379–96 (see 184).

1107 RICHARD, MICHAEL P., 'The ideology of Negro physicians: a test of mobility and status crystallization theory', *Social Problems*, vol. 17, no. 1 (Summer, 1969), pp. 20–9.

1108 RIEFF, PHILIP, *Freud: The Mind of the Moralist*, New York: Viking Press, 1959.

1109 RIES, RAYMOND E., 'Social science and ideology', *Social Research*, vol. 31, no. 2 (Summer, 1964), pp. 234–43.

1110 RIESMAN, DAVID, 'Some observations on community plans and utopia', in RIESMAN, D., *Individualism Reconsidered and Other Essays*, Chicago: Free Press, 1954.

1111 RITTER, JOACHIM, *Hegel und die Französische Revolution*, Cologne-Opladen: Westdeutscher Verlag, 1957.

1112 ROSEN, STANLEY, 'Philosophy and ideology: reflections on Heidegger', *Social Research*, vol. 35, no. 2 (Summer, 1968), pp. 260–85.

1113 ROSENBERG, M., 'Misanthropy and political ideology', *American Sociological Review*, vol. XXI, no. 6 (December, 1956), pp. 690–5.

1114 ROSTOW, W. W., 'A note on "the diffusion of ideologies" ', *Confluence*, vol. II, no. 1 (March, 1953), pp. 31–42.

1115 ROSZAK, THEODORE, *The Making of a Counter-Culture*, New York: Doubleday, 1969.

1116 ROUCEK, JOSEPH S., 'A history of the concept of ideology', *Journal of the History of Ideas*, vol. 5 (October, 1944), pp. 479–88.

1117 ROUCEK, JOSEPH S., 'The component parts of ideological forces', *Sociologia*, vol. 22, no. 3 (September, 1960), pp. 290–7.

1118 ROUCEK, JOSEPH S., *Contemporary Political Ideologies*, New York: Philosophical Library, 1961.

1119 ROUCEK, JOSEPH and HODGE, CHARLES, 'Ideology as the implement of purposive thinking in the social sciences', *Social Science*, vol. XI, no. 1 (1936), pp. 25–34.

1120 ROUSSEAS, STEPHEN W. and FARGANIS, JAMES, 'La política estadounidense y el fin de la ideología', *Revista Mexicana de Sociologia*, vol. 27, no. 3 (September–December, 1965), pp. 951–68.

1121 RUYER, RAYMOND, *L'utopie et les utopistes*, Paris: Presses Universitaires de France, 1950.

1122 SABINE, GEORGE H., 'Beyond ideology', *Philosophical Review*, vol. 57, no. 1 (January, 1948), pp. 1–26.

1123 SABINE, GEORGE H., *A History of Political Theory*, New York: Holt, 1950.

1124 SADE, DONATIEN ALPHONSE FRANÇOIS, *Aline et Valcour, ou le roman philosophique*, Brussels: J. J. Gay, 1883.

1125 SALOMON, GOTTFRIED, 'Historischer Materialismus und Ideologienlehre', in *Jahrbuch für Soziologie*, vol. 2 (ed. by G. Salomon), Karlsruhe: G. Braun, 1926, pp. 386–423.

1126 SARTORI, GIOVANNI, 'Politics, ideology and belief systems', *American Political Science Review*, vol. 63 (June, 1969), pp. 398–411.

1127 SAURAMIS, DEMOSTHENES, 'Soziale Utopien', *Soziale Welt*, vol. 8, no. 4 (1957), pp. 294–310.

1128 SCHEIBERT, P., *Von Bakunin zu Lenin: Geschichte der russischen revolutionären Ideologien 1840–95*, vol. I, Leiden: Brill, 1956.

1129 SCHELER, H., *Philosophische Probleme des Übergangs vom Kapitalismus zum Kommunismus*, Berlin: Verlag der Wissenschaften, 1959.

1130 SCHELER, MAX, *Vom Umsturz der Werte*, Leipzig: Der Neue Geist Verlag, 1923.

1131 SCHELSKY, HELMUT, 'Planung der Zukunft: Die Rationale Utopie und die Ideologie der Rationalität', *Soziale Welt*, vol. 17, no. 2 (1966), pp. 155–72.

1132 SCHLATTER, R., *Private Property: The History of an Idea*, New Brunswick: Rutgers University Press, 1951.

1133 SCHORER, M., 'The necessity of myth', *Daedalus*, vol. 88, no. 2 (1959), pp. 359–62.

1134 SCHORR, KARL-EBERHARD, 'Die Legitimation des praktischen Bewusstseins in den Sozialwissenschaften', *Soziale Welt*, vol. 20, no. 2 (1969), pp. 181–98.

1135 SCHRENCK-NOTZING, CASPAR, 'Zukunftsmacher: Die neue Linke in Deutschland und ihre Herkunft', Stuttgart: Seewald, 1968.

1136 SCHULTE HERBRUGGEN, HUBERTUS, *Utopie und Anti-Utopie*, Bochum Langendreer: H. Poppinghaus, 1960.

1137 SCHULZE, ROLF, 'The recession of ideology?', *Sociological Quarterly*, vol. 5 (Spring, 1964), pp. 148–56.

1138 SCHULZE, ROLF, 'Some social-psychological and political functions of ideology', *Sociological Quarterly*, vol. 10, no. 1 (Winter, 1969), pp. 72–83. Reprinted in REMMLING, GUNTER W. (ed.), *Towards the Sociology of Knowledge*, pp. 115–28 (see 184).

1139 SCHUMPETER, JOSEPH A., *Imperialism and Social Classes*, New York: Augustus M. Kelley, 1951.

1140 SCHUMPETER, JOSEPH A., 'Science and ideology', in CLEMENCE, RICHARD V. (ed.), *Essays of Joseph Schumpeter*, Cambridge: Addison-Wesley Press, 1951, pp. 267–81.

1141 SCHWEITZER, A., 'Ideological strategy', *Western Political Quarterly*, vol. XV (March, 1962), pp. 46–66.

1142 SCHWONKE, M., *Vom Staatsroman zur Science Fiction: eine Untersuchung über Geschichte und Funktion der naturwissenschaftlich-technischen Utopie*, Stuttgart: F. Enke Verlag, 1957.

1143 SCOTT, W. A., 'Empirical assessment of values and ideologies', *American Sociological Review*, vol. XXIV, no. 3 (June, 1959), pp. 299–310.

1144 SCOTT, W. A., 'International ideology and interpersonal ideology', *Public Opinion Quarterly*, vol. XXIV (Fall, 1960), pp. 419–35.

1145 SEEMAN, MELVIN, 'On the meaning of alienation', *American Sociological Review*, vol. 24, no. 6 (December, 1959), pp. 783–91.

1146 SHARABI, H., 'The transformation of ideology in the Arab world', *Middle East Journal*, vol. 19, no. 11 (Autumn, 1965), pp. 471–86.

1147 SHILS, EDWARD, 'Primordial, personal, sacred and civil ties', *British Journal of Sociology*, vol. 8, no. 2 (1957), pp. 130–45.

1148 SHKLAR, JUDITH N., *After Utopia: The Decline of Political Faith*, Princeton University Press, 1957.

1149 SHKLAR, JUDITH N., *Political Theory and Ideology*, New York: Macmillan, 1966.

1150 SHUMELDA, J., 'Postwar ideological difficulties in the Soviet Union', *Ukrainian Quarterly*, vol. XI, no. 3 (Summer, 1955), pp. 227–38.

1151 SHUVAL, JUDITH T., 'The role of ideology as a pre-disposing frame of reference for immigrants', *Human Relations*, vol. XII, no. 1 (1959), pp. 51–63.

1152 SIGMUND, PAUL E. (ed.), *The Ideologies of the Developing Nations*, New York: Praeger, 1963.

1153 SKINNER, BURRHUS FREDERIC, *Walden Two*, New York: Macmillan, 1948.

1154 SOREL, GEORGES, *Les illusions du progrès*, Paris: M. Rivière, 1908.

1155 SPIRO, MELFORD E., *Kibbutz: Venture in Utopia*, Cambridge, Massachusetts: Harvard University Press, 1956.

1156 SPIRO, MELFORD E., 'The Sabras and Zionism: a study in personality and ideology', *Social Problems*, vol. V, no. 2 (Fall, 1957), pp. 100–10.

1157 SPRANGER, EDUARD, 'Wesen und Wert politischer Ideologien', *Vierteljahrshefte für Zeitgeschichte*, vol. II, no. 2 (April, 1954), pp. 118–36.

1158 SRINIVAS, P. R., 'Hindu sociology and modern ideologies', *Bulletin of the Rama Krishna Mission Institute of Culture*, vol. VI, no. 5 (May, 1955), pp. 115–19.

1159 STAMMER, OTTO, 'Die Entstehung und die Dynamik der Ideologien', *Kölner Zeitschrift für Soziologie und Sozialpsychologie*, vol. 3, no. 3 (1951), pp. 281–97).

1160 STAMMER, OTTO, 'Ideologische Bindungen', in STAMMER, OTTO, *et al.*, *Verbände und Gesetzgebung*, Cologne-Opladen: Westdeutscher Verlag, 1965.

1161 STARK, WERNER, 'The psychology of social messianism', *Social Research*, vol. XXV, no. 2 (Summer, 1958), pp. 145–57.

1162 STECKLER, GEORGE A., 'Authoritarian ideology in Negro college students', *Journal of Abnormal Social Psychology*, vol. LIV, no. 3 (May, 1957), pp. 396–9.

1163 STEIN, J. W., 'Beginnings of ideology', *South Atlantic Quarterly*, vol. LV (April, 1956), pp. 163–70.

1164 STERN, F. R., *Cultural Despair and the Politics of Discontent: A Study of the 'Germanic' Ideology*, Ann Arbor, Michigan: Michigan University Press, 1954.

1165 SUTTON, F. X., *et al.*, *The American Business Creed*, Cambridge: Harvard University Press, 1956.

1166 SUZIKI, HIROSHI, 'Conception of ideology and utopia', *Japanese Sociological Review*, vol. VII, no. 1 (November, 1957), pp. 50–4.

1167 SZENDE, PAUL, 'Verhüllung und Enthüllung; der Kampf der Ideologien in der Geschichte', *Grünbergs Archiv für die Geschichte des Sozialismus und der Arbeiterbewegung*, vol. 10 (1922), pp. 183–270.

1168 TANDON, B. C., 'Some ideological approaches towards planned economics', *Indian Journal of Economics*, vol. XXXIX, no. 1 (July, 1958), pp. 141–9.

1169 THEBAUD, FRANTZ, 'Katholizismus, Vaudou und Ideologie im soziokulturellen Entwicklungsprozess der Republik Haiti', *Kölner Zeitschrift für Soziologie und Sozialpsychologie*, supplement 13 (1969), pp. 122–35.

1170 THOMAS, LOUIS-VINCENT, 'Une idéologie moderne: La négritude', *Revue de Psychologie des Peuples*, vol. 18, nos 3 and 4, pp. 264–72 and 367–98.

1171 THRUPP, SYLVIA (ed.), *Millennial Dreams in Action*, The Hague: Mouton, 1962.

1172 TILLICH, PAUL, 'Ideologie und Utopie', *Die Gesellschaft*, vol. 6 (October, 1929), pp. 348–55.

1173 TILLICH, PAUL, *Politische Bedeutung der Utopie im Leben der Völker*, Berlin: Gebrüder Weiss, 1951.

1174 TOCH, HANS H., 'Crisis situations and ideological revaluations', *Public Opinion Quarterly*, vol. XIX, no. 1 (Spring, 1955), pp. 53–67.

1175 TOMASIC, D., 'Ideologies and the structure of Eastern European society', *American Journal of Sociology*, vol. 5 (March, 1948), pp. 366–75.

1176 TOMLINSON, T. M., 'The development of a riot ideology among urban Negroes', *American Behavioral Scientist*, 2 (March, 1968), pp. 27–31.

1177 TOPITSCH, ERNST, *Sozialphilosophie zwischen Ideologie und Wissenschaft*, Berlin and Neuwied: Luchterhand Verlag, 1964.

1178 TORRES, J. A., 'Political ideology of guided democracy', *Review of Politics*, vol. XXV (January, 1963), pp. 34–63.

1179 TREVES, R., *Spirito critico e spirito dogmatico*, Milano: Casa Editrice Nuvoletti, 1954.

1180 TUVESON, ERNEST LEE, *Millennium and Utopia*, Berkeley: University of California Press, 1949.

1181 UCCELLI, SANTE ELIO, 'Ideologia e pratica dell'addestramento', *Quaderni di Sociologia*, vol. 25 (Summer, 1957), pp. 147–57.

1182 VAN DUZER, CHARLES HUNTER, *Contribution of the Ideologues to French Revolutionary Thought*, Baltimore: Johns Hopkins Press, 1935.

1183 VENTURI, F., *Roots of Revolution: A History of the Populist and Socialist Movements in 19th Century Russia* (trans. by F. Haskell), London: Weidenfeld & Nicolson, 1960.

1184 VIDICH, ARTHUR J. and BENSMAN, JOSEPH, *Small Town in Mass Society*, Princeton University Press, 1958.

1185 VILLEGAS, OSCAR URIBE, 'En materia de ideología', *Revista Mexicana de Sociología*, vol. 27, no. 3 (September–December, 1965), pp. 941–50.

1186 WALSBY, HAROLD, *The Domain of Ideologies: A Study of the Origin, Development and Structure of Ideologies*, Glasgow: MacLellan, 1947.

1187 WALSH, CHAD, *From Utopia to Nightmare*, New York: Harper, 1962.

1188 WARNER, W. LLOYD, *American Life: Dream and Reality*, University of Chicago Press, 1953.

1189 WATTS, ALAN, *The Book on the Taboo Against Knowing Who You Are*, New York: Random House, 1966.

1190 WAXMAN, CHAIM I. (ed.), *The End of Ideology Debate*, New York: Funk & Wagnall, 1968.

1191 WEBBER, EVERET, *Escape to Utopia: The Communal Movement in America*, New York: Hastings House, 1959.

1192 WEITLING, W. C., *Das Evangelium eines armen Sünders*, Berne: Jenni, 1845.

1193 WEITLING, W. C., *Die Menschheit, wie sie ist und wie sie sein sollte*, Berne: Jenni, 1845.

1194 WHITE, FREDERIC RANDOLPH (ed.), *Famous Utopias of the Renaissance*, New York: Packard, 1946.

1195 WHITE, WINSTON, *Beyond Conformity*, New York: Free Press, 1961.

1196 WILENSKY, HAROLD L. and EDWARDS, HUGH, 'The skidders: ideological adjustments of downward mobile workers', *American Sociological Review*, vol. 24, no. 2 (April, 1957), pp. 215–31.

1197 WILLIAMS, B., 'Democracy and ideology', *Political Quarterly*, vol. XXXII (October, 1961), pp. 374–84.

1198 WINTER, G., 'Conception of ideology in the theory of action', *Journal of Religion*, vol. XXXIX (January, 1959), pp. 43–9.

1199 WIRTH, LOUIS, 'Ideological aspects of social disorganization', *American Sociological Review*, vol. 5, no. 4 (August, 1940), pp. 472–82.

1200 WORSLEY, PETER, *The Trumpet Shall Sound: A Study of Cargo Cults in Melanesia*, London: MacGibbon & Kee, 1957.

1201 WRIGHT, D. M., 'Democracy and economics in American ideology', *Confluence*, vol. II, no. 1 (March, 1953), pp. 55–65.

1202 WYLLIE, I. G., *The Self-Made Man in America: The Myth of Rags to Riches*, New Brunswick, New Jersey: Rutgers University Press, 1954.

1203 ZEITLIN, IRVING M., *Ideology and the Development of Sociological Theory*, Englewood Cliffs, New Jersey: Prentice-Hall, 1968.

1204 ZELTNER, HERMANN, *Ideologie und Wahrheit: Zur Kritik der politischen Vernunft*, Stuttgart-Bad Cannstatt: Frommann, 1966.

1205 ZHDANOV, A. A., *Essays on Literature, Philosophy, Music*, London: Lawrence & Wishart, 1950.

1206 ZIEGLER, HEINZ O., 'Ideologienlehre', *Archiv für Sozialwissenschaft und Sozialpolitik*, vol. 57 (1927), pp. 657–700.

1207 ZITTA, VICTOR, *Georg Lukács' Marxism: Alienation, Dialectics, Revolution: A Study in Utopia and Ideology*, The Hague: M. Nijhoff, 1964.

Selected publications on élites and intellectuals

1208 ANDERSON, CHARLES H., 'The intellectual subsociety hypothesis', *Sociological Quarterly*, vol. 9 (Spring, 1968), pp. 210–27.

1209 ANDERSON, CHARLES H., 'Marginality and the academic', *Sociological Inquiry*, vol. 39, no. 4 (Winter, 1969), pp. 77–83.

1210 ANDERSON, CHARLES H. and MURRAY, JOHN D. (eds), *The Professors: Work and Life Styles among Academicians*, Cambridge, Massachusetts: Schenkman Publishing Company, 1971.

1211 ANDINA, R., *Die Stellung des Akademikers in Gesellschaft und Beruf*, Zürich: Regio, 1951.

1212 ARON, RAYMOND, 'Social structure and the ruling class', *British Journal of Sociology*, vol. I, no. 1 (March, 1950), pp. 1–17; vol. I, no. 2 (June, 1950), pp. 126–44.

1213 ARON, RAYMOND, *The Opium of the Intellectuals* (trans. by Terence Kilmartin), Garden City, New York: Doubleday, 1957.

1214 AVINERI, SHLOMO, 'Marx and the intellectuals', *Journal of the History of Ideas*, vol. XXVIII, no. 2 (April–June, 1967), pp. 269–278.

1215 BARAN, P. A., FRIED, E. and SALVATORE, G., *Intellektuelle und Sozialismus*, Berlin: Wagenbach Verlag, 1968.

1216 BARBER, BERNARD, 'Sociological aspects of anti-intellectualism', *Journal of Social Issues*, vol. 11, no. 3 (1955), pp. 25–30.

1217 BARBUSSE, HENRI, *Manifeste aux intellectuels*, Paris: Les Écrivains Réunis, 1927.

1218 BARKLEY, R., 'The theory of the élite and the mythology of power', *Science and Society*, vol. 19, no. 2 (1955), pp. 97–106.

1219 BARZUN, JACQUES, *The House of Intellect*, New York: Harper, 1959.

1220 BECK, CARL, MALLOY, JAMES M. and CAMPBELL, WILLIAM R., *A Survey of Élite Studies*, Washington, DC: Special Operations Research Office, American University, 1965.

1221 BELOFF, M., 'Intellectual classes and ruling classes in France', *Occidente*, vol. 10, no. 1 (1954), pp. 54–60.

1222 BENDA, JULIEN, *The Treason of the Intellectuals* (trans. by Richard Aldington), New York: William Morrow, 1928.

1223 BERGER, BENNETT M., 'Sociology and the intellectuals: an analysis of a stereotype', in LIPSET, S. M. and SMELSER, NEIL (eds), *Sociology: The Progress of a Decade*, Englewood Cliffs, New Jersey: Prentice-Hall, 1961, pp. 37–46.

1224 BIRNBAUM, NORMAN, 'Die Intellektuellen in der gegenwärtigen Politik der Vereinigten Staaten', *Zeitschrift für Politik*, vol. 2, no. 2 (1955), pp. 118–32.

1225 BODIN, L., *Les intellectuels*, Paris: Presses Universitaires de France, 1964.

1226 BOTTOMORE, T. B., *Élites in Society*, New York: Basic Books, 1964.

1227 BUSCH, ALEXANDER, *Die Geschichte den Privatdozenten*, Stuttgart: F. Enke, 1959.

1228 CAPLOW, THEODORE and MCGEE, REECE J., *The Academic Marketplace*, New York: Basic Books, 1958.

1229 CARLETON, W. G., 'American intellectuals and American democracy', *Antioch Review*, vol. 19, no. 2 (1959), pp. 185–204.

1230 CHARTEER, BARBARA, 'The social role of the literary élite', *Social Forces*, vol. 29, no. 2 (December, 1950), pp. 179–86.

1231 CHATELAIN, ABEL, 'Pour une géographie sociologique de la culture intellectuelle', *Revue de Géographie de Lyon*, vol. 33, no. 2 (1958), pp. 201–8.

1232 CHIAROMONTE, NICOLA, 'On modern tyranny: a critique of Western intellectuals', *Dissent*, vol. XVI, no. 2 (March–April, 1969), pp. 137–50.

1233 CHU WANG, Y., 'The intelligentsia in changing China', *Foreign Affairs*, vol. 36, no. 2 (January, 1958), pp. 315–29.

1234 COSER, LEWIS A., *Men of Ideas: A Sociologist's View*, New York: Free Press, 1965.

1235 CURTI, M., *American Paradox: The Conflict of Thought and Fiction*, New Brunswick: Rutgers University Press, 1956.

1236 DAVIS, JAMES A., 'Locals and cosmopolitans in American graduate schools', *International Journal of Comparative Sociology*, vol. 2, no. 2 (September, 1961), pp. 212–23.

1237 DEAK, ISTVAN, *Weimar Germany's Left-Wing Intellectuals*, Berkeley, California: University of California Press, 1968.

1238 DEMAN, HENDRIK, *Die Intellektuellen und der Sozialismus*, Jena: E. Diederichs, 1926.

1239 DORST, TANKRED, *Die Münchener Räterepublik*, Frankfurt: Suhrkamp Verlag, 1966.

1240 DREITZEL, HANS PETER, *Elitebegriff und Sozialstruktur: Eine soziologische Begriffsanalyse*, Stuttgart: F. Enke, 1962.

1241 ESSLIN, MARTIN, *Brecht: The Man and His Work*, Garden City, New York: Doubleday, 1959.

1242 FAVA, SYLVIA FLEIS, 'The status of women in professional sociology', *American Sociological Review*, vol. 25, no. 2 (April, 1960), pp. 271–6.

1243 FEUER, LEWIS S., *The Scientific Intellectual: The Psychological and Sociological Origins of Modern Science*, New York: Basic Books, 1963.

1244 FOGARASI, ADALBERT, 'Die Soziologie der Intelligenz und die Intelligenz der Soziologie', *Unter dem Banner des Marxismus*, vol. 4, no. 3 (1930).

1245 FOUGEYROLLAS, PIERRE, 'Le mot intellectuel', *Arguments*, vol. 4, no. 20 (1960), pp. 47–9.

1246 FRIEDMAN, NORMAN L., 'The problem of the "runaway Jewish intellectuals"', *Jewish Social Studies*, vol. 31 (January, 1969), pp. 3–19.

1247 GAY, PETER, *Weimar Culture: The Outsider as Insider*, New York: Harper & Row, 1968.

1248 GEIGER, THEODOR, *Aufgaben und Stellung der Intelligenz in der Gesellschaft*, Stuttgart: F. Enke, 1949.

1249 GEIGER, THEODOR, *Den danske intelligens fra Reformationen til Nutiden: en studie in empirisk kultursociologi*, Copenhagen: Munksgaard, 1949.

1250 GEIGER, THEODOR, 'An historical study of the origins and structure of the Danish intelligentsia', *British Journal of Sociology*, vol. 1, no. 3 (September, 1950), pp. 209–20.

1251 GEIGER, THEODOR, 'Intelligentsia', *Acta Sociologica*, vol. 1, no. 1 (1955), pp. 49–61.

1252 GEIGER, THEODOR, 'Der Intellektuelle in der europäischen Gesellschaft von heute', *Acta Sociologica*, vol. 1, no. 1 (1955), pp. 62–74.

1253 GLASER, BARNEY G., 'The local-cosmopolitan scientists', *American Journal of Sociology*, vol. 19, no. 3 (November, 1963), pp. 249–60.

1254 GRAMSCI, ANTONIO, *Gli intellettuali e l'organizzazione della cultura*, Turin: G. Einaudi, 1953.

1255 GROPIUS, WALTER, *The New Architecture and the Bauhaus* (trans. by P. Morton Shand), New York: Museum of Modern Art, and London: Faber & Faber, 1937.

1256 HAJDA, JAN, 'Alienation and integration of student intellectuals', *American Sociological Review*, vol. 26, no. 5 (October, 1961), pp. 758–77.

1257 HARTSHORNE, EDWARD Y., *The German Universities and National Socialism*, Cambridge, Massachusetts: Harvard University Press, 1937.

1258 HEEREN, JOHN, 'Karl Mannheim and the intellectual élite', *British Journal of Sociology*, vol. 22, no. 1 (March, 1971), pp. 1–15.

1259 HENNESSY, C. A. M., 'Intellectuals and politics in Spain', *Occidente*, vol. II, no. 2 (1955), pp. 100–20.

1260 HOFFMANN, K. (ed.), *Macht und Ohnmacht der Intellektuellen*, Hamburg: Wegner, 1968.

1261 HOFSTADTER, RICHARD, *Anti-intellectualism in American Life*, New York: Alfred A. Knopf, 1963.

1262 HOROWITZ, IRVING LOUIS, 'Establishment sociology: the value of being value-free', in HOROWITZ, IRVING LOUIS, *Professing Sociology: Studies in the Life Cycle of Social Science*, Chicago: Aldine, 1968, pp. 159–66.

1263 HOROWITZ, IRVING LOUIS, 'Social science yogis and military commissars', in *Professing Sociology*, pp. 340–54 (see 1262).

1264 HOWE, I. (ed.), *Voices of Dissent: A Collection of Articles from Dissent Magazine*, New York: Grove-Evergreen, 1958.

1265 HUGHES, H. STUART, 'Is the intellectual obsolete? The freely speculating mind in America', *Commentary*, vol. 22, no. 4 (October, 1956), pp. 313–19.

1266 HUMPHREY, R., *Georges Sorel: Prophet without Honour; A Study in Anti-Intellectualism*, Cambridge: Harvard University Press, 1951.

1267 HUSZAR, GEORGE B. DE (ed.), *The Intellectuals: A Controversial Portrait*, Chicago: Free Press, 1960.

1268 JAEGGI, URS, *Die gesellschaftliche Elite: Eine Studie zum Problem der sozialen Macht*, Berne: Haupt, 1960.

1269 JENNINGS, KENT M., *Community Influentials: The Élites of Atlanta*, New York: Free Press, 1964.

1270 JOLL, JAMES, *Intellectuals in Politics: Blum, Rathenau, Marinetti*, London: Weidenfeld & Nicolson, 1960.

1271 KAPLAN, NORMAN, 'The role of the research administrator', *Administrative Science Quarterly*, vol. 4 (June, 1959), pp. 20–42.

1272 KELLER, SUZANNE, *Beyond the Ruling Class: Strategic Élites in Modern Society*, New York: Random House, 1963.

1273 KENT, DONALD PETERSON, *The Refugee Intellectual: The Americanization of the Immigrants of 1933–1941*, New York: Columbia University Press, 1953.

1274 KOESTLER, ARTHUR, *Arrow in the Blue: An Autobiography*, New York: Macmillan, 1952.

1275 KRAUS, W., *Der fünfte Stand: Aufbruch der Intellektuellen in West und Ost*, Berne and Munich: Scherz, 1966.

1276 KRIEGER, LEONARD, 'The intellectuals and European society', *Political Science Quarterly*, vol. LXVII (1952), pp. 225ff.

1277 KUHN, HELMUT, 'Das geistige Gesicht der Weimarer Zeit', *Zeitschrift für Politik*, Neue Folge, vol. VIII (1961), pp. 1–10.

1278 KURUCZ, JENÖ, *Struktur und Funktion der Intelligenz während der Weimarer Republik*, Cologne: Grote, 1967.

1279 LABBENS, JEAN, 'The role of the sociologist and the growth of sociology in Latin America', *International Social Science Journal*, vol. 21, no. 3 (1969), pp. 428–32.

1280 LAQUEUR, WALTER and MOSSE, GEORGE L. (eds), *The Left-Wing Intellectuals between the Wars 1919–1939*, Harper Torchbooks, New York: Harper & Row, 1966.

1281 LASSWELL, HAROLD, LERNER, DANIEL and ROTHWELL, C. EASTON, *The Comparative Study of Élites: An Introduction and Bibliography*, Stanford University Press, 1952.

1282 LASSWELL, HAROLD D. and LERNER, DANIEL (eds), *World Revolutionary Élites: Studies in Coercive Ideological Movements*, Cambridge, Massachusetts: MIT, 1965.

1283 LAZARSFELD, PAUL F. and THIELENS, WAGNER, *The Academic Mind: Social Scientists in a Time of Crisis*, Chicago: Free Press, 1958.

1284 LE GOFF, JACQUES, *Les intellectuels au moyen âge*, Paris: Éditions du Seuil, 1957.

1285 LENK, KURT, 'Die Rolle der Intelligenzsoziologie in der Theorie Mannheims', *Kölner Zeitschrift für Soziologie und Sozialpsychologie*, vol. 15, no. 2 (1963), pp. 323–38.

1286 LEPSIUS, RAINER, 'Kritik als Beruf: zur Soziologie der Intellektuellen', *Kölner Zeitschrift für Soziologie und Sozialpsychologie*, vol. 16 (1964).

1287 LINDENLAUB, D., *Richtungskämpfe im Verein für Sozialpolitik*, Wiesbaden: F. Steiner, 1967.

1288 LIPSET, SEYMOUR MARTIN, 'American intellectuals: their politics and status', in *Political Man* (see 1006).

1289 LIPSET, SEYMOUR MARTIN and SOLARI, ALDO (eds), *Élites in Latin America*, New York: Oxford University Press, 1967.

1290 LOWRY, RITCHIE P., 'The functions of alienation in leadership', *Sociology and Social Research*, vol. 46, no. 4 (July, 1962), pp. 426–35.

1291 LUKÁCS, GEORG, 'Von der Verantwortung der Intellektuellen', in

Aufbau-Verlag (ed.), *George Lukács zum siebzigsten Geburtstag*, Berlin: Aufbau-Verlag, 1955, pp. 232–42.

1292 MANNHEIM, KARL, 'The problem of the intelligentsia: an inquiry into its past and present role', in *Essays on the Sociology of Culture*, pp. 91–170 (see 21).

1293 MANUEL, F. E., *The New World of Henri Saint-Simon*, Cambridge, Massachusetts: Harvard University Press, 1956.

1294 MARCHI, E., 'Nota sugli intellettuali italiani e la politica', *Occidente*, vol. 10, no. 1 (1954), pp. 13–18.

1295 MARTIN, DAVID ALFRED, 'El pacifismo y la intelligentsia durante la "guerra de treinta años" (1914–1945)', *Revista Mexicana de Sociología*, vol. 26, no. 2 (May–August, 1964), pp. 457–82.

1296 MARTINDALE, DON, 'Society, civilization, and the intellectual', in MARTINDALE, DON, *Social Life and Cultural Change*, Princeton, New Jersey: D. Van Nostrand, 1962, pp. 60–92.

1297 MAZZOLA, MICHEL, 'De l'intellectuel chez Marx au marxisme des intellectuels', *Arguments*, vol. 4, no. 20 (1960), pp. 22–6.

1298 MERTON, ROBERT K., 'The role of the intellectual in public bureaucracy', *Social Forces*, vol. 27, no. 4 (May, 1945), pp. 405–15.

1299 MERTON, ROBERT K., 'Patterns of influence: local and cosmopolitan influentials', in MERTON, ROBERT K., *Social Theory and Social Structure* (revised and enlarged edition), Chicago: Free Press, 1957, pp. 387–420.

1300 MICHEL, KARL MARKUS, *Die sprachlose Intelligenz*, Frankfurt: Suhrkamp Verlag, 1968.

1301 MICHELS, ROBERTO, 'Intellectuals', in *Encyclopaedia of the Social Sciences*, vol. 8 (ed. by Edwin R. A. Seligman and Alvin Johnson), New York: Macmillan, 1932, pp. 118–26.

1302 MICHELS, ROBERTO, 'Zur Soziologie der Boheme und ihrer Zusammenhänge mit dem geistigen Proletariat', *Jahrbuch für Nationalökonomie und Statistik*, 3rd series, vol. 81, no. 6 (1932).

1303 MICHELS, ROBERTO, 'Historisch-kritische Untersuchungen zum politischen Verhalten der Intellektuellen', *Schmollers Jahrbuch*, vol. 57 (1933).

1304 MILLER, DELBERT C., 'Town and gown: the power structure of a university town', *American Journal of Sociology*, vol. 68, no. 4 (January, 1963), pp. 432–43.

1305 MILLS, C. WRIGHT, 'The powerless people: the role of the intellectual in society', *Politics*, vol. I, no. 3 (April, 1944), pp. 68–72. Reprinted in MILLS, C. WRIGHT, *Power, Politics and People: The Collected Essays of C. Wright Mills* (ed. by Irving Louis Horowitz), New York: Ballantine Books, 1963, pp. 292–304.

1306 MILLS, C. WRIGHT, 'Intellectuals and Russia', *Dissent*, vol. VI, no. 3 (Summer, 1959), pp. 295–8.

1307 MILLS, C. WRIGHT, 'On intellectual craftsmanship', in GROSS, LLEWELLYN (ed.), *Symposium on Social Theory*, Evanston, Illinois: Row, Peterson, 1959, pp. 25–53; reprinted in *The Sociological Imagination* (see 1052).

1308 MITCHELL, ALLAN, *Revolution in Bavaria: 1918–1919; The Eisner Regime and the Soviet Republic*, Princeton University Press, 1965.

1309 MOLNAR, THOMAS, *The Decline of the Intellectual*, Cleveland: World Publishing, 1961.

1310 MORIN, EDGAR, 'Intellectuels: critique du mythe et mythe de la critique', *Arguments*, vol. 4, no. 20 (1960), pp. 35–40.

1311 MOSSE, GEORGE L., *The Crisis of German Ideology: Intellectual Origins of the Third Reich*, New York: Grosset & Dunlap, 1964.

1312 MUKERJI, D., 'The intellectuals in India', *Confluence*, vol. 4, no. 4 (1956), pp. 443–55.

1313 MYERS, BERNARD S., *The German Expressionists: A Generation in Revolt*, New York: McGraw-Hill, 1963.

1314 NEGT, O., *Universität und Arbeiterbewegung*, Frankfurt: Europäische Verlagsanstalt, 1969.

1315 NEUMANN, FRANZ L., *et al.*, *The Cultural Migration: The European Scholar in America*, University of Pennsylvania Press, 1953.

1316 ORTEGA Y GASSET, JOSÉ, *Der Intellektuelle und der Andere*, Stuttgart: Verlagsanstalt, 1949.

1317 OXAAL, IVAR (ed.), *Black Intellectuals Come to Power: A Study of Creole Nationalism and the Ambiguities of Equality in Trinidad*, Cambridge, Massachusetts: Schenkman, 1968.

1318 PARTISAN REVIEW (eds), *America and the Intellectuals*, PR series, no. 4 (1953).

1319 PIPES, R. (ed.), *The Russian Intelligentsia*, New York: Columbia University Press, 1961.

1320 PISCATOR, ERWIN, *Das politische Theater*, Berlin: A. Schultz, 1929.

1321 POOR, HAROLD L., *Kurt Tucholsky and the Ordeal of Germany, 1914–1935*, New York: Charles Scribner, 1968.

1322 RAINA, P. K., 'Poland: intellectuals vs. the party; a report on the Kolakowski case', *Dissent*, vol. XIV, no. 5 (September–October, 1967), pp. 576–89.

1323 RECORD, WILSON, 'Intellectuals in social and racial movements', *Phylon*, vol. 15, no. 3 (September, 1954), pp. 231–42.

1324 REMMLING, GUNTER W., 'Georg Wilhelm Friedrich Hegel: God in Prussia', in *Road to Suspicion*, pp. 63–71 (see 182).

1325 REMMLING, GUNTER W., 'Wilhelm Dilthey: the fragmentary nature of life', in *Road to Suspicion*, pp. 72–84 (see 182).

1326 REMMLING, GUNTER W., 'The French encyclopedists: subversion of the established order', in *Road to Suspicion*, pp. 128–44 (see 182).

1327 REMMLING, GUNTER W., 'Friedrich Nietzsche: panegyrist of the lie', in *Road to Suspicion*, pp. 165–80 (see 182).

1328 RICHTER, HANS, *Dada: Art and Anti-Art*, New York: McGraw-Hill, 1965.

1329 RIEFF, PHILIP (ed.), *On Intellectuals: Theoretical Studies/Case Studies*, Garden City, New York: Doubleday, 1969.

1330 RIESMAN, DAVID and GLAZER, NATHAN, 'The intellectuals and the discontented classes', *Partisan Review*, vol. 22, no. 1 (Winter, 1955), pp. 47–72.

1331 RIESMAN, DAVID, 'The college professor', in BLANSHARD, BRAND (ed.), *Education in the Age of Science*, New York: Basic Books, 1959.

1332 ROGIN, MICHAEL PAUL, *The Intellectuals and McCarthy: The Radical Specter*, Cambridge, Massachusetts: MIT, 1967.

1333 ROSENBERG, BERNARD, 'Thorstein Veblen: portrait of the intellectual as a marginal man', *Social Probability*, vol. 2, no. 3 (1955), pp. 181–7.

1334 ROSENBERG, HAROLD, 'Twilight of the intellectuals', *Dissent*, vol. V, no. 3 (Summer, 1958), pp. 221–8.

1335 RÜEGG, W., *Die studentische Revolte gegen die bürgerliche Gesellschaft*, Stuttgart: E. Rentsch, 1968.

1336 RUSSELL, BERTRAND, 'The role of the intellectual in the modern world', *American Journal of Sociology*, vol. 44, no. 4 (January, 1939), pp. 491–8.

1337 SCHISCHKOFF, G., *Die gesteuerte Vermassung*, Meisenheim am Glan: A. Hain, 1964.

1338 SCHOENBERGER, FRANZ, *The Inside Story of an Outsider*, New York: Macmillan, 1949.

1339 SCHORSKE, CARL E., *German Social Democracy, 1905–1917: The Development of the Great Schism*, Cambridge: Harvard University Press, 1955.

1340 SCHWARZ, EGON and WEGNER, MATTHIAS (eds), *Verbannung: Aufzeichnungen deutscher Schriftsteller im Exil*, Hamburg: C. Wegner, 1964.

1341 SEEMAN, MELVIN, 'The intellectual and the language of minorities', *American Journal of Sociology*, vol. LXIV, no. 1 (July, 1958), pp. 25–35.

1342 SHILS, EDWARD, 'The intellectuals and the powers: some perspectives for comparative analysis', *Comparative Studies in Social History*, vol. I, no. 1 (1958), pp. 5–22.

1343 SHILS, EDWARD, 'Ideology and civility: on the politics of the intellectual', *Sewanee Review*, vol. LXVI (Summer, 1958), pp. 450–80.

1344 SHILS, EDWARD, 'The traditions of intellectual life: their conditions of existence and growth in contemporary societies', *International Journal of Comparative Sociology*, vol. I, no. 2 (September, 1960), pp. 177–94.

1345 SIMSON, UWE, 'Typische ideologische Reaktionen arabischer Intellektueller auf das Entwicklungsgefaelle', *Kölner Zeitschrift für Soziologie und Sozialpsychologie*, supplement 13 (1969), pp. 136–62.

1346 SOARES-DILLON, G. A., 'Intellectual identity and political ideology among university students', in *Élites in Latin America*, pp. 431–53 (see 1289).

1347 SOLOTAROFF, THEODORE, 'The graduate student: a profile', *Commentary*, vol. 32, no. 6 (1961), pp. 482–90.

1348 SPEIER, HANS, 'Zur Soziologie der bürgerlichen Intelligenz in Deutschland', *Die Gesellschaft*, vol. VI (1929), pp. 58–72.

1349 SPEIER, HANS, 'Die Intellektuellen und ihr sozialer Beruf', *Neue Blätter für den Sozialismus*, vol. 1 (1930), pp. 549–57.

1350 SPEIER, HANS, 'The social conditions of the intellectual exile', in *Social Order and the Risks of War*, pp. 86–94 (see 386).

1351 STEMBER, HERBERT, 'Why they attack intellectuals', *Journal of Social Issues*, vol. 11, no. 3 (1955), pp. 22–4.

1352 VIERECK, PETER, *Shame and Glory of the Intellectuals: Babbitt Jr. versus the Rediscovery of Values*, Boston: Beacon Press, 1953.

1353 WEBER, ALFRED, *Der dritte oder der vierte Mensch: Vom Sinn des geschichtlichen Daseins*, Munich: Piper, 1953.

1354 WEYL, N., *The Creative Élite in America*, Washington, DC: Public Affairs Press, 1966.

1355 WILENSKY, HAROLD L., *Intellectuals in Labor Unions: Organizational Pressures on Professional Roles*, Chicago: Free Press, 1956.

1356 WILENSKY, HAROLD L., 'Mass society and mass culture: interdependence or independence', *American Sociological Review*, vol. 29, no. 2 (April, 1964), pp. 173–97.

1357 WILENSKY, HAROLD L., *Organizational Intelligence: Knowledge and Policy in Government and Industry*, New York: Basic Books, 1967.

1358 WILFERT, O., *Lästige Linke: Ein Überblick über die APO der Intellektuellen, Studenten und Gewerkschafter*, Mainz: Asche, 1968.

1359 WILSON, F. G., 'Public opinion and the intellectuals', *American Political Science Review*, vol. 48, no. 2 (1954), pp. 321–39.

1360 WILSON, LOGAN, *The Academic Man: A Study in the Sociology of a Profession*, New York: Oxford University Press, 1942.

1361 WINETROUT, KENNETH, 'Mills and the intellectual default', in HOROWITZ, IRVING LOUIS (ed.), *The New Sociology: Essays in Social Science and Social Theory in Honor of C. Wright Mills*, New York: Oxford University Press, 1964, pp. 147–61.

1362 WOLPERT, J. F., 'Notes on the American intelligentsia', *Partisan Review*, vol. 14 (1947), pp. 472–85.

1363 WOOD, N., *Communism and the British Intellectuals*, New York: Columbia University Press, 1952.

1364 WOODWARD, C. VANN, 'The populist heritage and the intellectual', *American Scholar* (Winter, 1959–60), pp. 55–72.

1365 WOOLSTON, HOWARD B., 'American intellectuals and social reform', *American Sociological Review*, vol. 1, no. 3 (June, 1936), pp. 363–72.

1366 ZAPF, WOLFGANG, *Wandlungen der deutschen Elite: Ein Zirkulationsmodell deutscher Führungsgruppen 1919–1961*, Munich: Piper, 1963.

1367 ZEHRER, HANS, 'Revolution der Intelligenz', *Die Tat*, vol. 21 (1929), pp. 486–507.

Selected publications on social planning

Background and general aspects

1368 ALLEN, B. W., 'Is planning compatible with democracy?', *American Journal of Sociology*, vol. 42 (June, 1937), pp. 510ff.

1369 BAUER, R. A., SOLA POOL, I. DE and DEXTER, L. A., *American Business and Public Policy*, New York: Atherton Press, 1963.

1370 BOGUSLAW, ROBERT, *The New Utopians*, Englewood Cliffs, New Jersey: Prentice-Hall, 1965.

1371 BOWLEY, ARTHUR L. and HOGG, MARGARET H., *Has Poverty Diminished?*, London: P. S. King, 1925.

1372 BRONFENGRENNER, MARTIN, 'Values and planning: economic consequences of technological change', in BAIER, KURT and RESCHER, NICHOLAS (eds), *Values and the Future: The Impact of Technological Change on American Values*, New York: Free Press, 1969, pp. 453–72.

1373 BROWDER, EARL RUSSELL, *Is Planning Possible under Capitalism?*, New York: Workers Library Publishers, 1933.

1374 CARR-SAUNDERS, A. M. and CARADOG, JONES D., *A Survey of the Social Structure of England and Wales*, London: Oxford University Press, 1927.

1375 CHAMBERLAIN, NEIL W., *Private and Public Planning*, New York: McGraw-Hill, 1965.

1376 COLE, GEORGE D. H. and COLE, MARGARET I., *The Condition of Britain*, London: Victor Gollancz, 1937.

1377 DAHL, ROBERT A. and LINDBLOM, CHARLES E., *Politics, Economics, and Welfare*, New York: Harper, 1953.

1378 DOOB, L. *Plans of Men*, New Haven, Connecticut: Yale University Press, 1944.

1379 ETZIONI, AMITAI, *The Active Society: A Theory of Societal and Political Processes*, New York: Free Press, 1968.

1380 FRIEDMANN, JOHN, *Retracking America: A Theory of Transactive Planning*, Garden City, New York: Anchor/Doubleday, 1973.

1381 GROSS, BERTRAM M. (ed.), *Action under Planning: The Guidance of Economic Development*, New York: McGraw-Hill, 1967.

1382 HAGEN, EVERETT E. and WHITE, STEPHANIE T., *Great Britain: Quiet Revolution in Planning*, National Planning Series, vol. 6, Syracuse University Press, 1966.

1383 HOLCOMBE, A. N., *Government in a Planned Democracy*, New York: W. W. Norton, 1935.

1384 KAHN, HERMANN and WIENER, ANTHONY J., *Toward the Year 2000*, New York: Macmillan, 1967.

1385 KEYNES, JOHN M., *The End of Laissez-Faire*, London: Hogarth, 1926.

1386 LAWLEY, FRANCIS E., *The Growth of Collective Economy*, 2 vols, London: P. S. King, 1938.

1387 LÖWE, ADOLF, *The Price of Liberty: A German on Contemporary Britain*, London: Hogarth, 1937.

1388 LYND, ROBERT, 'The implications of economic planning for sociology', *American Sociological Review*, vol. 9, no. 1 (February, 1944), pp. 14–20.

1389 MACKENZIE, FINDLAY (ed.), *Planned Society: Yesterday, Today, Tomorrow*, New York: Prentice-Hall, 1937.

1390 MCNAMARA, K., *Bibliography of Planning, 1928–1935*, Cambridge, Massachusetts: Harvard University Press, 1936.

1391 MANNING, CHARLES ANTHONY WOODWARD (ed.), *Peaceful Change: An International Problem*, New York: Macmillan, 1937.

1392 MARQUAND, HILARY A. and MEARA, GWYNNE, *South Wales Needs a Plan*, London: George Allen & Unwin, 1936.

1393 MERRIAM, CHARLES EDWARD, 'The possibilities of planning', *American Journal of Sociology*, vol. 49, no. 5 (March, 1944), pp. 397–407.

1394 MYRDAL, GUNNAR, *Beyond the Welfare State: Economic Planning in the Welfare State and Its International Implications*, New Haven, Connecticut: Yale University Press, 1960.

1395 PATRICK, GEORGE THOMAS WHITE, *The Psychology of Social Reconstruction*, Boston: Houghton Mifflin, 1920.

1396 PIGOU, ARTHUR C., *Socialism versus Capitalism*, London: Macmillan, 1938.

1397 PRESIDENT'S RESEARCH COMMITTEE ON SOCIAL TRENDS, *Recent Social Trends in the United States*, 2 vols, New York: McGraw-Hill 1933.

1398 REMMLING, GUNTER W., 'Automation als technisches und soziales Problem', *Schmollers Jahrbuch für Gesetzgebung, Verwaltung und Volkswirtschaft*, vol. 77, no. 2 (1957), pp. 39–60.

1399 REMMLING, GUNTER W., 'Zur Soziologie der Macht: Der Beitrag Karl Mannheims zur politischen Soziologie', *Kölner Zeitschrift für Soziologie und Sozialpsychologie*, vol. 12, no. 1 (1960), pp. 53–64.

1400 REMMLING, GUNTER W., 'Das Unbehagen an der Gesellschaft: Karl Mannheims Beitrag zur Theorie der Gesellschaftsplanung', *Soziale Welt*, vol. 14, nos 3–4 (1963), pp. 241–63.

1401 REMMLING, GUNTER W., *Wissenssoziologie und Gesellschaftsplanung: Das Werk Karl Mannheims*, Dortmund: Verlag Fr. Wilh. Ruhfus, 1968.

1402 RIEMER, SVEND, 'Social planning and social organization', *American Journal of Sociology*, vol. 52, no. 6 (May, 1947), pp. 508–16.

1403 ROBBINS, LIONEL CHARLES, *Economic Planning and International Order*, London: Macmillan, 1937.

1404 ROBSON, W. A. (ed.), *Public Enterprise: Developments in Social Ownership and Control in Great Britain*, London: New Fabian Research Bureau, 1937.

1405 RUGG, HAROLD O., *The Great Technology: Social Chaos and the Public Mind*, New York: John Day, 1933.

1406 SINGH, TARLOK, *Towards an Integrated Society: Reflections on Planning, Social Policy and Rural Institutions*, Bombay: Orient Longmans, 1969.

1407 SKINNER, B. F., *Walden Two*, New York: Macmillan, 1962.

1408 SOULE, GEORGE H., *A Planned Society*, New York: Macmillan, 1932.

1409 TAWNEY, R. H., *Education: The Socialist Policy*, London: Independent Labour Party, 1924.

1410 VEBLEN, THORSTEIN B., *The Instinct of Workmanship and the State of Industrial Arts*, New York: B. W. Huebsch, 1918.

1411 WOOD, ARTHUR LEWIS, 'The structure of social planning', *Social Forces*, vol. 22 (May, 1944), pp. 388–98.

1412 WOOTTON, BARBARA, *Plan or No Plan? A Comparison of Existing Socialist and Capitalist Economic Systems*, New York: Farrar & Rinehart, 1935.

1413 WOOTTON, BARBARA, *Freedom Under Planning*, Chapel Hill: University of North Carolina Press, 1945.

1414 ZWEIG, FERDYNAND, *The Planning of Free Societies*, London: Secker & Warburg, 1942.

Housing and urban renewal planning

1415 ABERCROMBIE, SIR PATRICK, *Town and Country Planning*, London: T. Butterworth, 1933.

1416 ABRAMS, CHARLES, 'Housing in the year 2000', in EWALD, WILLIAM R., JR (ed.), *Environment and Policy*, Bloomington: Indiana University Press, 1968, pp. 209–38.

1417 ANDERSON, MARTIN, *The Federal Bulldozer*, Cambridge: Massachusetts Institute of Technology Press, 1965.

1418 BOARDMAN, P., *Patrick Geddes: Maker of the Future*, Chapel Hill: University of North Carolina Press, 1944.

1419 ELDREDGE, H. WENTWORTH, 'Toward a national policy for planning the environment', in ERBER, ERNEST (ed.), *Urban Planning in Transition*, New York: Grossman, 1970, pp. 3–21.

1420 EWALD, WILLIAM R., JR (ed.), *Environment for Man*, Bloomington: Indiana University Press, 1967.

1421 FELSENSTEIN, JACOB, 'A citizen pleads case for participation in renewal', *Journal of Housing*, vol. 17 (March, 1960), pp. 105–8.

1422 FRIEDEN, BERNARD J. and MORRIS, ROBERT (eds), *Urban Planning and Public Policy*, New York: Basic Books, 1968.

1423 GANS, HERBERT, 'The failure of urban renewal: a critique and some proposals', *Commentary*, vol. XXXIX, no. 4 (April, 1965), pp. 29–37.

1424 GANS, HERBERT J. (ed.), *People and Plans: Essay on Urban Problems and Solutions*, New York: Basic Books, 1968.

1425 GROSSMAN, DAVID A., 'The community renewal program: policy development, progress and problems', *Journal of the American Institute of Planners*, vol. XXIX (November, 1963), pp. 259–69.

1426 HUNTER, DAVID R., *The Slums: Challenge and Response*, New York: Free Press, 1964.

1427 LE CORBUSIER (CHARLES EDOUARD JEANNERET), *The City of To-morrow and Its Planning*, London: J. Rodker, 1929.

1428 MEYERSON, MARTIN and BANFIELD, EDWARD C., *Politics, Planning and the Public Interest: The Case of Public Housing in Chicago*, New York: Free Press, 1964.

1429 NATIONAL COUNCIL OF SOCIAL SERVICE, NEW ESTATES COMMITTEE, *New Housing Estates and Their Social Problems*, London: The Council, 1935.

1430 ROBINOVITZ, FRANCINE F. (ed.), *City Politics and Planning*, New York: Atherton Press, 1969.

1431 ROSSI, PETER and DENTLER, ROBERT A., *The Politics of Urban Renewal: The Chicago Findings*, New York: Free Press, 1961.

1432 SCOTT, MEL, *American City Planning Since 1890*, Berkeley, California: University of California Press, 1969.

1433 U.S. DEPARTMENT OF HOUSING AND URBAN DEVELOPMENT, *Abstracts of 701 Studies, July–September 1968*, Washington, DC: US Government Printing Office, 1969.

1434 WARNER, SAM B., JR (ed.), *Planning for a Nation of Cities*, Cambridge, Massachusetts: MIT, 1966.

1435 WHEATON, WILLIAM, MILGRAM, L. C. and MEYERSON, MARGY, *Urban Housing*, New York: Free Press, 1966.

Land use planning and new communities

1436 BEST, ROBIN H., *Land for New Towns: A Study of Land Use, Densities, and Agricultural Displacement*, London: Town and Country Planning Association, 1964.

1437 CHAPIN, F. STUART, JR, *Urban Land Use Planning*, 2nd edition, Urbana: University of Illinois Press, 1965.

1438 DOXIADES, KONSTANTINOS, *Ekistics: An Introduction to the Science of Human Settlements*, New York: Oxford University Press, 1968.

1439 JONES, BARCLAY G., 'Land uses in the United States in the year 2000', in WEISS, CHARLES M. (ed.), *Man's Environment in the Twenty-First Century*, Chapel Hill: University of North Carolina Press, 1965.

1440 KAISER, EDWARD J., MASSIE, RONALD H., WEISS, SHIRLEY F. and SMITH, JOHN E., 'Predicting the behavior of predevelopment landowners on the urban fringe', *Journal of the American Institute of Planners*, vol. XXXIV, no. 5 (September, 1968), pp. 328–33.

1441 LANDSBERG, HANS H., FISCHMAN, LEONARD L. and FISHER, JOSEPH L., *Resources in America's Future: Patterns of Requirements and Availabilities 1960–2000*, Baltimore: Johns Hopkins Press for Resources for the Future, 1963.

1442 MAYER, ALBERT, 'Ingredients of a effective program for new towns', *Proceedings of the 1964 Conference of the American Institute of Planners*, Washington, DC: American Institute of Planners, 1964, pp. 186–92.

1443 MONTAGUE, ROBERT L. and WREN, TONY P., *Planning for Preservation*, Chicago: American Society of Planning Officials, 1966.

1444 NAIM, JAN, *The American Landscape*, New York: Random House, 1965.

1445 OWINGS, NATHANIEL ALEXANDER, *The American Aesthetic*, New York: Harper & Row, 1969.

1446 PERLOFF, HARVEY S., *Education for Planning: City, State and Region*, Baltimore: Johns Hopkins University Press for Resources for the Future, 1957.

1447 PERLOFF, HARVEY S., 'New towns intown', *Journal of the American Institute of Planners*, vol. XXXII, no. 3 (May, 1966), pp. 155–61.

1448 WHYTE, WILLIAM H., *The Last Landscape*, Garden City, New York: Doubleday, 1968.

1449 WINGO, LOWDON, JR, *Cities and Space*, Baltimore: Johns Hopkins Press, 1963.

Participatory, social, and social welfare planning

1450 BENNIS, W. G., BENNE, K. D. and CHIN, R. (eds), *The Planning of Change*, New York: Holt, Rinehart & Winston, 1961.

1451 BURKE, EDMUND M., 'Citizen participation strategies', *Journal of the American Institute of Planners*, vol. XXXIV, no. 5 (September, 1968), pp. 287–94.

1452 DYCKMAN, JOHN W., 'Social planning, social planners, and planned societies', *Journal of the American Institute of Planners*, vol. XXXII (March, 1966), pp. 66–76.

1453 DYCKMAN, JOHN W., 'Social planning in the American democracy', in *Urban Planning in Transition*, pp. 27–44 (see 1419).

1454 ERLICH, JOHN L., 'Breaking the dole barrier: the lingering death of the American welfare system', *Social Work*, vol. 14, no. 3 (July, 1969), pp. 49–57.

1455 FELLOWS, ERWIN W., 'The sociologist and social planning', *Sociology and Social Research*, vol. 36 (March–April, 1952), pp. 220–6.

1456 FRANCK, L. R., *L'expérience Roosevelt et le milieu social américain*, Paris: Alcan, 1937.

1457 FRIEDEN, BERNARD J., 'The changing prospects for social planning', *Journal of the American Institute of Planners*, vol. XXXIII, no. 5 (September, 1967), pp. 311–35.

1458 KAHN, ALFRED J., *Theory and Practice of Social Planning*, New York: Russell Sage Foundation, 1969.

1459 KANTOROVICH, L. V., *The Best Uses of Economic Resources*, Cambridge, Massachusetts: Harvard University Press, 1965.

1460 LIPPITT, RONALD, WATSON, JEANNE and WESTLEY, BRUCE, *Dynamics of Planned Change*, New York: Harcourt, Brace & World, 1958.

1461 MCCLENAHAN, BESSIE A., 'Sociology and social planning', *Sociology and Social Research*, vol. 38, no. 1 (September–October, 1953), pp. 7–13.

1462 MAYER, ROBERT R., *Social Planning and Social Change*, Englewood Cliffs, New Jersey: Prentice-Hall, 1971.

1463 MERRIAM, CHARLES EDWARD, 'Planning agencies in America', *American Political Science Review*, vol. 29 (1935), pp. 197–212.

1464 NORTH, CECIL C., *Social Problems and Social Planning*, New York: McGraw-Hill, 1932.

1465 REMMLING, GUNTER W., 'Social change and social problems', in *Basic Sociology*, pp. 262–82 (see 362).

1466 ROOS, CHARLES F., *N.R.A. Economic Planning*, Bloomington, Indiana: Principia Press, 1937.

1467 SMITH, HERBERT H., *The Citizen's Guide to Planning*, West Trenton, New Jersey: Chandler-David, 1961.

1468 WILSON, JAMES Q., 'Planning and politics: citizen participation in urban renewal', *Journal of the American Institute of Planners*, vol. XXIX (November, 1964), pp. 242–9.

Planning for community facilities: health, education, recreation

1469 AMERICAN SOCIETY OF PLANNING OFFICIALS, 'Planning for medical facilities', *Planning 1964*, Chicago: The Society, 1964, pp. 190–206.

1470 BAUMOL, WILLIAM J. and BOWEN, WILLIAM G., *Performing Arts: The Economic Dilemma*, New York: Twentieth Century Fund, 1966.

1471 COMMITTEE FOR ECONOMIC DEVELOPMENT, *The Schools and the Challenge of Innovation*, New York: McGraw-Hill, 1969.

1472 DIMOCK, H. S. and SORENSON, ROY, *Designing Education in Values:*

A Case Study in Institutional Change, New York: Association Press, 1955.

1473 FRENCH, RUTH W., *Dynamics of Health Care*, New York: McGraw-Hill, 1968.

1474 HAHN, K., *Education for Leisure*, London: Oxford University Press, 1938.

1475 HILLEBOE, HERMAN E. and SCHAEFER, MORRIS, 'Comprehensive health planning', *Medical Times*, vol. 96 (November, 1968), pp. 1072–80.

1476 HOVNE, AVRER, 'Manpower planning and the restructuring of education', in FRIEDEN, BERNARD J. and MORRIS, ROBERT (eds), *Guidelines for Social Policy in Education*, New York: Basic Books, 1968, pp. 404–22.

1477 KLARMAN, HERBERT E., *The Economics of Health*, New York: Columbia University Press, 1965.

1478 KOHN, ALFRED J. (ed.), *Planning Community Services for Children in Trouble*, New York and London: Columbia Press, 1963.

1479 KOTSCHNIG, WALTER M., *Unemployment in the Learned Professions: An International Study of Occupational and Educational Planning*, London: Oxford University Press, 1937.

1480 NATIONAL CONFERENCE, ARTS COUNCILS OF AMERICA, *The Arts: Planning for Change*, New York: Associated Councils of the Arts, 1966.

1481 REMMLING, GUNTER W., 'Automation und Volksgesundheit', *Deutsche Gesundheitspolitik*, vol. 1, no. 1 (1959), pp. 11–20.

1482 ROCKEFELLER PANEL, *The Performing Arts: Problems and Prospects*, New York: McGraw-Hill, 1965.

1483 SILBERMAN, CHARLES E., *Crisis in the Classroom*, New York: Random House, 1970.

Transportation planning

1484 BRANCH, MELVILLE C., *Transportation Development, Cities, and Planning*, Chicago: American Society of Planning Officials, 1965.

1485 FITCH, LYLE C. AND ASSOCIATES, *Urban Transportation and Public Policy*, San Francisco: Chandler, 1964.

1486 MEYER, J. R., *et al.*, *The Urban Transportation Problem*, Cambridge, Massachusetts: Harvard University Press, 1965.

1487 OWEN, WILFRED, *The Metropolitan Transportation Problem*, revised edition, Washington, DC: Brookings Institute, 1966.

1488 SCHRIEVER, BERNARD A. and SEIFERT, WILLIAM W., *Air Transportation 1975 and Beyond, A Systems Approach: Report of the Transportation Workshop, 1967*, Cambridge, Massachusetts: MIT, 1968.

1489 SMITH, WILBUR AND ASSOCIATES, *Future Highways and Urban Growth*, New Haven, Connecticut: Smith and Associates, 1961.

1490 STEERING GROUP OF THE MINISTRY OF TRANSPORT, *Cars for Cities: A Study of Trends in the Design of Vehicles with Particular Reference to Their Use in Towns*, London: HMSO, 1967.

1491 WINGO, LOWDON, *Transportation and Urban Land*, Washington, DC: Resources for the Future, 1961.

Notes

1 The significance and development of Mannheim's sociology

1 Herbert Spencer, *The Study of Sociology*, 9th edition, London and Edinburgh: Williams & Norgate, 1880, p. 73.
2 Wilhelm Dilthey, *Weltanschauungslehre: Abhandlungen zur Philosophie der Philosophie*, *Gesammelte Schriften*, vol. VIII, Leipzig and Berlin: B. G. Teubner, 1931, p. 224 (my translation).
3 See Wilhelm Dilthey, *Einleitung in die Geisteswissenschaften: Versuch einer Grundlegung für das Studium der Gesellschaft und der Geschichte*, *Gesammelte Schriften*, vol. I, Stuttgart: B. G. Teubner, 1923, p. 413.
4 Arthur Schopenhauer, *The World as Will and Idea*, vol. I (trans. by R. B. Haldane and J. Kemp), 9th impression, London: Routledge & Kegan Paul, 1948, p. 530.
5 See Karl Marx and Friedrich Engels, *The German Ideology*, parts I and III (ed. with an introduction by R. Pascal), New York: International Publishers, 1939, p. 6.
6 Émile Durkheim, *Suicide* (trans. by John A. Spaulding and George Simpson), London: Routledge & Kegan Paul, 1963, p. 245.
7 Karl Marx, *Economic and Philosophic Mansucripts of 1844*, Moscow: Foreign Languages Publishing House, 1961, p. 119 (emphasis in original).
8 For a more detailed analysis of Mannheim's first phase see Gunter W. Remmling, 'The radical sociology of knowledge and beyond', in Gunter W. Remmling, *Road to Suspicion: A Study of Modern Mentality and the Sociology of Knowledge*, New York: Appleton-Century-Crofts, 1967; Englewood Cliffs, New Jersey: Prentice-Hall, 1974, pp. 40–9. For the general problems of Mannheim's sociology see Gunter W. Remmling, *Wissenssoziologie und Gesellschaftsplanung: Das Werk Karl Mannheims*, Dortmund: Verlag Fr. Wilh. Ruhfus, 1968. For the general structural context of the sociology of knowledge see Gunter W. Remmling 'The intellectual heritage of sociology', in Gunter W. Remmling and Robert B. Campbell, *Basic Sociology: An Introduction to the Study of Society*, Totowa, New Jersey: Littlefield, Adams, 1970, pp. 25–57. For overall orientation see Gunter W. Remmling, 'Existence and

thought', in Gunter W. Remmling (ed.), *Towards the Sociology of Knowledge: Origin and Development of a Sociological Thought Style*, London: Routledge & Kegan Paul, and New York: Humanities Press, 1973, pp. 3–43.

2 Philosophical parameters of Mannheim's sociology of knowledge

1 On the origin of positivist philosophy in Saint-Simon's thought see Émile Durkheim, *Socialism* (ed. with an introduction by Alvin W. Gouldner; trans. by Charlotte Sattler), Collier Books, New York: Macmillan, 1962, p. 142.

2 As the following chapter will demonstrate the sociological stage in Mannheim's early work was dominated by his efforts on behalf of the utilization of ideologically defused conceptual resources provided by Karl Marx's method of ideological analysis, the general Marxist skill in the socio-existential grounding of theory, and Georg Lukács's partial relativization of historical materialism. For the discussion of Mannheim's sociology of knowledge and its connections with the Marxist universe of discourse, see also Gunter W. Remmling, 'Marxism and Marxist sociology of knowledge', in Gunter W. Remmling (ed.), *Towards the Sociology of Knowledge: Origin and Development of a Sociological Thought Style*, London: Routledge & Kegan Paul, and New York: Humanities Press, 1973, pp. 135–52, and Gunter W. Remmling, 'Ideology: the twilight of ideas', in Gunter W. Remmling, *Road to Suspicion: A Study of Modern Mentality and the Sociology of Knowledge*, New York: Appleton-Century-Crofts, 1967; Englewood Cliffs, New Jersey: Prentice-Hall, 1974, pp. 105–17; see also 'The French encyclopedists: subversion of the established order', in ibid., pp. 128–44.

3 See Georg Lukács, 'Mein Weg zu Marx', in *Georg Lukács zum siebzigsten Geburtstag*, Berlin: Aufbau-Verlag, 1955, p. 228.

4 See Karl Mannheim, 'Seele und Kultur' (trans. by Ernest Manheim), in Karl Mannheim, *Wissenssoziologie: Auswahl aus dem Werk* (ed. and with an introduction by Kurt H. Wolff), Berlin: Hermann Luchterhand Verlag, 1964, p. 68 and pp. 83–4.

5 See ibid., p. 68. See also Karl Mannheim, 'Historicism', in Karl Mannheim, *Essays on the Sociology of Knowledge* (ed. by Paul Kecskemeti), London: Routledge & Kegan Paul, 1952, p. 124.

6 See Karl Mannheim, 'Besprechung von Georg Lukács, Die Theorie des Romans', in Karl Mannheim, *Wissenssoziologie: Auswahl aus dem Werk*, p. 85.

7 For the discussion of Mannheim's Hungarian experience I am indebted to Lewis Coser's *Masters of Sociological Thought*, New York: Harcourt Brace Jovanovich, 1971. See also Zoltan Horvath, *Die Jahrhundertwende in Ungarn*, Neuwied and Berlin: Luchterhand, 1966; A. Kaas and F. de Lazarovics, *Bolshevism in Hungary: The Bela Kun Period*, London: Grant Richards, 1931; David Kettler, *Marxismus und Kultur: Mannheim und Lukács in den ungarischen Revolutionen 1918/19*, Neuwied and Berlin: Luchterhand, 1967; Georg Lukács, *Schriften zur Literatursoziologie* (ed. and introduced by Peter Ludz), Neuwied and Berlin: Luchterhand, 1961.

8 Among the numerous works on the Weimar Republic I have profited especially from the following books: Prinz Max von Baden, *Memoirs*, 2 vols (trans. by W. M. Calder and C. W. H. Sutton), London: Constable, 1928; Stephen M. Bouton, *And the Kaiser Abdicates: The German Revolution, November, 1918–August, 1919*, New Haven: Yale University Press, 1920; Karl Dietrich Bracher, *Die Auflösung der Weimarer Republik*, Stuttgart: Ring-Verlag, 1955; Istvan Deak, *Weimar Germany's Left-Wing Intellectuals*, Berkeley: University of California Press, 1968; Erich Eyck, *A History of the Weimar Republic*, 2 vols (trans. by H. P. Hanson and R. L. G. Waite), Cambridge: Harvard University Press, 1962–3; Emil J. Gumbel, *Vom Fememord zur Reichskanzlei*, Heidelberg: Schneider, 1962; William S. Halperin, *Germany Tried Democracy*, New York: Crowell, 1946; Harold L. Poor, *Kurt Tucholsky and the Ordeal of Germany, 1914–1935*, New York: Charles Scribner, 1968; Hans Richter, *Dada*, New York: McGraw-Hill, 1965; Philipp Scheidemann, *The Making of the New Germany*, 2 vols, New York: Appleton, 1929; Hugo Sinzheimer and Ernst Fraenkel, *Die Justiz in der Weimarer Republik*, Neuwied and Berlin: Luchterhand, 1968; Louis L. Snyder, *The Weimar Republic*, Princeton: Van Nostrand, 1966; Eric Sutton (ed.), *Gustav Stresemann: His Diaries, Letters, and Papers*, 3 vols, New York: Macmillan, 1935–40; Ernst Troeltsch, *Spektator-Briefe*, Tübingen: Mohr, 1924; Henry A. Turner, Jr, *Stresemann and the Politics of the Weimar Republic*, Princeton University Press, 1963; Robert G. L. Waite, *Vanguard of Nazism: The Free Corps Movement in Post-War Germany, 1918–1923*, Cambridge: Harvard University Press, 1952; John W. Wheeler-Bennett, *The Nemesis of Power: The German Army in Politics, 1918–1945*, London and New York: St Martin's Press, 1954.

9 See Karl Mannheim, *Ideology and Utopia: An Introduction to the Sociology of Knowledge* (trans. by Louis Wirth and Edward Shils), New York: Harcourt, Brace & World, 1936, p. 241.

10 See ibid., p. 59.

11 See Karl Mannheim, *Essays on Sociology and Social Psychology* (ed. by Paul Kecskemeti), London: Routledge & Kegan Paul, 1953, pp. 15–30.

12 See Wilhelm Dilthey, *Einleitung in die Geisteswissenschaften: Versuch einer Grundlegung für das Studium der Gesellschaft und der Geschichte*, *Gesammelte Schriften*, vol. I, Stuttgart: B. G. Teubner, 1923. See also Wilhelm Dilthey, *Der Aufbau der geschichtlichen Welt in den Geisteswissenschaften*, *Gesammelte Schriften*, vol. VII, Leipzig and Berlin: B. G. Teubner, 1927.

13 See Karl Mannheim, *Essays on the Sociology of Knowledge*, p. 81 n.

14 See ibid., pp. 43–63.

15 On the concept of 'central attitude' see Kurt H. Wolff, 'The sociology of knowledge: emphasis on an empirical attitude', *Philosophy of Science*, vol. 10, no. 2 (April, 1943), p. 112. Mannheim's 'documentary method of interpretation' has been acknowledged by Harold Garfinkel as an important element in the analysis of 'common understandings' which underlie the routine 'activities of everyday life'. See Harold Garfinkel, *Studies in Ethnomethodology*, Englewood Cliffs, New Jersey: Prentice-Hall, 1967, p. 40 and pp. 76–103.

16 Mannheim attempts to mitigate the relativistic implications of documentary interpretation with the dubious distinction between historical periods that are closer in essence to a particular age and others that are more distant to that age. He concludes arbitrarily that the interpretation of the historical period with the closest affinity will 'prevail'. See Karl Mannheim, *Essays on the Sociology of Knowledge*, p. 61.

17 See Karl Mannheim, 'Zum Problem einer Klassifikation der Wissenschaften', in Karl Mannheim, *Wissenssoziologie: Auswahl aus dem Werk*, pp. 155–65.

18 See Karl Mannheim, 'Historicism', pp. 84–133. For Dilthey's historicism see Wilhelm Dilthey, *Der Aufbau der geschichtlichen Welt in den Geisteswissenschaften*. See also Wilhelm Dilthey, *The Essence of Philosophy* (trans. by Stephen A. Emery and William T. Emery), Chapel Hill: University of North Carolina Press, 1954, and William Kluback, *Wilhelm Dilthey's Philosophy of History*, New York: Columbia University Press, 1956.

19 The French Revolution of 1789 and the resulting social conflict influenced the development of new, conflicting socio-historical perspectives. For these connections see Karl Mannheim, 'Conservative thought', in Karl Mannheim, *Essays on Sociology and Social Psychology*, pp. 74–164.

20 See Ernst Troeltsch, 'Moderne Geschichtsphilosophie', in Ernst Troeltsch, *Gesammelte Schriften*, vol. II, Tübingen: J. C. B. Mohr, 1912–25, pp. 673–728. See also Ernst Troeltsch, *Der Historismus und seine Probleme*, vol. I, Tübingen: J. C. B. Mohr, 1922, and Ernst Troeltsch, *Der Historismus und seine Überwindung*, Berlin: R. Heise, 1924.

21 Karl Mannheim, 'Historicism', p. 102.

22 Ibid., p. 102. The historicist fusion of past, present, and future is formally similar to George Herbert Mead's symbolic interactionist treatment of thinking, intelligence, and knowledge as processes; Mead's formulations appeared in printed form ten years after the publication of Mannheim's article on 'Historicism'. As McKinney points out Mead interprets intelligence essentially as the capacity for problem solving; this activity is guided by past experience and the desire to solve contemporary problems with attention to future consequences. See John C. McKinney, 'The contribution of George H. Mead to the sociology of knowledge', *Social Forces*, vol. 34, no. 2 (December, 1955), p. 148. Mead describes thinking as a process within the individual: this process, however, has its basis and origin external to the individual, that is, in the experiential matrix of social relations and interactions among people. See George Herbert Mead, *Mind, Self, and Society* (ed. by Charles W. Morris), University of Chicago Press, 1934, p. 156.

23 Karl Mannheim, 'Historicism', p. 104 (emphasis in original).

24 See Johann Gustav Droysen, *Outline of the Principles of History* (trans. by E. Benjamin Andrews), Boston: Ginn, 1893, pp. 12–13.

25 Karl Mannheim, 'Historicism', p. 105. See also Edmund Husserl, *Ideas: General Introduction to Pure Phenomenology* (trans. by W. R. Boyce Gibson), New York: Macmillan, 1952, pp. 130–8.

26 See Louis Wirth, 'Preface', to Karl Mannheim, *Ideology and Utopia*,

p. xxix; Robert K. Merton, *Social Theory and Social Structure*, enlarged edition, New York: Free Press, 1968, p. 562; John C. McKinney, op. cit., pp. 144–9; Peter L. Berger, 'Identity as a problem in the sociology of knowledge', *European Journal of Sociology*, vol. VII (1966), pp. 105–15; Peter L. Berger and Thomas Luckmann, *The Social Construction of Reality: A Treatise in the Sociology of Knowledge*, Garden City, New York: Doubleday, 1966. See also Harvey A. Farberman, 'Mannheim, Cooley, and Mead: toward a social theory of mentality', *Sociological Quarterly*, vol. 11, no. 1 (Winter, 1970), pp. 3–13; James E. Curtis and John W. Petras, 'Introduction' to James E. Curtis and John W. Petras (eds), *The Sociology of Knowledge: A Reader*, New York: Praeger, 1970, pp. 28–31; and Leon Shaskolsky, 'The development of sociological theory in America: a sociology of knowledge interpretation', in Larry T. Reynolds and Janice M. Reynolds (eds), *The Sociology of Sociology*, New York: David McKay, 1970, pp. 16–20.

27 Wilhelm Windelband and even more so Heinrich Rickert maintained that *any* object matter may ultimately be analyzed either through the optic of the idiographic method or that of the nomothetic method. In opposition to Dilthey this line of demarcation was designed to cut across any distinction made with regard to the different qualities of scientific object matter. See Wilhelm Windelband, *Geschichte und Naturwissenschaft*, Strassburg: J. H. E. Heitz, 1894. See also Heinrich Rickert, *Kulturwissenschaft und Naturwissenschaft*, Tübingen: J. C. B. Mohr, 1899.

28 See Alfred Weber, 'Prinzipielles zur Kultursoziologie: Gesellschaftsprozess, Zivilisationsprozess und Kulterbewegung', *Archiv für Sozialwissenschaft und Sozialpolitik*, vol. 47 (1920), pp. 1–49. For a discussion of Weber's principles see Robert K. Merton, 'Civilization and culture', *Sociology and Social Research*, vol. 21 (November–December, 1936), pp. 103–13. Weber's third concept of 'social process' had no relevance for the methodological problems pursued by Mannheim. See also Alfred Weber, *Prinzipien der Geschichts- und Kultursoziologie*, Munich: Piper, 1951, and Alfred Weber, *Fundamentals of Culture-Sociology* (trans. by G. H. Weltner and C. F. Hirschman), New York: Progress Administration and Columbia University, 1939 (mimeographed); partially reprinted in Talcott Parsons, *et al.* (eds), *Theories of Society: Foundations of Modern Sociological Theory*, vol. II, New York: Free Press, 1961, pp. 1274–83.

29 Karl Mannheim, 'Historicism', p. 118.

30 Ibid., p. 119.

31 Ibid., p. 124.

32 Ibid.

33 See Peter Gay, *Weimar Culture: The Outsider as Insider*, New York: Harper & Row, 1968, p. xiv. See also Franz Schoenberger, *The Inside Story of an Outsider*, New York: Macmillan, 1949.

34 See Jean-Paul Sartre, *Being and Nothingness: An Essay in Phenomenological Ontology* (trans. by Hazel E. Barnes), 5th edition, New York: Citadel Press, 1968, p. 529.

35 Karl Mannheim, 'Historicism', pp. 128–9.

36 See Alvin W. Gouldner, 'The sociologist as partisan: sociology and the

welfare state', *American Sociologist*, vol. 3, no. 2 (May, 1968), pp. 103–16. For a general presentation see Robert G. Snyder, 'Knowledge, power and the university: notes on the impotence of the intellectual', in Gunter W. Remmling (ed.), *Towards the Sociology of Knowledge: Origin and Development of a Sociological Thought Style*, pp. 339–59.

3 The development of the conceptual matrix

1 Karl Mannheim, 'Historicism', in Karl Mannheim, *Essays on the Sociology of Knowledge* (ed. by Paul Kecskemeti), London: Routledge & Kegan Paul, 1952, p. 125.
2 Ibid., p. 126.
3 See Peter Gay, *Weimar Culture: The Outsider as Insider*, New York: Harper & Row, 1968, p. xiv.
4 Karl Mannheim, 'The problem of a sociology of knowledge', in Karl Mannheim, op. cit., p. 136 (emphasis in original).
5 See ibid., pp. 137–44.
6 See ibid., pp. 149–90.
7 Ibid., p. 190.
8 See Karl Mannheim, 'The ideological and the sociological interpretation of intellectual phenomena' (trans. by Kurt H. Wolff), in *From Karl Mannheim* (ed. and with an introduction by Kurt H. Wolff), New York: Oxford University Press, 1971, pp. 116–31.
9 Karl Mannheim, 'Conservative thought', in Karl Mannheim, *Essays on Sociology and Social Psychology* (ed. by Paul Kecskemeti), London: Routledge & Kegan Paul, 1953, p. 101.
10 Ibid., p. 91.
11 See ibid., pp. 84–119.
12 See Karl Mannheim, 'The problem of generations', in Karl Mannheim, *Essays on the Sociology of Knowledge*, pp. 276–320.
13 See Arnhelm Neusüss, *Utopisches Bewusstsein und freischwebende Intelligenz*, Meisenheim am Glan: Verlag Anton Hain, 1968, p. 45.
14 See also Karl Mannheim, 'Towards the sociology of the mind: an introduction', in Karl Mannheim, *Essays on the Sociology of Culture* (ed. by Ernest Manheim and Paul Kecskemeti), London: Routledge & Kegan Paul, 1956, pp. 15–89.
15 Karl Mannheim, 'Competition as a cultural phenomenon', in Karl Mannheim, *Essays on the Sociology of Knowledge*, pp. 196–7.
16 See Karl Marx and Friedrich Engels, *The Communist Manifesto* (ed. by Samuel H. Beer), New York: Appleton-Century-Crofts, 1955, p. 30; see also Friedrich Nietzsche, *Gesammelte Werke*, vol. XV, Munich: Musarion Verlag, 1920–9, p. 284.
17 Karl Mannheim, 'Competition as a cultural phenomenon', p. 208.
18 See ibid., pp. 221–9.
19 See Auguste Comte, *The Positive Philosophy* (freely trans. and condensed by Harriet Martineau), New York: Calvin Blanchard, 1858, pp. 453–68. On the role of the French Enlightenment philosophers in the social analysis of knowledge see Gunter W. Remmling, 'The French encyclopedists: subversion of the established order', in Gunter W. Remmling, *Road to Suspicion*, New York: Appleton-Century-Crofts,

1967; Englewood Cliffs, New Jersey: Prentice-Hall, 1974, pp. 128–44. For further developments in Marxist social theory see Gunter W. Remmling, 'Marxism and Marxist sociology of knowledge', in Gunter W. Remmling (ed.), *Towards the Sociology of Knowledge*, London: Routledge & Kegan Paul, and New York: Humanities Press, 1973, pp. 135–52.

20 See Georg G. Iggers, 'Elements of a sociology of ideas in the Saint-Simonian philosophy of history', in Gunter W. Remmling (ed.), *Towards the Sociology of Knowledge*, pp. 60–7.

21 See Émile Durkheim and Marcel Mauss, *Primitive Classification* (trans. by Rodney Needham from 'De quelques formes primitives de classification', *L'Année Sociologique*, 1902), University of Chicago Press, 1963; Émile Durkheim and Célestin Bouglé, 'Les conditions sociologiques de la connaissance', *L'Année Sociologique*, vol. 11 (1906–9), pp. 41–8; Émile Durkheim, 'Sociologie religieuse et théorie de la connaissance', *Revue de Métaphysique et de Morale*, vol. 17, no. 6 (November, 1909), pp. 733–58; Émile Durkheim, 'Subject of our study: religious sociology and the theory of knowledge', Introduction to Émile Durkheim, *The Elementary Forms of the Religious Life* (trans. by Joseph Ward Swain), New York: Free Press, 1965, pp. 13–33; and 'Conclusion', ibid., pp. 462–96. See also Maurice Halbwachs, *Les cadres sociaux de la mémoire*, Paris: F. Alcan, 1925; Marcel Granet, *La pensée chinoise*, Paris: La Renaissance du Livre, 1934.

22 For Max Weber's unsystematic contributions to the developing sociology of knowledge perspective see Alexander von Schelting, *Max Webers Wissenschaftslehre*, Tübingen: J. C. B. Mohr, 1934. See also Werner Stark, *The Sociology of Knowledge*, London: Routledge & Kegan Paul, 1958.

23 See Max Scheler, *Die Wissensformen und die Gesellschaft*, *Gesammelte Werke*, vol. 8 (ed. with commentaries by Maria Scheler), Berne and Munich: Francke Verlag, 1960, pp. 61–4.

24 See ibid., pp. 66–8; see also Karl Mannheim, 'The problem of a sociology of knowledge', pp. 151–75, and Karl Mannheim, 'Competition as a cultural phenomenon', p. 199. For a similar view, supported by anthropological observations, see Bronislaw Malinowski, *Magic, Science, and Religion and Other Essays*, Anchor Books, Garden City, New York: Doubleday, 1954, pp. 29–32. The contemporary counter culture has a strong basis in types of thought derived from centers of experience that remained untouched by scientific-technological reality constructions; see for example Theodore Roszak, *The Making of a Counter Culture: Reflections on the Technocratic Society and Its Youthful Opposition*, Garden City, New York: Doubleday, 1969.

4 The establishment of the sociology of knowledge

1 See Karl Mannheim, *Ideologie und Utopie*, Bonn: Friedrich Cohen, 1929, pp. 67–8.

2 See Karl Mannheim, 'The sociology of knowledge', in Karl Mannheim, *Ideology and Utopia: An Introduction to the Sociology of Knowledge* (trans. by Louis Wirth and Edward Shils), New York: Harcourt, Brace & World, 1936, p. 242.

3 See Karl Mannheim, *Ideology and Utopia*, p. 72.
4 See ibid., p. 40.
5 See Wilhelm Dilthey, *Der Aufbau der geschichtlichen Welt in den Geisteswissenschaften*, *Gesammelte Schriften*, vol. VII, Leipzig and Berlin: B. G. Teubner, 1927, p. 191.
6 See Wilhelm Dilthey, *Die Geistige Welt: Einleitung in die Philosophie des Lebens*, *Gesammelte Schriften*, vol. V, Leipzig and Berlin: B. G. Teubner, 1924, pp. 4–5. See also Karl Mannheim, 'The sociology of knowledge', p. 250.
7 See ibid., p. 239. See also Wilhelm Dilthey, *Einleitung in die Geisteswissenschaften: Versuch einer Grundlegung für das Studium der Gesellschaft und der Geschichte*, *Gesammelte Schriften*, vol. I, Stuttgart: B. G. Teubner, 1923, p. 413.
8 See Karl Mannheim, 'The sociology of knowledge', p. 243. See also Max Scheler, *Die Wissensformen und die Gesellschaft*, *Gesammelte Werke*, vol. 8 (ed. by Maria Scheler), Berne and Munich: Francke Verlag, 1960, pp. 21–58.
9 According to Boulding's theory of *eiconics* our responses to reality are always mediated by the *image* which combines the projections of personality with the normative expectations maintained by social groups. See Kenneth E. Boulding, *The Image: Knowledge in Life and Society*, Ann Arbor: University of Michigan Press, 1956, p. 14 and pp. 174–5. Mannheim's approach also invites comparison to Festinger's 'cognitive dissonance' theory; Festinger assumes that individuals avoid dissonance and seek consonance among their cognitions in order to maintain their psychic structure which consists of an organized set of cognitions. See Leon Festinger, *A Theory of Cognitive Dissonance*, Evanston, Illinois: Row, Peterson, 1957.
10 See Karl Mannheim, 'The sociology of knowledge', pp. 263–4; see also Karl Mannheim, *Ideology and Utopia*, p. 77. Recently Brunner has developed perspective contexts of a specifically sociological nature; see Otto Brunner, *Neue Wege der Verfassungs- und Sozialgeschichte*, 2nd edition, Göttingen: Vandenhoeck & Ruprecht, 1968.
11 On Durkheim's position and the criticism of sociological reinterpretations of Kantian epistemology see Gunter W. Remmling, *Road to Suspicion*, New York: Appleton-Century-Crofts, 1967; Englewood Cliffs, New Jersey: Prentice-Hall, 1974, pp. 12–15. Mannheim's assumption of an historical changeability of the categories also continues Dilthey's attempts to 'historicize the *a priori*'. See ibid., p. 79.
12 See Karl Mannheim, 'The sociology of knowledge', pp. 240–3.
13 See ibid., pp. 275–8. On the use of statistics in contemporary methods of imputation see Hans Jürgen Krysmanski, 'Metrische Vorstellungen: Zur wissenssoziologischen Beschreibung modernen Bewusstseins', *Soziale Welt*, vol. 14, nos 3–4 (1963), pp. 298–9.
14 See Ernst Niekisch, *Gewagtes Leben*, Cologne and Berlin: Kiepenheuer & Witsch, 1958; see also Ernst Jünger, *Der Arbeiter*, Hamburg: Hanseatische Verlagsanstalt, 1932. Generally see Karl Dietrich Bracher, *Die deutsche Diktatur*, Cologne and Berlin: Kiepenheuer & Witsch, 1969, pp. 155–66, and Walter Z. Laqueur, *Young Germany*, New York: Basic Books, 1962, pp. 179–87.

15 See Karl Mannheim, 'The prospects of scientific politics: the relationship between social theory and political practice', in Karl Mannheim, *Ideology and Utopia*, pp. 103–30.
16 See Karl Mannheim, *Ideology and Utopia*, pp. 57–8.
17 See Gunter W. Remmling, 'Ideology: the twilight of ideas', in Gunter W. Remmling, op. cit., pp. 105–17, and, Gunter W. Remmling, 'Francis Bacon and the French Enlightenment philosophers', in Gunter W. Remmling (ed.), *Towards the Sociology of Knowledge*, London: Routledge & Kegan Paul, and New York: Humanities Press, 1973, pp. 47–59. See also George Lichtheim, 'The concept of ideology', *History and Theory*, vol. IV, no. 2 (1965), pp. 164–95, and, George H. Sabine, *A History of Political Theory*, New York: Holt, 1950.
18 This interpretation of Mannheimian concepts leads to a question inviting further research: Does the psychic-individualistic fixation of contemporary American sociology of knowledge represent regressive tendencies or does it reflect a social situation devoid of strongly integrated groups?
19 See Claude Adrien Helvétius, *De l'homme*, *Oeuvres complètes*, vol. II, Paris: Lepetit, 1818, p. 566.
20 See Karl Mannheim, *Ideology and Utopia*, p. 66.
21 See Karl Marx and Friedrich Engels, *The German Ideology*, parts I and III (ed. by R. Pascal), New York: International Publishers, 1939, p. 181.
22 See Karl Marx and Friedrich Engels, *Die deutsche Ideologie*, Berlin: Dietz Verlag, 1953, pp. 196–9.
23 For the differentiation of particular and total conceptions of ideology see Karl Mannheim, *Ideology and Utopia*, pp. 49–53.
24 See ibid., pp. 67–9.
25 See for example Karl Marx and Friedrich Engels, *The German Ideology*, pp. 21–7; Karl Marx, *Capital*, vol. I (trans. by Samuel Moore and Edward Aveling, ed. Friedrich Engels), 4th edition, New York: D. Appleton, and London: Swan Sonnenschein, 1891, pp. xxx and 43–51; Karl Marx, *The Poverty of Philosophy* (trans. by H. Quelch), Chicago: Charles H. Kerr, 1910, p. 119; Karl Marx and Friedrich Engels, *Werke*, vol. 2, 4th edition, Berlin: Dietz Verlag, 1962, pp. 195–6.
26 See Karl Marx, 'Zur Kritik der Hegelschen Rechtsphilosophie', in Marx and Engels, *Historisch-Kritische Gesamtausgabe*, I/1 (ed. by D. Rjazanov), Frankfurt: Marx-Engels-Archiv Verlagsgesellschaft, 1927, pp. 617–21.
27 See Georg Lukács, *Geschichte und Klassenbewusstsein*, Berlin: Malik-Verlag, 1923, pp. 217–23. On the cognitive privileges of the proletarian thinker see also Friedrich Engels, *Ludwig Feuerbach and the Outcome of Classical German Philosophy* (ed. by C. P. Dutt), New York: International Publishers, 1934, p. 70, and F. Engels, 'Juristic socialism', in Marx and Engels, *On Religion*, Moscow: Foreign Languages Publishing House, 1957, p. 270.
28 See Karl Mannheim, 'The sociology of knowledge', p. 240.
29 See Max Horkheimer, 'Ein neuer Ideologiebegriff?', *Archiv für die Geschichte des Sozialismus und der Arbeiterbewegung*, vol. XV, 1930, pp. 33–56. Reprinted in Kurt Lenk (ed.), *Ideologie: Ideologiekritik und*

Wissenssoziologie, 4th edition, Neuwied and Berlin: Hermann Luchterhand Verlag, 1970, pp. 283–303.

30 Ibid., pp. 287–92.

31 See ibid., pp. 300–3; see also Theodor W. Adorno, 'Das Bewusstsein der Wissenssoziologie', in Theodor W. Adorno, *Prismen: Kulturkritik und Gesellschaft*, Berlin and Frankfurt: Suhrkamp Verlag, 1955, pp. 32–50, and, more generally Herbert Marcuse, 'Über das Ideologieproblem in der hochentwickelten Industriegesellschaft', in Kurt Lenk, op. cit., pp. 395–419.

32 See Hans-Joachim Lieber and Peter Furth, 'Wissenssoziologie', in H.-J. Lieber, *Philosophie – Soziologie, Gesellschaft: Gesammelte Studien zum Ideologieproblem*, Berlin: Walter De Gruyter, 1965, pp. 82–105. See also Hans-Joachim Lieber, *Wissen und Gesellschaft: Die Probleme der Wissenssoziologie*, Tübingen: Max Niemeyer Verlag, 1952. In *Wissen und Gesellschaft*, Lieber was closer to Mannheim's idealistic position; he also shared Eduard Spranger's subjectivist belief in the 'scientific ethos' as a bridge to truth. The recent West German *rapprochement* between contemporary sociologists and Marxism is also reflected in Kurt Lenk, 'Nachwort', in Kurt Lenk, op. cit., pp. 421–39, and Arnhelm Neusüss, *Utopisches Bewusstsein und freischwebende Intelligenz*, Meisenheim am Glan: Verlag Anton Hain, 1968.

33 See Hans-Joachim Lieber and Peter Furth, op. cit., pp. 97–8.

34 Karl Mannheim, *Ideology and Utopia*, p. 76. See also Karl Mannheim, 'The sociology of knowledge', pp. 274–5.

35 Karl Mannheim, *Ideology and Utopia*, p. 85.

36 Ibid., p. 86.

37 Ibid., p. 84.

38 Ibid.

5 Beyond ideology and utopia

1 Karl Mannheim, *Ideology and Utopia: An Introduction to the Sociology of Knowledge* (trans. by Louis Wirth and Edward Shils), New York: Harcourt, Brace & World, 1936, p. 132.

2 Ibid.

3 See Richard Drews and Alfred Kantorowicz (eds), *Verboten und Verbrannt: Deutsche Literatur 12 Jahre unterdrückt*, Berlin and Munich: Heinz Ullstein–Helmut Kindler Verlag, 1947.

4 See Martin Esslin, *Brecht: The Man and His Work*, Garden City, New York: Doubleday, 1959; Walter Gropius, *The New Architecture and the Bauhaus* (trans. by P. Morton Shand), New York: Museum of Modern Art, and London: Faber & Faber, 1937; Siegfried Kracauer, *From Caligari to Hitler: A Psychological History of the German Film*, Princeton University Press, 1947; Bernard S. Myers, *The German Expressionists: A Generation in Revolt*, New York: McGraw-Hill, 1963; Erwin Piscator, *Das politische Theater*, Berlin: A. Schultz Verlag, 1929; Hans Richter, *Dada: Art and Anti-Art*, New York: McGraw-Hill, 1965.

5 See Carl Grünberg, *Festrede, Gehalten zur Einweihung des Instituts für Sozialforschung . . . Juni 22, 1924*, Frankfurter Universitätsreden, XX (1924). See also Max Horkheimer, *Die gegenwärtige Lage der Sozial-*

philosophie und die Aufgaben eines Instituts für Sozialforschung, Frankfurter Universitätsreden, XXXVII (1931).

6 Max Horkheimer, personal communication, July 20, 1969.

7 Ernest Manheim, personal communication, May 14, 1969.

8 According to Bracher the leading German universities lost many faculty members during the first year of Nazi rule. In Berlin and Frankfurt over 32 per cent of the professoriat were dismissed and over 24 per cent of the faculty were forced from their positions at Heidelberg university. See Karl Dietrich Bracher, *Die deutsche Diktatur: Entstehung, Struktur, Folgen des Nationalsozialismus*, Cologne and Berlin: Kiepenheuer & Witsch, 1969, p. 294.

9 As far as the extreme Right is concerned Mannheim's discussion of 'modern currents of thought' is limited to a brief analysis of Mussolini's fascism, but contains no references to Hitler or National Socialism. See Karl Mannheim, op. cit., pp. 119–30.

10 Ibid., p. 135.

11 Ibid., p. 137 (emphasis in original).

12 Ibid., p. 142.

13 Ibid., p. 143.

14 See Karl Dietrich Bracher, op. cit., pp. 182 and 291. On the social and political obscurantism of German academicians see also Franz L. Neumann, 'The social sciences', in Franz L. Neumann, *et al.*, *The Cultural Migration: The European Scholar in America*, Philadelphia: University of Pennsylvania Press, 1953, pp. 21–2.

15 See Peter Gay, *Weimar Culture*, New York: Harper & Row, 1968, pp. 30–43.

16 Kurt Tucholsky, 'Fünfundzwanzig Jahre', *Die Weltbühne*, vol. XXVI, no. 37 (September 9 1930), p. 382 (my translation).

17 See Istvan Deak, *Weimar Germany's Left-Wing Intellectuals: A Political History of the Weltbühne and Its Circle*, Berkeley and Los Angeles: University of California Press, 1968, p. 1. See also Leonhard Frank, *Heart on the Left* (trans. by Cyrus Brooks), London: A. Barker, 1954.

18 Karl Mannheim, op. cit., p. 232.

19 Ibid., p. 168.

20 See Peter Gay, op. cit., p. xiv.

21 Karl Mannheim, op. cit., p. 179.

22 Ibid., p. 236.

23 See Ernst Robert Curtius, 'Die Soziologie und ihre Grenzen', *Neue Schweizer Rundschau*, vol. 22 (October, 1929), pp. 729 and 732.

24 See Ernst Robert Curtius, *Deutscher Geist in Gefahr*, Stuttgart: Deutsche Verlagsanstalt, 1932, p. 86 and p. 131. From a Marxian position, however, Lewalter argued that it was precisely his skepticism which separated Mannheim from Marxist social theory. See Ernst Lewalter, 'Wissenssoziologie und Marxismus', *Archiv für Sozialwissenschaft und Sozialpolitik*, vol. 64, no. 1 (April, 1930), p. 118.

25 See Karl Mannheim, 'Problems of sociology in Germany' (trans. by Kurt H. Wolff), in *From Karl Mannheim* (ed. by Kurt H. Wolff), New York: Oxford University Press, 1971, pp. 265–6.

26 See ibid., pp. 267–8.

27 See ibid., p. 270.
28 See ibid., pp. 262–4.
29 See Wolfgang J. Mommsen, *Max Weber und die deutsche Politik, 1890–1920*, Tübingen: J. C. B. Mohr, 1959; Ernst Troeltsch, *Aufsätze zur Geistesgeschichte und Religionssoziologie, Gesammelte Schriften*, vol. IV (ed. by Hans Baron), Tübingen: J. C. B. Mohr, 1925, p. 653; John Raphael Staude, *Max Scheler 1874–1928: An Intellectual Portrait*, New York: Free Press, 1967, pp. 152 and 223.
30 Karl Mannheim, 'On the nature of economic ambition and its significance for the social education of man', in Karl Mannheim, *Essays on the Sociology of Knowledge* (ed. by Paul Kecskemeti), London: Routledge & Kegan Paul, 1952, p. 233.
31 Ibid., p. 243.
32 Ibid., p. 244.
33 See ibid., p. 236.
34 For the 'end of ideology' thesis see for example Daniel Bell, *The End of Ideology*, Chicago: Free Press, 1960; Lewis S. Feuer, 'Beyond ideology', in Lewis S. Feuer, *Psychoanalysis and Ethics*, Springfield, Illinois: Charles C. Thomas, 1955, pp. 126–30; Seymour M. Lipset, 'The end of ideology?', in Seymour M. Lipset, *Political Man*, Garden City, New York: Doubleday, 1960, pp. 403–17; Edward Shils, 'The end of ideology?', *Encounter*, vol. 5 (November, 1955), pp. 52–8. For critiques of the 'end of ideology' theme see for example Gerhard Lenski, *Power and Privilege*, New York: McGraw-Hill, 1966; Rolf Schulze, 'The recession of ideology?', *Sociological Quarterly*, vol. 5 (Spring, 1964), pp. 148–56; Dusky Lee Smith, 'The sunshine boys: toward a sociology of happiness', in Larry T. Reynolds and Janice M. Reynolds, *The Sociology of Sociology*, New York: David McKay, 1970, pp. 371–87; Sylvan Tomkins, 'Left and right: a basic dimension of ideology and personality', in Robert W. White (ed.), *The Study of Lives*, New York: Atherton Press, 1966.
35 Karl Mannheim, 'On the nature of economic ambition and its significance for the social education of man', p. 245.
36 Ibid., p. 247.
37 See ibid., pp. 252–3.
38 See ibid., pp. 271–4.
39 Ibid., p. 275.
40 Ibid.
41 See Karl Mannheim, *Die Gegenwartsaufgaben der Soziologie: Ihre Lehrgestalt*, Tübingen: J. C. B. Mohr (Paul Siebeck), 1932.
42 See ibid., pp. 9–27.
43 See ibid., pp. 11–13.
44 See ibid., pp. 17–21.
45 See ibid., pp. 36–48.
46 See Karl Mannheim, 'American sociology. Review of Stuart A. Rice (ed.), *Methods in Social Science*, Chicago: University of Chicago Press, 1931', *American Journal of Sociology*, vol. 38, no. 2 (September, 1932), pp. 273–82. Reprinted in Karl Mannheim, *Essays on Sociology and Social Psychology* (ed. by Paul Kecskemeti), London: Routledge & Kegan Paul, 1953, pp. 185–94.

47 See Karl Mannheim, 'German sociology (1918–1933)', *Politica*, vol. I (February, 1934), pp. 12–33. Reprinted in Karl Mannheim, *Essays on Sociology and Social Psychology*, pp. 209–28. Mannheim's interest in problems concerning the nature and tasks of sociology also informs his discussion of 'The place of sociology', paper presented at a conference held under the auspices of the Institute of Sociology and World University Service, British Committee, London, 1936. Reprinted in Karl Mannheim, *Essays on Sociology and Social Psychology*, pp. 195–208.

48 See Karl Mannheim, 'American Sociology', in Karl Mannheim, *Essays on Sociology and Social Psychology*, pp. 185–6.

49 Ibid., p. 189.

50 Ibid. See Robert K. Merton, *Social Theory and Social Structure*, enlarged edition, New York: Free Press, 1968, p. 496.

51 Karl Mannheim, 'American sociology', p. 190. See C. Wright Mills, *The Sociological Imagination*, New York: Oxford University Press, 1959.

52 The concept of 'isolating empiricism' was coined later in a similar comparative context, but fits the analytical intentions of the review essay on 'American sociology'. For this concept see Karl Mannheim, 'German sociology (1918–1933)', in Karl Mannheim, *Essays on Sociology and Social Psychology*, p. 225. In his *Sociological Imagination* Mills conceptualized similar problems as 'abstracted empiricism'.

53 Karl Mannheim, 'American sociology', p. 191.

54 Ibid., p. 193.

55 Ibid., p. 194.

6 The sociology of social planning

1 J. Alcock, personal communications, December 22, 1972 and January 15, 1973.

2 Karl Mannheim, 'German sociology (1918–1933)', in Karl Mannheim, *Essays on Sociology and Social Psychology* (ed. by Paul Kecskemeti), London: Routledge & Kegan Paul, 1953, p. 226.

3 Among the numerous works on British social conditions I have profited especially from the following books: Noreen Branson and Margot Heinemann, *Britain in the Nineteen Thirties*, London: Weidenfeld & Nicolson, 1971; British Association For the Advancement of Science, *Britain in Depression*, London: Pitman, 1935; G. D. H. and Margaret I. Cole, *Condition of Britain*, London: V. Gollancz, 1937; Bentley B. Gilbert, *British Social Policy, 1914–1939*, Ithaca, New York: Cornell University Press, 1970; Pauline Gregg, *A Social and Economic History of Britain, 1760–1965*, London: Harrap, 1965; Benjamin Seebohm Rowntree, *The Human Needs of Labour*, revised edition, London and New York: Longmans, Green, 1937; Benjamin Seebohm Rowntree, *Poverty and Progress*, London and New York: Longmans, Green, 1941; A. J. Youngson, *The British Economy, 1920–1957*, London: Allen & Unwin, 1960.

4 See J. E. Meade, *Efficiency, Equality and Ownership of Property*, London: Allen & Unwin, 1964, p. 27.

5 See Thomas Jones, *A Diary with Letters, 1931–1950*, London and New York: Oxford University Press, 1954, p. 286. See also Harold Macmillan, *Winds of Change, 1914–1939*, London: Macmillan, 1966, p. 197.
6 See Walter Citrine, *Men and Work*, London: Hutchinson, 1964, p. 316.
7 See Noreen Branson and Margot Heinemann, op. cit., p. 18.
8 See Karl Mannheim, *Man and Society in an Age of Reconstruction* (trans. by Edward Shils), New York: Harcourt, Brace & World, 1940, pp. 251, 259, 261, 263, 266, 323, 339.
9 See Fred Copeman, *Reason in Revolt*, London: Blandford Press, 1948, and T. H. Wintringham, *Mutiny: Being a Survey of Mutinies from Spartacus to Invergordon*, London: S. Nott, 1936.
10 See R. Page Arnot, *The Miners in Crisis and War*, vol. II, London: Allen & Unwin, 1961, p. 211.
11 See G. D. H. Cole (ed.), *British Trade Unionism Today*, London: V. Gollancz, 1939, p. 242.
12 See Noreen Branson and Margot Heinemann, op. cit., pp. 197–200.
13 On upper-class sympathy for Fascism see ibid., p. 161.
14 See ibid., pp. 213–14.
15 See ibid., pp. 209–11. See also John Boyd Orr, *Food, Health and Income*, London: Macmillan, 1936.
16 See J. B. Priestley, *English Journey*, New York and London: Harper, 1934, p. 249.
17 See Noreen Branson and Margot Heinemann, op. cit., pp. 275–8.
18 See Karl Mannheim, *Rational and Irrational Elements in Contemporary Society* (Hobhouse Memorial Lecture, delivered on March 7, 1934 at Bedford College for Women, University of London), London: Oxford University Press, 1934.
19 See Karl Mannheim, 'The crisis of culture in the era of mass-democracies and autarchies', *Sociological Review*, vol. XXVI, no. 2 (April 1934), pp. 105–29. Enlarged and reprinted as 'Social causes of the contemporary crisis in culture', in *Man and Society in an Age of Reconstruction*, pp. 78–114.
20 See Karl Mannheim, *Mensch und Gesellschaft im Zeitalter des Umbaus*, Leiden: A. W. Sijthoff's Uitgeversmaatschappij N. V., 1935.
21 See ibid., pp. 16–18. See also Karl Mannheim, *Man and Society in an Age of Reconstruction*, pp. 41–4.
22 See Karl Mannheim, *Mensch und Gesellschaft im Zeitalter des Umbaus*, p. 23.
23 See ibid., p. 25.
24 See ibid., pp. 53–4. See also Karl Mannheim, *Man and Society in an Age of Reconstruction*, pp. 73–4.
25 See Karl Mannheim, *Mensch und Gesellschaft im Zeitalter des Umbaus*, pp. 28–32. See also Karl Mannheim, *Man and Society in an Age of Reconstruction*, pp. 51–5.
26 See Karl Mannheim, *Mensch und Gesellschaft im Zeitalter des Umbaus*, pp. 57–90. See also Karl Mannheim, *Man and Society in an Age of Reconstruction*, pp. 79–114.
27 See Karl Mannheim, *Mensch und Gesellschaft im Zeitalter des Umbaus*, p. 100 and *Man and Society in an Age of Reconstruction*, p. 149. See also John Dewey, *Reconstruction in Philosophy*, New York: H. Holt, 1920,

p. 156, and John Dewey, *The Quest for Certainty: A Study of the Relation of Knowledge and Action*, New York: Minton, Balch, 1929, p. 37.

28 Karl Mannheim, *Man and Society in an Age of Reconstruction*, pp. 154–5. See also Karl Mannheim, *Mensch und Gesellschaft im Zeitalter des Umbaus*, p. 152.

29 Karl Mannheim, *Man and Society in an Age of Reconstruction*, p. 193. See also Karl Mannheim, *Mensch und Gesellschaft im Zeitalter des Umbaus*, p. 152.

30 Karl Mannheim, *Man and Society in an Age of Reconstruction*, p. 177.

31 Ibid., p. 181.

32 Ibid., p. 204. See also Karl Mannheim, *Mensch und Gesellschaft im Zeitalter des Umbaus*, p. 169.

33 Karl Mannheim, *Man and Society in an Age of Reconstruction*, p. 216.

34 Ibid., p. 220.

35 Ibid., p. 222.

36 Ibid., p. 236 (emphasis in original).

37 See ibid., pp. 117–43. See also Karl Mannheim, 'The psychological aspect', in C. A. W. Manning (ed.), *Peaceful Change: An International Problem*, London and New York: Macmillan, 1937, pp. 101–32.

38 Karl Mannheim, *Man and Society in an Age of Reconstruction*, p. 121.

39 Adorno and Horkheimer adopt a similar view of the relationships between political liberalism and monopolistic capitalism on the one hand and anti-Semitism on the other. See Max Horkheimer and Theodor W. Adorno, 'Elemente des Antisemitismus: Grenzen der Aufklärung', in Max Horkheimer and Theodor W. Adorno, *Dialektik der Aufklärung: Philosophische Fragmente*, Amsterdam: Querido Verlag, 1947, pp. 199–244.

40 On the function of symbols in social life see C. G. Jung, *Psychology of the Unconscious* (trans. by Beatrice M. Hinkle), London: Kegan Paul, Trench, Trubner & Co., 1916.

41 Karl Mannheim, *Man and Society in an Age of Reconstruction*, p. 142.

42 Ibid., p. 129.

43 See ibid., pp. 239–366.

44 Ibid., p. 315.

45 Ibid., p. 336.

46 See ibid., p. 337.

47 Ibid., p. 347.

48 See ibid., p. 350.

49 See ibid., p. 351.

50 See ibid.

51 See ibid.

52 See C. Wright Mills, *The Power Elite*, New York: Oxford University Press, 1959, pp. 62–8. For my participant observations of English public-school life see Gunter W. Remmling, *Wissenssoziologie und Gesellschaftsplanung*, Dortmund: Ruhfus, 1968, pp. 272–3.

53 See Karl Mannheim, *Man and Society in an Age of Reconstruction*, pp. 249–51.

54 See ibid., pp. 293, 323, 352.

55 Ibid., p. 370.

56 See ibid., p. 366.

57 See Theodor W. Adorno, *Prismen: Kulturkritik und Gesellschaft*, Berlin and Frankfurt: Suhrkamp Verlag, 1955, p. 50.
58 Karl Mannheim, *Man and Society in an Age of Reconstruction*, p. 369.
59 Ibid., p. 372.
60 Ibid., p. 378.
61 See ibid., pp. 377–80.

7 The values and the education of democratic men

1 For my description of Mannheim's activities in wartime England and the evolution of war-related social policy I found the following sources especially valuable: Angus Calder, *The People's War: Britain 1939–1945*, New York: Pantheon, 1969; Michael Foot, *Aneurin Bevan*, vol. I, New York: Atheneum, 1963; T. O. Lloyd, *Empire to Welfare State: English History 1906–1967*, London: Oxford University Press, 1970; George Orwell, *The Lion and the Unicorn*, London: Secker & Warburg, 1941; J. B. Priestley, *Postscripts*, 17, London: W. Heinemann, 1940; J. B. Priestley, *Margin Released*, London: W. Heinemann, 1962; Edward Shils, 'Karl Mannheim', in *International Encyclopedia of the Social Sciences*, New York: Macmillan, 1968, pp. 557–62; Thomas Henry Wintringham, *New Ways of War*, Harmondsworth, Middlesex: Penguin, 1940. See also *Social Insurance and Allied Services*: Report by Sir William Beveridge, 1942 (Cmd. 6404).
2 See Karl Mannheim, 'Mass education and group analysis', in J. I. Cohen and R. M. W. Travers (eds), *Educating for Democracy*, London: Macmillan, 1939, pp. 329–64. Reprinted in Karl Mannheim, *Diagnosis of Our Time: Wartime Essays of a Sociologist*, London: Kegan Paul, Trench, Trubner & Co., 1943, pp. 73–94.
3 See also Karl Mannheim and W. A. C. Stewart, *An Introduction to the Sociology of Education*, London: Routledge & Kegan Paul, 1962. This posthumous volume is based on Mannheim's manuscript and lecture notes, organized and rewritten by his friend and student, Professor Stewart.
4 See Karl Mannheim, *Diagnosis of Our Time*, pp. ix, 64, 67.
5 This chapter 'Diagnosis of our time', in *Diagnosis of Our Time*, pp. 1–11, was first presented in January, 1941 as a lecture at a Conference of Federal Union at Oxford; also read in July, 1941 at the Week-End Summer Meeting of the Delegacy for Extra-Mural Studies at Oxford and in August, 1941 at the International Gathering of Friends Service Council at Woodbrooke.
6 Ibid., p. 72.
7 See Victor Branford, 'The drift to revolution', in V. Branford, *Papers for the Present*, London: Headley, 1917–20.
8 See Wilhelm Röpke, *Die Gesellschaftskrisis der Gegenwart*, Erlenbach-Zürich: Rentsch, 1942.
9 See Karl Mannheim, *Diagnosis of Our Time*, p. 6.
10 Ibid., p. 38.
11 Ibid., p. 6. See also Karl Mannheim, *Man and Society in an Age of Reconstruction* (trans. by Edward Shils), New York: Harcourt, Brace & World, 1940, pp. 350–2.

12 See Karl Mannheim, *Diagnosis of Our Time*, p. 38.
13 Ibid., p. 38. See also ibid., p. 70.
14 Ibid., p. 16.
15 Ibid., p. 17.
16 See Charles Horton Cooley, *Social Organization: A Study of the Larger Mind*, New York: Charles Scribner, 1909, pp. 32–57.
17 Karl Mannheim, *Diagnosis of Our Time*, pp. 18–19.
18 Ibid., p. 21.
19 See William Graham Sumner, *Folkways: A Study of the Sociological Importance of Usages, Manners, Customs, Mores, and Morals*, Boston: Ginn, 1906.
20 Karl Mannheim, *Diagnosis of Our Time*, p. 22.
21 Ibid., p. 25.
22 See ibid., pp. 17–26.
23 See ibid., pp. 26–30.
24 See ibid., p. 112.
25 Mannheim first used the concept of substantial morality in 1935; see Karl Mannheim, *Mensch und Gesellschaft im Zeitalter des Umbaus*, Leiden: Sijthoff, 1935, p. 45. See also Karl Mannheim, *Man and Society in an Age of Reconstruction*, p. 67.
26 See Karl Mannheim, *Freedom, Power, and Democratic Planning*, New York: Oxford University Press, 1950, p. 198.
27 See F. Warren Rempel, *The Role of Value in Karl Mannheim's Sociology of Knowledge*, The Hague: Mouton, 1965, pp. 112–13.
28 See ibid., pp. 35, 103.
29 See Karl Mannheim, *Diagnosis of Our Time*, pp. 74, 132.
30 See ibid., pp. 60–4, 115.
31 See Karl Mannheim, *Systematic Sociology: An Introduction to the Study of Society* (ed. by J. S. Erös and W. A. C. Stewart), London: Routledge & Kegan Paul, 1957, pp. 131–5.
32 Karl Mannheim, *Diagnosis of Our Time*, p. 144. See also pp. 46–53.
33 See ibid., p. 23.
34 Ibid., p. 6.
35 See ibid., p. 49.
36 Ibid., p. 72.
37 See ibid., p. 11.
38 Ibid., p. 38. See also ibid., p. 70.
39 See ibid., p. 52.
40 See ibid., pp. 157–8.
41 Ibid., p. 110.
42 See ibid., p. 18.
43 See ibid., p. 105. See also Karl Mannheim, *Man and Society in an Age of Reconstruction*, pp. 357–8.
44 See Karl Mannheim, 'The problem of youth in modern society', in Karl Mannheim, *Diagnosis of Our Time*, p. 36.
45 See ibid., pp. 46–53.
46 See Karl Mannheim, 'Education, sociology and the problem of social awareness', in Karl Mannheim, *Diagnosis of Our Time*, pp. 54–5.
47 For the distinction between personality-centered and group-centered social problems see Gunter W. Remmling, 'Social change and social

problems', in G. W. Remmling and R. B. Campbell, *Basic Sociology*, Totowa, New Jersey: Littlefield, Adams, 1970, pp. 278–9.

48 Karl Mannheim, *Diagnosis of Our Time*, p. 164.
49 See ibid., p. 64.
50 See ibid.
51 See ibid., pp. 65–8.
52 See ibid., pp. 8, 76, 164.
53 Karl Mannheim, 'Mass education and group analysis', in Karl Mannheim, *Diagnosis of Our Time*, p. 87.
54 See Frederick M. Thrasher, *The Gang: A Study of 1,313 Gangs in Chicago*, University of Chicago Press, 1927; August Aichhorn, *Wayward Youth*, New York: Viking Press, 1935; Erich Fromm, *The Fear of Freedom*, London: Kegan Paul, Trench, Trubner, 1942; Gustav Ichheiser, *Die Kritik des Erfolges*, Leipzig: C. I. Hirschfeld, 1930; Paul Schilder, 'The analysis of ideologies as a psycho-therapeutic method especially in group treatment', *American Journal of Psychiatry*, vol. 93, no. 3 (November, 1936), pp. 601–15.
55 Karl Mannheim, *Diagnosis of Our Time*, p. 94.
56 See Auguste Comte, *System of Positive Polity*, vol. 4 (trans. by R. Congreve and H. D. Hutton), London: Longmans, Green, 1877; Émile Durkheim, *The Elementary Forms of the Religious Life* (trans. by Joseph Ward Swain), London: Allen & Unwin, 1915; Benjamin Kidd, *Social Evolution*, new edition, New York and London: Macmillan, 1894; Benjamin Kidd, *The Control of the Tropics*, New York: Macmillan, 1898; Karl Mannheim, 'Towards a new social philosophy: a challenge to Christian thinkers by a sociologist', in Karl Mannheim, *Diagnosis of Our Time*, pp. 100–65.
57 Ibid., p. 110.
58 Ibid.
59 See ibid., p. 106.
60 See ibid., pp. 109–11.
61 See ibid., pp. 18, 78, 116.
62 See ibid., pp. 100, 101, 129, 143.
63 See ibid., p. 114.
64 See ibid., pp. 123, 128.
65 Ibid., p. 119.
66 Ibid., p. 133.
67 Ibid., p. 172 n. 7.
68 See ibid., pp. 125, 135, 172 n. 10.
69 See ibid., p. 143.

8 Political power and human freedom

1 See Karl Mannheim, *Freedom, Power, and Democratic Planning* (ed. by Hans Gerth and Ernest K. Bramstedt), New York: Oxford University Press, 1950, pp. 3–21.
2 See ibid., pp. 22–37.
3 Ibid., p. 43.
4 See ibid., p. 45.
5 Ibid., p. 47.

6 See ibid., pp. 48–76.
7 See ibid., pp. 77–107.
8 See ibid., pp. 108–69.
9 See ibid., pp. 173–313.
10 Ibid., p. 244.
11 See ibid., pp. 246–65. See also W. L. Warner, R. J. Havighurst, and M. B. Loeb, *Who Shall Be Educated?*, New York: Harper, 1944, p. 55.
12 Karl Mannheim, op. cit., p. 247.
13 See ibid., pp. 266–74.
14 Ibid., p. 274. See also Herbert Read, *Education Through Art*, London: Faber & Faber, 1943.
15 See Karl Mannheim, op. cit., pp. 275–84.
16 Ibid., p. 284.
17 Ibid., p. 286.
18 Ibid., p. 295.
19 Ibid., p. 313.
20 See ibid., p. xviii.
21 See ibid., pp. 124–5.
22 See ibid., p. 116.
23 See Karl Mannheim, *Essays on Sociology and Social Psychology* (ed. by Paul Kecskemeti), London: Routledge & Kegan Paul, 1953, pp. 74–164.
24 See Karl Mannheim, *Freedom, Power, and Democratic Planning*, pp. 116, 119, 288. See also Karl Mannheim, *Diagnosis of Our Time*, London: Routledge & Kegan Paul, 1943, p. 6, where he calls for the blending of the 'new leadership' with the older élites.
25 See Karl Mannheim, *Freedom, Power, and Democratic Planning*, pp. 166–7. According to Jean Floud, who was Mannheim's graduate assistant in London, he concluded his career as a 'utopian of the right'. See Jean Floud, 'Karl Mannheim (1893–1947)', in Timothy Raison (ed.), *The Founding Fathers of Social Science*, Baltimore, Maryland: Penguin, 1969, p. 204.
26 See Karl Mannheim, *Freedom, Power, and Democratic Planning*, pp. 8–10.
27 See ibid., p. 71.
28 Ibid., p. 57.
29 See ibid., pp. 45–7.
30 See ibid., p. 71.
31 See ibid., pp. 108–44.
32 Ibid., pp. 112–13.
33 Ibid., p. 127.
34 See ibid., pp. 127–31.
35 See ibid., pp. 131–4.
36 Ibid., p. 135.
37 See ibid., pp. 138–43.
38 Ibid., p. 144. Mannheim obviously equates existing patterns of representative government with popular democracy; this naïvety is especially noticeable in his analysis of government which quickly deteriorates to the level of a 'chamber of commerce' luncheon speech. (See ibid., pp. 145–69.)

9 Retrospect and prospect

1 According to some observers Mannheim's overarching concern for meaning and structure places him in the immediate vicinity of social action theory and functionalism. See Don Martindale, *The Nature and Types of Sociological Theory*, Boston: Houghton Mifflin, 1960, pp. 414–418; Edward A. Tiryakian, 'Existential phenomenology and the sociological tradition', in Gunter W. Remmling (ed.), *Towards the Sociology of Knowledge: Origin and Development of a Sociological Thought Style*, London: Routledge & Kegan Paul, and New York: Humanities Press, 1973, p. 287.

2 See Karl Mannheim, *Ideology and Utopia: An Introduction to the Sociology of Knowledge* (trans. by Louis Wirth and Edward Shils), New York: Harcourt, Brace & World, 1936, pp. 65, 84, 278–9; Karl Mannheim, *Man and Society in an Age of Reconstruction: Studies in Modern Social Structure* (trans. by Edward Shils), New York: Harcourt, Brace & World, 1940, p. 206.

3 See Karl Mannheim, *Freedom, Power, and Democratic Planning* (ed. by Hans Gerth and Ernest K. Bramstedt), New York: Oxford University Press, 1950, p. 87.

4 See Claude Adrien Helvétius, *Oeuvres complètes*, vol. II: *De l'homme*, Paris: Lepetit, 1818, p. 566.

5 See Karl Mannheim, *Freedom, Power, and Democratic Planning*, pp. 64–5.

6 See Karl Mannheim, *Diagnosis of Our Time: Wartime Essays of a Sociologist*, London: Routledge & Kegan Paul, 1943, pp. 135–7.

7 See Karl Mannheim, *Freedom, Power, and Democratic Planning*, pp. 26–8, 77–107.

8 See ibid., p. 117.

9 See ibid., pp. 164–5.

10 See ibid., pp. 79–80.

11 See ibid., p. 125.

12 See ibid., p. 149.

13 See C. Wright Mills, *The Sociological Imagination*, New York: Oxford University Press, 1959.

14 See for example Alvin W. Gouldner, *The Coming Crisis of Western Sociology*, New York: Basic Books, 1970; Irving Louis Horowitz (ed.), *The New Sociology: Essays in Social Science and Social Theory in Honor of C. Wright Mills*, New York: Oxford University Press, 1964; Irving Louis Horowitz, *Professing Sociology: Studies in the Life Cycle of Social Science*, Chicago: Aldine, 1968; Gunter W. Remmling, op. cit.

15 For summary interpretations of the counter culture see Charles A. Reich, *The Greening of America*, New York: Random House, 1970; Theodore Roszak, *The Making of a Counter Culture: Reflections on the Technocratic Society and Its Youthful Opposition*, New York: Doubleday, 1969. See also Keith Melville, *Communes in the Counter Culture: Origins, Theories, Styles of Life*, New York: William Morrow, 1972. For a retrospective analysis see Harvey C. Greisman, 'Requiem for the Counter Culture', unpublished Ph.D. dissertation, Syracuse University, 1972.

16 See John Friedmann, *Retracking America: A Theory of Transactive Planning*, Anchor Books, Garden City, New York: Anchor Press/ Doubleday, 1973.
17 See John Friedmann, 'Precursor: Karl Mannheim', in J. Friedmann, op. cit., pp. 22–48.
18 See ibid., p. 19.
19 See ibid., p. 227.

Index